JOURNAL FOR THE STUDY OF THE NEW TESTAMENT
SUPPLEMENT SERIES
65

Executive Editor
David Hill

JSOT Press
Sheffield

THE RHETORIC
OF RIGHTEOUSNESS
IN ROMANS 3.21-26

Douglas A. Campbell

Journal for the Study of the New Testament
Supplement Series 65

Copyright © 1992 Sheffield Academic Press

Published by JSOT Press
JSOT Press is an imprint of
Sheffield Academic Press Ltd
The University of Sheffield
343 Fulwood Road
Sheffield S10 3BP
England

Typeset by Sheffield Academic Press
and
Printed on acid-free paper in Great Britain
by Billing & Sons Ltd
Worcester

British Library Cataloguing in Publication Data

Campbell, Douglas A.
    Rhetoric of Righteousness in Romans 3:
    21-26.—(JSNT Supplement Series, ISSN
    0143-5108; No. 65)
    I. Title II. Series
    227.106

    ISBN 1-85075-294-x

CONTENTS

PREFACE

This study is a modification of my doctoral dissertation, which was accepted by the University of Toronto in 1989 (and therefore only takes account of literature published up to that date). It grew out of a fascinating and very popular course on Romans given at Wycliffe College by my eventual supervisor, Professor Richard Longenecker. It was he who first posed the question: 'What exactly *is* going on in Rom. 3.21-26?' My deepest thanks are due to him: he has been both a personal and a scholarly inspiration. A particular debt of thanks is also owed to the Rev. Dr Michael Knowles, whose insight into Rom. 3.21-26 at the syntactical level catalyzed this project, to Professor Robert Jewett, who provided vital encouragement and support, and to Dr David Hill, for graciously accepting this book into the JSNT Supplement Series. It is dedicated to my wife, Rachel, who sacrificed five precious years to make it possible, and also to my son, Rupert, who wasn't all that interested.

Douglas A. Campbell
University of Otago
Dunedin, New Zealand
January 1992

VERSIFIED GREEK TEXT OF ROMANS 3.21-26

Throughout this study Rom. 3.21-26 will be cited as follows:

21a	νυνὶ δὲ
b	χωρὶς νόμου
c	δικαιοσύνη θεοῦ πεφανέρωται
d	μαρτυρουμένη ὑπὸ τοῦ νόμου καὶ τῶν προφητῶν
22a	δικαιοσύνη δὲ θεοῦ
b	διὰ πίστεως Ἰησοῦ Χριστοῦ
c	εἰς πάντας τοὺς πιστεύοντας
d	οὐ γάρ ἐστιν διαστολή
23	πάντες γὰρ ἥμαρτον καὶ ὑστεροῦνται τῆς δόξης τοῦ θεοῦ
24a	δικαιούμενοι δωρεὰν τῇ αὐτοῦ χάριτι
b	διὰ τῆς ἀπολυτρώσεως τῆς ἐν Χριστῷ Ἰησοῦ
25a	ὃν προέθετο ὁ θεὸς ἱλαστήριον
b	διὰ τῆς πίστεως ἐν τῷ αὐτοῦ αἵματι
c	εἰς ἔνδειξιν τῆς δικαιοσύνης αὐτοῦ
d	διὰ τὴν πάρεσιν τῶν προγεγονότων ἁμαρτημάτων
26a	ἐν τῇ ἀνοχῇ τοῦ θεοῦ
b	πρὸς τὴν ἔνδειξιν τῆς δικαιοσύνης αὐτοῦ
c	ἐν τῷ νῦν καιρῷ
d	εἰς τὸ εἶναι αὐτὸν δίκαιον καὶ δικαιοῦντα τὸν ἐκ πίστεως Ἰησοῦ

ABBREVIATIONS

ATR	*Anglican Theological Review*
AusBR	*Australian Biblical Review*
BAGD	W. Bauer, W.F. Arndt, F.W. Gingrich and F.W. Danker, *Greek–English Lexicon of the NT*
BDF	F. Blass, A. Debrunner and R.W. Funk, *A Greek Grammar of the NT*
CBQ	*Catholic Biblical Quarterly*
CIG	*Corpus Inscriptionum Graecarum* (ed. A. Boeckh; Berlin, 1828–77)
ConNT	*Coniectanea neotestamentica*
CTM	*Concordia Theological Monthly*
EvQ	*Evangelical Quarterly*
EvT	*Evangelische Theologie*
ExpTim	*Expository Times*
HeyJ	*Heythrop Journal*
HibJ	*Hibbert Journal*
HTR	*Harvard Theological Review*
HUCA	*Hebrew Union College Annual*
IDB	G.A. Buttrick (ed.), *Interpreter's Dictionary of the Bible*
IDBSup	*IDB*, Supplementary Volume
IG	*Inscriptiones Graecae* (1873–)
Inscr. Magn.	*Die Inschriften von Magnesia am Mäander* (ed. O. Kern; Berlin, 1900)
Int	*Interpretation*
JAC	Jahrbuch für Antike und Christentum
JBC	R.E. Brown *et al.* (eds.), *The Jerome Bible Commentary* (Englewood Cliffs, NJ: Prentice–Hall, 1968)
JBL	*Journal of Biblical Literature*
JQR	*Jewish Quarterly Review*
JR	*Journal of Religion*
JRH	*Journal of Religious History*
JSNT	*Journal for the Study of the New Testament*
JSNTSup	*Journal for the Study of the New Testament* Supplement Series
JTS	*Journal of Theological Studies*
LNSM	J.P. Louw, E.A. Nida, R.B. Smith and K.A. Munson, *Greek–English Lexicon of the NT Based on Semantic Domains*

LSJ	H.G. Liddell, R. Scott and H.S. Jones, *A Greek–English Lexicon*
NIDNTT	C. Brown (ed.), *The New International Dictionary of New Testament Theology*
NKZ	*Neue kirchliche Zeitschrift*
NovT	*Novum Testamentum*
NTS	*New Testament Studies*
OGIS	*Orientis Graecae Inscriptiones Selectae* (ed. W. Dittenberger; Leipzig, 1903–1905)
RelSRev	*Religious Studies Review*
ResQ	*Restoration Quarterly*
RTR	*Reformed Theological Review*
SBL	Society of Biblical Literature
SBLSP	*Society of Biblical Literature Seminar Papers*
SJT	*Scottish Journal of Theology*
ST	*Studia theologica*
Str–B	[H. Strack and] P. Billerbeck, *Kommentar zum Neuen Testament aus Talmud und Midrasch*
TDNT	G. Kittel and G. Friedrich (eds.), *Theological Dictionary of the New Testament*
TLG	Thesaurae Linguae Graecae computerized data-base
TLZ	*Theologische Literaturzeitung*
TP	*Theologie und Philosophie*
TR	*Theologische Rundschau*
TSK	*Theologische Studien und Kritiken*
TWNT	G. Kittel and G. Friedrich (eds.), *Theologisches Wörterbuch zum Neuen Testament*
TZ	*Theologische Zeitschrift*
VC	*Vigiliae christianae*
VD	*Verbum domini*
VKGNT	K. Aland (ed.), *Vollständige Konkordanz zum griechischen Neuen Testament*
WA	M. Luther, Kritische Gesamtausgabe (= 'Weimar' edn)
WTJ	*Westminster Theological Journal*
ZNW	*Zeitschrift für die neutestamentliche Wissenschaft*
ZTK	*Zeitschrift für wissenschaftliche Theologie*

Introduction

PRELIMINARIES AND OUTLINE OF THE PROJECT

1. *Romans 3.21-26 as* Crux Interpretum

The importance of Paul's letter to the Romans need hardly be stated; it is still, however, the subject of serious interpretative disputes. In particular, Paul's meaning in a number of critical passages within the letter is still far from settled. One such—or perhaps even 'the'—pivotal and disputed text in Romans is 3.21-26.

The importance of 3.21-26 within the broader argument of Paul's letter to the Romans is almost universally affirmed. The section has constantly attracted designations like 'thesis paragraph', because it stands at the heart of a sustained theological discourse.[1] C.E.B. Cranfield may be taken as representative: it is, he says, 'the centre and heart of the main division to which it belongs. We may go farther and say that it is the centre and heart of the whole of Rom. 1.16b–15.13.'[2]

But the actual meaning of Rom. 3.21-26 is a far less settled issue than the shared evaluation of its importance, as the slightly less frequent declarations by scholars of its difficulty suggest.[3] In fact, the

1.   It is the symmetrical development of Paul's dramatic opening statement of 1.16-17; it is his response to the powerful arguments deployed through 1.18–3.20; it prefaces the exegetical discourse of 3.27–4.25; and it is probably the basis for the summation of 5.1-11. Thus it dominates, at the least, one third of Paul's letter to the Romans: that is, 1.16 through to 5.11, although, depending on how we reconstruct Paul's argument, its influence may extend much further.

2.   C.E.B. Cranfield, *A Critical and Exegetical Commentary on the Epistle to the Romans* (2 vols.; Edinburgh: T. & T. Clark, 1975, 1979), p. 199; cf also E. Käsemann, 'the thesis proper' (*Commentary on Romans* [trans. G. Bromiley; Grand Rapids: Eerdmans, 1980 (1975)], p. 91); and H. Ridderbos, 'the great programmatic summary of his gospel' (*Paul: An Outline of his Theology* [trans. J.R. de Witt; Grand Rapids: Eerdmans, 1975 (1966)], p. 144).

3.   Cf. J.A.T. Robinson, 'He [Paul] is by no means always lucid' (*Wrestling

passage is an arena for constant scholarly disputation. Conflict has been particularly heated over the passage's convoluted syntax, its possible dependence on early confessional material, the function of πίστις, and its use of various significant atonement and righteousness terms. Peter Stuhlmacher voices the opinion of many when he states, 'Exegesis on Rom. 3.24-26 appears today more than ever to end inconclusively. It has not been clarified decisively whether and to what extent Paul is citing traditional material in these verses, what this tradition means for him and for his theology of justification, and in what manner the text connects justification and the death of Jesus.'[1] In sum, 3.21-26 is a strategically critical but essentially unresolved section within Paul's letter to the Romans. It seems appropriate, therefore, to subject it to yet another detailed investigation.

2. *Questions of Provenance*

Before focusing on 3.21-26, certain standard questions of provenance for the letter as a whole should be addressed, although, as it turns out, few of them concern us directly. It is widely agreed that Paul wrote the letter to the Romans—probably as dictated to the scribe Tertius (Rom. 16.22), and so he bears ultimate responsibility for it.[2] If a

---

with Romans [London: SCM Press, 1970], p. 43)—but he concludes more confidently: 'Romans 3.21-26 is the most concentrated and heavily theological summary of the Pauline gospel, and every word has to be wrestled with. But if we take the trouble it demands and really enter into the background of his words it is not, I believe, obscure, however profound' (p. 48). Cf. also Käsemann (quoting Weiss): 'this section has rightly been called one of the most obscure and difficult in the whole epistle' (*Romans*, p. 92); and J.C. O'Neill: 'vv. 21-26 are so overloaded with ideas that it is hard to see clearly what Paul is getting at' (*Paul's Letter to the Romans* [London: Penguin Books, 1975], p. 70). Some of the Reformation theologians obviously felt the same way. So (on the book as a whole) Gagney: 'this one to the Romans is much the most difficult [of all Paul's epistles]', and Sadoleto: 'a book so full of divine thoughts that it seems scarcely possible for the human mind to enter into its understanding' (cited by T.H.L. Parker, *Commentaries on the Epistle to the Romans, 1532–1542* [Edinburgh: T. & T. Clark, 1986], p. 203).

   1.   'Recent Exegesis on Romans 3:24-26', in *idem, Reconciliation, Law and Righteousness* (trans. E. Kalin; Philadelphia: Fortress Press, 1986), p. 94.

   2.   Pauline authorship was disputed by Evanson in England (1792), by Bruno Baur in Germany (1852), and by the Swiss and Dutch scholars, Loman (1882) and Steck (1888). But, as Sanday and Headlam comment, 'these theories. . . will seem

degree of historicity in Acts is assumed,[1] and its narrative in chapters eighteen to twenty is coordinated with the externally attested proconsulship of Gallio[2] (and a few other dates),[3] a reasonably accurate date for the letter's composition can be deduced of 57 CE (give or take a year). There is also considerable evidence that Corinth is the point of origin for the letter.[4] There is some dispute concerning

probably to most readers hardly worth while repeating; so subjective and arbitrary is the whole criticism' (W. Sanday and A.C. Headlam, *A Critical and Exegetical Commentary on the Epistle to the Romans* [Edinburgh: T. & T. Clark, 2nd edn, 1896], p. lxxxvii). Even the radical nineteenth-century Tübingen school held Paul to be the author of Romans.

1. This assumption has been disputed by certain schools of NT interpretation since the advent of F.C. Baur's Tübingen school; in recent times most notably by John Knox and his followers. In any case, it matters little for the present study. If Knox's chronology is followed, a wider zone of possible dates should be adopted. Knox himself suggests 53–54 CE (*Chapters in a Life of Paul* [New York: Abingdon Press, 1950], p. 86). Following such an approach, I would argue on internal grounds for a date of *c.* 58 or 59 CE, since 58 was marked by strenuous public complaint concerning indirect taxes (cf. J.G.D. Dunn, *Romans 1–8* [Dallas: Word Books, 1988], pp. liii-liv, citing Tacitus, *Annals* 13.50-51).

2. Gallio's praefecture can be fixed reasonably precisely in 51–52 CE. With Paul's trial before Gallio located somewhere in this period, Acts suggests a lapse of about five years until his brief sojourn at Corinth (and Cenchreae), suggesting 56–57 CE as the letter's date of composition. J.A. Fitzmyer has recently argued that the trial was definitely in 52 CE, since this was the exact year of Claudius's twenty-sixth acclamation as imperator, attested to by a little-known inscription at Kys ('The Pauline Letters and the Lucan Account of Paul's Missionary Journeys', *SBLSP* [1988], pp. 82-90). Gallio's correspondence with his younger brother, Seneca, suggests that he left office in the same year as his appointment and returned home by sea because of an illness. This would shift the writing of Romans, on an Acts dating, more firmly into 57 CE.

3. R. Jewett notes certain analyses of Paul's departure from Philippi on his fifth journey to Jerusalem, recorded by Acts 20.6, which can be co-ordinated with feast days and astronomical tables. 54 and 57 CE seem the best dates, this last corroborating the previous suggestion of 57 (*A Chronology of Paul's Life* [Philadelphia: Fortress Press, 1979], pp. 49-50).

4. The place from which Paul wrote can be roughly ascertained from ch. 16— assuming that it belongs to the original letter. Phoebe, who is to carry the letter, is from Cenchreae, Corinth's eastern port city (Rom. 16.1). Gaius, 'whose hospitality. . . [Paul] enjoys', sends his greetings (Rom. 16.23). If he is the Gaius of 1 Cor. 1.14, Paul would seem to be writing from Corinth, the more so if Gaius is to be identified with the Titius Justus of Acts 18.7 (cf. E.J. Goodspeed, 'Gaius Titius

the exact form of the original letter, but this debate has little relevance for the interpretation of 3.21-26 and its context—although we will address this dispute briefly in the following chapter. One question of provenance, however, does require a more detailed examination for this study, namely, the basic cultural and religious identity of the recipients of the letter. This information is critical for any reasoning from the nature of the readership—a neglected factor in much traditional interpretation. Here we are interested primarily in whether the letter's recipients included a significant number of Jewish Christians.[1] A more detailed breakdown of the nature of the letter's recipients is not necessary, even if, indeed, it were possible.[2] It seems, moreover, that several considerations imply that Paul's addressees included a substantial number of Jewish Christians:[3]

Justus', *JBL* 69 [1950], pp. 382-83). In addition to this, Erastus, 'the city's director of public works' (16.23), is probably identifiable with the official mentioned in a Latin inscription found at Corinth: 'Erastus laid this pavement at his own expense, in appreciation of his appointment as aedile'. Even without the evidence of ch. 16, Corinth seems the logical point of origin as the place from which Paul probably left for Jerusalem with the collection from the Gentile churches; cf. 2 Cor. 1.15-17; 9.4-5; Rom. 15.25-28.

    1.   We are not able to engage here with the crucial but very difficult question for the broader interpretation of Romans of why Paul seems to be writing to Jewish Christians at Rome, and also why he is interacting with Jewish concerns throughout the letter, when he is the apostle to the Gentiles and seems to address the letter directly to Gentiles in the epistolary opening and closing (and at various points throughout the letter). Two recent attempts to engage with this 'double character' in the letter include L.A. Jervis, *The Purpose of Romans: A Comparative Letter Structure Investigation* (JSNTSup, 55; Sheffield: JSOT Press, 1991), and N. Elliott, *The Rhetoric of Romans: Argumentative Constraint and Strategy and Paul's Dialogue with Judaism* (JSNTSup, 45; Sheffield: JSOT Press, 1990). At this point we must also set aside the interesting but irrelevant question concerning the precise nature of Jewish Christianity and its relationship with Judaism. For a discussion of this delicate issue, cf. R.N. Longenecker, *The Christology of Early Jewish Christianity* (London: SCM Press, 1970), pp. 1-12.

    2.   Perhaps the most ambitious such attempt is by P. Minear in his *The Obedience of Faith* (London: SCM Press, 1971), but most judge his delineation of seven separate groups at Rome to be unsubstantiated.

    3.   We must limit ourselves here mainly to internal arguments—a procedure which is also followed wherever possible throughout the following study, for reasons of method. Because of the fluid nature of language and meaning, it is impor-tant to give textual data in the immediate vicinity of a problem (first, in the immediate

(1) Paul addresses Jews directly at various points in the letter. One instance of this is his aside at 7.1, γινώσκουσιν γὰρ νόμον λαλῶ.[1] This is supplemented by 1.14 and 16, where Paul states that he is obligated to both Greeks *and non-Greeks*, that is (v. 16), Ἰουδαίῳ τε πρῶτον καὶ Ἕλληνι (repeated in 2.9, 10 and 3.9).[2] Similarly, in 4.1 Paul refers to Abraham as '*our* forefather *according to the flesh*' (τὸν προπάτορα ἡμῶν κατὰ σάρκα).[3] The diatribe of 2.17-24 also directly addresses a hypothetical Jew: εἰ δὲ σὺ Ἰουδαῖος ἐπονομάζῃ καὶ ἐπαναπαύῃ νόμῳ καὶ καυχᾶσαι ἐν θεῷ κτλ.[4] Further, certain of Paul's occasional second person remarks elsewhere (2.9, 10; 3.8, 9) suggest that he was conscious of Jews within his audience. Thus, Paul's frequent manner of address within the letter suggests at least a partial Jewish presence among the letter's recipients.

(2) Paul discusses Jewish themes extensively in Romans, but this is a strategy which would make little sense if his audience were entirely

context, and then in the same document) priority over all other evidence, including documents written by the same author but at different times and to different situations. We are fortunate that the length and complexity of Romans probably gives us more local information than any of Paul's other letters. Consequently, the application of the principle of 'internal determination' is easier.

1.   This comment is a little vague, but a specific reference to the Mosaic Law seems likely, and a broader reference including the Mosaic Law is almost certain; cf. A.J.M. Wedderburn, *Baptism and Resurrection: Studies in Pauline Theology against its Graeco-Roman Background* (Tübingen: Mohr [Paul Siebeck], 1987), p. 41, esp. n. 4. Wedderburn cites Althaus, Diezinger, Leenhardt, Lietzmann, Murray, Räisänen, Schlatter and Wilckens in favour of a Mosaic reference, and Best, Denney, Käsemann, Knox, Lagrange, Michel and Sanday and Headlam, in support of a more general reference. Cranfield is also confident that the reference is Mosaic (citing Aquinas in support, *Romans*, I, p. 333) as is Dunn (citing v. 4 [*Romans 1–8*, p. 359]).

2.   This point is often overlooked, but is it not curious that the Apostle to the Gentiles would explicitly (and repeatedly) claim a similar obligation and prerogative with respect to the Jews?

3.   The easiest way to read this statement is to assume the presence of Jews in Paul's audience—although many scholars have shrunk from the reading's implications. *Contra* Dunn, *Romans 1–8*, p. liii. His comments on pp. 199 and 226-27 seem almost at cross-purposes. Cf. the comments of R.B. Hays, '"Have we Found Abraham to be our Fore-Father according to the Flesh?' A Reconsideration of Rom. 4:1', *NovT* (1985), pp. 76-98.

4.   We may allow for the fact that this is the style of diatribal argument. But note that for the diatribe to be effective it must somehow engage the audience.

Gentile (and had not been subject to Jewish teaching).[1] If he intended much of his letter to be understood, it would seem that he was expecting at least some Jews to be present.[2] We may note two of these themes in particular:[3]

a. Paul quotes the OT frequently in Romans (approximately 54 of 83 citations in his corpus).[4] Only Galatians approaches the density of the scriptural citations in Romans (10 references),[5] and Jewish influence is certainly obvious in Galatia! The Corinthian correspondence also utilizes Scripture, although far less frequently;[6] yet, once again, this church had been subject to Jewish-Christian instruction. The implication from this correlation is that Paul only cited Scripture when writing to churches that either had Jewish-Christian members, or had been taught by Jewish Christians. The saturation of Romans with such quotations consequently suggests a Jewish audience rather strongly.

1.   It is insufficient to argue against this that Paul is merely defining the correct relationship between a Gentile group and the Jewish religion, because for this purpose ch. 11 alone would suffice. In addition to this, many of his discussions, some of them famously impassioned, seem peripheral to such an objective (e.g. ch. 7): cf. Dunn, *Romans 1–8*, pp. liii-liv.

2.   This unusually heavy emphasis on Jewish materials is particularly obvious when Romans is compared with some of Paul's other letters that seem to be directed to Gentiles. For example, the Thessalonian correspondence is largely devoid of these themes. The implication in these letters is that Paul knows his audience will neither understand such issues nor be interested in them. And the converse applies to Romans. Paul's high expectation with respect to the recipients' comprehension of Jewish issues suggests a significant Jewish-Christian presence at Rome.

3.   Many more could be noted, for example, Paul's extensive discussions of the law (2.17-24; 4.13-15; 7.1-25), of circumcision (2.25-29; 4.9-12) and of Israel (9.1–11.32).

4.   Citations from R.N. Longenecker, *Biblical Exegesis in the Apostolic Period* (Grand Rapids: Eerdmans, 1975), pp. 108-11; cf. 65 citations according to the index in Nestle–Aland (p. 899).

5.   Eleven in Nestle–Aland (p. 900).

6.   Fifteen quotations in 1 Corinthians, 7 in 2 Corinthians; cf. 17 in 1 Corinthians, and 11 in 2 Corinthians according to Nestle–Aland (pp. 899-900). Longenecker observes: 'The great bulk of his biblical quotations are to be found in the so-called *Hauptbriefe* (Romans, I and II Corinthians, Galatians), with only six appearing elsewhere (four in Ephesians, one in I Timothy and one in II Timothy)' (*Biblical Exegesis*, p. 107; cf. six in Ephesians according to Nestle–Aland, p. 900).

b. There seems to be a scarlet thread of Levitical imagery running through Romans. Martin Hengel, among others, has discerned a muted theme of high-priestly activity that surfaces occasionally within the letter in relation to Christ. In 1.4 Christ is appointed Son of God by the πνεῦμα ἁγιωσύνης, 'the Spirit of sanctification', which is perhaps a deliberate evocation of the cultically resonant ἁγιάζω word group.[1] And in 5.2 Christ obtains 'access', προσαγωγή, for the believer into the presence of God.[2] In 8.3 Jesus' death is described as περὶ ἁμαρτίας, the standard LXX rendering of 'sin-offering' (*ḥaṭṭā't*).[3] Similarly, in 8.34 Christ fulfils the priestly function of interceding at the right hand of God for his people.[4]

The word διάκονος, used in 15.8, may also align with these cultically resonant terms and phrases.[5] And Hengel notes that the theme of καταλλαγή had cultic connotations in certain Graeco-Roman texts.[6] Finally, this use of Levitical and sacrificial imagery even seems to extend, on occasion, to Paul and to the believer.[7]

1. It is a point not noted by Hengel, but cf. the great significance of 'the Spirit of Holiness' at Qumran, a community with marked priestly interests (1QS 4.21; 8.16; 9.3; 1QH 7.6-7; 9.32; 12.12; cf. also *T. Levi* 18.11): cf. M. Hengel, *The Atonement* (trans. J. Bowden; London: SCM Press, 1981), pp. 45-47.

2. Cf. Eph. 2.18; 3.2; Heb. 4.16, and 1 Pet. 3.18—in view of these references, Dunn's objection seems forced (*Romans 1–8*, p. 248).

3. Cf. 1 Jn 2.2; 4.10, where περὶ ἁμαρτίας is combined with ἱλασμός. Cf. also Lev. 5.6-7, 11; 16.3, 5, 9; Num. 6.16; 7.16; 2 Chron. 29.23-24; Neh. 10.33; Ezek. 42.13; 43.19. Dunn cites Wright, Wilckens, Denney and Michel here *contra* Lagrange, Lietzmann, Barrett, Murray, Black, Cranfield and Zeller. He himself finds a sacrificial reference 'wholly natural and unremarkable in a first-century context' (*Romans 1–8*, p. 422).

4. A muted reference to Ps. 110?

5. Cf. BADG, pp. 184-85. The word can mean simply 'helper', but, particularly in view of the foregoing (and 15.16), it is just as appropriately rendered by 'deacon', with the attendant connotations of priestly ministry and officiation (so LSJ, p. 398, meaning 2: cf. also Paul's self-reference at 11.13, which is also cultically reinforced by 15.16).

6. In 5.1-10 it occurs in the context of αἷμα, a word already sacrificially nuanced by ἱλαστήριον in 3.25: see Sophocles, *Ajax* 744, and *OGIS* 218.105 (LSJ, p. 899), but cf. especially 2 Macc. 1.5; 5.20; 7.33; 8.3-5 and 29. So Dunn: 'a sharp distinction between the language of sacrifice and that of reconciliation should be avoided; in martyr theology the two had already merged' (*Romans 1–8*, p. 259)—cf. also Eph. 2.16.

7. In 9.1-5 Paul grieves over Israel and recounts its earlier privileges, which

It seems fair, therefore, to claim that a theme of Levitical and sacrificial imagery runs, partially submerged, throughout the text of Romans. Although not overt (as, for example, in the manner of Hebrews),[1] it is nevertheless present. But such imagery would only make sense if at least some of the readers of Romans were Jews. Paul's subtlety here would be lost on Gentiles.

(3) A further, although weaker, observation is that the greetings of ch. 16 seem to include references to a number of Jewish Christians. The apostles Andronicus and Junia were 'in Christ' before Paul (Rom. 16.7), and so presumably were not the fruit of Paul's Gentile mission. They are also called his fellow countrymen. Similarly, Ἡρῳδίωνα in v. 11 is Paul's συγγενῆ.[2] And it is worth noting that Priscilla and Aquila had a Jewish background according to Acts.[3]

Admittedly, however, for this argument to hold, these references would have to have been within the original letter, and, while the weight of scholarly opinion would favour this, it is only fair to note

include ἡ δόξα καὶ αἱ διαθῆκαι καὶ ἡ νομοθεσία καὶ ἡ λατρεία. In 12.1 Paul exhorts the believers, παραστῆσαι τὰ σώματα ὑμῶν θυσίαν ζῶσαν ἁγίαν εὐάρεστον τῷ θεῷ τὴν λογικὴν λατρείαν ὑμῶν. And in 15.16 he states: εἰς τὸ εἶναί με λειτουργὸν Χριστοῦ Ἰησοῦ εἰς τὰ ἔθνη ἱερουργοῦντα τὸ εὐαγγέλιον τοῦ θεοῦ ἵνα γένηται ἡ προσφορὰ τῶν ἐθνῶν εὐπρόσδεκτος ἡγιασμένη ἐν πνεύματι ἁγίῳ. This last passage is saturated with sacrificial and liturgical motifs. It also stylistically evokes 1.4, locking the body of the letter between its two personal sections in an overarching pattern of the cultically resonant idea of 'sanctification'. Cf. the similar evocation of 1.1-4 and 1.5 by 15.25-27 (εὐαγγέλιον, οἱ προφῆται, αἱ γραφαί, ὑπακοὴν πίστεως).

1. The precise correlation between these motifs, and the argument and terminology of Hebrews is very striking. Cf. Stuhlmacher's comments in 'Recent Exegesis' (pp. 98-100), especially the observation that 'Hebrews 9 confirms to a tee the Jewish-Christian message the tradition intends to convey' (p. 103).

2. In Rom. 9.3 this clearly means a fellow Jew: cf. BADG, LSJ.

3. Acts 18.2 calls Aquila a Jew, and v. 4 suggests that Paul and Aquila continued to frequent the synagogue together. It is speculative but intriguing to note that Rufus (Rom. 16.13) might be the son of Simon of Cyrene (Mk 15.21). People of Cyprus and Cyrene founded the church at Antioch (Acts 11.20), and they were Jewish Christians. Furthermore, the household of Aristobulus may have belonged to the grandson of Herod the Great who bore this name, and who lived under royal favour during the reign of Claudius (Sanday and Headlam, *Romans*, pp. 425-26). Paul Trebilco argues that, in fact, every name in Rom. 16 may be attested as Jewish: 'Women as Co-Workers and Leaders in Paul's Letters', *Journal of the Christian Brethren Research Fellowship* 112 (1990), pp. 27-36.

that the point is disputed—and not without reason: Rom. 16.1-20 reads like a very concise letter of commendation, with attached greetings and warnings.[1]

Consequently, it seems that several stylistic and substantive features of Romans assume a significant degree of Jewish knowledge on the part of at least some of its recipients. In what follows, therefore, I will assume at least a partially Jewish-Christian audience for Romans.[2] Any further specification of the nature of Roman Christianity, even if it is possible, does not affect the following argument overmuch.

1. H. Gamble argues that ch. 16 is an integral part of the original letter (*The Textual History of the Letter to the Romans* [Grand Rapids: Eerdmans, 1977]); cf. also B.N. Kaye, '"To the Romans and Others" Revisited', *NovT* 18 (1976), pp. 38-41. T.W. Manson suggests the converse ('St Paul's Letter to the Romans— and Others', in *The Romans Debate* [ed. K. Donfried; Minneapolis: Augsburg, 1977], pp. 1-16).

2. I have limited myself here to internal evidence; however, external evidence for the Jewish-Christian introduction of Christianity to Rome may be found in Suetonius's famous remark: *Judaeos impulsore Chresto assidue tumultuantes Roma expulit* (*Life of Claudius* 25). The fourth-century Ambrosiaster also makes the interesting remark that 'without seeing displays of mighty works, or any one of the apostles, they accepted the faith of Christ, *though with Jewish rites*' (emphasis added, trans. Dodd, with original quote from Sanday and Headlam, *Romans*, pp. xxv-xxvi). It is difficult to see how Ambrosiaster could have known this from the NT (without a modern critical reading)—the Church's later split with Judaism, and her glorification of Paul and of Rome, could hardly have encouraged such a comment (Cranfield still denies this [*Romans*, I, p. 20]).

Dunn gives a lucid, comprehensive and up-to-date evaluation of the question in his introduction (*Romans 1–8*, pp. xliv-lxix). He discusses the Jewish community in Rome after Pompey's annexation of Judaea, and argues for the probable origin of Roman Christianity from this local Judaism (citing the strong commercial, political and religious links between Rome and Palestine; the use of the Synagogue as a mission platform by the early church; Suetonius's remark; and so on). Dunn also argues points (2a) and (3) above. His conclusion concerning the composition of the Roman church(es), however, seems to go beyond the evidence, when he argues that it was primarily Gentile with a small minority of marginalized Jews (p. xlix). This under-values the evidence that suggests a strong Jewish presence, and seems to over-estimate the significance of Claudius's expulsion (in 49 CE?) about which we know very little, and even less concerning its sociological consequences. Dunn also gives a comprehensive bibliography (note esp. Romano Penna, 'Les juifs à Rome au temps de l'apôtre Paul', *NTS* 28 [1982], pp. 321-47; and E.A. Judge and G.S.R. Thomas, 'The Origin of the Church at Rome: A New Solution?', *RTR* 25 [1966], pp. 81-93).

3. The Development of the Argument

An interpretation of Rom. 3.21-26 is built up throughout the following study in four stages (which correspond to the four following chapters).

In Chapter 1, current attempts to interpret the passage are analysed. From this it becomes apparent that any interpretation of Rom. 3.21-26 must address an agenda of questions, ranging from a lexical to a theological level, but that, within this agenda, the critical preliminary item is the series of syntactical decisions which must be made concerning the mutual relations among the clauses and phrases that comprise 3.21-26.

There are two hypotheses current in the literature that attempt (at least partially) to resolve this syntactical confusion, and these are examined carefully. The first posits the quotation of early church confessional material within the middle section of the passage, either in vv. 24a-26a or in vv. 25a-26a. Such a view helps to explain the awkwardness of the syntactical transitions through the central section.

The second hypothesis suggests reading the phrase πίστις ’Ιησοῦ Χριστοῦ at v. 22b as a subjective genitive, rather than as a more traditional objective genitive. This eliminates the apparent redundancy within v. 22, and also influences the reading of the two subsequent occurrences of πίστις in the passage.

After these two theories have been evaluated, however, it is apparent that further insight into the section is still desirable, and indeed necessary. Chapter 2 is therefore devoted to the distinctive insight that rhetorical analysis provides. In this section, first of all the variegated use of rhetoric by biblical scholars is set in some kind of order, with the particular perspective adopted by the present study being defined. Then the passage itself is subjected to rhetorical scrutiny and, during this process, a series of syntactical and stylistic clarifications begins to accumulate. But it also becomes apparent that the meaning of certain key words must also be investigated further if the passage is to be fully understood. These key words fall into two groups, which are then analysed in two further chapters.

Chapter 3 analyses the three highly significant atonement words in the passage, that is, ἀπολύτρωσις, ἱλαστήριον and αἷμα. Previous analyses are scrutinized in view of the insights gained from a rhetorical perspective, and this results in a rather different slant on the various debates. Similarly, the complex and contentious righteousness debate is evaluated in Chapter 4 in terms of the semantic evidence given by 3.21-26, and by the rest of the letter, again resulting in new perspectives on existing issues.

When these lexical analyses have been completed, the results of the various investigations are drawn together and combined in a suggested reading of the text. At this point, perhaps not surprisingly, I argue that a rather different sense has emerged from 3.21-26 compared with its usual rendering. It would seem that in this section Paul is simply describing the eschatological revelation of the saving righteousness of God in Christ. That is, Christ reveals God's final salvation in his life of faithful obedience and, above all, in his faithful endurance of death on the Cross. It is this event that constitutes the revelation of God's saving power, particularly in its sacrificial removal of sin. Thus, it seems that a theology of the Cross lies beneath the surface of 3.21-26, though one cast in unusually elegant and Jewish terms.

Chapter 1

PREVIOUS SYNTACTICAL ANALYSES OF ROMANS 3.21-26

1. Previous Scholarly Study and the Interpretative Agenda

A brief review of previous scholarly study on Rom. 3.21-26, particularly that of the commentators, is perhaps the best place to begin this investigation, since such a review reveals those issues that are the subject of dispute, and allows the establishment of an 'interpretative agenda' that must be addressed if the passage is to be appropriately exegeted.[1] Here we will simply read through the passage in a linear fashion and address the interpretative questions which arise as they would occur to a reader or listener.

Most scholars note the contrast that this section presents over against the preceding argument suggested by Paul's opening phrase, νυνὶ δέ, in v. 21. James Dunn comments: 'no one disputes that with the νυνὶ δέ of v. 21 Paul intends a decisive shift in the argument to a new stage: the eschatological state of affairs brought about by Christ'.[2] But there is some dispute over whether the contrast is temporal or argumentative, or perhaps both. Most commentators, in fact, opt for a combined reading.[3]

---

1. The literature on Romans, which usually includes specific comment on 3.21-26, is so voluminous that it is unfortunately impossible to address it exhaustively here. We therefore confine ourselves largely to the following commentaries: Barth, Byrne, Cranfield, Dunn, Käsemann, Parker's summary of select Reformation commentators, Sanday and Headlam, Wilckens and Ziesler. Fuller lists of commentaries on Romans may be found in Cranfield, *Romans*, I, Dunn, *Romans 1–8*, p. 161, and in G. Davies, *Faith and Obedience in Romans* (JSNTSup, 39; Sheffield: JSOT Press, 1990), pp. 205-207.

2. *Romans 1–8*, p. 161.

3. Cranfield argues that some temporal sense is actually undeniable in view of the verb (*Romans*, I, p. 201), and Barth's rendering is particularly powerful: '*But now* directs our attention to time which is beyond time, to space which has no

Paul then prefaces the subject of the sentence, δικαιοσύνη θεοῦ, with the statement χωρὶς νόμου, which seems a deliberate contrast to the clause that immediately follows the subject, μαρτυρουμένη ὑπὸ τοῦ νόμου τῶν προφητῶν. Scholars generally seem untroubled by the theological tension implicit within this antithesis, usually explaining it in terms of different functions of the law, whether as a salvific system or as Scripture.[1]

The genitive construction δικαιοσύνη θεοῦ is the first major point of controversy in the section. Here a question arises concerning the nature of the genitive, that is, whether it is subjective, objective, or some other perhaps combined sense. The meaning of δικαιοσύνη itself is also unclear: Does it suggest justice, salvation, power, liberation, covenant-faithfulness, something else, or some combination of the foregoing?

In the earlier commentaries, an objective genitive reading is almost universally favoured,[2] and this finds a few modern supporters.[3] Most

---

locality, to impossible possibility, to the gospel of transformation, to the imminent coming of the Kingdom of God, to affirmation in negation, to salvation in the world, to acquittal in condemnation, to eternity in time, to life in death' (*The Epistle to the Romans* [trans. E.C. Hoskyns; London: Oxford University Press, 1952 (1933)], pp. 92-93).

1.   Perhaps a rabbi would feel these tensions more strongly than the predominantly Gentile commentators on Romans, who cheerfully assume that these two functions of the *torah* are separable: cf. Dunn, who talks of covenant-membership as no longer dependent on the possession and keeping of the law (*Romans 1–8*, pp. 161, 165, 176-77). A. Nygren has a particularly full discussion (*Commentary on Romans* [trans. C. Rasmussen; Philadelphia: Muhlenberg Press, 1974], pp. 147-49), but once again Barth is noteworthy. He argues that God is free to speak where he wills, therefore he can speak apart from the law if he so wishes: 'This "otherness" [of God's speaking] cuts sharply through all human sense of possession and semipossession. . .God speaks where there is *law*; but he speaks also where there is no law. . .God is free' (*Romans*, pp. 92, 95).

2.   Sanday and Headlam note that 'for some time past it has seemed to be almost an accepted exegetical tradition that the "righteousness of God" means here "a righteousness of which God is the author and man the recipient", a righteousness not so much "*of God*" as "*from God*", i.e. a state or condition of righteousness bestowed by God upon man' (*Romans*, p. 24). No doubt this tendency was in large measure attributable to Luther. He stated that 'here [Rom. 1.17 and following]. . . "the righteousness of God" must not be understood as that righteousness by which he is righteous in himself, but as that righteousness by which we are made righteous (justified) by Him, and this happens through faith in the gospel' (*Lectures on Romans* [trans.

twentieth-century commentators, however, incline towards a subjective construal, but argue that Paul's meaning rather exceeds the limitations of grammar at this point. It is as if the dynamic quality of God's righteousness bursts out of its subjective definition![1] There is also a virtual unanimity among modern commentators (over against the Mediaeval and Reformation traditions) that δικαιοσύνη is nuanced more in terms of salvation and liberation (probably with covenantal

W. Pauck; Philadelphia: Westminster Press, 1961], p. 18—written by Luther himself in 1515). Parker notes that Haresche, Melanchthon, and Bucer all take δικαιοσύνη θεοῦ as an objective genitive (variously nuanced), but it is interesting that Calvin is more cautious: 'It is doubtful why he calls the righteousness which we obtain by faith the righteousness of God. Either because it alone stands firm before God, or because it is that which the Lord in his mercy bestows on us. Either interpretation fits in well and we do not argue for the one side or the other.' That is, Calvin cannot decide between a righteousness *before* God and a righteousness *from* God. But Calvin, like his contemporaries, does not really consider a subjective genitive construction a serious possibility (Parker, *Commentaries*, pp. 145-46).

3.   Notably Cranfield: 'δικαιοσύνη θεοῦ is no doubt to be understood both here and in v. 22 in the same sense as it has in 1.17, that is, as meaning a status of righteousness before God which is God's gift' (*Romans*, I, p. 202). He is supported by Black (*Romans* [London: Marshall, Morgan & Scott, 1973] pp. 45, 66), and J. Knox ('The Epistle to the Romans', in *The Interpreter's Bible* [ed. G.A. Buttrick *et al.*; New York: Abingdon Press, 1957], IX, pp. 428-29; cf. pp. 393-94), who understand the phrase as a subjective genitive at 1.16-17, but, rather curiously, follow an objective reading at 3.21-22. O'Neill (*Romans*, pp. 72-73) and Schlier concur (but not Nygren; *contra* Cranfield, see Nygren, *Romans*, pp. 75, 76).

1.   Sanday and Headlam anticipated this perspective, commenting in 1896: 'The very cogency of the arguments on both sides is enough to show that the two views which we have set over against each other are not mutually exclusive but rather inclusive. The righteousness of which the Apostle is speaking not only proceeds from God but *is* the righteousness of God Himself: it is this, however, not as inherent in the Divine Essence but as going forth and embracing the personalities of men' (*Romans*, p. 25). They note two earlier arguments for a subjective reading by J. Barmby (*Romans* [London: Funk & Wagnalls, 1980], pp. x-xiv, 8-9, esp. x-xi), and A. Robertson (in *The Thinker*, Nov. 1893)—a view, they note, which is 'beginning to attract some attention in Germany' (!). The recent consensus is probably due in large measure to Ernst Käsemann's famous study: '"The Righteousness of God" in Paul', in *idem*, *New Testament Questions for Today* (trans. W.J. Montague; London: SCM Press, 1969 [1965]), pp. 168-82.

associations), than in terms of strictly forensic notions of justice and moral rectitude.[1]

In v. 22 a second ambiguous genitive is introduced within the expression διὰ πίστεως Ἰησοῦ Χριστοῦ εἰς πάντας τοὺς πιστεύοντας. In contrast to the customary reading of the first problematic genitive, however, διὰ πίστεως Ἰησοῦ Χριστοῦ has usually been interpreted as an objective genitive, hence meaning 'through faith in Jesus Christ'.[2] Verse 22 is therefore read as a strong statement concerning the role of the believer's faith in appropriating salvation through Christ: righteousness is available 'through faith in Jesus Christ, to all who have faith'.

A subjective understanding of the genitive would, admittedly, eliminate a nagging sense of redundancy within the verse (and throughout the passage), but this reading only surfaces, even as an interpretative possibility, in the occasional commentary, being argued primarily in specialized studies.[3] Cranfield exemplifies the confidence

1. See e.g. Barth (*Romans*, pp. 40-41), B. Byrne (*Reckoning with Romans* [Wilmington, DE: Michael Glazier, 1986], pp. 42-47, 93-94), Dunn (*Romans 1–8*, pp. 165-82, who emphasizes the covenantal aspect of the terminology), Käsemann (*Romans*, p. 93, God's right to his creation—probably an influence from Stuhlmacher's important study), Sanday and Headlam (*Romans*, pp. 24-25, 34-39, 82-83), and J.A.T. Ziesler (*Paul's Letter to the Romans* [London: SCM Press, 1989], pp. 70-71, 107-108).

2. Although the addition of ἐπὶ πάντας (to yield εἰς πάντας καὶ ἐπὶ πάντας τοὺς πιστεύοντας) suggested a subjective, or hypostasized, reading to some sixteenth-century commentators: Caietan said, 'the apostle proves that the righteousness of God by the faith of Jesus Christ is in all and upon all', and Haresche, 'whatever a Christian knows about the aforesaid righteousness of God he knows by the mediation of the Faith'. But Bullinger simply rolled all the references into a pleonasm, and Calvin stated, 'he repeats the same thing in different forms of expression *ad auxesim*' (for these quotations cf. Parker, *Commentaries*, pp. 147, 157). It is interesting that Nygren favours this longer reading (although the MS evidence is not particularly strong: D, G, K, a marginal gloss in S, 150). So does O'Neill, *Romans*, p. 73.

3. It is presented as a serious option only by Byrne (*Reckoning*, pp. 79-80), and cursorily by Ziesler (*Romans*, p. 109). Sanday and Headlam note a much earlier round in the same discussion, deciding against it. Cranfield, Dunn and Käsemann all dismiss the possibility rather abruptly. Apart from these commentators, the alternative is seldom even noted, although forthcoming commentaries by R. Jewett (Hermeneia) and R. Longenecker (New International Greek Testament Commentary) will probably treat the issue more sympathetically. For a detailed discussion of this point and bibliography, cf. section C, below.

of almost all commentators in the objective reading at this point: 'The suggestion that it should be understood as subjective. . . is altogether unconvincing'.[1]

At the close of v. 22 most commentators suggest that a break in the argument takes place as Paul makes a retrospective comment concerning the universality of salvation: οὐ γάρ ἐστιν διαστολή κτλ. Byrne, for example, comments that

> Paul has more to say about the role of Christ in the redeeming effects of God's righteousness. Before pursuing this, however, he turns aside (vv. 22d-23) for a moment to insist once more upon the universal and equal need for a gracious justification from God. . . [in a] terse résumé of 1.18–3.20.[2]

Consequently, the remark οὐ γάρ ἐστιν διαστολή seems to be expanded by the clause πάντες γὰρ ἥμαρτον καὶ ὑστεροῦνται τῆς δόξης τοῦ θεοῦ, both statements apparently referring to Paul's first use of πᾶς in v. 22.

The ensuing sentence is difficult for commentators to interpret, however, because what begins as an aside seems to end as a significant contribution to the passage, as Paul's discussion continues through vv. 24 and 25. Debate focuses particularly on the participle beginning v. 24, δικαιούμενοι, which provides a link to the statements that follow concerning grace and redemption.[3] Cranfield's solution here may be taken as representative (and he is more thorough than most!). He takes the participle in v. 24 as formally dependent on πάντες in v. 23, but adds that

> at the same time. . . [one must] recognize that in filling out the explanation of v. 22b Paul has, as a matter of fact, also made a substantial addition to the treatment of the main theme of the paragraph.[4]

---

1. Cranfield, *Romans*, I, p. 203 n. 2 (discussing Haussleiter's view). Ziesler is equivocal (*Romans*, p. 109), and, characteristically, Barth is quite original. He often takes 'faith' in Romans as a reference to God's faithfulness (cf. *Romans*, p. 96), but on one occasion refers it to Christ's obedience: 'His entering within the deepest darkness of human ambiguity and abiding within it is *THE* faithfulness. The life of Jesus is perfected obedience to the will of the faithful God' (p. 97).

2. *Reckoning*, p. 80.

3. Sanday and Headlam's discussion of four grammatical options for this section is particularly good (*Romans*, p. 85).

4. Cranfield (*Romans*, I, p. 205).

The problem is usually solved by the commentators along these lines, with the difficulties in the Greek text tending in any case to disappear within their respective translations.

An alternative explanation for the apparently awkward transition was proposed by Rudolph Bultmann, and was later considerably expanded and strengthened by his pupil, Ernst Käsemann, namely, that the participle marks a transition from Paul's free composition to the quotation of early church confessional material—perhaps a short creed, or something similar.[1] This theory, which has permutated into a number of variants, will be examined in the next section. Suffice it here to say that it has not been widely accepted by commentators, although it seems to be gaining ground.[2]

It should also be noted that this central section contains a number of lexical difficulties. In v. 23 the precise reference of δόξα is difficult to determine. Various alternatives have been suggested: God's glory; heaven as the realm of his reflected glory; humanity's lost state and image in paradise; God's good opinion; and so on. Some reference to the divine likeness or image which was enjoyed by Adam in paradise, but lost through the Fall, is the most widely favoured reading.[3]

Similarly, the precise nature of the 'rightness' given by δικαιού- μενοι in v. 24 raises both hotly disputed and theologically critical issues. The general alternatives presented vary between a forensic reading, which suggests relational restoration and acquittal, and a more ethical reading, which suggests inner transformation. At this

1. R. Bultmann, 'Glossen im Römerbrief', *TLZ* 4 (1947), pp. 197-202; *idem, Theology of the New Testament* (trans. K. Grobel; 2 vols.; New York: Scribners, 1951–55 [1948]), I, p. 46; and E. Käsemann, 'Zum Verständnis von Römer 3,24-26', *ZNW* 43 (1950–51), pp. 150-54.

2. Käsemann, of course, endorses it (*Romans*, pp. 92, 95), as does U. Wilckens (in a slightly different form: *Der Brief an die Römer* [3 vols.; Zürich: Neukirchener Verlag, 1978], I, pp. 183-84). Bruce (*The Letter of Paul to the Romans: An Introduction and Commentary* [Grand Rapids: Eerdmans, 1985], p. 102), Byrne (*Reckoning*, p. 84), Dunn (*Romans 1–8*, pp. 164, 179, 182-83), and Ziesler (*Romans*, pp. 110-11, 115) are more cautious, but tentatively in favour.

3. Barmby presents the options clearly (*Romans*, pp. 82-84). The various observations of Black (*Romans*, pp. 66-67: see also his 'The Pauline Doctrine of the Second Adam', *SJT* 7 [1954], pp. 170-79), Cranfield, who cites Jewish reflections on Adam (*Gen. R.* 12.5, *3 Bar.* 4.16, and *T. Moses* 21.6; *Romans*, I, pp. 205-206), and Käsemann (it is similar to εἰκών speculation in later Wisdom literature: cf. Wisd. 2.23ff.; *Romans*, pp. 94, 95) are engaging.

point, however, the commentators almost unanimously favour a relational reading, and thus seldom speak of ethical transformation or ability—suggesting that the 'Protestant' reading of the verb is enjoying some ascendancy.[1]

A third lexical problem in v. 24 concerns the rare word ἀπολύτρωσις. A reading in the widely-attested extra-biblical sense of 'ransom' seems to support a substitutionary conception of the atonement, and it has been followed by some commentators.[2] But the perception of various theological problems in this reading have forced others to argue for a definitive influence from the LXX, where a broader notion of 'liberation' or 'deliverance' is often apparent.[3] This dispute, however, is far from settled.

In v. 25 a further cluster of syntactical and lexical problems is presented to the reader. Most commentators believe that Paul should at this point begin a new sentence, although it entails starting a sentence with a relative pronoun in the accusative, ὅ v. This is somewhat awkward grammatically, but not unheard of,[4] and the semantic break

---

1. This is perhaps because the commentators are disproportionately Protestant. But various Catholic commentators also support such a reading, for example, Byrne: ' "Justification" is that verdict of acquittal, a declaration of legal right-standing that the faithful hope to hear at the time of the eschatological judgment. It means rescue— or "redemption"—from the captivity and oppression of the present, evil time and entrance into the blessing of salvation' (*Reckoning*, p. 81). Only specialized studies (discussed later) suggest a fundamentally ethical or transformational reading, although Barth is close with his strong emphasis on the creative power of the Word of God (*Romans*, pp. 102-103), as is Käsemann (*Romans*, p. 96).

2. E.g. Dunn (*Romans 1–8*, pp. 169, 170, 180), L. Morris (*The Epistle to the Romans* [Grand Rapids: Eerdmans, 1988], p. 179), J. Murray (*The Epistle to the Romans: The English Text with Introduction, Exposition, and Notes* [2 vols.; Grand Rapids: Eerdmans, 1959], pp. 115-16), and Sanday and Headlam (who emphasize costliness rather than price: *Romans*, p. 86). Cranfield notes the further support of Lagrange, Moffatt and Warfield for this position (although he himself thinks that the question must be left open: *Romans*, pp. 206-208).

3. E.g. Black (*Romans*, pp. 67-68), Byrne (*Reckoning*, p. 81), Nygren (*Romans*, pp. 155-56), and Ziesler (*Romans*, p. 111). Käsemann speaks of a 'liturgical' use in comparison to 1 Cor. 1.30 (*Romans*, p. 96). Cranfield notes further support for this position by F. Büchsel (*TWNT*, IV, p. 357) and D. Hill (*Greek Words and Hebrew Meanings* [Cambridge: Cambridge University Press, 1967], p. 76) (*Romans*, I, p. 206 n. 2).

4. Cf. A.T. Robertson, *A Grammar of the Greek New Testament in the Light of Historical Research* [London: Hodder & Stoughton, 1914], pp. 719-20.

is usually indicated in translations of the passage by a full stop. But Cranfield seems to undermine this suggestion by observing (correctly) that the pronoun in v. 25 is dependent grammatically on the preceding phrase, where it has an appropriate antecedent. Consequently, 'the whole of 25 and 26 is a single relative clause depending on Χριστῷ ᾽Ιησοῦ in v. 24. It consists of a main element followed by three formulations equivalent to final clauses which together serve to clarify the key word ἱλαστήριον.[1] Whatever alternative is finally followed, the syntactical nature and function of v. 25 remain rather obscure.

Irrespective, however, of whether vv. 25-26 is read as a relative clause or a sentence, ἱλαστήριον is emphasized as the dominant image in the section. ἱλαστήριον, the first of three further lexical problems within v. 25, is a rare word, attested elsewhere in the NT only at Heb. 9.5. Nevertheless, as the apparently critical atonement word in Rom. 3.21-26, considerable effort has been expended by commentators on ascertaining its meaning. Broadly speaking, two axes of dispute are observable. (1) Is the word a specific allusion to 'the mercy seat' that was central to the annual Jewish Festival of Atonement (*Yom Kippur*: cf. Lev. 16)?[2] Or, is it a more general sacrificial term, as easily understood by a Graeco-Roman audience as by a Jewish one? Further, (2) does the word carry the connotation of appeasing an angry deity, hence 'means of propitiation',[3] or is it to be read in the expiatory sense of cleansing, hence 'means of expiation'?[4]

Little convergence is apparent within this dispute, beyond a basic agreement that the word has sacrificial nuances. The specific sense of that sacrifice, and hence the specific function of the Cross of Christ (according to Paul), is a far from settled issue.

Verse 25 also contains the troublesome phrase διὰ [τῆς] πίστεως,

1. *Romans*, I, p. 208
2. So Barth (*Romans*, pp. 104-105), Bruce—'perhaps' (*Romans*, p. 101), Dunn (*Romans 1-8*, less confidently on p. 171 than on p. 180), and Nygren (*Romans*, pp. 156-58). Ziesler is open to the suggestion but unsure (*Romans*, pp. 113-14).
3. So Barmby (*Romans*, p. 84), Bruce (*Romans*, p. 101), Cranfield (*Romans*, I, pp. 214-18), Morris (*Romans*, pp. 180-82), and Murray (*Romans*, I, p. 117).
4. So E. Best (*The Letter of Paul to the Romans* [Cambridge: Cambridge University Press, 1967], p. 43), Käsemann (*Romans*, p. 97), O'Neill (*Romans*, pp. 74-75), and Ziesler (*Romans*, pp. 112-14).

which is awkward in that it separates two phrases that seem to belong together: ὅν προέθετο ὁ θεὸς ἱλαστήριον... ἐν τῷ αὐτοῦ αἵματι. Consequently, most commentators read διὰ πίστεως as a clumsily placed assertion of the importance of faith, comparable to v. 22 in meaning, but properly read apart from the main flow of the argument. So Käsemann concludes that 'the phrase διὰ πίστεως, which is not accidentally dropped from A... should be treated as a parenthesis'.[1] Conversely and somewhat atypically, Sanday and Headlam state that 'it is a quite legitimate combination'.[2] But O'Neill is the most candid about the difficulty: 'Most commentators prefer to take "through faith" with expiation and this produces the sense given by the RSV... but the Greek does not really allow it'.[3]

Another lexical problem within this verse is the meaning of the word προέθετο. Ordinarily the verb means either 'purposed' and 'intended', or 'demonstrated' and 'set forth publicly', although most have agreed with Sanday and Headlam in favouring 'set forth':[4]

> Both meanings would be in full accordance with the teaching of St Paul both elsewhere and in this Epistle... But when we turn to the immediate context we find it so full of terms denoting publicity (πεφανέρωται εἰς ἔνδειξιν, πρὸς τὴν ἔνδειξιν) that the latter sense [i.e. 'whom God set forth publicly'] seems preferable.[5]

1. *Romans*, pp. 97-98; cf. also Cranfield (*Romans*, I, p. 210), Dunn (*Romans*, I, p. 172), and Taylor (*The Epistle to the Romans* [London: Epworth Press, 1955], p. 33)—cf. also his 'Great Texts Reconsidered', *ExpTim* 50 (1938–39), pp. 297. Dunn (a little reluctantly) and Käsemann both reject Alfons Pluta's suggestion that πίστις refers here to God's covenant faithfulness, although Pluta's position is also argued, independently, by Barth (A. Pluta, *Gottes Bundestreue: Ein Schlüsselbegriff in Röm 3.25a* [Stuttgart: Katholisches Bibelwerk, 1969]). Dunn reasons: 'Pluta's suggestion that πίστις here refers to God's covenant faithfulness is attractive, in view of the emphasis of 3.3-4, 7... The possibility is not to be entirely excluded, but it is much more likely that Paul took the opportunity to stress once again that God reaches out to faith' (*Romans 1–8*, pp. 172-73)—but is it?
2. *Romans*, p. 89.
3. He himself omits the phrase as a marginal note, on the basis of A and 2127 (*Romans*, p. 76).
4. For example, Dunn (*Romans 1–8*, pp. 170-80), Käsemann (*Romans*, p. 97), O'Neill (*Romans*, p. 75).
5. *Romans*, p. 87. Cranfield (*Romans*, I, pp. 208-209) and others dissent, but they are in the minority. Calvin writes (supported by Pellicanus and Bucer), 'Here *proponere* does not mean to produce or display (*proferre*) or to present openly (*in*

The meaning of αἷμα in v. 25 is also disputed. Scholars disagree over whether the basic idea involves the release of life, or simply death. There is also some discussion over whether the word is sacrificially nuanced, or whether it simply refers to the loss of life (in some sense).[1] The majority accept the meaning of death in context,[2] and allow for a sacrificial allusion.

The interpretation of the final two semantic units within the passage (vv. 25c-26d) depends largely on the meaning given to πάρεσις. The almost universally accepted meaning is 'pass over' or 'overlook', as against a meaning more equivalent to ἄφεσις.[3] The clause in which πάρεσις occurs is consequently assumed to refer to a previous aeon in which sins are graciously overlooked by God in his forbearance (ἀνοχή; cf. 2.4) until proper action can be taken with the coming of Christ.[4] διά in the accusative is interpreted here in its usual causal sense of 'because of',[5] and ἔνδειξις is taken to mean 'proof' or

medium repraesentare), but to pre-ordain and pre-determine; so that it refers to God's mercy which spontaneously sought out a way to help our wretchedness' (Parker, *Commentaries*, p. 151). Ziesler is attracted by a technical, sacrificial reading, as found in the LXX (*Romans*, p. 114).

1.   So, e.g., Cranfield (*Romans*, I, p. 210), Dunn (*Romans 1–8*, p. 171), Käsemann (*Romans*, p. 87), and Ziesler (*Romans*, p. 114) support a sacrificial nuance, whereas Morris (*Romans*, p. 182) does not.

2.   Ziesler (*Romans*, p. 114) prefers 'life'.

3.   The only dissenters among the commentators are Barth and (somewhat ambiguously) Ziesler (*Romans*, pp. 115-16; cf. his *The Meaning of Righteousness in Paul* [Cambridge: Cambridge University Press, 1972], p. 210). They are supported by the KJV, G.A. Deissmann (*Paul: A Study in Social and Religious History* [trans. W.E. Wilson; New York: Harper & Harper, 2nd edn, 1957 (1912)], p. 172), W.G. Kümmel ('πάρεσις and ἔνδειξις: Ein Beitrag zum Verständnis der paulinischen Rechtfertigungslehre', in *idem, Heilgeschehen und Geschichte* [Marburg: Elwert, 1965], I, pp. 260-70, first published in *ZTK* 49 [1952], pp. 154-67), and J.A. Fitzmyer, 'Pauline Theology', *JBC*, p. 815 (s. 86).

4.   Given that the immediate context speaks of a present action against sin by means of Christ, it follows that any overlooking of sin must have taken place before his coming. And this links up neatly with the retrospective focus of the participle in v. 25d, προγεγονότων, which is linked with πάρεσις in a genitive construction.

5.   Other options do not really need to be explored, although some commentators favour them, namely, an instrumental sense analogous to διά in the genitive, which is followed by Käsemann (*Romans*, p. 99, citing Rom. 8.20; Rev. 11.14 and 12.13); and a prospective or future sense, which Paul seems to employ again in 4.24 and 25, but which is not widely attested in extra-biblical literature: cf. H.G. Meecham,

'vindication', rather than merely 'display' or 'demonstration'. The repeated δικαιοσύνη is also universally acknowledged to be God's (αὐτοῦ) at this point.[1]

This statement about God's action in the past is then usually read as a deliberately constructed counterpoint to the immediately following section, v. 26, that clearly deals with the present (cf. νῦν in v. 26ċ). Verse 26b-c suggests that, just as the gracious overlooking of past sin revealed God's merciful righteousness (vv. 25c-26a), so the death of Christ reveals his just (and merciful) righteousness in the present, because sins are not overlooked indefinitely but are appropriately dealt with in the Cross.

These two perspectives are then taken to be combined in a climactic concluding section, which essentially outlines a theodicy: εἰς τὸ εἶναι αὐτὸν δίκαιον καὶ δικαιοῦντα τὸν ἐκ πίστεως Ἰησοῦ. Here the adversative function of the καί which separates the conclusion's two δικ- terms, δίκαιος and δικαιοῦντα, tends to be emphasized. God is δίκαιος in that his justice is preserved as sin is punished on the Cross, 'and' he is δικαιοῦντα, in the sense of mercifully righteous, because he actively saves those who believe in Christ. Thus, on the one hand, God's abhorrence of sin is preserved because sin is atoned for by Christ's sacrificial death, while, on the other hand, God is able to show mercy to believing sinners by saving them in Christ. Justice and mercy, therefore, have been united in the Cross. Cranfield summarizes this reading of the passage as follows:

> For God to have forgiven men's sins lightly—a cheap forgiveness which would have implied that moral evil does not matter very much—would have been altogether unrighteous, a violation of His truth and profoundly unmerciful and unloving toward men. . . The purpose of Christ's being ἱλαστήριον was to achieve a divine forgiveness, which is worthy of God, consonant with His righteousness. . . It involves nothing less than God's bearing the intolerable burden of that evil Himself in the person of his own dear Son, the disclosure of the fulness of God's hatred of man's evil at the same time as it is its real and complete forgiveness.[2]

'Romans 3.25f.; 4.25—The Meaning of διάc. Acc.', *ExpTim* 50 (1938–39), p. 564.

1.   Even Cranfield concedes this: 'The reference to God's being righteous in the last part of v. 26 would seem to tell strongly in favour of understanding δικαιοσύνη in these two verses as referring to God's own righteousness' (*Romans*, I, p. 211).

2.   *Romans*, I, pp. 213-14.

This was the standard reading of Rom. 3.25-26 throughout the Middle Ages and Reformation,[1] and its influence is still apparent in most modern commentators, particularly those arising from the English-speaking tradition.[2] For many, Rom. 3.21-26 is simply the *locus classicus* for a 'satisfactory' (in the full theological sense of the word) understanding of the atonement.[3]

Other scholars, however, argue for a more continuous under-standing of Paul's depiction of the righteousness and righteous actions of God, and so suggest that the connective καί in v. 26d is more additive than adversative.[4] For example, Sanday and Headlam comment: 'It is not that "God is righteous *and yet* declares righteous the believer in Jesus", but that "He is righteous *and also*, we might almost say *and therefore*, declares righteous the believer"'. These scholars downplay the notion of divine justice and its strict demands, and tend to emphasize instead a constant divine action in terms of faithfulness and mercy (supporting this understanding of righteousness from the LXX).[5] Such a reading hinders the emergence of a classical picture of theodicy from the passage, where differing notions of δικαιοσύνη are reconciled in the Cross, although it is not without its own

1. See Parker, *Commentaries*, pp. 156-200.
2. So Dunn—rather nuanced (*Romans 1–8*, pp. 172, 181), Murray (*Romans*, I, pp. 116-20), Sanday and Headlam (*Romans*, p. 82), and Taylor (*Romans*, p. 299).
3. The classic expression of this theory is by Anselm, in his famous *Cur Deus Homo*, but there have been numerous, subsequent restatements (and criticisms!); cf. R.H. Culpepper, *Interpreting the Atonement* (Grand Rapids: Eerdmans, 1966); M. Barth, *Justification* (trans. A.M. Woodruff; Grand Rapids: Eerdmans, 1971); P.T. Forsyth, *The Work of Christ* (London: Independent Press, 1938); *idem, The Cruciality of the Cross* (London: Independent Press, 1948).
4. Sanday and Headlam (*Romans*, p. 91). Also Byrne (*Reckoning*, pp. 81-82, 86), Cranfield (*Romans*, I, p. 213), Käsemann (*Romans*, p. 101), and O'Neill (*Romans*, pp. 77-78—although it is the work of a glossator).
5. See esp. C.H. Dodd (*The Epistle of Paul to the Romans* [London: Hodder & Stoughton, 1932], p. 83—who naturally refers to the basis for this in his *The Bible and the Greeks* [London: Hodder & Stoughton, 1935]), and Ziesler (*Romans*, pp. 115-16). Some commentators simply emphasize Christ's revelation of God's δικαιοσύνη, whatever the nuancing and sense of that revelation, e.g. Byrne (*Reckoning*, pp. 78, 85-86). Käsemann prefers to talk of the Jewish theme of the patience of God, as against the divine *iustitia distributiva*, which seems tantamount to a rejection of the theodicy reading (*Romans*, p. 100: he cites Exod. 34.6; CD 2.4; 1QS 11.12 and *4 Ezra* 8.31-36).

problems (notably, what to do with Paul's references to the wrath of God in the immediate context of 3.21-26; cf. 1.18–2.12; 5.9-10).[1]

In view of this survey, it can be seen that any interpreter of Rom. 3.21-26 must make a series of decisions concerning what are often extremely difficult, not to mention controversial, questions. This interpretative agenda may be clarified by noting that these questions fall into four main groups: (1) lexical; (2) grammatical; (3) syntactical; and (4) theological. All the interpretive issues within the passage occur under one of these headings. To summarize:

(1) Lexically, the meanings of no less than eight words and four phrases (because of a disputed word) are uncertain in Rom. 3.21-26. The individual words are: δικαιοσύνη, δικαιόω, ἀπολύτρωσις, ἱλαστήριον, αἷμα, προτίθημι, ἔνδειξις, and καί (in v. 26d). The problematic phrases are the two νόμος units of v. 21, where the precise meaning of νόμος is uncertain although its broad sense is clear enough; the meaning of ὑστεροῦνται τῆς δόξης τοῦ θεοῦ in v. 23, where, although the words themselves are again clear at the literal level, the reference to the lost glory is not; and the extremely difficult διὰ τὴν πάρεσιν τῶν προγεγονότων ἁμαρτημάτων of v. 25d, where the meaning of πάρεσις is awkward.[2]

(2) What I have termed 'grammatical' decisions concerns the precise reading of two genitive phrases, δικαιοσύνη θεοῦ in vv. 21 and 22, and πίστεως Ἰησοῦ Χριστοῦ in v. 22. It is uncertain whether these substantives relate in a subjective or an objective sense. This subtle decision concerning the genitive relation has profound ramifications for the interpretation of the passage, as well as for Paul's soteriology as a whole.[3]

(3) Syntactically, there is one major and overriding problem within the passage, namely, the construal of Paul's central section. A smooth reading of vv. 22c-25b has simply proved to be impossible for most commentators. This difficulty will be discussed in detail later on. Suffice it here to note that (i) the section probably incorporates a

---

1. This primary soteriological point is also invariably supplemented by the point that this salvation is not achieved by works or through law, but is received by faith in Christ. The commentators are almost unanimous here.

2. One could also easily add a ninth word to the list of problematic lexical decisions because of this clause, namely, the meaning of διά with the accusative in v.25d.

3. Note the differences between a righteousness *from* and the righteousness *of* God, and between faith *in* and the *faith* (*-fulness*) *of* Christ.

parenthesis, although its precise extent is disputed, and (ii) given the usual reading, the next two sentences seem to begin respectively with a dangling participle (δικαιούμενοι at v. 24), and an accusative relative pronoun. The syntactical convolutions settle into some sort of order only in v. 25c, where a clear parallelism between two ἔνδειξις clauses anchors the end of the section. But before this, v. 22c to v. 25b certainly comprises a tortuous syntactical journey.

A second area of syntactical clumsiness is related to Paul's use of πίστις. In v. 22b his statement seems almost amusingly redundant: 'by means of belief in Jesus Christ, to all who believe'. Even worse, the phrase διὰ πίστεως in v. 25 is essentially unreadable where it stands. It interrupts a smooth semantic connection between ἱλαστήριον and ἐν τῷ αὐτοῦ αἵματι, functioning like a misplaced insertion or a random aside (which is how it is usually read). Moreover, by the end of what is not a particularly long section, Paul seems to have made this point about πίστις no less than four times.

(4) Finally, any theological interpretation of the section sits on top of this teetering pile of lexical and syntactical decisions. In particular, along with the resolution of these more localized questions, it must try to bring some overall coherence to the three extremely significant clusters of terms that Paul uses: a. righteousness terminology, which is scattered throughout the passage in the form of four nouns (vv. 21, 22, 24c and 26a), two participles (vv. 24a and 26b) and an adjective (v. 26b); b. atonement terminology, because three rare but pregnant terms, and an unusual phrase, are tightly correlated in vv. 24b-25; and c. πίστις terminology, which, as we have seen, occurs four times in the passage (twice in v. 22, and once in v. 25b and v. 26b respectively).

In view of these difficulties, it is perhaps not surprising that many suggested interpretations have been somewhat awkward. For example (and as we have seen), many commentators have claimed that Paul is setting forth a theodicy of atonement in Rom. 3.24-26 (a reading that depends heavily on the translation of πάρεσις in v. 25d as 'pass over' or 'overlook'). This reading does succeed in integrating God's right-eousness (which is both just and merciful) with Christ's atonement and with faith. Yet such a reading also seems to generate a multitude of questions given much of Paul's argument in the rest of Romans, and the basic drift of his theology as a whole.[1] In short, the reading does not really sound like Paul himself.

Thus, at the end of a long process of interpretative decision-making, it often seems that the derived readings of Rom. 3.21-26 are often far from satisfactory. It is important to note, however, that some sort of causality obtains between the various decisions and their interpretative consequences. Fundamentally, it seems that the disjointed syntax of vv. 22-25 blocks interpretation of the passage. Without an intelligible transition between v. 21 and the following material, it is difficult either to sustain the preliminary meaning of the section, or to give an integrated sense to the two ἔνδειξις clauses and the concluding colon that follow. Given this fundamental syntactical quandary, it is also not surprising that any interpretation of the individual righteousness and atonement words in the passage tends to be insensitive. In the absence of a clear correlation of words and phrases, it is never absolutely certain what the immediate context and argument are.

The best point of entry into the passage's interpretative agenda, therefore, is probably at the level of syntax. If the mutual relations between the various phrases and clauses can be established, then both the narrower and the broader levels of interpretation will be greatly clarified. At the narrower level, the determination of the meaning of individual words can be helped by a consideration of their context and their argumentative function. At the broader level of theological interpretation, the overall point (or points) of the passage should become more apparent.

These difficulties within Rom. 3.21-26 have not gone unnoticed and, as we have seen, two solutions are particularly favoured within the secondary literature on the passage. The first, using form-critical analysis, attempts to deal with the syntactical difficulties in the central section by positing Paul's citation of early church confessional material. It is argued that this mode of composition may explain its awkward syntax and vocabulary—particularly so if Paul does not

---

1.   Does Paul's God really 'overlook' sin in the past? Does he need the require-ments of justice satisfied in the present (perhaps through an atonement that functions like a ransom payment)? How does God's righteousness, in the sense of his covenant-faithfulness to Israel, integrate with this reading? Why is human faith now so significant?—was it absent in the past? or unimportant? Is it fundamentally dif-ferent from Torah-righteousness? (and so on).

entirely agree with its theology, and so feels bound to correct it later on.[1] As Ernst Käsemann confidently states,

> The jumbled nature of the passage can be explained only if it be noted that we have here a heaping up of non-Pauline terms and liturgical motifs. In other words, fixed tradition is drawn on by way of both introduction and conclusion to support the doctrine of justification both here and in 4.25.[2]

The second solution proposes a subjective reading of the πίστις genitive construction in v. 22, which would eliminate the troublesome redundancy in the verse, and would also allow a much more significant play on the meaning of πίστις throughout the passage. Consequently, before investigation of the passage can proceed further, these two proposals must be addressed. If they prove successful, a significant portion of the passage will already have been explained, namely, v. 22b-c and, depending on the precise reconstruction of the quoted fragment, at least v. 25, and possibly as much as vv. 24-26a. If they prove unsound, however, some resolution of the syntax is still probably the best place to begin analysis of the passage.

2. Form-Critical Analyses

Two form-critical analyses of Rom. 3.21-26 are influential today: the solution first suggested by Rudolph Bultmann, which was then expanded by Ernst Käsemann and John Reumann, and the significant modification of this solution suggested by Eduard Lohse. I will examines these in turn.

a. *Bultmann's Hypothesis and its Development*
Rudolph Bultmann first initiated discussion of a form-critical approach to Rom. 3.24-26a. His actual analysis, however, is surprisingly brief. In 1936 he simply suggested in passing that Rom. 3.24-26a was an early community creed.[3] Later he marshalled three points in support of his earlier hypothesis: he claimed that (1) the use of

---

1. The converse of this theory is that some clumsy later redactor concerned with un-Pauline problems has interpolated a fragment: so G. Fitzer, 'Der Ort der Versöhnung nach Paulus', *TZ* 22 (1966), pp. 161-83; and C.H. Talbert, 'A Non-Pauline Fragment at Romans 3:24-26?', *JBL* 85 (1966), pp. 287-96.

2. *Romans*, p. 92.

3. R. Bultmann, 'Neueste Paulusforschung', *TR* 8 (1936), pp. 11-12 (p. 12).

ἱλαστήριον was un-Pauline; (2) so also was the use of blood, since Paul usually employs σταυρός to characterize Christ's death (he argued that 1 Cor. 10.16; 11.25 and 27 follow tradition, with Rom. 5.9 being the only other instance); and (3) the idea of the divine righteousness demanding expiation for former sins was also foreign to Paul.[1]

Ernst Käsemann accepted Bultmann's hypothesis, but, noting its slender justification, stated 'that one can and must strengthen such arguments'.[2] He supplements Bultmann's observations with three additional contentions: (1) the awkwardness of the transition from v. 23 to v. 24, where 'the emphatic πάντες is without a counterpart in v. 24, which a real antithesis would actually require'; (2) 'the accumulation of what is uncharacteristic terminology—at least for Paul', namely, πάρεσις, προγεγόνοτα ἁμαρτήματα, προτίθεσθαι in the sense of manifestation, δικαιοσύνη as a divine attribute, and ἀπολύτρωσις; and (3) the 'überladene Stil' with its high concentration of genitive constructions and prepositional connections, which Käsemann characterizes as 'Near Eastern hymnic-liturgical'.[3]

But Käsemann's main argument for the presence of an early confessional fragment is (4), the nuanced recapitulation of vv. 25c-26a by v. 26b-c, which he believes is Paul correcting a quoted theological statement that he does not entirely agree with. Käsemann is aware of a perception of tension between v. 25c-d and v. 26b-c by certain previous analyses (e.g. by Jülicher, Zahn and Lietzmann), but he feels that these scholars have not entered into the implications of the contradiction fully. As we have seen, v. 25c-d is usually read in terms of God overlooking sins committed in the past (πάρεσις). This reveals his righteousness in the sense of his tolerance and forbearance (ἀνοχή) as he withholds his just wrath from the sinner, and such a statement is in

---

1. Buttmann, *Theology of the New Testament*, I, pp. 46-47.
2. 'Zum Verständnis von Römer 3,24-25', in *idem*, *Exegetische Versuche und Besinnungen* (Göttingen: Vandenhoeck & Ruprecht, 1970), p. 96. The study first appeared in *ZNW* 43 (1950–51), pp. 150-54; see also his 'Liturgische Formeln im NT', in *idem*, *Die Religion in Geschichte und Gegenwart* (Tübingen: Mohr [Paul Siebeck], 3rd edn, 1958), II, pp. 993-96; and *Romans*, pp. 91-101.
3. Käsemann, 'Zum Verständnis', p. 96. Here he is dependent on E. Percy, *Die Probleme der Kolosser- und Epheserbriefe* (Lund: Gleerup, 1946), pp. 191, 213.

perfect continuity with OT Jewish piety. But, Käsemann asserts, it is not Pauline, because Paul was not interested in covenant restoration or atonement after a long period of divine patience. Paul's perspective was eschatological, discontinuous, present, universalist and individual.[1] Consequently, vv. 25c-26a cannot be Pauline and must be a quotation. But Paul wishes to nuance the quotation in a more strongly eschatological direction, and so qualifies it with a parallel phrase: πρὸς τὴν ἔνδειξιν τῆς δικαιοσύνης αὐτοῦ ἐν τῷ νῦν καιρῷ. Here δικαιοσύνη no longer signifies a quality in God himself analogous to patience, but is something that God does as he breaks into the present. It is now an eschatological power. Paul originally appropriated the traditional unit, Käsemann asserts, because it used δικαιοσύνη terminology in relation to the work of Christ. Beyond this general support, however, its theology is apparently a little questionable.[2]

Käsemann's suggestion is characteristically brilliant and provocative, but its textual basis is fairly fragile. It depends heavily on the interpretation of v. 25d as oriented towards the past (and hence on rendering πάρεσις as 'overlook'), and also on Käsemann's broader understanding of Paul's thought as eschatological.[3]

The theory was introduced to English-speaking scholarship by John Reumann, who reproduces the main arguments of Bultmann and Käsemann but also adds some further supporting considerations.[4] Reumann deepens Käsemann's contention concerning the abruptness of

1. 'Zum Verständnis', pp. 99-100.
2. In his commentary, published 25 years later, Käsemann maintains his earlier commitment to an underlying traditional fragment without a great deal of development in the supporting evidence (*Romans*, pp. 96-97, 99).
3. Perhaps sensing this vulnerability, Käsemann criticizes Lietzmann's alternative reading of πάρεσις as 'remission', which would shift it out of the past into a present act, and thereby severely weaken his own perception of tension in the passage. This, he argues, generates a redundancy, since v. 26a needlessly repeats v. 25; it leaves the relationship between God's wrath and his patience unclear; it reduces v. 26a to a subordinate final sentence; it breaks the parallelism; and it does not specify the relationship between the forgiveness of earlier sins and present righteousness ('Zum Verständnis', p. 98). In addition to this, Käsemann cites Zahn's 'detachment' of ἀνοχή from v. 26a and πάρεσις (*Romans*, pp. 97-98, citing T. Zahn, *Der Brief des Paulus an die Römer* [Leipzig: Deichert, 3rd edn, 1925], p. 198).
4. J. Reumann, 'The Gospel of the Righteousness of God: Pauline Reinterpretation in Romans 3:21-26', *Int* 20 (1966), pp. 432-52.

the participle that begins v. 24. He argues that it is not the grammatical construction that one would expect in Paul (i.e. an aorist participle, a third use of πάντες, or an indicative construction with a conjunction), nor does it complete the sense of the previous phrase smoothly. Consequently, the participle must mark the beginning of an interpolation of some sort, with v. 24 functioning as a discrete unit: 'Being justified freely by his grace, through the redemption which is in Christ Jesus'. Both this sentence and the following one (v. 25) are clumsy, reinforcing the idea that a liturgical fragment is present.[1]

Reumann also adds to the 'accumulation' of uncharacteristically Pauline words in the passage. Bultmann noted αἷμα and ἱλαστήριον, and Käsemann cited an additional five words and phrases, but Reumann suggests that no less than eight are distinctly un-Pauline, adding ἔνδειξις and ἀνοχή to the list (although he omits Käsemann's emphasis on δικαιοσύνη in the attributive sense).[2] And, like other advocates of the theory, Reumann excises certain awkward phrases from the text, arguing that they are Pauline insertions or glosses.[3] After these modifications, the reconstructed fragment reads:

> δικαιούμενοι [δωρεὰν]
> διὰ τῆς ἀπολυτρώσεως τῆς ἐν Χριστῷ Ἰησοῦ
> ὃν προέθετο ὁ θεὸς ἱλαστήριον ἐν τῷ αὐτοῦ αἵματι
> εἰς ἔνδειξιν τῆς δικαιοσύνης αὐτοῦ
> διὰ τὴν πάρεσιν τῶν προγεγονότων ἁμαρτημάτων
> ἐν τῇ ἀνοχῇ τοῦ θεοῦ
>
> [24] Being declared righteous (as a gift)
> through the redemption which is through Messiah Jesus,
> [25] whom God put forward, a *hilasterion* in his blood,

1. Reumann, 'The Gospel', p. 435.
2. Reumann, 'The Gospel', pp. 436-37.
3. διὰ πίστεως in v. 25 is invariably dropped as a Pauline addition that clearly interrupts the smooth connection between ἱλαστήριον and αἷμα. Bultmann also eliminates δωρεὰν τῇ αὐτοῦ χάριτι in v. 24a. Reumann and Käsemann concur that this phrase incorporates a redundancy, but they retain δωρεὰν, eliminating only τῇ αὐτοῦ χάριτι. Significantly, Bultmann, Käsemann and Reumann all elect to leave the troublesome τῆς ἐν Χριστῷ Ἰησοῦ of v. 24b within the formula (although, of course, without its later Pauline significance and meaning), because the accusative ὅν of v. 25a needs an antecedent, and because the double article and ἀπολύτρωσις of v. 24b read best with an object. Reumann, however, allows the possibility of a substitution here by Paul (following Lohse).

for a demonstration of his (i.e. God's) righteousness,
because of the passing-over of previously committed sins,
[26] in the forbearance of God.[1]

We may draw together the evidences adduced by Bultmann and his followers in favour of seeing a traditional confessional formula in 3.24-26a as follows: (1) the abrupt participle at the beginning of v. 24; (2) the unusual terminology (as many as eight words); (3) the unusual theology of v. 25c-d; and (4) the 'liturgical' style.

b. *Lohse's Reformulation of the 'Quoted Fragment'*
Eduard Lohse, in a study published in 1963,[2] maintains a commitment to the presence of a traditional fragment in Rom. 3.21-26, but he reorients the theory significantly. He disputes the limits of Bultmann's reconstruction, contending that the start of the formula is not v. 24a but v. 25a, because the linguistic peculiarities in the section (with the exception of ἀπολύτρωσις) all fall within v. 25, and not in v. 24.[3] Viewed soberly, δικαιούμενοι δωρεὰν τῇ αὐτοῦ χάριτι διὰ τῆς ἀπολυτρώσεως τῆς ἐν Χριστῷ Ἰησοῦ is an acceptably Pauline statement.[4]

In addition to his criticism of the perception of non-Pauline material in v. 24, Lohse supplies a positive argument for the beginning of the quotation at v. 25: this section begins with a tell-tale relative pronoun. A relative pronoun begins several other almost unanimously accepted early church confessions, argues Lohse (e.g. Phil. 2.5, 1 Pet. 2.23 and 1 Tim. 3.16), so its presence at Rom. 3.25 may well signal

1. Cf. esp. Reumann, 'The Gospel', p. 442.
2. E. Lohse, *Märtyrer und Gottesknecht: Untersuchungen zur urchristlichen Verkündigung vom Sühntod Jesu Christi* (Göttingen: Vandenhoeck & Ruprecht, 2nd edn, 1963 [1955]).
3. He also observes that the deletion of τῷ αὐτοῦ χάριτι from v. 24 as a Pauline addition is inconsistent with the maintenance of τῆς ἐν Χριστῷ Ἰησοῦ. Following Lohse's logic to its conclusion, we may note that little is actually left in the quoted clause if τῆς ἐν Χριστῷ Ἰησοῦ is also cut as an obvious addition by Paul: only δικαιούμενοι διὰ τῆς ἀπολυτρώσεως—yet who would deny that Paul uses δικαιόω?! Consequently, at the end of a consistent editing it seems that almost the entire verse must be deleted as a Pauline gloss, leaving ἀπολύτρωσις standing alone as the quoted fragment. It is simpler to concede that Paul wrote v. 24.
4. Lohse does not comment on the participle in v. 24. He probably feels that enough has been said to shift the fragment's opening from v. 24 to v. 25.

the beginning of a confessional fragment here as well. Beyond these modifications, however, Lohse accepts the previous arguments from diction and theology.[1] The original confession according to Lohse would look (or sound) as follows:

ὃν προέθετο ὁ θεὸς ἱλαστήριον
ἐν τῷ αὐτοῦ αἵματι
εἰς ἔνδειξιν τῆς δικαιοσύνης αὐτοῦ
διὰ τὴν πάρεσιν τῶν προγεγονότων ἁμαρτημάτων
ἐν τῇ ἀνοχῇ τοῦ θεοῦ

[25] Whom God set forth (or purposed), to be a *hilasterion*,
in his blood,
to demonstrate his righteousness,
through the passing-over of previously occurring sins,
[26] in the kindness of God.

Lohse's analysis has found strong support in K. Wengst's stylistic analysis of early Christian confessions.[2] Wengst strengthens Lohse's study at one of its weaker points, namely, its failure to deal specifically with Käsemann's (and Reumann's) arguments concerning the awkwardness of the participle δικαιούμενοι that begins v. 24. Against this assertion, Wengst observes that it is not unusual for Paul to continue a phrase with a participle—in fact, he 'loves' to use coordinating participles after finite verbs.[3] Thus, the perception of a

1.   It is important to note Lohse does not replace Käsemann's determination of the end of the traditional fragment with some other justification. He merely assumes that the confession ends at v. 26a, and that the remainder of the verse is Paul's interpretation and commentary (*Märtyrer und Gottesknecht*, p. 153).

2.   *Christologische Formeln und Lieder des Urchristentums* (Gütersloh: Mohn, 1972), esp. pp. 87-91. At about the same time, one of Lohse's students, H. Koch, contextualized the theory within a history of the passage's exegesis: 'Römer 3:21-26 in der Paulusinterpretation der letzten 150 Jahre' (doctoral dissertation, University of Göttingen, 1971). This thesis is an excellent resource, although primarily for German-speaking studies, and only up to 1971.

3.   Citing BDF §468 (p. 245): 'Paul is fond of continuing a construction begun with a finite verb by means of co-ordinated participles, sometimes in a long series'. Cf. 2 Cor. 5.12; 7.5; 10.14-15. Käsemann's assertion that 'the emphatic πάντες' in v. 23 is 'without a counterpart in v. 24, which a real antithesis would actually require' is similarly spurious. Wengst replies, 'the "actually" shows how insubstantial this reason is. What would we expect for a counterpart in v. 24? πάντες clearly relates back to εἰς πάντας τοὺς πιστεύοντας in v. 22, which therefore makes all believers, who are also the subject of the co-ordinating participle δικαιούμενοι in

break in the syntax at v. 24 really amounts to wishful thinking.[1]

After this, the mere occurrence of ἀπολύτρωσις is insufficient for establishing a pre-Pauline fragment in v. 24. As Wengst points out, this word is not particularly unusual for Paul.[2] The assertion that all the other occurrences in his letters are liturgical is never actually proved. Indeed, Rom. 8.23 is 'surely a Pauline formulation', and 'it is also impossible to prove that 1 Cor. 1.30 is a stereotyped formula, since sonorous language and the accumulation of substantives—which are neither in themselves nor in the present use unpauline—do not constitute sufficient indicators'[3] (although Wengst is perhaps less convincing here than when confronting the issue of the participle).

In an article published in 1975, Peter Stuhlmacher drew together much of the debate concerning Rom. 3.21-26. Although he himself is primarily interested in substantive issues, particularly the meaning of ἱλαστήριον, Stuhlmacher suggests that Lohse's analysis is still the soundest and most influential literary-critical point of departure for any analysis of the passage.[4] Stuhlmacher's study shows that, at least at the syntactical level, the form-critical debate has progressed little

v. 24' (*Formeln*, p. 87). Cf. also Cranfield, who argues, as we have seen, that the participle has an acceptable prior determination in terms of grammar (*Romans*, I, p. 205).

1. However, it is important to note that although Wengst points out that the use of the participle is probably authentically Pauline, he does not really explain how it integrates into the section, and hence how we are to understand the section's syntax as a whole.

2. He has three out of ten NT occurrences (Rom. 8.23; 1 Cor. 1.30), but considerably more (i.e. seven) if the Pauline canon is broadened to include Colossians and Ephesians (Eph. 1.7, 14; 4.30; Col. 1.14).

3. Wengst, *Formeln*, p. 87. Lohse's reconstruction also receives support from the analysis of C.H. Talbert ('A Non-Pauline Fragment at Romans 3:24-26?', pp. 287-96). Talbert seems unaware of Kümmel's and Lohse's studies, but his own reasoning exactly reproduces Lohse's critique of Bultmann and also Lohse's positive suggestion for the relocation of the beginning of the fragment to v. 25.

4. Here he specifically emphasizes the success of Lohse's criticism of v. 24 as the fragment's starting point, and the positive evidence for its beginning at v. 25 because of its diction and the relative pronoun. Stuhlmacher quotes a raft of scholars who have been convinced by Lohse: H. Koch, H. Conzelmann, W. Schrage, K. Wengst, G. Delling, G. Klein, E. Schweizer, U. Wilckens and G. Eichholz ('Recent Exegesis on Romans 3:24-26', p. 96 nn. 15-23).

beyond the analyses of Bultmann, Käsemann and Lohse. Their arguments, and in particular Lohse's modification of the original hypothesis of Bultmann and Käsemann, still dominate discussion.[1] We may

1. Talbert has suggested a rather different reconstruction of the 'original fragment' based on the symmetry between vv. 25-26 (thereby, rather significantly, using their parallelism *not* as an argument for incongruity and disjunction, but for their deliberate association). It is less influential than the German solutions, but still an important contribution:

ὃν προέθετο θεὸς ἱλαστήριον
ἐν τῷ αὐτοῦ αἵματι, εἰς ἔνδειξιν τῆς δικαιοσύνης αὐτοῦ
διὰ τὴν πάρεσιν τῶν προγεγονότων ἁμαρτημάτων
ἐν τῇ ἀνοχῇ τοῦ θεοῦ, πρὸς τὴν ἔνδειξιν τῆς δικαιοσύνης αὐτοῦ
εἰς τὸ εἶναι αὐτὸν δίκαιον καὶ δικαιοῦντα.

There are, however, two clusters of related problems with Talbert's ingenious reconstruction. (1) He has excised all the phrases that do not fit his symmetrical pattern, namely, διὰ πίστεως in v. 25b (which is usually removed), ἐν τῷ νῦν καιρῷ in v. 26c, and τὸν ἐκ πίστεως Ἰησοῦ from v. 26d. These excisions total 10 out of 48 words, or more than 20% of the material. If textual excisions of up to 20% are permitted, one suspects that many texts could be shaped into some symmetry or pattern. This procedure seems rather like an ignoring of awkward evidence (cf. George Howard's brief criticisms in 'Romans 3:21-31 and the Inclusion of the Gentiles', *HTR* 63 [1970], pp. 223-33, esp. p. 225)—and if the edited material is reinserted into Talbert's 'fragment', a very different text is produced: one that is unsymmetrical and means something quite different! (2) But even granting Talbert his methodology, the final text does not read convincingly. First, the phrase ἐν τῷ αὐτοῦ αἵματι is detached from its obvious relation with ἱλαστήριον, and becomes associated instead with the demonstration of righteousness in v. 25c. Following from this rearrangement is the inconsistency that ἐν τῷ αὐτοῦ αἵματι is set in parallel to ἐν τῇ ἀνοχῇ τοῦ θεοῦ. Talbert argues that these phrases function in a parallel instrumental sense, and to a certain extent this may be granted. But the one refers to Christ and his death, and the other to God and his patience. These are very different 'instruments' in the drama of salvation, and hardly function there in parallel. More importantly, however, αὐτοῦ functions ambiguously in line two of Talbert's reconstruction. The first αὐτοῦ clearly refers to Christ, but the second should also probably be read in its immediate context with reference to Christ. This, however, disrupts the parallelism with the second occurrence of the phrase, where the αὐτοῦ obviously refers to God. Even worse, this reading is contradicted by the context of Rom. 3.21-26, where vv. 21-22 anchors the phrase δικαιοσύνη αὐτοῦ firmly to θεός. Thus, Paul seems to have changed radically the meaning of his quotation—an unlikely procedure. Thus, excessive excisions and some awkward ambiguities cripple Talbert's reconstruction—as a Greek text it just does not seem to work very well.

summarize the elements of the reformulated case for Paul's quotation of an early church confession in 3.25-26a as follows: (1) the unusual theology, for Paul, of vv. 25c-26a; (2) the unusual terminology; (3) the 'liturgical' style; and (4) the fact that v. 25a begins with a relative pronoun.

c. *Evaluation of the Form-Critical Arguments in vv. 25c-26a*

In evaluating the form-critical analyses, we begin with what is probably the strongest contention in favour of the presence of a quoted fragment in 3.21-26: argument (1), namely, Käsemann's reading of vv. 25d-26a in terms of an un-Pauline Jewish-Christian theology of covenant-restoration. Here it is extremely significant that, almost simultaneous with the appearance of Käsemann's study, Werner Georg Kümmel published a study which included a careful analysis of the meaning of the critical word within the disputed section, namely, πάρεσις. Kümmel's conclusions (perhaps without his deliberate intent) seriously challenge the position taken by his German colleague.[1]

Kümmel begins by noting that πάρεσις may legitimately be translated as 'overlook, pass over, close one's eye to' (*hingehenlassen*). This meaning generates the interpretation of v. 25d assumed by Käsemann, and Kümmel notes the large number of scholars who follow it:[2] in the age before Christ, God graciously *overlooked* sin, but this oversight called his concern for sin and hence justice into question. With the event of the Cross, however, God's hatred and horror of sin is proved, and he is thereby vindicated—and, admittedly, this notion does seem a little strange for Paul.

Kümmel notes, however, that πάρεσις may also be translated as 'remission' or 'forgiveness' (*Erlass*). This meaning would suggest a significantly different reading of vv. 25c-26a. God's righteousness is demonstrated or shown forth through the present remission of previously committed sins, and such a remission is clearly a result of the

1. Kümmel, 'Πάρεσις und ἔνδειξις'. In what follows I will concentrate on Kümmel's analysis of πάρεσις, since the meaning of this word largely determines the meaning of ἔνδειξις in the context (a review of Kümmel's analysis of ἔνδειξις may be found in D.A. Campbell, 'The Rhetoric of Romans 3.21-26' [PhD dissertation, University of Toronto, 1989], pp. 64-66).

2. 'Ein Beitrag', p. 260 n. 1; namely, Zahn, Althaus, Dodd, Haering, Bardenhewer, Brunner, Gaugler, Wizsäcker and Albrecht, Moffatt, Holtzmann, Feine, Bultmann, BADG, Steiger, Karner and Taylor.

forbearance and clemency of God.[1] This reading shifts the focus of v. 25d into the present, alongside v. 26a. It also suggests that ἀνοχή relates not so much to a previous period of forbearance, but to a present act of forgiveness.

The readings clearly turn on the meaning given to πάρεσις. Kümmel observes that BADG only lists the meanings 'pass over' and 'let go unpunished' (p. 626), but LSJ offers several other possible meanings for the word including 'release, let go, dismiss' (in a nominal form), 'paralysis', 'neglect', and 'remit' (p. 1337). Given the word's single occurrence in the NT, the extra-biblical references are highly significant when evaluating these alternatives.

There are three classical occurrences of the noun in comparable senses to Rom. 3.25.[2] One simply means 'release'.[3] The two other occurrences also suggest the meaning 'release', but nuanced in the direction of 'remission' or 'forgiveness', rather than the notion of 'overlook'.

In the first, a statement by Dio Chrysostom,[4] God out of graciousness and clemency is said to grant a select few some relief from the adamantine chain of fate. In this context πάρεσις can conceivably take

---

1. Kümmel cites as previous authorities the Vulgate and Luther; also C.A.A. Scott, H. Lietzmann, K. Barth, W. Mundle, H.D. Wendland, E. Stauffer and A. Nygren (this last citation is questionable).

2. The noun occurs most frequently with the meaning of 'paralysis'. This is its sense throughout the period's medical literature, and also when it occurs in Josephus (*Ant.* 9.238; 11.234) and Philo (*Det. Pot. Ins.* 168; *Vit. Mos.* 26.143, 145). For exhaustive citations, cf. TLG. The medical evidence is so extensive that the meaning 'paralysis' is perhaps worth reconsidering as a possible translation in Rom. 3.25d, but it just does not seem to fit—'because of the paralysis of previously-occurring sins'?

3. Plutarch (c. 80 CE), *Comp. Dion. Brut.* 2: Δίωνα δ' ἡ Διονυσίου πάρεσις ἐκ Συρακουσιῶν καὶ τὸ μὴ κατασκάψαι τοῦ προτέρου τυράννου τὸν τάφον ἐπαίτιον μάλιστα πρὸς τοὺς πολίτας ἐποίησεν. Plutarch also uses the noun in the sense of paralysis in *Quaestiones Convivales* 112.652.

4. τινὰς μέντοι καὶ λίαν ὀλίγους πάρεσίν τινα ἔχειν ἐκ τοῦ θεοῦ, καὶ δεδέσθαι μέν, ἐλαρῶς δὲ πάνυ δι' ἐπιείκειαν (*Thirtieth Discourse: Charidemus,* 80 [30], 19). The Loeb translation by J.W. Cohoon attaches 'gentleness' to the privileged few, but both the sentence and the reference in §24 suggest that it is a description of God: ἐκ τούτων ἐνίοτε οἱ θεοί τινας καὶ παρέδρους ἑαυτοῖς ποιοῦνται δι' ἀρετὴν καὶ σοφίαν, καθόλου τῆς τιμωρίας ἀπαλλάξαντες. Here ἀπαλλάξαντες also seems equivalent to the earlier πάρεσις.

the general meaning 'release' or 'relief', and possibly the sense of 'remission', but not the meaning 'overlook'.

The second nuanced occurrence of πάρεσις, in Dionysius of Halicarnassus, is more difficult to evaluate.[1] The word occurs in the midst of the famous account of Coriolanus. At the point in the story where the word is used, the Roman consuls are hoping to avoid the trial of Coriolanus before the assembled tribes of plebeians, and so ask the tribunes to drop the charges against him. There seems to be less thought here of overlooking or passing over the incident that took place in the senate than of releasing Marcius from its consequences.[2] This is probably closer to the idea of acquittal than to passing over in the sense of overlooking, although it is difficult to be certain. Perhaps more significant is the observation that ἀφίημι and ἀπολύω seem to function in the context as parallel notions.[3] It should also be noted, however, that in a fourth occurrence in Appian (which was overlooked by Kümmel) the meaning clearly seems to be 'overlook' or 'pass over' (*Basilica* 13.1).

Thus, the rather sparse extra-biblical evidence is balanced between the two ideas of 'overlook' and 'remit'—with a possible leaning towards the meaning 'remittance', but not a strong or even certain one. The basic meaning, however, seems to be simply that of 'release', and one wonders if it would not simply be best to translate the word thus in v. 25d, allowing the context to colour the idea with hints of either remittance or oversight. Kümmel's survey does establish that 'remittance' is a possible interpretation for πάρεσις; that is, it cannot be excluded *a priori* from consideration.[4] But the

1. παρὰ δὲ τῶν δημάρχων πολλὰ λιπαρήσαντες τὴν μὲν ὁλοσχερῆ πάρεσιν οὐχ εὕροντο τὴν δ' εἰς χρόνον ὅσον ἠξίουν ἀναβολὴν ἔλαβον (*The Roman Antiquities* 7.37.2).

2. J.M. Creed notes that the context is the story of Coriolanus, but he seems to misappropriate it: 'ΠΑΡΕΣΙΣ in Dionysius of Halicarnassus and in St Paul', *JTS* 41 (1940), pp. 28-30.

3. Minicius's previous speech (34.2, 3) had almost induced the plebeians to release (ἀπολύειν) Marcius, and Marcius himself was given the opportunity ἄφεσιν αἰτῆσθαι τῆς τιμωρίας. Similarly, at his later trial, Minucius requests ἀφέσεως ἀπολύσωσι, ἀφεικέναι, and for the tribes to forgive (ἀφεῖναι) him (60.3, 4, 5)—and Dionysius himself comments that Marcius was almost acquitted (ἀπολυούσας ἀπελέλυτα: 64.6).

4. The traditional reading of πάρεσις as 'overlook' seems to have been overly

debate seems overly polarized in his account.

When Kümmel completes his largely extra-biblical analysis, he nevertheless correctly insists that any translation in Rom. 3.24-26 still depends primarily on the context. The extra-biblical survey merely establishes a range of interpretative possibilities. And, with reference to the translation of πάρεσις in Rom. 3.25d, Kümmel does argue (although not at great length) that 'remission' is a better translation than 'overlook' or 'pass over'. But it is important to nuance Kümmel's suggestion here rather considerably.

πάρεσις must be interpreted in its immediate context, which means primarily in relation to the 'demonstration of his righteousness [i.e. God's]' that Paul speaks of in the preceding phrase (and this relationship also includes the other three instances of righteousness present in the section, in vv. 21c, 22a and 26b, which Paul seems to have arranged in parallel[1]). There is little dispute among scholars today that the righteousness of God which Paul speaks of in 3.21-26 (along with its occurrences in 1.16-17 and 3.3-5) carries strong connotations of salvation, and even of liberation—the observation that it is revealed through Christ is enough to establish this, for Christ brings salvation. πάρεσις in v. 25c should therefore be linked to this demonstration of God's salvation, especially in view of the preposition governing its phrase: διά with the accusative, which usually means

---

influenced by the verb, which occurs elsewhere in the LXX and NT: at Lk. 11.42 and Heb. 12.12 in the NT, with 22 occurrences in the LXX, usually with one of three general areas of meaning: (1) 'weak', 'feeble', in Num. 13.21; Deut. 32.36; 2 Sam. 4.1; Jer. 4.21; 20.9; Zeph. 3.16; Sir. 2.12, 13 (2×); 25.23; *3 Macc.* 2.13; (2) 'pass by', 'leave', in Exod. 14.12; 1 Sam. 2.5; Prov. 9.15; 15.10; Ps. 137.8 [LXX]; (3) 'release', 'discharge', or 'remit', in Jdt. 12.12; Sir. 4.29; 23.2 [?], 1 Macc. 11.35 (and *4 Macc.* 5.29). Yet it is unwise to place too much emphasis on the verb because, fundamentally, it is a different word from the noun. In any case, 'remitting' is also a possible translation for the verb, as Josephus, *Ant.* 15.48, and 1 Macc. 11.35 also show quite clearly (the latter statement is parallel to 10.29-30 where again ἀπολύω [once] and ἀφίημι [twice] occur as cognates for παρίημι: cf. also Dionysius of Halicarnassus, *The Roman Antiquities*, 7.68, and *Ant.* 12 *passim*, for similar uses of ἀφίημι, ἀπολύω, τελέω). The usual rendering also seems to have been influenced by Acts, where a similar point concerning God's 'oversight' is made at 14.16 and 17.30. But the wisdom of this procedure is seriously questionable, when two remarks in a secondary source are used to interpret a primary text.

1.   To a certain extent here conclusions actually argued for later on are anticipated, but this is unavoidable in dealing with this question.

'because of' and has causal and explanatory force.

In what sense can πάρεσις demonstrate the salvation of God in Christ? It seems unlikely that God's 'overlooking' previously-committed sins really reveals or demonstrates his saving righteousness in Christ.[1] But if God 'releases' or 'remits' sins in a public event, then this is a clear demonstration of his saving righteousness. Thus, the translation 'release' or 'forgive' perhaps makes the best sense in context.

We may add to this the observation that vv. 25c-26a are constructed in an almost perfect parallelism to v. 26b-c, which speaks of a demonstration in the present time (literally, 'the now time'). We should therefore try, at least initially, to read the two units in parallel. The interpretation of πάρεσις in terms of 'release' or 'remittance' integrates effortlessly with such an approach: God's saving righteousness is demonstrated because of the release from, or remittance of, previously-committed sins through Christ, and this demonstration is certainly taking place 'in the present time'. But 'passing over' previously-committed sins cannot possibly reveal anything in the present. It is rooted in the past, thus (as Käsemann correctly says) it drives a wedge between the two discussions of righteousness. This wedge is removed, however, if πάρεσις is rendered in terms of a deliverance or remittance, which takes place in the present.

Consequently, a translation of πάρεσις in terms either of release or of remittance seems easily the best rendering in the immediate context. It aligns smoothly both with Paul's surrounding use of δικαιοσύνη, and with its following clause. Conversely, a rendering in terms of 'overlook' or 'passing over' is awkward, grating with both these aspects of the context. Clearly, the former reading should be preferred.

At this point it can be seen that Käsemann's argument has begun to work against his own position. He notes, as we have seen, that a rendering of πάρεσις in terms of oversight is in tension with Paul's surrounding statements, and he concludes that therefore Paul did not compose the statement in which it appears. But if an alternative rendering of πάρεσις can avoid this contextual tension—an alternative Käsemann does not really explore—then it should be

---

1.   This would be a reference to another act altogether, and then a rather puzzling one, in which the passive event of 'passing over' sin actively demonstrated God's salvation—a curious idea, to say the least.

preferred as the solution to the tension. Thus, Käsemann's observation of tension in the one alternative drives interpretation to the other, which has the effect of undermining the conclusion he wishes to establish from the difficulty of the first.

We should note one final point in relation to πάρεσις before moving on. It is sometimes argued in support of the non-Pauline nature of v. 25d that Paul usually employs the word ἄφεσις when he wishes to speak of 'forgiveness', hence πάρεσις is uncharacteristic. But a quick survey of Paul's letters suggests that this contention verges on the irresponsible. Paul does *not* use ἄφεσις, or even the verbal form ἀφίημι, at all frequently. ἄφεσις only occurs in Eph. 1.7 and Col. 1.14—letters which the main proponents of this argument (Bultmann, Käsemann, and Lohse) do not hold to be authentically Pauline.[1] Thus, the extant instances of ἄφεσις in the authentic Pauline letters for many scholars is zero, and, even resorting to a ten-letter canon, a meagre two instances is not enough to justify the claim that Paul always uses ἄφεσις when speaking of forgiveness[2]—it is perhaps more consistent with this evidence to argue that πάρεσις *is* Paul's word for forgiveness.[3]

Consequently, in view of Kümmel's study and these arguments, it seems fair to conclude that argument (1) in favour of a quotation (or interpolation)[4] in vv. 25c-26a does not hold—and also that πάρεσις

1. Cf. Bultmann, *Theology of the New Testament*, p. 190; E. Käsemann, *Perspectives on Paul* (trans. M. Kohl; London: SCM Press, 1971), pp. 107, 109-10, 118, and 120-21; and E. Lohse, *The Formation of the New Testament* (trans. M.E. Boring; Nashville: Abingdon Press, 1981 [1972]), pp. 87-97.

2. Even the verb ἀφίημι, which is not strictly relevant, occurs only in Rom. 1.27, 4.7 (quoting Ps. 32.1), and in the highly specialized context of 1 Cor. 7.11-13 (here three times).

3. It should also be noted that ἄφεσις can easily take the meaning 'release', rather than 'forgive', in these contexts.

4. This is the theory of Fitzer in 'Der Ort der Versöhnung nach Paulus, pp. 161-83. Fitzer argues, on the basis of Käsemann's observation, that v. 25 is a *later* interpolation, not an earlier confession. The 'particle-conscious Paul' would surely have used a conjunction to connect vv. 25 and 26 (p. 163). In addition to this, v. 24 reads smoothly on to v. 26, hence v. 25 is more readily understandable as an early response to an implication generated by Paul's statement concerning the forgiveness of sins: if we are forgiven because of Jesus' sacrifice, what of those who sinned before Christ (p. 164). This question is, asserts Fitzer, decidedly un-Pauline. Consequently, Fitzer neatly reverses Käsemann's thesis while using the same

should probably be rendered in terms of 'release', or perhaps 'forgiveness'. But what of the three other arguments supporting the theory? It is also frequently asserted that a quoted fragment must be present at Rom. 3.24-25 because of its 'accumulation' of non-Pauline terminology (argument [2]). There are ten words that have on one occasion or the other been so characterized: ἀπολύτρωσις, ἱλαστήριον, αἷμα, ἀνοχή, ἔνδειξις, προτίθημι, ἁμάρτημα, πάρεσις, προγίνομαι and δικαιοσύνη (in an attributive sense). On closer examination, however, this case may be less impressive than its initial barrage makes it seem.

As we have already seen in part, ἀπολύτρωσις occurs in six other places within the Pauline corpus (twice in undisputed letters).[1] So Wengst observes with respect to the occurrence of ἀπολύτρωσις, 'This word is, in relation to its occurrence in the NT overall, not so unusual in Paul, that it must be termed "uncharacteristic terminology for Paul"'.[2] The occurrence of the word in Romans at 8.23 seems to be the final nail in the non-Pauline coffin as far as ἀπολύτρωσις is concerned—although one may detect a slightly different meaning here. Clearly he was familiar with it.

Likewise, with respect to ἀνοχή and προτίθημι, although these words are unusual, both occur in Romans (at 2.4 and 1.13 respectively[3]), making any argument for their non-Pauline usage somewhat strained. ἔνδειξις and ἁμάρτημα are also admittedly rare, but they are attested in some of Paul's undisputed letters: ἔνδειξις at 2 Cor. 8.24 and Phil. 1.28, and ἁμάρτημα at 2 Cor. 6.18—again effectively

evidence. But Fitzer's imaginative proposal, because it rests on the same lexical foundation as Käsemann's, is also undermined by Kümmel's analysis and my supporting considerations. Given a reading of πάρεσις in terms of forgiveness or release, the awkwardness of v. 25d evaporates. And in the absence of any creaking textual joints, theories of interpolation are unnecessary.

1. Rom. 8.23; 1 Cor. 1.30; Eph. 1.7, 14; 4.30; Col. 1.14.

2. *Formeln*, p. 87. The counterargument that at these points Paul is quoting traditional material begs the question and cannot account for Rom. 8.23. In any case, 1 Cor. 1.30 and Eph. 4.30 are not undisputably traditional.

3. προτίθημι also occurs in Eph. 1.13: cf. the substantive πρόθεσις in Rom. 8.28; Eph. 1.11; 3.11 (cf. 2 Tim. 1.9 and 3.10).

negating any argument for non-Pauline usage.

The 'attributive' reading of δικαιοσύνη is a little more difficult, but Kümmel's argument applies here as well: why can the word not simply take the unexceptionable meaning it has in its three other immediate occurrences, which makes good sense in context? Then the difficulty vanishes.

αἷμα, like ἀπολύτρωσις, is relatively common in Paul (twelve occurrences).[1] Bultmann asserts that where Paul is not dependent on traditional material (as in 1 Cor. 10 and 11) he refers to Christ's death in terms of the Cross, not blood. Linguistically, Paul's use of σταυρός does not of course preclude him using αἷμα if he wishes to when speaking of Christ's death.[2] But Romans itself is a fundamental embarrassment to Bultmann's argument, because in it Paul uses αἷμα twice (3.25; 5.9), but doesn't use σταυρός at all.[3] Besides, to deny the use of αἷμα in a sacrificial setting to a pre-Destruction rabbi seems a little dubious in itself.

As a result of these objections, the argument from diction really reduces itself to the three (Pauline) *hapax legomena* in the passage; ἱλαστήριον (its only other NT occurrence being Heb. 9.5), πάρεσις and προγεγονότων (the perfect participle of προγίνομαι). At this point, with the 'hard' linguistic data in place, we must carefully evaluate the claims of the form critics. In particular, attention will briefly be devoted to two issues:

(1) Can the raw datum of a certain percentage of unusual words in a passage suggest its quotation (or interpolation)? Furthermore, *does* Rom. 3.24-25 have a particularly high percentage of such words?

(2) Can an argument from *diction* or *vocabulary* say anything about

1. Rom. 3.15 (quoting the LXX); 5.9; 1 Cor. 10.19; 11.25, 27; 15.10; Gal. 1.16; Eph. 1.7; 2.13; 6.12; and Col. 1.20 (the references in 1 Cor. 15, Gal. 1 and Eph. 6 are rather idiomatic).

2. Col. 1.20 is highly significant—if it is by Paul—because here σταυρός is combined with αἷμα: εἰρηνοποιήσας διὰ τοῦ αἵματος τοῦ σταυροῦ αὐτοῦ. The words are also closely associated in Eph. 2.13 and 16.

3. It could be argued that σταυρός is as influenced by circumstance as αἷμα for Paul, since he uses it primarily in the polemical contexts of 1 Corinthians and Galatians (1 Cor. 1.17, 18; Gal. 5.11; 6.12, 14). Outside these letters, there are only five references in Paul to the Cross (Eph. 2.16; Phil. 2.8; 3.18; Col. 1.20; 2.14), compared with five references in 1 Corinthians to blood. Thus, Paul's usage is really very evenly balanced.

the origin of *sentences*? We will suggest following that the answer to both these questions is 'no'.

With respect to our first question concerning the implications of raw lexical percentages, it is clearly fundamental that an objective criterion must be in place against which to measure any such percentages. Past statistical analyses of authorship suggest, however, that for any distributional analysis of style to be effective, the quantities of disputed and authentic text must be sufficiently large to generate some sense of predictability.[1] The rule of thumb is 100,000 words of undisputed text as a reservoir, against which to compare a disputed text preferably of a length not less than 10,000 words itself. Rom. 3.24-26 is 61 words long, thus any objective statistical analysis of this type is clearly impossible. Consequently, statements of lexical percentages and so on, in statistical terms, mean nothing.

But even granting the attempt, the ratio of unique words to frequent words in Rom. 3.21-26 is unremarkable. For the passage as a whole, it is 3:45, or one in 15 (6.7%). Bearing in mind that the smaller the section the more distorted the ratio, as small a section as 3.25a-26a still only yields a ratio of 3:17, or 17.6%. This is not a particularly high ratio or percentage. Paul's letters average a ratio of 17.4% peculiar vocabulary to total vocabulary, and in Romans the ratio is 26.3%. Thus, meaning as little as it does in any case, the percentage figure is not significant.[2] Any argument from the mere incidence of

1.   The definitive study of statistical analysis of authorship in Paul is now by K. Neumann, *The Authenticity of the Pauline Epistles in the Light of Stylo-Statistical Analysis* (Atlanta: Scholars Press, 1990).

2.   Cf. J.J. O'Rourke, 'Some Considerations about Attempts at Statistical Analysis of the Pauline Corpus', *CBQ* 35 (1973), pp. 485, 487. It is significant to note that in Rom. 1.29-31, a vice list, the ratio is much higher, namely, 7:26, or 26%—and if the evidence of the Pastorals is removed (and note, *only* that evidence), the ratio jumps to 12:26, or nearly a 50% incidence of *hapax legomena*. Yet only one scholar suggests that the vice list is un-Pauline (among the many who do not accept the Pastorals as Pauline), namely, O'Neill (*Romans*, pp. 40-42). His reasoning is a little forced; for example: 'it is very hard to see how the argument would fit into the train of thought so strikingly begun in 1.1-17'. The statistics he quotes, however, do emphasize my main point (*Romans*, p. 41); 29 words in 1.18-32 are Pauline *hapax legomena*, and 49 in 1.18–2.29. Nineteen Pauline *hapaxes* occur in an 'equivalent stretch of Romans around this chapter and a half'. Thus, if *hapax legomena* are to be the measure of authorship, Rom. 1.18–2.29 must be a mosaic of confessions and early church hymns, yet this seems unlikely and even rather

unusual words proves nothing in the case of Rom. 3.21-26.

Perhaps more importantly, it must be seriously questioned what such a percentage would prove in any case. Form-critical hypotheses assume the quotation of complete syntactical units, that is, of phrases, clauses and (most probably) of sentences. Consequently, the presence of unusual words in and of themselves would seem to carry few direct implications for their syntactical contexts. It makes little sense to say that Paul is quoting words, and if he is quoting longer linguistic units, these themselves need to be examined. Here, word-studies are not much help: an unusual word does not necessarily show that the sentence in which it occurs is unusual as well. Thus, it would seem wiser when unusual terminology occurs to argue that Paul is involved with simply that—namely, he has appropriated unusual *terminology* (and this could well be the case in v. 25).

But this is a major concession for any form-critical hypothesis. Even if Paul is using words found elsewhere, he is clearly in complete control of their syntactical combination within his argument. The insight is not lost that (1) the origin of the material is pre-Pauline (yet what material is not, in some sense or other?), and that (2) Paul may well be recombining motifs from the thought and language of the early church, seeing that much of his theology no doubt takes this form. But it is inaccurate to characterize it as a process of quotation. Furthermore, Paul's use of unusual lexical reservoirs cannot help us with most of the problems we face in the passage, namely, the awkward syntax and the way in which he has combined his terminology.

Thus, argument (2) from unusual terminology is really incapable of establishing a form-critical theory with respect to 3.25a-26 for theoretical reasons—and even if it were methodologically sound, the actual data would not bear it out. The hypothesis really leads to an interpretative cul-de-sac.

The two remaining arguments for a quotation in 3.25a-26a may be dealt with more quickly.

Argument (3) is the argument from style. The passage's style has been termed 'liturgical'. Three characteristics are cited: (1) its high frequency of prepositions; (2) its preponderance of genitive construc-

ludicrous. Nevertheless, if a 50% instance of *hapax legomena* does not suggest non-Pauline authorship in this case, lesser ratios cannot consistently be asserted to do so.

tions; and (3) its measured, 'liturgical' rhythm.[1] This argument also proves less convincing when examined more closely, also for three reasons.

The argument works best for the more extended version of the fragment (vv. 24-26a), which has seven prepositions (διά occurs three times, ἐν three times, and εἰς once) and seven genitive constructions.[2] But this delimitation has already been challenged, and the fragment's probable starting-point has been shifted to v. 25. This redefinition eliminates two of the prepositions and one genitive construction. In addition to this, one of the prepositions is excised as a later Pauline gloss (διὰ τῆς πίστεως), reducing the number of prepositional constructions to two. Thus:

1. It is not particularly convincing to argue for a preponderance of genitive constructions and prepositional phrases on the basis of two prepositions, two further ἐν constructions, and four genitives—of which three are merely possessives.

2. Furthermore, these stylistic features are not confined to the section of text in question, but extend throughout the passage.[3] Consequently, either the argument from style suggests a pre-Pauline provenance for vv. 21-26 as a whole, or it signifies something other than a process of quotation.

3. The final flaw within the stylistic argument is the contradiction between its claim that the fragment is liturgically crafted, and its actual reconstructed state. The ostensible confession reads:

---

1. Käsemann, 'Zum Verständnis', p. 96. Reumann echoes this ('The Gospel', p. 436).
2. But even this summary is overstated. Little significance can be accorded the incidence of ἐν constructions in Paul, given his fondness for them, and also the preposition's frequency in the NT. It is the fifth most common word with 2757 occurrences. Of these, 1006 can be found in Paul—164 times in his famous ἐν Χριστῷ phrase, or its equivalent—with total occurrences in Romans of 173. Up to this point in the epistle he has used ἐν 46 times (*VKGNT*, II, p. 407). Two of the genitive constructions are dependent on a preposition (διά), while four are merely possessives (αὐτοῦ 3×, in vv. 24, 25 [2×]). Nevertheless it may be conceded that the passage is given a measured tone with the remaining prepositions and genitives.
3. The preceding verse has two prepositions and two genitives. Similarly, v. 21 has one preposition and two genitives, v. 22 two prepositions and two genitives, the shorter v. 23 a genitive, and v. 26 five prepositions and three genitives.

ὃν προέθετο ὁ θεὸς ἱλαστήριον
ἐν τῷ αὐτοῦ αἵματι
εἰς ἔνδειξιν τῆς δικαιοσύνης αὐτοῦ
διὰ τὴν πάρεσιν τῶν προγεγονότων ἁμαρτημάτων
ἐν τῇ ἀνοχῇ τοῦ θεοῦ

Charles Talbert has pointed out that this fragment is, in fact, not particularly balanced or measured: it seems quite unremarkable, and perhaps even rather clumsy.[1] Certainly, there is no rhyme or equivalence of clauses, with only the two ἐν phrases possibly being stylistically crafted in any sense (although this is also dubious, given Paul's fondness for that preposition). Thus, any characterization of the style of the text as liturgical is exaggerated and imprecise.

Lohse, among others, has made a final argument (4), claiming that the relative pronoun in v. 25 signals the beginning of quoted confessional material, just as it does in several other texts widely regarded as early church confessions.[2] But it should be recalled that the primary function of relative pronouns is to avoid the needless repetition of nouns through the initiation of relative clauses.[3] Consequently, the mere presence of a relative pronoun cannot be taken as suggesting the

1.   'A Non-Pauline Fragment', p. 288: 'Over against the evidence of what could be a liturgical style, however, we must note that as long as vss. 24 and 25 are linked together there is no possibility of a formal, balanced structure like that which so often characterizes traditional fragments in Paul's letters (e.g., Rom. 1.3-4; 4.25; Col. 1.15-20)'. His own theory makes much better sense of the stylistic argument when it repeats the last three lines of the fragment in an elegant isocolon.

2.   E.g. Rom. 4.25; Phil. 2.6; Col. 1.13, 15; 1 Tim. 3.16; Tit. 2.14; 1 Pet. 2.23 and 3.22. Note, there is a severe danger of circularity in the argument at this point, not to mention an obscuring of significant stylistic, theological and lexical differences between these passages. Rom. 3.25-26a only really shares similarities in some of these areas with Rom. 1.2-4; 4.25; Col. 1.12-13; 1 Pet. 3.22, and perhaps 1 Cor. 15.3-4, and then it approximates none of them closely.

3.   Robertson: 'The relative becomes. . . the chief bond of connection between clauses. . . [It] plays a very important part in the structure of the subordinate sentence in Greek' (*Grammar*, p. 711); cf. BDF, pp. 152-55 (§§292-97); and C.F.D. Moule, *An Idiom Book of NT Greek* (Cambridge: Cambridge University Press, 2nd edn, 1959), pp. 130-34. Paul uses it 318 times (excluding only the Pastorals), and 89 times in Romans alone. In the material preceding Rom. 3.21-26, he uses a relative pronoun 15 times, and three of the instances are even masculine, nominative and singular (1.25; 2.6; 2.23; with another such occurrence in 3.30)—a feature often cited as an indicator for the presence of quoted material.

presence of a confessional fragment or quoted material, or the consequences would be absurd; neither is it really being suggested by scholars that it does. The pronoun only indicates where a quotation begins when such a section's presence has already been established on other grounds.[1] In Rom. 3.25 the presence of a relative pronoun in the accusative at the beginning of the quotation also seems rather awkward.[2]

To draw the discussion at this stage to a conclusion, an evaluation of the leading form-critical hypotheses concerning Rom. 3.24-26a suggests that the four considerations commonly cited in their support are, without exception, unsound. As a result, while we may admit that Paul's terminology has been influenced by the early church, any theory positing a quotation or interpolation somewhere within vv. 24-26a must be abandoned.[3] There is simply not enough solid evidence given to support such theories. Some alternative explanation for the section's difficulties—and its difficulties remain—must be found.

1.   And even in the cited texts the occurrence of a relative pronoun is often irrelevant: cf. Rom. 1.2-4, which has a relative pronoun at the start of v. 2, but clearly not with reference to Christ or God; and also Col. 1.12-13 where three occur (in separate confessions, combined in one, or alternately?). Conversely, two of the most confidently held pre-Pauline fragments, 1 Cor. 15.3-4 and 2 Tim. 2.11-13, have none.

2.   Again, if read in isolation as a quotation, it simply does not seem to function very well, running into Talbert's problem that the αὐτοῦ in v. 25c is ambiguous. θεός is also awkward, since the subject of the quotation seems to occur midway through the first line—a strange arrangement for an early church creed or hymn.

3.   The hypothesis has also been rejected by, among others, Cranfield, W.A. Maier ('Paul's Concept of Justification and Some Recent Interpretations of Rom. 3.21-26', *The Springfielder* 37 [1974], pp. 248-64), J. Piper ('The Demonstration of the Righteousness of God in Romans 3.24-26', *JSNT* 7 [1980], pp. 2-32), and Schlier. Schlier's criticisms are summarized in Piper and B.F. Meyer ('The Pre-Pauline Formula in Rom. 3.25-26a', *NTS* 29 [1983], pp. 198-208)—Piper feels that they are cogent; Meyer not so, with the truth probably lying somewhere in between. A little-known study, however, is the most thorough critique, namely, N.H. Young, 'Did St Paul Compose Romans III.24f.?', *AusBR* 22 (1974), pp. 23-32.

3. The πίστις Ἰησοῦ Χριστοῦ Dispute

a. Background to the Christological Reading

A solution to some of the interpretative problems of Rom. 3.21-26 may lie in a different reading of its πίστις phrases. Paul uses the noun πίστις three times in Rom. 3.21-26, each time in a prepositional phrase, and twice in a genitive construction with Ἰησοῦς. He uses a participle construction built from πιστεύω once, also within a prepositional phrase:

22a	δικαιοσύνη θεοῦ πεφανέρωται
22b	διὰ πίστεως Ἰησοῦ Χριστοῦ
22c	εἰς πάντας τοὺς πιστεύοντας κτλ
25a	ὃν προέθετο ὁ θεὸς ἱλαστήριον
25b	διὰ τῆς πίστεως ἐν τῷ αὐτοῦ αἵματι κτλ
26d	εἰς τὸ εἶναι αὐτὸν δίκαιον καὶ δικαιοῦντα τὸν ἐκ πίστεως Ἰησοῦ

Each instance of πίστις here creates its own interpretative difficulties. The standard reading understands all four occurrences of πιστ- language to refer to the faith of the individual Christian in Christ—suggesting immediately a certain heavy-handedness on Paul's part. There is, however, a growing body of opinion that at least one, and possibly as many as three, of these occurrences should be read as the faith—or, perhaps better, the faithfulness—of Christ.[1] The genitive relation between *Christ* and *faith* is therefore one in which he is subject, not object.[2] In my opinion, this reading does eliminate the various problems associated with the πίστις clauses in the section.

Such an interpretation of πίστις and its genitive constructions in Paul has a long history. George Howard argues that the Peshitta

---

1. Previous attempts to establish the subjective genitive reading have often tried to prove too much. It is not being denied here that in Paul's letters πίστις designates, quite frequently, the believer's faith in Christ. It is simply being argued that the word is also sometimes best applied to Christ himself.

2. For a discussion of the genitive by the standard grammars, see A.J. Hultgren, 'The *PISTIS CHRISTOU* Formulation in Paul', *NovT* 22 (1980), p. 249 n. 3. The grammars admit that the distinction between a subjective and objective genitive is often blurred, since the very categories of subject and object are somewhat indistinct.

understood the phrase as a subjective genitive,[1] and this reading also circulated in the Mediaeval and Reformation periods.[2] The origin of the modern debate was a monograph by Johannes Haussleiter, published in 1891, entitled *Der Glaube Jesu Christi und der christliche Glaube*.[3] Haussleiter's conclusions were endorsed by Gerhard Kittel[4] and Adolf Deissmann.[5] A wave of rejections, however, so effectively buried the proposal that many later works did not even refer to its possibility.[6] The 1950s saw a resurgence of the question in English-speaking scholarship (seemingly in independence from the German debate) in articles by A.G. Hebert and T.F. Torrance.[7] Instead of the Germans' textual approach, these scholars argued that the connotations of fidelity and trustworthiness associated with the Hebrew *'ᵉmûnâ* underlay Paul's use of the Greek πίστις, so that the subjective reading was a more appropriate rendering of the genitive constructions.[8] But once again a wave of opposition smothered the suggestion, at least

1. 'Notes and Observations on the "Faith of Christ"', *HTR* 60 (1967), p. 460—although Hooker is not convinced, pointing out that genitive constructions in Latin and Greek versions and commentators are as ambiguous as the original ('ΠΙΣΤΙΣ ΧΡΙΣΤΟΥ', *NTS* 35 [1989], pp. 321-22, esp. 322 n. 1).

2. For example, Caietan's 1532 commentary on Romans translates *per fidem Iesu Christi* in 3.22 clearly as 'by the faith of Jesus Christ' (Parker, *Commentaries*, p. 157).

3. *NKZ* 2 (1891), pp. 109-45, 205-30. The following account of the history of the dispute is indebted to R.B. Hays's excellent summary in *The Faith of Jesus Christ* (Chico, CA: Scholars Press, 1983), pp. 158-62. There were earlier comments (for example, by MacKnight in 1810, and Lange in 1869: see Howard, 'Notes and Observations', *HTR* 60 [1967], p. 461). But Haussleiter's monograph seems to have catalyzed the ongoing modern debate.

4. 'πίστις Ἰησοῦ Χριστοῦ bei Paulus', *TSK* 79 (1906), pp. 419-36.

5. *Paul: A Study in Social and Religious History* (trans. W.E. Wilson; New York: Harper, 2nd edn, 1957 [1912]), pp. 161-65.

6. Hays lists the opposition of W.H.P. Hatch, O. Schmitz, E. Wissman and W. Mundle (*Faith of Jesus Christ*, p. 185 n. 88). Bultmann's cognizance of the debate in his *TDNT* article on πίστις is limited to one footnote (*TDNT*, VI, p. 204 n. 230).

7. Hebert, 'Faithfulness and Faith', *Theology* 58 (1955), pp. 373-79; Torrance, 'One Aspect of the Biblical Conception of Faith', *ExpTim* 68 (1957), pp. 111-14.

8. 'Faithfulness in Christ' does not make much sense, whereas '[the] faithfulness of Christ' is readily understandable.

initially, by focusing particularly on the proposal's somewhat dubious methodology.[1]

Nevertheless, the suggestion has been raised repeatedly since Torrance and Hebert, creating a third round in the modern debate that is still very much in progress,[2] and perhaps the only explanation for this hydra-like propensity is 'that the nature of the evidence requires it: "Faith *in* Jesus Christ" is not the most natural translation of πίστις Ἰησοῦ Χριστοῦ'.[3] While Gaston's recent statement is over-optimistic, it does exemplify the growing support for the subjective reading: 'The correctness of the translation of πίστις Ἰησοῦ Χριστοῦ as the "faith or faithfulness *of* Jesus Christ" has by now been too well established to need any further support'.[4]

The christological reading of πίστις in Paul also—although this is

1. For example, C.F.D. Moule, 'The Biblical Conception of Faith' [a letter to the editor in response to Torrance's article], *ExpTim* 68 (1957), p. 157; Murray, 'Appendix B: From Faith to Faith', *Romans*, I, pp. 363-74; and in particular, J. Barr, *The Semantics of Biblical Language* (London: Oxford University Press, 1961), pp. 161-205.

2. For example, by G.M. Taylor, 'The Function of ΠΙΣΤΙΣ ΧΡΙΣΤΟΥ in Galatians', *JBL* 85 (1966), pp. 58-76; G. Howard, 'Notes and Observations on the "Faith of Christ"', *HTR* 60 (1967), pp. 459-65; *idem*, 'Rom. 3.21-31 and the Inclusion of the Gentiles', *HTR* 63 (1970), pp. 223-33; *idem*, 'The "Faith of Christ"', *ExpTim* 85 (1974), pp. 212-25; *idem, Paul: Crisis in Galatia—A Study in Early Christian Theology* (Cambridge: Cambridge University Press, 1979), pp. 46-65; M. Barth, 'The Faith of the Messiah', *HeyJ* 10 (1969), pp. 363-70; D.W.B. Robinson, 'Faith of Jesus Christ', *RTR* 29 (1970), pp. 71-81; J.J. O'Rourke, *'Pistis* in Romans', *CBQ* 35 (1973), pp. 188-94; R.N. Longenecker, 'The Obedience of Christ in the Theology of the Early Church', in *Reconciliation and Hope* (ed. R. Banks; Grand Rapids: Eerdmans, 1974), pp. 142-52; and of particular relevance for this study, L.T. Johnson, 'Rom. 3.21-26 and the Faith of Jesus', *CBQ* 44 (1982), pp. 77-90; S.K. Williams, 'Again *Pistis Christou*', *CBQ* 49 (1987), pp. 321-42; and Morna Hooker, 'ΠΙΣΤΙΣ ΧΡΙΣΤΟΥ'. For further references, see Hays, *Faith of Jesus Christ*, pp. 186-87 nn. 105 and 106; and K. Barth, *Romans*, p. 364 n. 2. The catalyst for 'round three' is probably due in large measure to Hays's study and ongoing advocacy.

3. Hays, *Faith of Jesus Christ*, p. 162.

4. *Paul and the Torah* (Vancouver: University of British Columbia Press, 1987), p. 12. Hooker's study, the 1988 SNTS Presidential Address, is also probably a significant indicator (although her response to this comment of Gaston's is interesting: cf. 'ΠΙΣΤΙΣ ΧΡΙΣΤΟΥ', p. 321). Until the reading is seriously discussed in the commentaries, or even accepted, the issue cannot be considered closed.

not evidence in its support—integrates well with contemporary scholarship's re-evaluation of the nature of first century Judaism. As is well known, since World War Two and the Holocaust, Pauline scholarship has been reorienting its presentation of late Second Temple Jewish soteriology away from a depiction in terms of crabbed legalism.[1] Several studies have revealed this portrait to be a gross caricature,[2] and have replaced the catch-word 'legalism' with phrases like 'covenantal nomism' that convey the devout spirit of much of Second Temple Judaism more accurately.[3]

This has in turn necessitated a reorientation of Paul (something still far from complete),[4] but within this reorientation it has often been overlooked that Paul and Second Temple Judaism now share the principle of individual faith, since it exists at the heart of the covenant relationship.[5] Consequently, it no longer seems necessary for Paul to

1. This view still dominates large areas of scholarship. Surveys are given in W.D. Davies, 'Introduction: Paul and Judaism since Schweitzer', in *idem, Paul and Rabbinic Judaism* (Philadelphia: Fortress Press, 5th edn, 1980 [1948]), pp. vii-xv; E.P. Sanders, *Paul and Palestinian Judaism* (Philadelphia: Fortress Press, 1977), pp. 33-59; R. Kraft and G.E. Nickelsburg, 'Introduction: The Modern Study of Early Judaism', in *idem, Early Judaism and its Modern Interpreters* (Atlanta: Scholars Press, 1986), pp. 1-33; and Dunn, *Romans 1-8*, pp. lxiii-lxxii.

2. Notably Davies and Sanders ('Introduction'; *Paul and Rabbinic Judaism*), but also H.J. Schoeps, *Paul: The Theology of the Apostle in the Light of Jewish Religious History* (trans. H. Knight; London: Lutterworth, 1961); and an early voice of protest, G.F. Moore, *Judaism in the First Centuries of the Christian Era: The Age of the Tannaim* (3 vols.; Cambridge, MA: Harvard University Press, 1966 [1927-30]).

3. The phrase was coined by Sanders; however, it should not be employed monolithically. Our understanding of Second Temple Judaism must still be nuanced, and there were 'weeds' as well as 'flowers' present in it. For a more sophisticated reading, see R.N. Longenecker, *Paul, Apostle of Liberty* (New York: Harper & Row, 1964), pp. 65-85 (and for Sanders's legalistic rebuttal, cf. *Paul*, pp. 56-57).

4. This is a complex issue, but suffice it to say that many scholars have argued for a developmental or 'fulfilled' relationship between Paul and the *torah*, rather than an antithetical or hostile stance that a negative portrait of Judaism necessitates (so e.g. Davies and Longenecker). And this certainly seems to make better sense of several previously puzzling Pauline statements (like Rom. 3.31; 2 Cor. 3.7-11; 11.22; and, most importantly, Phil. 3.4-6). For a more radical reorientation, see Gaston's *Paul and the Torah*, and John Gager's *The Origins of Anti-Semitism: Attitudes toward Judaism in Pagan and Christian Antiquity* (Oxford: Oxford University Press, 1973).

5. Cf. the comment of G.N. Davies: 'the appropriate response of men and women to God is always faith and obedience. . . Although faith towards God finds

state, particularly to a Jewish or Jewish-taught audience, that God requires a response of faith. This would be not merely superfluous, but banal and perhaps even insulting.[1] This is not to be taken as belittling the principle of believing faith, because it remains fundamental.[2] But it is to recognize that faith would have been largely presupposed by both Paul and his Jewish and Jewish-Christian colleagues.[3]

If the nature and role of faith in Paul's theology has frequently been overstated in the past (in deliberate contrast to an outmoded and inaccurate picture of the soteriology of Second Temple Judaism), then it may now be in need of fundamental revision. Furthermore, since Jews already believe, the more distinctive and contentious idea of Christ's messianic faithfulness may be a more appropriate antithesis to the notion of '*torah*-works' when Paul speaks of πίστις. This assertion would give Paul's statements a substantive impact rather than an aura of superfluity.

b. *Evidence for a Christological Reading in Rom. 3.21-26*

Eight observations may be made here concerning our three disputed πίστις constructions—the participle construction in v. 22c is not disputed, clearly referring to 'everyone who believes'. We begin with v. 22b.

1. Verse 22 contains a needless redundancy if the reference of both phrases is to the same type of faith. Paul is presumably not above repeating himself, and it may also be argued that the emphasis in v. 22c is on πάντας and not on the fact of belief.[4] Nevertheless, it must be admitted that, if this is Paul's intention, the construction is clumsy. This needless repetition is doubly unusual in that the surrounding text is compact and carefully crafted, as indicated by its frequent description as 'liturgical'. This oscillation between prosaic

---

a more specific focus under the new covenant, with respect to the fulfilment of God's promises, it is not qualitatively different from that faith which was exercised by believers in the days of old covenant. . .' (*Faith and Obedience in Romans*, p. 18).

1. 'Even the demons believe that!' (Jas. 2.19).

2. And Paul does note it frequently in passing, e.g., in Rom. 1.16b; 3.3; 4.3, 23-25; 11.17-24; and so on.

3. So Schoeps, *Paul*, pp. 200-12. Schoeps specifically states that, while faith is a principle shared between Paul and Judaism, it is the *object* of faith that has changed for Paul.

4. So Cranfield (*Romans*, I, p. 203) and Dunn (*Romans 1–8*, p. 167).

brevity and verbose repetition in the same section is an embarrassment for an objective genitive reading.

Conversely, a subjective reading of the first phrase produces a very neat progression: the righteousness of God has been revealed through the faithfulness of Christ, with the goal of faith in all. Instead of redundancy, we have an elegant wordplay.

2. The objective reading also creates what we might term a problem of causality. Paul's εἰς clause in v. 22c is generally understood to be purposive; the goal of the revelation of God's righteousness through Christ is 'that everyone might believe', and presumably become ongoing believers. But if v. 22b is read as 'through belief in Jesus Christ', then the believers' faith functions as both means and goal. It is more than a little awkward to suggest that one reaches the goal or end of faith through faith itself—in fact, it is nonsense: if one goes through something, one already has it, and if one has yet to get there, one does not have it. Thus, Paul's prepositional progression is not merely redundant—it is a semantic garble.

But a subjective reading also eliminates this problem. The faith of Jesus clearly precedes the faith of everyone else, so the means precedes the end and goal quite appropriately. Once again it would seem that a subjective reading allows a smooth progression to replace a nonsense.

3. A further difficulty with the objective reading is, as D.W.B. Robinson has pointed out, that it cannot really complete the main sense of the passage.[1] In v. 21 Paul states νυνὶ ... δικαιοσύνη θεοῦ πεφανέρωται. All that follows in the section derives grammatically from this statement. But an objective construal of the πίστις genitive cannot really complete the sense of this statement. Clearly, the faith of the individual believer does not actually reveal the righteousness of God, that is, his eschatological saving righteousness. To accord this role to a believer's faith would be to strain the credulity of even the most ardent supporter of the objective genitive reading—and also to fragment and to scatter this revelation throughout history.[2]

---

1.   Robinson, 'Faith of Jesus Christ', p. 80. Hays makes the same point (*Faith of Jesus Christ*, p. 172), noting the same observation in H.W. Schmidt, *Der Brief des Paulus an die Römer* (Berlin: Evangelische Verlagsanstalt, 2nd edn, 1966), p. 66.

2.   Käsemann's observations on 1.16-17 are also appropriate here.

The perfect tense of the verb exacerbates the problem. The event of faith takes place in the present as an act of decision, but it is supposed to have revealed God's righteousness in the immediate past! This temporal sequence is not merely difficult: it is incoherent.

A subjective genitive reading, however, is in perfect continuity with this basic notion, both semantically and temporally. The faithfulness of Christ clearly does reveal the righteousness of God (according to the gospel), in the sense that it is the point at which God's final salvation becomes objectively apparent in history. And this revelation within the life and death of Jesus clearly took place in the immediate past, hence the appropriateness of the perfect tense.

Thus, a subjective reading of διὰ πίστεως Ἰησοῦ Χριστοῦ in v. 22b achieves three significant advantages over an objective reading: it effortlessly eliminates a nagging sense of redundancy, a contradictory causality, and a fundamental semantic and temporal incoherence. We may now note the arguments in support of a subjective or christological reading of πίστις in v. 25b—although they are perhaps not as decisive as those pertaining to v. 22b.[1]

4. Most commentators recommend that διὰ τῆς πίστεως be read as a parenthesis or aside, but, as some have admitted, this puts an intolerable strain on Paul's Greek: πίστις then has no object, unless we read it in relation to ἐν τῷ αἵματι, but this strange expression has no equivalent elsewhere in Paul, and so really gets us no further (and it also disrupts any parenthesis around διὰ τῆς πίστεως).

Another solution is to read πίστις with reference to the faithfulness of God (so Alfons Pluta), but this attractive alternative encounters the same problems as the foregoing: it really needs some implied participle or verb to make sense where it stands (like 'revealed': ἐφανέρωσεν or its equivalent), and it is even more awkward than the idea of human belief if it is read with reference to 'in his blood'—it almost seems as if it is God's (as in 'the Father's') blood that is being spoken of!

There are really only two solutions: (1) διὰ τῆς πίστεως ἐν τῷ αὐτοῦ αἵματι must refer back to the participle δικαιούμενοι in v. 24a, hence 'being rightwized... by faith in his death'; or (2) πίστις refers to Christ, and then the phrase makes perfect sense where it

---

1.   The arguments here depend more on my syntactical solution to vv. 24a-25b: something not yet discussed or established.

stands: 'through the faithfulness in his death'—an eminently Pauline idea (cf. Phil. 2.5-11).

The former reading is perhaps less satisfactory than the latter, however, because it is awkward to refer the phrase back to the participle over the intervening material (and most commentators do not, in fact, do this). It seems more obvious to read αἷμα in v. 25b with ἱλαστήριον in v. 25a. The reading also fails to resolve or to explain why Paul speaks of faith in blood, and why αἷμα stands in the dative case.

Given these problems, it seems better simply to refer πίστις in v. 25b to the faithfulness of Christ, at which point they disappear; the phrase reads smoothly where it stands, and the link with blood (cast in the dative), is appropriate, since the faith being spoken of is Christ's own faithfulness, revealed supremely in his 'obedience unto death'. Thus, it seems that, even without any resolution of the section's syntax, a christological reading makes the best sense of an otherwise very awkward πίστις phrase in v. 25b.[1]

5. The syntactical solution to be proposed below for 3.24-25b also has implications for this question. The suggested syntax will (among other things) align διὰ τῆς πίστεως in v. 25a with the preceding διά phrase in v. 22b-c, which suggests in turn interpreting the two phrases in parallel. At this point, therefore, any arguments that establish a christological reading in v. 22b draw v. 25b automatically into its train as well.[2]

In addition to this, argument (3) for v. 22b becomes directly applicable to v. 25b. That is, διὰ τῆς πίστεως must also in some sense complete the section's subject and verb, that is, the idea of the revelation of the eschatological saving righteousness of God in the immediate past. And, as we have seen, only a christological reading really makes sense of this idea.

Thus, the christological reading of πίστις also seems best in v. 25b. It remains only to address the expression τὸν ἐκ πίστεως Ἰησοῦ in v. 26d. Here three further points are relevant.

6. It is significant for the meaning of the πίστις constructions within the section as a whole that they are bracketed by πίστις genitive

---

1. My syntactical solution greatly strengthens this argument, because it removes any possible connection between v. 25b and the participle in v. 24a.

2. As G. Davies suggests (although independently of our detailed resolution of this section) in *Faith and Obedience in Romans*, p. 110, esp. nn. 2 and 3.

constructions in Rom. 3.3 and 4.16. In 3.3 God is described as faithful in a clearly subjective construction: μὴ ἡ ἀπιστία αὐτῶν τὴν πίστιν τοῦ θεοῦ καταργήσει.[1] More importantly, in 4.16 an identical formulation to 3.26 is also clearly subjective; οὐ τῷ ἐκ τοῦ νόμου μόνον ἀλλὰ καὶ τῷ ἐκ πίστεως 'Αβραάμ.[2] This formulation strongly suggests a subjective reading in 3.26d, or else Paul has, within the space of 21 verses, radically changed the meaning of an

---

1.   In 4.5 a (generic) believer is also described as λογίζεται ἡ πίστις αὐτοῦ εἰς δικαιοσύνην—technically, a subjective genitive construction.

2.   Strikingly, Dunn uses this phrase to argue the opposite point, namely, the correctness of the objective genitive reading in 3.22. But it is important to note that his argument is not grammatical (nor can it be: the construction is clearly a subjective genitive) but *theological* (and somewhat Protestant at that!). Put bluntly, Abraham's faith must be interpreted, according to Dunn, as paradigmatic of the believer's faith in Christ, therefore πίστις, while expressed grammatically in a subjective construction in 4.16, nevertheless must receive an objective reading when combined with Jesus (*Romans 1–8*, pp. 176, 189-90, 216). We may note the following points against this not uncommon reasoning:

1. It does not follow necessarily or automatically from the premiss that πίστις is the believer's in ch. 4 (granting at this point its truth) that all occurrences of πίστις in Paul will be to references to this as well. Certain complex and far-reaching questions are begged by this claim.

2. It is also an overly monolithic reading of πίστις in Paul. Even as the word occurs in Romans up to ch. 4, we can distinguish easily at least three significantly different meanings: the faithfulness of God; initial, believing ('kerygmatic') faith; and ongoing steadfastness. This makes extrapolations from one text to another even more difficult.

3. The reading of Abraham as prototypical for the believer may be disputed. I would argue that Abraham is prototypical for the Jewish believer, but also for the Messiah, before he functions prototypically for the generic Gentile believer (although this reading would not be widely followed; but cf. R. Hays, '"Have We Found Abraham to be our Father according to the Flesh?": A Reconsideration of Rom. 4.1', *NovT* 27 [1985], pp. 77-98; and L. Gaston, 'Abraham and the Righteousness of God', in *idem*, *Paul and the Torah*, pp. 45-63, for the beginnings of a significant re-evaluation of the role of Abraham in Paul's thought).

4. Dunn's procedure is methodologically highly suspect, since the claims of (neo-Protestant) theology are being asserted over those of both the immediate context and grammar. Context precedes both these factors, but it may be argued that grammar (where it is unambiguous) should probably also precede the rather subjective and potentially deeply biased claims of theology.

identically constructed phrase—not an impossible feat linguistically, but an unlikely one.[1]

7. Given the cogency of the syntactical solution to be proposed below, τὸν ἐκ πίστεως Ἰησοῦ should also be interpreted in parallel to its two preceding πίστις phrases. This, conditional on the success of the relevant previous arguments, should also draw the meaning of v. 26d into the christological theme already established.

8. We cannot explore this point fully here—and so it is not really being offered as an argument so much as a suggestion—but the meaning of ἐκ πίστεως in Paul generally has important implications for the present discussion.

It is seldom noted that Paul only uses ἐκ πίστεως in those letters that also quote Hab. 2.4 (i.e. Galatians and Romans), but in those letters the phrase occurs 21 times.[2] It therefore seems probable that it is Paul's use of Hab. 2.4 that underlies his use of ἐκ πίστεως elsewhere,[3] a text which has already been cited by this point in Romans (1.17).[4] Given this possible connection,[5] the interpretation of Rom. 1.17 assumes key importance.

The complex task of exegeting this text cannot be entered into in detail here, so it must suffice to suggest that, for many reasons to be argued elsewhere, a christological reading of Hab. 2.4 in Rom. 1.17[6]

1. A broader argument is also made here by J.W. Pryor: 'Paul's Use of *Iesous*—A Clue for the Translation of Rom. 3.26?', *Colloquium* 16 (1983), pp. 31-45.

2. This is only noted (but not developed) in a study by B. Corsani, 'ΕΚ ΠΙΣΤΕΩΣ in the Letters of Paul', in *The New Testament Age: Essays in Honor of Bo Reicke* (ed. W.C. Weinrich; Macon, GA: Mercer University Press, 1984), I, pp. 87-93.

3. This is more probable than the opposite relationship, namely, that Paul used the phrase ἐκ πίστεως frequently—although it only appears in Romans and Galatians among his extant letters for some reason—and then 'found' Hab. 2.4 in the Scriptures, which text he then used to support authoritatively his key phrase.

4. See Hays's suggestion: *Faith of Jesus Christ*, pp. 139-91, esp. pp. 150-57.

5. Which I argue at much greater length in 'The Meaning of ΠΙΣΤΙΣ and ΝΟΜΟΣ in Paul: A Linguistic and Structural Perspective', *JBL* (forthcoming). S. Stowers proposes a different, more general reading: 'ἐκ πίστεως and διὰ τῆς πίστεως in Romans 3.30', *JBL* 108 (1989), pp. 665-74, which I have criticized in some detail.

6. A similar, though not quite as strong, case can be made for Gal. 3.11.

is to be regarded not only as possible, but even as necessary.[1] Such a reading not only gives the best sense to 1.17a, with its dramatic sense of eschatological disclosure,[2] but it also seems a good interpretation of Hab. 2.4, given Paul's use of Scripture and of certain key terms elsewhere in Romans.[3]

In conclusion, even apart from any discussion of Hab. 2.4 in Paul, it seems that an almost irresistible weight of evidence has built up in favour of a subjective reading of Paul's πίστις Χριστοῦ genitives in Rom. 3.21-26. As a result of this, in what follows the traditional reading of πίστις Ἰησοῦ Χριστοῦ as 'faith in Jesus Christ' will be laid aside, and the christological reading 'the faithfulness of Jesus Christ' will be adopted.[4] As Byrne comments, 'An interpretation according a role to the personal faith of Jesus opens up this passage, which has always been significant, in fresh and illuminating ways'[5]—

---

1.   Cf. my 'Ambiguity and Apocalypse in Rom. 1.17—Hab. 2.4 Revisited', (forthcoming), and Appendix 1 below.

2.   A christological reading avoids many of the problems that we have already observed the traditional reading encounters in 3.21-26, namely, how does individual faith reveal the eschatological saving righteousness of God? Here a reading of ἐκ πίστεως in terms of God's faithfulness is also possible, but it seems difficult, and, on occasion, impossible (e.g. in Rom. 3.26) to sustain elsewhere.

3.   For example, ὁ δίκαιος may be functioning in Paul's use of Hab. 2.4 as a stereotyped titular reference to Christ (see Acts 3.14; 7.52; and, most significantly, 22.14, where Luke places it on the lips of Paul, although its use is ascribed to Ananias. If Luke can be trusted, Paul was obviously familiar with it: cf. also R.N. Longenecker, *The Christology of Early Jewish Christianity* [London: SCM Press, 1970], pp. 46-47, and Hays, *Faith of Jesus Christ*, pp. 151-54). Paul's tendency to use articular substantives as titles for Christ also supports a titular use of ὁ δίκαιος in Rom. 1.17: cf. ὁ υἱός (Rom. 1.3, 4, 9; 5.10; 8.3, 29, 32), ὁ Χριστός (Rom. 9.3, 5; 14.18; 15.3, 7, 19; 16.16), ὁ εἷς (Rom. 5.15, 17, 18, 19), and so on.

4.   Paul, in fact, seems to be nuancing his use of πίστις throughout Romans in a fourfold sense: (1) the faithfulness of God (3.3) reveals itself in (2) the faithfulness of Christ (1.17; 3.22b, 25b), and is appropriated by (3) the faith of the believer (1.16, 17a; 3.22c), who lives 'out of' (or, 'on the ground of') the faithfulness of Jesus (3.26d), and so lives a life of (4) steadfast faithfulness (1.5, 12). Cf. Byrne, *Reckoning*, p. 80. Such wordplay may be a little confusing or irritating theologically, but it is certainly permissible—and even elegant—from a stylistic perspective.

5.   Byrne, *Reckoning*, p. 80 (cf. also p. 79). As we have seen, Barth consistently translates the phrase by 'the faithfulness of God', and on one occasion he refers it to Christ. But he never justifies this reading—a sound intuition perhaps (*Romans*, p. 97)?

and also, one might add, in less troublesome ways.

A subjective understanding of the word πίστις and its genitive constructions does not, however, eliminate all the problems in the passage. Several difficulties still remain that obstruct a clear understanding of the text (although solutions to some of them have been anticipated in a few of the preceding arguments), so we turn to Graeco-Roman rhetoric in the hope that it will supply a key to the fundamental syntactical conundrum that hampers the attempt at a coherent reading of Rom. 3.21-26.

Chapter 2

RHETORICAL ANALYSIS AND ROMANS 3.21-26

1. *Previous Rhetorical Analysis of Paul*

Somewhat surprisingly, particularly in view of comments by some of the Church Fathers[1] and various Reformation commentators,[2] and the classical training of many NT scholars, the rhetorical dimension in Paul's letters has been largely ignored until quite recently.[3] Apart from a few isolated early studies,[4] the importance of rhetoric for

---

1. For example, Augustine comments: ' "Antithesis" provides the most attractive figures in literary composition: the Latin equivalent is "opposition", or, more accurately, "contraposition". The Apostle Paul makes elegant use of antithesis in developing a passage in the Second Epistle to the Corinthians. . . [2 Cor. 6.7ff.]. The opposition of such contraries gives an added beauty to speech' (*City of God* [trans. H. Bettenson; Reading, England: Cox & Wyman, 1972], p. 449).

2. Various Reformation commentators utilized rhetorical categories extensively in analysing Romans: e.g. Melanchthon, Bullinger, Bucer and Calvin. Their interpretations, however, tend towards a static categorization of Paul's argument in terms of stases, propositions and causes (see Parker, *Commentaries*, pp. 156-200).

3. Cf. M. Kessler, 'A Methodological Setting for Rhetorical Criticism', *Semitics* 4 (1974), p. 24; W. Wuellner, 'Greek Rhetoric and Pauline Argumentation', in *Early Christian Literature and the Classical Intellectual Tradition* (ed. W.R. Schoedel and R.L. Wilken; Paris: Editions Beauchesne, 1979), pp. 178-79.

4. An eighteenth-century precursor was Johann Bengel's *Gnomon of the New Testament* (trans. C.T. Lewis and M.R. Vincent; 2 vols.; Philadelphia: Perkinpine & Higgins, 1860–62 [1742]). Somewhat later came a series of German studies: E. König, *Stilistik, Rhetorik, Poetik* (Leipzig: Theodor Weicher, 1900); some work by J. Weiss, e.g., his 'Beiträge zur paulinischen Rhetorik', in *Theologische Studien: Bernhard Weiss Festschrift* (ed. C.R. Gregory *et al.*; Göttingen: Vandenhoeck & Ruprecht, 1897); E. Norden, *Die Antike Kunstprosa* (Leipzig: Teubner, 2nd edn, 1909); and F. Blass, *Die Rhythmen der asianischen und römischen Kunstprosa* (Hildesheim: Gerstenberg, 1972 [1905]). These were followed by some studies in

understanding Paul only began to be widely appreciated in the 1960s.
At this point three precursors for the rhetorical analysis of the Bible
can be distinguished:[1] (1) a theoretical (or, occasionally, an anti-theo-
retical) group strongly influenced by Perelman and Olbrechts-Tyteca;[2]
(2) a small cluster of Continental scholars who were influenced
primarily by modern literary theory and Structuralism, but who also
used rhetorical insights;[3] and (3) what has been termed 'the Berkeley

English-speaking scholarship: F.H. Colson, 'Μετεσχημάτισα 1 Cor. iv 6', *JTS* 17
(1915–16), pp. 379-84; N.W. Lund, *Chiasmus in the New Testament: A Study in
Formgeschichte* (Durham, NC: University of North Carolina Press, 1942);
J.S. Callaway, 'Paul's letter to the Galatians and Plato's *Lysias*', *JBL* 67 (1948),
pp. 353-56; D. Daube, 'Rabbinic Methods of Interpretation and Hellenistic
Rhetoric', *HUCA* 22 (1949), pp. 239-64; R.M. Grant, 'Like Children', *HTR* 39
(1946), pp. 71-73; *idem*, Hellenistic Elements in I Corinthians', in *Early Christian
Origins: Studies in Honour of Harold R. Willoughby* (ed. A. Wikgren; Chicago:
Quadrangle Books, 1961), pp. 60-66; and A.N. Wilder, *Early Christian Rhetoric*
(New York: Harper & Row, 1964); *idem*, 'The Rhetoric of Ancient and Modern
Apocalyptic', *Int* 25 (1971), pp. 436-53.
    1.   Much of the following depends on the excellent summary article by
W. Wuellner, 'Where is Rhetorical Criticism Taking us?', *CBQ* 49 (1987),
pp. 448-63.
    2.   C. Perelman and L. Olbrechts-Tyteca, *The New Rhetoric: A Treatise on
Argumentation* (trans. J. Wilkinson and P. Weaver; Notre Dame, IN: Notre Dame
University Press, 1969 [1958]). Cf. Kessler's use of the term in 'A Methodological
Setting for Rhetorical Criticism' and 'An Introduction to Rhetorical Criticism of the
Bible: Prolegomena', *Semitics* 7 (1980), pp. 1-27; and also W. Booth, *The Rhetoric
of Fiction* (Chicago: University of Chicago Press, 2nd edn, 1982), and
P. de Man, *The Rhetoric of Romanticism* (New York: Columbia University Press,
1984). Wuellner summarizes the implications of this approach: 'The discipline of
rhetorical criticism will emerge as "a dynamic process", not as a system. . . It will
be imaginative criticism. . . a criticism of the dialogical imagination. . . which is cog-
nizant of the Bible as "ideological literature". . . and of biblical hermeneutics as part
of the "politics of interpretation" ('Rhetorical Criticism', pp. 463-64). A recent study
of Romans utilizing rhetoric in this sense is Elliott's *The Rhetoric of Righteousness
in Romans*, cf. esp. pp. 15-21; cf. also G.W. Hansen, *Abraham in Galatians:
Epistolary and Rhetorical Genres* (JSNTSup, 29; Sheffield: JSOT Press, 1989),
pp. 79-93.
    3.   The group included L. Alonso-Schökel, R. Alter, A. Berlin, and D. Rhoads:
cf. L. Alonso-Schökel, *The Inspired Word: Scripture in the Light of Language and
Literature* (trans. F. Martin; New York: Herder, 1965); R. Alter, *The Art of Biblical
Narrative* (New York: Basic Books, 1981); *idem*, *The Art of Biblical Poetry* (New
York: Basic Books, 1985); A. Berlin, *Poetics and Interpretation of Biblical Narrative*

School'. In 1968 the founding father of the school, James Muilenburg, made a programmatic appeal to the Society of Biblical Literature in his presidential address entitled 'After Form Criticism What?', responding (of course) 'rhetorical criticism, that's what'.[1] Largely under his impetus, Berkeley fostered a vigorous exploration of rhetoric and the Bible by scholars such as Wilhelm Wuellner, William J. Brandt and Edward P.J. Corbett.[2]

We may also distinguish three more immediate precursors to the rhetorical analysis of Paul: (1) Hans Dieter Betz, (2) George Kennedy and (3) Edwin A. Judge.[3]

(Sheffield: Almond Press, 1983); and D. Rhoads and D. Michie, *Mark as Story* (Philadelphia: Fortress Press, 1982), pp. 35-62. This group was probably (at least in part) stimulated by the French Structuralists' rediscovery of ancient rhetoric; see T. Todorov, *Theories of the Symbol* (trans. C. Porter; New York: Cornell University Press, 1977).

1. Wuellner highlights Muilenburg's address as epochal, noting particularly that 'the answer to this question—rhetorical criticism, that's what—led to the rise of a veritable Muilenburg School, whose publications have done much to make the reference to rhetoric acceptable, if not fashionable, again in biblical exegesis' ('Rhetorical Criticism', p. 454). The address was published as 'Form Criticism and Beyond', *JBL* 88 (1969), pp. 1-18. Muilenburg's observations in this study emphasize (among other things) that rhetorical devices are not necessarily consciously derived from the classical tradition, although the classical theorists developed the most sophisticated systems for their recognition and use. Many tropes were universal, or at least widespread in the orient, so a 'classical' classification does not necessarily imply a 'classical' education or derivation. (For a bibliography of Muilenburg's work and some interesting comments on its development, cf. J.R. Lundbom, *Jeremiah: A Study in Ancient Hebrew Rhetoric* [Missoula, MT: Scholars Press, 1975], p. 129 n. 3.)

2. W.J. Brandt, *The Rhetoric of Argumentation* (New York: Bobbs–Merrill, 1970); Edward P.J. Corbett, *Classical Rhetoric for the Modern Student* (New York: Oxford University Press, 1965); *idem* (ed.), *Rhetorical Analyses of Literary Works* (New York: Oxford University Press, 1969). See also Lundbom, *Jeremiah*.

3. One should also note the various chiastic analyses of Paul that have been undertaken as part of a wider investigation of biblical literature in terms of this figure. The seminal biblical work is Lund's *Chiasmus in the New Testament*; cf. also J. Bligh's later chiastic investigation of Galatians: *Galatians in Greek: A Structural Analysis of St Paul's Epistle to the Galatians with Notes on the Greek* (Detroit: University of Detroit Press, 1966); and J. Jeremias, 'Chiasmus in den Paulusbriefen', *ZNW* 49 (1958), pp. 145-56. A good survey (and employment) of this approach is given by Hansen, *Abraham in Galatians*, pp. 73-79.

(1) In 1960 Lausberg published an important classification of ancient rhetoric,[1] which strongly influenced (among others) Hans Dieter Betz. Betz's work, particularly his commentary on Galatians, constitutes the first major modern study of Paul from an explicitly rhetorical perspective.[2] Betz argues specifically that Paul's letters (and Galatians in particular) are structured in accordance with the ideal juridical speech, along with its formal rhetorical divisions into an *exordio, narratio, propositio, probatio* (an optional *partitio*, and/or *digressio*, or *transitio*) and *peroratio*.

But many have failed to be convinced by Betz's approach—despite its originality and appeal.[3] His commentary remains a landmark in

---

1. *Handbuch der literarischen Rhetorik* (2 vols.; Munich: Hueber, 1960), supplemented by his *Elemente der literarischen Rhetorik* (Munich: Hueber, 8th edn, 1984). Lausberg's compilations received mixed reviews. Wuellner calls them 'one-sided', citing a Dutch critic, Spies, to the effect that 'the influence of Heinrich Lausberg's recodification of rhetoric [was not] beneficial in one particular, since he asserts that epideictic rhetoric was designed mainly for praise of beauty, and had little importance in argumentation' ('Rhetorical Criticism', p. 452).

2. *Galatians: A Commentary on Paul's Letter to the Churches in Galatia* (Hermeneia; Philadelphia: Fortress Press, 1979). Betz's commentary was prefigured by *Der Apostel Paulus und die sokratische Tradition* (Tübingen: Mohr, 1972); and 'The Literary Composition and Function of Paul's Letter to the Galatians', *NTS* 21 (1974–75), pp. 353-79. He has also published another Hermeneia commentary that argues from a similar rhetorical standpoint, *Second Corinthians 8 and 9: A Commentary on Two Administrative Letters of the Apostle Paul* (Hermeneia; Philadelphia: Fortress Press, 1985). Possibly Bligh's analysis of Galatians in chiastic terms pre-empts Betz's analyses as the first modern rhetorical work on Paul.

3. The formal categories make good sense of the opening phases of Paul's Galatian letter, especially Paul's strategy in his introduction of 1.6-10, his thesis statement of 1.11-12, the subsequent *narratio* of 1.13–2.14, and even the *propositio* of 2.15-21 (Kennedy's comments at this point, however, are interesting: the particular events recounted by Paul, he suggests, do not conform precisely to a *narratio*, but to the external evidence often used in a deliberative speech intended to establish a thesis based on *ethos*: cf. *New Testament Interpretation through Rhetorical Criticism* [Chapel Hill, NC: University of North Carolina Press, 1984], p. 145). Beyond this point in the letter, however, Betz's analysis begins to break down, since the ensuing discourse seems fundamentally different from the rhetorical categories that he claims are moulding it. For example, the arguments of the *probatio* are not symmetrically structured around a digression, and the mythical category of *exhortatio* must be introduced to explain Paul's paraenetic discourse that starts at 5.13 (the ideal juridical speech had no *exhortatio*, but moved directly from *probatio* to *peroratio*: certainly I

Pauline scholarship, and has led to a generation of imitators, but his specific analytic framework, in our opinion, should not be followed too closely.

(2) Another mode of rhetorical interpretation in Paul stems from the work of George Kennedy, one among a small number of classical scholars who have focused on the NT in rhetorical terms.[1] Kennedy's writings are an excellent resource for rhetorical analysis, and he makes a number of useful methodological comments.[2] But his specific analytical proposals also seem methodologically flawed.[3] Furthermore, his actual analyses of the Pauline letters are inadequate.[4] Consequently,

---

have never seen the category mentioned in any of the manuals on ancient rhetorical theory; cf. again Kennedy's comments, *New Testament Interpretation*, pp. 145-46; cf. also the comments by W.A. Meeks, Review of *Galatians*, by H.D. Betz, *JBL* 100 [1981], p. 306; D. Aune, Review of *Galatians*, by H.D. Betz, *RelSRev* 7 [1981], pp. 323-28; R.N. Longenecker, *Commentary on Galatians* [Dallas: Word Books, 1990] pp. cix-cxii; Hansen, *Abraham in Galatians*, pp. 58-71: cf. also Quintilian's very appropriate comments, *Inst.* 1.8.1-2, 14-16).

1.   G.A. Kennedy, 'An Introduction to the Rhetoric of the Gospels', *Rhetorica* 1 (1983), pp. 17-31; *idem, New Testament Interpretation.* Wuellner also notes the work of the Swedish classicist, A. Wifstrand, and German classicist, W. Jens ('Rhetorical Criticism', p. 449 n. 7).

2.   His suggestion, to discern textual units and then to explore their argumentative arrangement from the level of tropes and figures up to the level of their overall interaction, is sound. And his notion of 'linearity' is also significant, because it emphasizes a factor frequently overlooked in NT texts (Kennedy, *New Testament Interpretation*, p. 5):

> A speech is linear and cumulative, and any context in it can only be perceived in contrast to what has gone before, especially what has immediately gone before, though a very able speaker lays the ground for what he intends to say later and has a total unity in mind when he first begins to speak. We need to keep in mind that the Bible in early Christian times was more often heard when read aloud to a group than read privately; very few Christians owned copies of the Bible, and some did not know how to read.

See also p. 37, where he points out that an important stylistic consequence of orality is repetition (note, linearity is a point distinct from 'orality' and 'aurality', although they are related).

3.   His advice (1) to define the 'rhetorical situation', and (2) to follow the process of invention through from problem to text by way of the author's intention, seems blatant instances of both the sociological and biographical fallacies. We have no access to these prior to analysing the text itself (cf. A. Warren and R. Wellek, *Theory of Literature* [New York: Harcourt, Brace & World, 1942], pp. 65-106).

4.   For example, he seems unaware of the function of paraenetic discourse,

his recommendations should also, in our opinion, not be followed too literally.

(3) Edwin A. Judge argues that Paul's rhetorical style and mission practice are closely correlated with that of first-century philosophers and their schools (who, of course, also used rhetoric extensively), and that this model can therefore be used to explain the Pauline mission.[1]

But such a reconstruction may be overly constricting the rhetorical features apparent in Paul. Rhetoric was simply part of the culture of ancient Graeco-Roman society, hence everyone, whether formally educated or simply exposed to the ructions of the marketplace and the forum, was probably influenced by its categories and figures to some degree. Paul's use of rhetoric may be no more than that of an intelligent citizen of the empire who was educated in the usual manner to the 'secondary' level (perhaps before continuing with specialized

suggesting that the paraenesis of chs. 5–6 is the heart of the argument in Galatians: 'What Paul is leading to in [Galatians] chapters 1–4 is the exhortation of chapters 5–6. That is the point of the letter' (*New Testament Interpretation*, p. 146). This is an observation not well supported by other NT scholars. Similarly, his applications of the three classical categories of deliberative, juridical and epideictic argument seem strained, since Galatians is not merely deliberative, and therefore concerned with future actions, but also contains extensive references to past and present behaviour (cf. the argument from the Spirit in 3.2-5, from Abraham in 3.6-9, 14, 15-20, and from the law as a pedagogue in 3.21-25). Kennedy's statement that 'the question to be decided by the Galatians was not whether Paul had been right in what he had said and done, but what they themselves were going to believe and to do' (*New Testament Interpretation*, p. 146)—presumably intended to preserve the future, deliberative nature of the letter—ignores the organic connection between these two factors (it also renders Paul's *exordio* and thesis statement of 1.6-12, as well as the following *narratio* of 1.13–2.14, dysfunctional).

1.   E.A. Judge, 'The Early Christians as a Scholastic Community', *JRH* 1 (1960–61), pp. 4-15, 125-37; *idem*, *The Social Pattern of Christian Groups in the First Century* (London: Tyndale, 1960); *idem*, 'Paul's Boasting in Relation to Contemporary Professional Practice', *AusBR* 16 (1968), pp. 37-50; *idem*, 'St Paul and Classical Society', *JAC* 15 (1972), pp. 19-36. A more recent representative of this line of thought (among others) is S.K. Stowers, 'Social Stature, Public Speaking and Private Teaching: The Circumstances of Paul's Preaching Activity', *NovT* 26 (1984), pp. 60-82. It is particularly significant for this view that the philosophers used letters to propagate their teaching, both publicly (often pseudonymously) and among their disciples, and also that Tarsus was a famous 'university town', having a large Stoic school.

rabbinic training),[1] who travelled extensively, and who used what he found appropriate when he needed to.[2] Thus, there is no real need to posit a specialized philosophical education and social dynamic for Paul and his mission; broader cultural considerations provide an adequate social-dynamic explanation.[3]

In my opinion, the work of Abraham Malherbe represents a more balanced approach than these explicitly rhetorical exemplars. Malherbe is not a rhetorical analyst *per se*, but he has made several illuminating studies of various difficult Pauline statements from the perspective of the philosophico-rhetorical texts of Paul's time (often in conjunction with epistolary theory). Malherbe's orientation is therefore fundamentally textual. His insights usually contribute to an understanding of specific, localized phrases and expressions. In short, his approach is stylistic, rather than architectonic (Betz or Kennedy) or sociological (Judge). As such, he is an important methodological exemplar for the following analysis.[4] Rhetorical analyses are now rather fashionable,

---

1.   Cf. Longenecker's reading of Acts 22.3 (*contra* van Unnik), which takes Paul to Jerusalem in his teens (*Paul, Apostle of Liberty*, pp. 25-26). That Paul received rabbinic training is also a direct claim: cf. Gal. 1.14 and Phil. 3.5-6. Note also that the variable scope of a 'secondary' education taught by a *grammaticus* makes it possible that Paul had also received some more advanced 'tertiary' rhetorical training at this stage (cf. Quintilian, *Institutes* 1.1.1-6: 'the teachers of literature have undertaken tasks which rightly belonged to others. . . Consequently subjects which once formed the first stages of rhetoric have come to form the final stages of a literary education'; see also 3.11.23-24).

2.   A.J. Malherbe, *Social Aspects of Early Christianity* (Philadelphia: Fortress Press, Press, 2nd [enlarged] edn, 1983 [1977]), pp. 33-35, 41-45.

3.   It is also significant (of course!) that Paul himself does not claim to be a trained speaker (as some of his opponents are): cf. esp. 1 Cor. 2.1-5, 13-16, and 2 Cor. 10.10-11. Similarly, many of the well-educated and rhetorically proficient Church Fathers (notwithstanding their occasional recognition of a trope or figure) do not recognize in Paul a polished style, but are forced in effect to apologize for its somewhat rude timbre. C. Forbes argues that Paul's rhetorical skill in the Corinthian correspondence suggests a more advanced rhetorical education: 'Comparison, Self-Praise and Irony: Paul's Boasting and the Conventions of Hellenistic Rhetoric', *NTS* 32 (1986), pp. 1-30.

4.   Cf. esp. his 'The Beasts at Ephesus', *JBL* 87 (1968), pp. 71-80; ' "Gentle as a Nurse": the Cynic Background of I Thess. ii', *NovT* 12 (1970), pp. 203-17; 'Exhortation in First Thessalonians', *NovT* 25 (1983), pp. 238-56; and *idem, Paul and the Philosophers* (Philadelphia: Fortress Press, 1988).

and so are proliferating through the literature rapidly, but few share the approach outlined above.[1]

2. *The Chosen Rhetorical Method and Sources*

The central interpretative contribution of rhetoric to this study is mainly at the level of style. The question is whether rhetorical principles can explain how Paul has arranged his phrases and clauses in Rom. 3.21-26, which is to focus on just one of the five divisions of rhetoric as classically defined, namely, on ornamentation or *elocutio*.[2] If a knowledge of *elocutio* can unravel Paul's syntax and style in this section, then the major obstruction to its further analysis will have been removed. We will then be able to proceed to an investigation of Paul's key terms, and, beyond that, to a final, integrated interpretation of the section as a whole. Thus, rhetorical insights at the stylistic level are really the interpretative pivot upon which the whole of the present investigation turns.

Investigation of the rhetorical possibilities available to Paul at the level of style will be primarily through the standard rhetorical manuals and treatises.[3] It is not assumed that he read these directly,[4] but if 'two

1. Two excellent studies from this perspective are F.F. Church, 'Rhetorical Structure and Design in Paul's Letter to Philemon', *HTR* 71 (1978), pp. 17-33; and D.E. Garland, 'The Composition and Unity of Philippians: Some Neglected Literary Factors', *NovT* 27 (1985), pp. 141-73. Cf. also A.H. Snyman, 'Style and the Rhetorical Situation of Rom. 8.31-39', *NTS* 34 (1988), pp. 218-31; *idem*, 'The New Testament and Greco-Roman Rhetoric: A Bibliography', *JETS* 31 (1988), pp. 465-72; and R. Jewett, *The Thessalonian Correspondence: Pauline Rhetoric and Millenarian Piety* (Philadelphia: Fortress Press, 1986).

2. The five divisions were invention, disposition or arrangement, ornamentation, memory and delivery. An excellent but largely unnoticed study focusing on this issue is A.H. Snyman and J.v.W. Cronje, 'Toward a New Classification of the Figures (ΣΧΗΜΑΤΑ) in the Greek New Testament', *NTS* 32 (1986), pp. 113-21.

3. Rhetoric in the ancient world was, of course, conditioned by experience as well as by theory (and perhaps primarily so), but to undertake an exhaustive survey of the entire ancient rhetorical corpus is clearly impossible within the limits of the present study. It will be assumed that the theoretical treatments alone provide sufficient information to note the handful of devices that occur in Rom. 3.21-26.

4. Although a case can be made, not only for Demetrius's first-century provenance, but for his origin from Tarsus, unfortunately it cannot be proved sufficiently to allow much weight to be placed on it. See W.R. Roberts, 'Introduction', in *idem*

or more' speak of a given principle or technique, and Paul also uses it, then it may probably be assumed that a rhetorical device is operative in the text that can be used to explain it.

The best source for rhetorical theory at this time is Quintilian, who (c. 95 CE) published a magnificent twelve-volume discussion of rhetoric, the *Institutes of Oratory*.[1] His discussion is closely followed in importance by certain theoretical works of Cicero, namely, his early *On Invention* (which he later disowned), the five-volume exposition of his mature years entitled *On the Orator, Brutus,* and *Orator,* and also the useful *Partitions of Oratory*.[2] Further significant studies are the anonymous *Rhetorica ad Herennium*,[3] Demetrius's *On Style*,[4] Dionysius of Halicarnassus's *On Literary Composition*,[5] Aristotle's *Art of Rhetoric*,[6] and Pseudo-Aristotle's *Rhetoric to Alexander*.[7] Secondary but still significant discussions include Plato's *Phaedrus* and *Gorgias*,[8] Longinus's *On the Sublime*,[9] Tacitus's *Dialogue on*

(ed. and trans.), *Demetrius On Style* (Cambridge: Cambridge University Press, 1902), pp. 49-64, who argues for a date c. 100 BCE–100 CE. In his later Loeb edition, however (Cambridge, MA: Harvard University Press, 1953 [1927], pp. 269-81), he suggests that the author might be the first-century Demetrius of Tarsus. G.M.A. Grube, in *A Greek Critic: Demetrius on Style* (Toronto: University of Toronto Press, 1961), pp. 39-56, argues against Roberts for a much earlier date, namely, around 270 BCE. Both viewpoints seem overstated.

1. Quintilian, *Institutes of Oratory* (trans. H.E. Butler; 4 vols.; London: Heinemann, 1933, 1939, 1943 [1921]).

2. Cicero, *Two Books on Rhetoric, Commonly Called On Invention* (trans. H.M. Hubbell; London: Heinemann, 1949), II, pp. 1-345; *idem, On the Orator* (trans. H. Rackham; London: Heinemann, 1968), III, and IV, pp. 2-185; *idem, Brutus* (trans. G.L. Hendrickson; London: Heinemann, 1939), V, pp. 2-293; *Orator* (trans. H.M. Hubbell; London: Heinemann, 1939), V, pp. 297-509; *idem, Partitions of Oratory* (trans. H. Rackham; London: Heinemann, 1968), IV, pp. 305-421.

3. *Rhetorica ad Herennium* (trans. H. Caplan; London: Heinemann, 1954).

4. Demetrius, *On Style* (trans. W. Rhys Roberts; Cambridge, MA: Harvard University Press, 1953 [1927]), pp. 294-487.

5. Dionysius of Halicarnassus, *On Literary Composition* (trans. W. Rhys Roberts; London: Macmillan, 1910).

6. Aristotle, *The 'Art' of Rhetoric* (trans. J.H. Freese; Cambridge, MA: Harvard University Press, 1947 [1926]).

7. In *The Complete Works of Aristotle: Revised Oxford Translation*, II, pp. 2270-315 (ed. J. Barnes; trans. W.R. Roberts; Princeton: Princeton University Press, 1984).

8. Plato, *Phaedrus* (trans. H.N. Fowler; London: Heinemann, 1971), I,

Oratory,[1] treatises by Hermogenes and Philodemus,[2] and some of Cicero's less important treatises (*Topics*, *On the Best Kind of Orator*, and so on[3]).[4]

3. *The Setting*

The first point at which the rhetorical manuals prove useful is in their description of different literary styles. This allows us to delimit Rom. 3.21-26 within its immediate context as a discrete literary entity. It also suggests an explanation for the passage's unusual and distinct style, which has so often attracted designations like 'liturgical'.

Several of the theorists note that rhetorical argument can proceed in one of three (or four) styles; the plain, the middle, and the grand (and, according to Demetrius, the forcible).[5] Each style is suited to

pp. 407-579; *idem, Gorgias* (trans. W.R.M. Lamb; London: Heinemann, 1983), III, pp. 249-533.

9.   Longinus, *On the Sublime* (trans. W.H. Fyfe; London: Heinemann, 1953).

1.   Trans. W. Peterson; rev. M. Winterbottom; London: Heinemann, 1970 (1893), pp. 229-347.

2.   Cf. Hermogenes' *On Stases*, in R. Nadeau (trans. and ed.), 'Hermogenes *On Stases*: A Translation with Introduction and Notes', *The Speech Teacher* 31 (1964), pp. 361-424 (also in L. Spengel [ed.], *Rhetores Graeci* [3 vols.; Leipzig: Teubner, 1853–56]), and 'The Rhetorica of Philodemus', trans. H.M. Hubbell, *Transactions of the Connecticut Academy of Arts and Sciences* 23 (1920), pp. 243-382.

3.   *The Best Kind of Orator* (trans. H.M. Hubbell; London: Heinemann, 1949), II, pp. 347-73; *idem, Topics* (trans. H.M. Hubbell; London: Heinemann, 1949), II, pp. 375-459. One might also include at this point a set of commentaries on Cicero's speeches written by Asconius for his children (c. 54–57 CE) which are only available in Latin (ed. A.C. Clark; Oxford: Clarendon Press, 1907). B. Marshall has written an extensive commentary on these: *A Historical Commentary on Asconius* (Columbia, MO: University of Missouri Press, 1985).

4.   For another review of sources and of other translations, and for further sources, cf. C. Forbes, 'Comparison, Self-Praise and Irony, pp. 1-30; and C.S. Rayment, 'A Current Study of Ancient Rhetoric (1939–1957)', and 'Ancient Rhetoric (1957–63)', in *The Classical World Bibliography of Philosophy, Religion, and Rhetoric* (London: Garland, 1978), pp. 371-96.

5.   See W. Rhys Roberts, 'Introduction', in *Demetrius' On Style*, pp. 257-93, esp. pp. 259-69. Demetrius is the only instance of a fourfold classification, which introduces the 'forcible' style. The other theorists all speak in terms of three (cf. Cicero, *Orator* 69: 'to prove is the first necessity, to please is charm, to sway is victory; for it is the one thing of all that avails most in winning verdicts. For these

different argumentative intentions,[1] and utilizes different literary techniques.

Cicero, the *Auctor ad Herennium*, Dionysius and Quintilian all agree in emphasizing the variability that should characterize style: 'It is certainly obvious that totally different styles must be used, not only in the different parts of the speech, but also that whole speeches must be in one style, now in another'.[2] Or, as Cicero says later at some length:

> This. . . is the form of wisdom that the orator must especially employ—to adapt himself to occasions and persons. In my opinion one must not speak in the same style at all times, nor before all people, nor against all opponents, nor in defence of all clients, nor in partnership with all advocates. He therefore, will be eloquent who can adapt his speech to fit all conceivable circumstances. When this is determined, he will speak each part as it should be spoken; a rich subject will not be treated meagrely, nor a grand subject in a paltry way, nor vice versa, but the speech will be proper and adequate to the subject.[3]

It is clear that Paul is varying his style in the opening chapters of Romans, just as the theorists recommend. On the one hand, certain sections are plainly cast in a diatribal form.[4] In fact, up to 3.20 the

---

three functions of the orator there are three styles, the plain style for proof, the middle style for pleasure, the vigorous style for persuasion').

1. Cicero, *Orator* 101: 'He. . . will be an eloquent speaker. . . who can discuss trivial matters in a plain style, matters of moderate significance in the tempered style, and weighty affairs in the grand manner'.

2. Cicero, *Orator* 74.

3. *Orator* 122–23.

4. S.K. Stowers has designated large sections of Paul's letter to the Romans as diatribal: 1.18-32 (indictment); 2.1-5 ('the inconsistent Judge'); 2.17-24 ('the inconsistent Jew'); and 3.27–4.2; 9.19-21; 11.17-24; and so on (in *The Diatribe and Paul's Letter to the Romans* [Chico, CA: Scholars, 1981]). Diatribal features also occur at 6.1, 15; 7.7, 13; 8.2; 14.4, 10, 13, 15, 19, 20 and 22. Following this, Stowers published an important analysis of Rom. 3.1-9, 'Paul's Dialogue with a Fellow Jew in Romans 3.1-9', *CBQ* 46 (1984), pp. 707-22, thus extending his recognition of diatribal material in the opening chapters from 1.18 through to 4.2 almost without interruption (excepting 2.7-16, 25-29, and 3.10-26). Cf. R. Bultmann, *Der Stil der paulinische Predigt und die kynisch-stoische Diatribe* (Göttingen: Vandenhoeck & Ruprecht, 1910), for the earlier, still widely prevalent, view.

argument is perhaps primarily diatribal (although the diatribe of 3.1-9 is somewhat obscured by the catena of scriptural citations running from vv. 10-18). This style resumes in 3.27 and continues into the opening verses of ch. 4. Such a use of the diatribe seems very close to Demetrius's forcible style, which uses short sentences (since 'length paralyses intensity') in an uninterrupted succession of periods.[1] Demetrius argues that this style originated in the 'vivid' and 'didactic' Socratic dialogue.[2]

Interspersing Paul's diatribal passages are sections composed in a quite different style. The sentences are more complex and use balanced cola and commata with a distinct rhythmical lilt. The diction is more elevated, and theological motifs (like νόμος) figure centrally in sweeping enthymemes.[3] Rom. 3.21-26 is one such section, comprising extended periodic syntax with a series of carefully formed clauses and phrases, and ending in v. 26 with a climactic concluding phrase. This seems more akin to the 'middle' style (also called the intermediate, or elegant style), which was supposed to be graceful, even verging at times on the genial and the humorous. The middle style used repetition and anaphora,[4] and was intended to be beautiful,

---

1. It may also use anaphora, asyndeton, homoeoteleuton, climax, rhetorical questions, picturesque words and covert allusion.

2. *On Style* 5.240-304.

3. Cicero: 'A vigorous dispute requires speech, exposition requires a slower rhythm', and, 'There is no style better or stronger than to strike with phrases of two or three words, sometimes with single words, and at other times with several, in the midst of which comes sparingly the rhythmical period with varying cadences' (*Orator* 212-13; 226). These suggestions capture the rhythm of the opening chapters of Romans perfectly, with their constant shift from rapid and vigorous diatribe to slower, more modulated argument.

4. Cicero, *Orator* 128-87. Cf. Dionysius's 'intermediate' and 'harmoniously blended' compositions, examples of the last being Homer, Herodotus, Demosthenes and Plato (*On Literary Composition* 232-47, 246-51). Certainly, Paul's passages are not Platonic, but their stylistic features do seem to suggest many of the characteristics of the intermediate style. According to Cicero, this style is 'fuller and somewhat more robust than the simple style. . . [with] a minimum of vigour and a maximum of charm' (*Orator* 91). It uses metaphor and metonymy, and in a most intriguing remark Cicero says, 'It is commonly the philosophical schools which produce such orators. . . [with] a brilliant and florid, highly coloured and polished style in which all the charms of language and thought are intertwined' (94-95). Paul is a little rougher than this would suggest, but the description is not impossible—and particu-

hence measure (i.e. rhythm) was important.[1]

But the section also seems to share features with the grand style. The grand or elevated style used rounded periods and long members, a complex diction, variable connectives (with frequent use of asyndeton), and was considered proper to the exposition of a vivid and elevated subject matter.[2] As Cicero says, it is 'magnificent, opulent, stately and ornate. . . the kind of eloquence which rushes along with the roar of a mighty stream'.[3]

Rom. 3.21-26 seems to combine features from both these styles. It is not really necessary for our purposes here to state which precise style it belongs to (if indeed Paul is consciously writing in a particular classical style). More important are two simpler points: (1) Rom. 3.21-26 is clearly separated from the surrounding discourse in terms of style, and so exists and may be evaluated as a discrete literary unit; and (2) the variation in Paul's style within Romans, and within 3.21-26 in particular, may be explicable in terms of a deliberate decision on his part to vary the nature of his discourse, just as good composition demanded. Consequently, its interpretation should arguably be sought first in any stylistic principles that Paul may be employing. The

---

larly as the sections are contrasted with the surrounding diatribes. Here the plain and forcible styles are clearly inappropriate descriptions.

1.   'The close of each member has something of a metrical cadence, but the fact is disguised through the linking of the words in one series; and great pleasure results. Now Plato in many passages owes his elegance directly to the rhythm, which is, so to speak, long drawn out, but free from either heaviness or lengthiness, of which the former suits the plain and forcible, and the latter the elevated style. His members seem to glide along and to be neither altogether metrical nor unmetrical' (Demetrius *On Style* 183-85).

2.   Demetrius *On Style* 38-127; cf. Dionysius, 'Smooth Composition', *On Literary Composition* 232-47.

3.   *Orator* 97—and Cicero's own speeches perhaps provide the best example of this grandiose 'Asiatic' style. Circa 50 BCE, rhetoric was engaged in a struggle between the Asiatic style, whose best representative was Cicero, and the purist school known as 'Atticism'. By the time of Paul, although precise characterizations are not possible, the more restrained Attic school was predominant, suggesting that the grand style had fallen into temporary disuse, or at least been significantly moderated. Asianism later staged a revival, and Atticism was eclipsed around the turn of the first century. Cf. G.A. Kennedy, *The Art of Rhetoric in the Roman World: 300 BC–AD 300* (Princeton: Princeton University Press, 1972), pp. 97-100, 241-43, 282-83, 299-300, 351-54, 366-68, 460-61, 553-54.

measured cadence and arrangement of 3.21-26 may be no more than an attempt on Paul's part to craft this section in a more elevated style than the surrounding discourse, presumably because of its more elevated subject matter.

4. A Rhetorical Analysis of Romans 3.21-26

Analysis specifically of Rom. 3.21-26 will take place in three stages: (1) v. 21 will be analysed in terms of antithesis and paronomasia, (2) vv. 22b-25b will be investigated in terms of parenthesis, antithesis and epanaphora, and (3) vv. 25c-26c will be described as an isocolic reduplication.

a. Antithesis in Verse 21
The first semantic unit within the section that must be addressed is v. 21 (although it need not detain us for long):

> νυνὶ δὲ
> χωρὶς νόμου
> δικαιοσύνη θεοῦ πεφανέρωται
> μαρτυρουμένη ὑπὸ τοῦ νόμου καὶ τῶν προφητῶν

Two νόμος phrases are arranged here in some sort of opposition or contrast, which immediately suggests the rhetorical device of antithesis—although this is not a particularly elegant one, because the two clauses are quite uneven in length.

An important and complex dimension within rhetorical theory was that dealing with sentence construction, which varied from style to style in accordance with purpose, as we have seen. The plain and forcible styles used accumulations of short, simple periods to generate a vigorous appearance, much in the manner of the diatribe. But the elegant and elevated styles employed complex periods, consisting of careful arrangements of cola and commata.[1] Given a complex periodic

---

1. Precise definitions of the colon and the comma differ, but perhaps the clearest meaning that can be given them is to equate the comma with the phrase and the colon with the clause, with the proviso that the two units possess some rhythmical self-sufficiency—here we follow Demetrius's definitions, which seem the clearest (*On Style* 1-29); but cf. Cicero, *Orator* 203-18 (where the discussion moves into an analysis of the closely related principle of rhythm); Quintilian, *Institutes* 9.4.122-25; and *Rhetorica* 4.9.26-27. Cicero asserts emphatically that the ear is the best test of

structure consisting of numerous subordinate phrases and clauses, various techniques could be utilized to link the sub-units of the sentence together. One such technique for linking clauses consisted in their opposition, which generated the figure of antithesis. Cicero writes in *Orator*:

> The juxtaposition of opposing ideas makes the verse. It would likewise be rhythmical in prose: 'What you know does not help; what you do not know greatly hinders'. Clauses of this sort which the Greeks call ἀντίθετα or 'antithetical', in which contrasted ideas are set off one against the other, necessarily produce a rhythm in prose even if it is not intentional. The ancients even before the time of Isocrates were fond of this style—Gorgias particularly so; in his prose symmetry of itself frequently produces rhythm. We, too, have made frequent use of this style, for example in the fourth speech of the *Accusation* [*In Verrem*, Actio Secunda, iv. 115]: 'Compare this peace with that war, the arrival of this praetor with the victory of that general, this abandoned retinue with that invincible army, the praetor's lust with the general's restraint; you will say that Syracuse was founded by its conqueror, and captured by its governor'.[1]

The early origin of the figure is confirmed by a statement in Aristotle:

> The clauses of the periodic style are divided or opposed... opposed in which, in each of the two clauses, one contrary is brought close to another, or the same word is coupled with both contraries; for instance, 'They were useful to both, both those who stayed and those who followed; for the latter they gained in addition greater possessions than they had in their own country'... This kind of style is pleasing, because contraries are easily understood and even more so when placed side by side, and also because antithesis resembles a syllogism; for refutation is a bringing together of contraries.[2]

---

measure ('Without theory the ear marks their limits with unconscious intuition', *Orator* 203; cf. *Partitions* 18, 72; *Institutes* 9.4.116 and 119-20; and Dionysius *On Literary Composition* 106-107). 'It [the period] should end, not because the speaker stops to breathe, or the copyist has placed a mark of punctuation, but because the rhythm brings it to a necessary close' (*Orator* 228). Consequently, the test for rhythm, and hence for cola and commata, resides in the intuitions of a native speaker of the language; a requirement made doubly difficult in the case of Greek, where the ancient intonations have been lost.

1.   *Orator* 167.
2.   *Art of Rhetoric* 3.9.7-9.

The figure is also a feature of Hebrew poetry, so its Hellenic origin need not be overly stressed. But, whatever its origin, the figure is common in Paul, and his two statements concerning νόμος in v. 21 seem another such occurrence: 'apart from law . . . [but] being witnessed to by the law and the prophets. . . '

The specific implications of Paul's opposition here give rise to difficult theological problems, although these are often not appreciated. But these may be dealt with in part if it is conceded that Paul can use terminology flexibly, that is, in more than one sense. This is certainly evident for other words in the letter (cf. πίστις at 1.16-17; 3.3, 22), and even seems to be the case for νόμος itself earlier on (cf. 3.19, 20, 21, esp. at v. 28; 7.22-23, 25). That Paul would be doing this is further suggested by its correlation with the rhetorical principle of paronomasia.[1]

Clever use of diction was a feature of rhetoric, particularly of the elegant and elevated styles. In an extremely compact enumeration, Cicero comments:

> For there is sometimes force and in other cases charm in iteration of words, in slightly changing and altering a word, and in sometimes repeating the same word several times at the beginning of clauses and sometimes repeating the same word several times at their end, and starting and ending clauses with the same words, and attachment of a word, and climax, and assigning a different meaning to the same word used several times, and repetition of a word, and the employment of words that rhyme or have the same case-ending or balance each other or sound alike.[2]

The *Auctor ad Herennium* defines paronomasia as 'the figure in which, by means of a modification of sound, or change of letters, a close resemblance to a given verb or noun is produced so that similar words express dissimilar things. There are others also [that is, forms of wordplay] in which the words lack so close a resemblance, and yet are not dissimilar. . . There is a third form of paronomasia, depending on a change of case in one or more proper nouns [polyptoton].'[3] So paronomasia actually embraces different forms of punning and

---

1. This principle also corroborates the earlier arguments concerning Paul's use of πίστις in Rom. 3.21-26.
2. *On the Orator* 3.54.206.
3. *Rhetorica* 4.21.29-32.

wordplay.[1] Thus, a broad principle derived from rhetorical theory and practice is the subtle and nuanced use of individual words.

The theory of paronomasia therefore suggests that, while the word νόμος appears in both flanking phrases in v. 21 and ties them together in a loose antithesis at the level of expression, at the semantic level differing concepts may be operative. The first phrase seems to speak of the fulfilment of the demands of the Mosaic Law by acting in accordance with its prescriptions, that is, by good works. Paul is stating that salvation is not linked to this activity and life-style (however this is construed in terms of motivation and reward), but is separate from it. The second phrase speaks conversely of the witness of the Scriptures to this salvation as inspired and authoritative documents. Thus, Paul shifts his use of the word νόμος within the antithesis, between the senses of ethical code and inspired oracle.

Both senses, of course, refer ultimately to the same books, and this is what makes the antithesis possible in the first place. Thus, it may be argued that Paul is contrasting different functions of the same set of writings. The law does not function to save, although it does function as a testimony to humanity's sin and salvation, and to the punishing and saving God. But Paul does not explain or explore the theological implications of his statements at this point in the letter. He leaves them in an essentially unresolved conceptual tension—and we probably should not push his meaning too far beyond the level at which this tension operates, that is, the stylistic level where the pun takes place.

b. *Epanaphora, Parenthesis and Antithesis in Verses 22-25b*
With the comment οὐ γάρ ἐστιν διαστολή in v. 22d, a short section begins that has traditionally proved to be a syntactical quagmire—and perhaps it is not exaggerating to say that the text's problems have never been resolved satisfactorily. It is this study's contention,

---

1. Homoeoteleuton and homoeoptoton, although usually listed separately, are really two variants within the broader category of wordplay, as Cicero's preceding quotation suggests. Quintilian notes that variants comprise similar words with equal length and similar terminations; clauses [and words] concluding alike (homoeo-teleuton); and those ending with similar case endings (ὁμοιόπτωτον; *Institutes* 3.3.57-80). The *Auctor* comments: 'These two figures, of which one depends on like word endings and the other on like case endings, are very much of a piece. And that is why those who use them well generally set them together in the same passage of a discourse' (*Rhetorica* 4.20.28).

however, that three rhetorical figures clarify the section's structure and syntax at this point, namely, parenthesis, antithesis and epanaphora. All three techniques are standard rhetorical devices, and all are used frequently by Paul in the argument of Romans. Paul's statement οὐ γάρ ἐστιν διαστολή in v. 22d seems to introduce a shift into the discourse. The comment cannot complete the sense of the section's opening clause, and so is clearly not directly aligned with Paul's present argument.[1] Its reference to the abolition of distinction evokes rather the πάντας of the immediately preceding clause: εἰς πάντας τοὺς πιστεύοντας. There, Paul lays down the principle that salvation is for 'all' who believe, and he adds that there is no difference between individuals under this principle. Thus, the clause seems to be functioning as an aside, and it has been characterized as such by certain commentators.[2] Such a function also conforms to the common rhetorical technique of parenthesis.[3]

Parenthesis, or apostrophe, is an apparently random but in fact quite deliberate violation of measured periodic syntax. It is the small incidental occurrence at the level of the sentence of the much broader technique of digression, or amplification. Cicero reserves parenthesis for a sidelong remark designed to appeal to the emotions, and thus it was often for him a vocative appeal to the gods or something similar (as it was also for the *Auctor*[4])—a 'brief divergence from the subject—not on the scale of the digression'.[5] Longinus merely refers to it as an incidental remark.[6] But Quintilian's comments are

---

1. 'The righteousness of God has been revealed by means of the faithfulness of Jesus Christ. . . for there is no difference. . . ' Here the phrase is clearly dysfunctional when read in dependence on the preceding subject and predicate, or even in relation to the first prepositional phrase about Christ. It only makes sense when we add 'for all who have faith'.

2. E.g., Byrne, *Reckoning*, p. 80; and Dunn, *Romans 1–8*, p. 178.

3. Cf. BDF: 'The parenthesis usually originates in a need which suddenly crops up to enlarge upon a concept or thought where it appears in the sentence; or it may be due to the difficulty of adapting an afterthought which suddenly comes to mind to the structure of the sentence as it was begun. The NT, especially the epistles of Paul, contains a variety of harsher parentheses, harsher than a careful stylist would allow' (p. 242, §465).

4. *Rhetorica* 4.15.22.

5. Cicero, *On the Orator* 3.53.205.

6. *On the Sublime* 16.2: adjuration or apostrophe.

particularly revealing. He defines digression (also interposition, *interclusio*, παρέκβασις) flexibly:

> Occasions for digression on points not involved by the question at issue arise when we amplify or abridge a topic, make any kind of emotional appeal or introduce any of those topics which add such charm and elegance to oratory, topics that is to say such as luxury, avarice, religion, duty.[1]

He also notes its oral dimension in an extremely interesting statement:

> If, however, some brilliant improvisation should occur to us while speaking, we must not cling superstitiously to our premeditated scheme. For premeditation is not so accurate as to leave no room for happy inspiration: even when writing we often insert thoughts which occur to us on the spur of the moment.[2]

One suspects that much in Paul will become clear if parentheses are correctly determined as such, instead of being characterized as 'blemishes', or even 'glosses'.[3] Certainly it would seem that he has begun a parenthesis in v. 22d.

Left in isolation, however, the statement that 'there is no difference' is a little puzzling. Paul clearly has not abolished all distinctions between Jew and Gentile in his previous argument, as his special treatments of law and circumcision have shown. And while the immediate reference of the phrase is to the universality of salvation by belief in Christ, which was stated in v. 22c, Paul has not yet established this notion at any length—it is merely implicit within his earlier argument. So he seems to introduce v. 23 as an explanation and reinforcement of this comment that humanity lacks distinction:

---

1. *Institutes* 4.3.14-15; cf. 9.2.15: '[parenthesis is] often employed by orators and historians. . . consisting in the insertion of one sentence in the midst of another', and '[parenthesis] consists in the interruption of the continuous flow of our language by the insertion of some remark' (9.3.23-24).

2. *Institutes* 10.6.5: cf. also 'space must also be left for jotting down the thoughts which occur to the writer out of due order, that is to say, which refer to subjects other than those in hand. For sometimes the most admirable thoughts break in upon us which cannot be inserted in what we are writing, but which, on the other hand it is unsafe to put by, since they are at times forgotten, and at times cling to the memory so persistently as to divert us from some other line of thought' (*Institutes* 10.3.33).

3. Cf. R. Bultmann, 'Glossen in der Römerbrief', *TLZ* 4 (1947), pp. 197-202.

πάντες γὰρ ἥμαρτον καὶ ὑστεροῦνται τῆς δόξης τοῦ θεοῦ.
With v. 23 Paul creates a twofold stylistic evocation. It begins with
πάντες, which clearly echoes the πάντας of v. 22c. Immediately the
reader (or listener) is prompted to link the two statements together,
with v. 23 being read as an expansion both of the notion of 'all'
introduced in v. 22c, and of the idea of 'lacking distinction' stated in
v. 22d. But the precise reference of πάντες in v. 23 has changed.
Here Paul recalls his previous argument in 1.18–3.20, as πάντες
ἥμαρτον repeats numerous earlier assertions about sin (cf. 1.18, 21-
32; 2.5-16, 17-19; 3.9, 20), some of them almost verbatim. Similarly,
the loss of δόξα evokes his previous use of the motif and, in particular, humanity's exchange of God's glory for idolatry (1.23). Thus,
v. 23 functions as something of a twist. Whereas one would expect
some direct expansion of the idea that all are saved by faith, Paul
refers to a different universality, namely, the universality of sin.

This movement, however, allows the statement to function as an
argumentative support for Paul's comment in v. 22c. It explains that
there is also no difference within humanity in that all have sinned and
exist in solidarity within the fallen condition (a position that Paul
established at some length earlier on). This fallen solidarity implies
the truth of Paul's radical claim that all are saved by faith, in that a
common predicament suggests a common solution.[1] So there are
really two senses in which 'there is no difference'. Verse 22c suggests
one sense, and its symmetrical counterpart is evoked by v. 23 and the
argument of 1.18–3.20.

I have presented this argumentative and stylistic relationship at
some length because it is critical to understand that v. 23 functions
in alignment with v. 22c-d. As we have seen, none of the stylistic or
argumentative associations in v. 23 link up with the dominant statements of v. 21. They all either spring from a single word in v. 22c
(πάντας), or recall 1.18–3.20. Thus, v. *23 is still clearly functioning
within the parenthesis inaugurated by v. 22d.*[2]

---

1. Although it does not necessitate it. Paul's point here is not logically
necessary.
2. An important additional support for the contention that v. 22d and v. 23 are
parenthetical is the observation that such incidental comments tend to be triggered
throughout Romans by πᾶς. A close parallel to the present argument is 2.9-11,
where the double occurrence of πᾶς is immediately followed by two occurrences of
the fixed phrase Ἰουδαίου τε πρῶτον καὶ Ἕλληνος. Similarly, in 1.16 πᾶς

The syntactical difficulties in 3.21-25—by no means inconsiderable in v. 23—greatly intensify with Paul's next statement in v. 24: δικαιούμενοι δωρεὰν τῇ αὐτοῦ χάριτι. This phrase is universally understood to be a resumption of the main argument in the section, and so most commentators have placed a period after θεοῦ in v. 23. I argue here, however, *that this phrase continues the parenthesis*, within which it functions in accordance with the rhetorical technique of antithesis, both to counterbalance Paul's statement in v. 23 concerning universal sinfulness, and to return Paul to his main argument (and I break Paul's discussion after χάριτι for reasons that will become clear shortly). Four considerations suggest this parenthetical reading of v. 24a:

1. There is a clear grammatical signal for this reading in the masculine nominative plural antecedent for the participle δικαιούμενοι in πάντες in v. 23.[1] In fact, it seems curious that this rather obvious connection has usually either been overlooked or its implications ignored. But to read the participle in accordance with its antecedent is not just grammatically faithful. It fits very well into the flow of the argument.

2. In v. 23 Paul has digressed momentarily, prompted, as we have seen, by the πάντας in εἰς πάντας τοὺς πιστεύοντας, to recapitulate his earlier conclusion concerning the universality of human sin. This universality reinforces his claim that salvation is also universal, which was made in v. 22c-d. Paul's main theme at this stage, however, is a further step in the argument, namely, God's salvific intervention in Christ (hence the νυνὶ δέ of v. 21). So by the end of v. 23 Paul is

triggers the same universalist maxim: Ἰουδαίῳ τε πρῶτον καὶ Ἕλληνι, and linked directly with πᾶς. 3.19-20 repeats πᾶς twice in the context of criticizing the Jew. Finally, while 10.10-14 admittedly appears much later in the letter, it is no doubt significant that here οὐ γάρ ἐστιν διαστολή is repeated exactly, and once again it is clearly triggered by πᾶς. Thus, πᾶς seems to function as a somewhat volatile catalyst throughout Romans for Paul's universalist theme (or obsession?) that God's salvation is for *all*. Within this idea he combines the universality of salvation with the universality of sin. Verses 22c-23 fit neatly into this pattern of an aside triggered by πᾶς (πᾶς is also frequently subject to attraction: BDF comments on the apparent Semitism that an anacoluthon often follows πᾶς [243, §466.3], but could this be the occurrence of parentheses instead?).

1. Which many of the commentators notice, e.g., Sanday and Headlam, *Romans*, p. 85; Cranfield, *Romans*, I, p. 205; and Byrne, *Reckoning*, pp. 77, 80.

caught within a deviation, and is some distance away from his main theme. He is talking about the solidarity of humanity in sin, when his main intention is to present Christ as the specific historical manifestation of God's righteousness.

Verse 24a resolves this dilemma by returning Paul to his main theme after this brief digression. It does this by means of an antithesis. The opposing nature of an antithesis allows Paul to state that the universality of falling short (v. 23) is counterbalanced by the universality of the free gift of being rightwized. This second contrasting statement brings Paul back to his argument concerning the revelation of this rightwizing (which Paul characteristically also describes in terms of grace[1]). Thus, the antithetical construction rebounds from a consideration of sin to righteousness, and thereby reorients the discussion neatly to the issue at hand.

3. Antithesis, as we have seen, is a standard rhetorical figure (it is also a favourite technique of Paul's in Romans, occurring some 12 times up to this, relatively early, stage in the argument).[2] That it is an antithesis is further suggested by the approximate rhythmical correlation between the two members: v. 23 has 17 syllables, and v. 24a has 14.

4. Finally, Paul seems to have a stylistic predilection for this connective use of participles. Paul, as BDF observes, 'is fond of continuing a construction begun with a finite verb by means of co-ordinated participles, sometimes in long series'.[3] In v. 24, this fondness combines with his comparable partiality for antitheses. As a result, it is not the neatest antithesis imaginable, but it is functional.

In sum, grammar, the argumentative context, rhetorical convention, and Paul's stylistic preferences, all suggest reading v. 24a and its

---

1. Cf. Rom. 1.5; 5.2; and especially 5.15-21. Note, this last passage may explain the apparent redundancy in δωρεὰν τῇ αὐτοῦ χάριτι, as Paul closely associates grace and the idea of gift, but nevertheless seems to distinguish them. The former is a more attributional quality of God, from which the latter springs as a concrete manifestation.

2. Cf. 1.3-4, 14-15, 16; 2.7-10, 12-14, 25-29.

3. BDF, p. 245, §468: e.g., Rom. 12.9ff.; 2 Cor. 5.12; 6.3-10; 7.5; 8.18ff.; 9.11, 13; Eph. 3.17; 4.1ff.; 5.21; Phil. 1.29-30; Col. 3.16-17. In the preceding chapters of Romans, Paul used co-ordinating participles at 1.1, 10b, 21 and 22.

opening participle as a continuation of the aside begun in v. 22d.[1] The complete parenthesis reads:

> εἰς πάντας τοὺς πιστεύοντας
> (οὐ γάρ ἐστιν διαστολή:
> πάντας γὰρ ἥμαρτον καὶ ὑστεροῦνται τῆς δόξης τοῦ θεοῦ
> δικαιούμενοι δωρεὰν τῇ αὐτοῦ χάριτι).

There are, however, two obstacles to this reading of δικαιούμενοι in v. 24a. The first is the aura that tends to surround δικ- terminology in the minds of some scholars. It seems to be simply assumed that whenever Paul uses such words he must be stating something important. This is exemplified in Cranfield's strange argument, which correctly notes the grammatical antecedents for δικαιούμενοι but then adds a 'significance' proviso: 'in filling out the explanation of v. 22b Paul has, as a matter of fact, also made a substantial addition to the treatment of the main theme of the paragraph'.[2] So Cranfield feels justified in treating v. 24 as part of Paul's main argument.

Against this it must be stated (i) that Paul is perfectly entitled to use δικ- words in retrospective summaries. This is not demeaning to the word group—and even if it were, it would still be acceptable. But, more importantly, (ii) Rom. 3.21-26 is *not* centred on δικ- terms in general, but on a phrase built from the specific noun δικαιοσύνη. It is this word that is repeated four times, and another repetition would certainly justify a 'substantial contribution' argument. The participle, however, is only utilized in combination with the relevant adjective in the passage's final clause, clearly in a subordinate sense to the noun. Thus, far from suggesting a substantial contribution, the abrupt appearance of a participle in v. 24a (and in the masculine nominative plural form), suggests incongruity more than importance. In short, the argumentative role of δικαιόω up to this point in Romans has not been significant enough to suggest that Paul is discussing something of central importance simply because it occurs.[3]

The second obstacle to our reading is the much more significant one that scholars have simply not known where to end the parenthesis. Interpreters have usually been oblivious to the subordinate status of

---

1.   It is not an anacoluthon because, as will be seen shortly, the original sentence resumes in v. 24b.

2.   *Romans*, I, p. 205.

3.   Cf. 2.13; 3.4 (Ps. 51.4); and 3.20.

v. 24a because it has always been assumed that the entire verse constitutes one united phrase: 'being justified freely by his grace through the redemption which is in Christ Jesus'. If it is conceded that v. 24 begins within the aside of vv. 22c-23, then so much apparently significant material is dragged in after it that at some unnoticed moment Paul seems to have twisted within the aside into his main argument. Not only the participle and the phrase concerning grace, but the characterization of Jesus as ἀπολύτρωσις would have to be included within the aside as well. In short, the parenthesis seems too weighty and substantial to be a parenthesis at all (hence perhaps Cranfield's reasoning).

But this difficulty is neatly resolved by noting the function of a third rhetorical technique within the section.[1] Paul's use of epanaphora is the key to the syntactical difficulties in Rom. 3.22b-25b.[2]

Epanaphora is another rhetorical figure, like antithesis, operative within the general area of sentence construction when the elegant co-ordination of cola and commata is a central problem. These are frequently connected through the repetition of key words, whether at the beginning, the end, or throughout the clauses and phrases. If the initial word in successive statements is repeated, the technique is termed epanaphora; if the last, antistrophe; and if one or more words are involved, reduplication. The *Auctor* concludes: 'In the four kinds of figures which I have thus far set forth, the frequent recourse to the same word is not dictated by verbal poverty; rather there inheres in the repetition an elegance which the ear can distinguish more easily

---

1. I am indebted to a former fellow-student at Wycliffe College, the Rev. Dr Michael Knowles, for originally pointing out to me the measured succession of διά clauses in the passage. Without this initial insight of his, the following interpretation would have been impossible.

2. In all fairness, it should be noted that certain Catholic Reformation commentators recognized that Paul was using anaphora at this point. Ironically, however, since their analyses depended on the Vulgate, the first term in the anaphora was misconstrued. The Vulgate renders the dative phrase in v. 24a with a preposition, translating it (and the following verse) *per gratiam ipsius, per redemptionem quae est in Christo Iesu. . .per fidem in sanguine ipsius. . .* Thus, although v. 22 was also rendered *per fidem Iesu Christi*, the anaphora that Caietan, for example, perceived derived from *per* in v. 24, which, of course, is not in the Greek text. But at least Caietan recognized the presence of the device, correctly noting two of the three parallel clauses (see Parker, *Commentaries*, p. 159).

than words can explain'.[1] Quintilian also comments that 'a number of clauses may begin with the same word for the sake of force and emphasis... Sometimes a whole clause is repeated, although the order of the words is altered' (*Institutes* 9.3.30-33, 86). Thus, the rhetorical technique of epanaphora is part of a broader rhetorical technique that links clauses and phrases by repeating key words, and it specifically dictates a connection by repeating the opening word.

Although it has seldom been noted, just such a repetition takes place throughout the central section of Romans where a repeated preposition, in this case διά with the genitive,[2] opens three successive clauses. The technique is clearest if the three repetitions are set out initially without the parenthetical material already isolated above:

> διὰ πίστεως Ἰησοῦ Χριστοῦ
> εἰς πάντας τοὺς πιστεύοντας...
> διὰ τῆς ἀπολυτρώσεως τῆς ἐν Χριστῷ Ἰησοῦ,
> ὃν προέθετο ὁ θεὸς ἱλαστήριον,
> διὰ τῆς πίστεως ἐν τῷ αὐτοῦ αἵματι.

The recognition that this rhetorical device is operative in the central section of Rom. 3.21-26 is particularly helpful to us, because it not only clarifies these successive clauses, but it also demarcates clearly where the parenthesis just identified should end, namely, just before the second occurrence of διά with the genitive at v. 24b. At this previously unnoticed point of syntactical transition, the aside terminates and Paul's main argument begins again, as signalled by the epanaphoric resumption. Consequently, material that scholars had previously assumed was being dragged into the parenthesis (namely, ἀπολύτρωσις), now functions exactly where it should, that is, within Paul's main argument.

As a result of this, διὰ τῆς ἀπολυτρώσεως τῆς ἐν Χριστῷ Ἰησοῦ

---

1. *Rhetorica* 4.13.19–14.21. He also notes that epanaphora and antistrophe may be combined in an interlacement, and that the reintroduction of a key word is transplacement.

2. As Robertson comments (independently of any rhetorical theory), 'Sometimes a word is repeated for special emphasis' (*Grammar*, p. 1184). The parallelism between the clauses is also signalled by their precise structural congruence, especially between the first and second units. The main differences between them are substantive, namely, the exclusive focus of the second on Christ, and its shift from πίστις to sacrificial terminology.

is not to be linked with δικαιούμενοι δωρεὰν τῇ αὐτοῦ χάριτι in v. 24a at all, as in the usual reading. It is to be connected with δικαιοσύνη θεοῦ πεφανέρωται in vv. 21 and 22, in parallel with διὰ πίστεως Ἰησοῦ Χριστοῦ in v. 22b. And with this observation that Paul's parenthesis is straddled by an epanaphoric construction, the second objection to a parenthetical reading of v. 24a collapses, and we may terminate the aside after χάριτι.

It is now possible to separate that parenthesis off from the statements it interrupts, and to address the clarified material in more detail. As we have seen, a threefold epanaphora constitutes the heart of Rom. 3.21-26. In a carefully crafted exposition, it unfolds the meaning of the subject and predicate Paul uses in v. 21:

> (νυνὶ δέ. . .) δικαιοσύνη θεοῦ πεφανέρωται
> διὰ πίστεως Ἰησοῦ Χριστοῦ
> εἰς πάντας τοὺς πιστεύοντας. . .
> διὰ τῆς ἀπολυτρώσεως τῆς ἐν Χριστῷ Ἰησοῦ
> ὃν προέθετο ὁ θεὸς ἱλαστήριον,
> διὰ τῆς πίστεως ἐν τῷ αὐτοῦ αἵματι.

To paraphrase:

> (But now) the righteousness of God has been revealed,
> *through* the faithfulness of Christ
> (for everyone who believes. . .);
> *through* the redemption that is in Christ Jesus
> (whom God purposed, or, set forth, as a *hilasterion*);
> *through* the faithfulness in his blood.

Because of this syntactical clarification we are now in position to address the critical words within the section, and also the question of the meaning of the section as a whole.

c. *Isocolic Reduplication in Verses 25c-26c*
The central section of vv. 22b-25b is followed by two parallel accusative constructions in vv. 25c-26c:

> εἰς ἔνδειξιν τῆς δικαιοσύνης αὐτοῦ
> διὰ τὴν πάρεσιν τῶν προγεγονότων ἁμαρτημάτων
> ἐν τῇ ἀνοχῇ τοῦ θεοῦ
> πρὸς τὴν ἔνδειξιν τῆς δικαιοσύνης αὐτοῦ
> ἐν τῷ νῦν καιρῷ.

Here the dominant δικ- phrases echo each other—although these

parallel statements are expanded by different subordinate prepositional phrases—and this is again in accordance with a standard
rhetorical technique, namely *reduplicatio* (and the construction in
equal length is an isocolon).

Isocolon gives two periods or cola the same number of syllables,
and thus balances them rhythmically. The *Auctor* states: 'To effect the
isocolon we shall not count the syllables—for that is surely childish—
but experience and practice will bring such a facility that by a sort of
instinct we can produce again a colon of equal length to the one before
it'.[1] And we have already seen how the repetition of more than one
word from clause to clause is termed *reduplicatio*. Rom. 3.25a-26a
therefore constitutes an isocolic reduplication (or *conduplicatio*). It
should be remembered, however, that this is simply a technical designation for the repetition of one or more words (in this case phrases),
in units of equal rhythmical length.[2]

Verses 25c-26c do just this, as εἰς ἔνδειξιν τῆς δικαιοσύνης αὐτοῦ
is almost exactly recapitulated by πρὸς τὴν ἔνδειξιν τῆς δικαιοσύνης
αὐτοῦ.[3] But a perfect figure again seems blurred by a parenthetical

---

1. *Rhetorica* 4.20.27; cf. *Institutes* 9.3.81-86; and Dionysius's πάρισον and οἱ
παραπλήσιοι, or parallel structure; *On Literary Composition* 246.

2. Cf. *Rhetorica* 4.28.38: 'Reduplication is the repetition of one or more words
for the purpose of Amplification or Appeal to Pity'; cf. 4.20.27: 'We call Isocolon
the figure comprised of cola. . . which consist of a virtually equal number of
syllables'.

3. Against this it may be objected that the prepositions in the two clauses differ,
and that the second iteration has an extra article (before ἔνδειξιν), hence the unit is
not a precise reduplication. But given the notorious flexibility of Greek prepositions,
the first argument is extremely fragile (cf. C.F.D. Moule's comments, *Idiom Book*,
pp. 48-49), and doubly so as Paul appears to use πρός and εἰς interchangeably at
2 Cor. 1.15-16 and Phlm. 5 (also in Rom. 15.2; Eph. 4.12). Furthermore, both
πρός and εἰς are capable of bearing equivalent meanings, in this case, probably a
purposive or goal-oriented suggestion (Moule, 'final or consecutive', *Idiom Book*,
p. 70), appropriately rendered 'with a view to', 'resulting in', 'in order that', or
some equivalent phrase (cf. for πρός: Rom. 8.31; 15.2; 1 Cor. 6.5; 7.35b;
2 Cor. 4.6; 7.3; 11.8; Eph. 4.12; 6.11a; 1 Thess. 2.9; 2 Thess. 3.8; for εἰς:
Rom. 5.18; 9.17 [quoting Exod. 9.16]; 10.1, 4, 10; 12.3; 13.4; 14.9; 2 Cor. 2.9;
5.5 [often in the phrase εἰς τοῦτο, or εἰς αὐτὸ τοῦτο], Phil. 1.11; Col. 3.10).

With respect to the second objection, Paul is not required to reproduce his phrases
exactly—in fact, some rhetorical theorists actually recommend incidental variation in
figures to avoid tedium. Cf. Quintilian, *Institutes* 9.3.27: 'Figures and the like,

insertion: in this instance, the fourth διά phrase in the section. The phrase may be intended to function exactly where it is placed. On the other hand, it may be another retrospective parenthesis, which would then have to be interpreted apart from the main flow of the text. This would introduce a much better symmetry into the *conduplicatio* by extending the isocolic repetition from two to four phrases:

εἰς ἔνδειξιν τῆς δικαιοσύνης αὐτοῦ
ἐν τῇ ἀνοχῇ τοῦ θεοῦ

πρὸς τὴν ἔνδειξιν τῆς δικαιοσύνης αὐτοῦ
ἐν τῷ νῦν καιρῷ.

The evidence for the two readings is very evenly balanced. On the one hand, the preposition is the fourth occurrence of διά in the passage, suggesting some sort of integration into the preceding section. The differing case is also perhaps not as awkward as it first seems, given the possible meanings of διά with the genitive and the accusative, and the possibility of attraction to the preceding accusative phrase. The phrase's reference is clearly retrospective, referring to the work of Christ just discussed, and its removal generates a much better symmetry in the unit. Moreover, numerous other Pauline texts demonstrate the organic connection understood by the Apostle (as by the entire early church) to stand between Christ's death and the forgiveness of sins (e.g. Rom. 4.25; 5.8; 8.3-4; 1 Cor. 15.3).

These arguments, however, are weaker than they first appear. Both the argument from anaphora and from the *conduplicatio* are uncon-

---

which consist in change, addition, omission, and the order of words, serve to attract the attention of the audience and do not allow it to flag, rousing it from time to time by some specially striking figure, while they derive something of their charm from their very resemblance to blemishes, just as a trace of bitterness in food will sometimes tickle the palate'. But most significant is the *Rhetorica*. Concerning isocolon, the *Auctor* says, 'To effect the isocolon we shall not count the syllables. . . but experience and practice will bring such a facility that by a sort of instinct we can produce again a colon of equal length to the one before it. . . In this figure *it may often happen that the number of syllables seems equal without being precisely so*—as when one colon is shorter than the other by one or even two syllables, or when one colon contains more syllables, and the other contains one or more longer or fuller-sounding syllables, so that the length or fullness of sound of these matches and counterbalances the greater number of syllables in the other' (4.20.28; emphasis added). The addition of an article thus seems a weak ground for rejecting the repetition of the other five words as deliberate.

vincing, because the text is not compelled to reproduce archetypal rhetorical patterns. Similarly, the retrospective reference to Christ in vv. 22b-25b, together with the strong thematic connection with his death, remains significant even given the phrase's separation from the material by an intervening phrase. The connection could be maintained easily from this distance, without suggesting a parenthesis or interpolation. Finally, and perhaps most significantly, a parenthetical reading renders ἀνοχή dysfunctional, because without the reference to the forgiveness of sins in v. 25d it has no purpose. It makes little sense in the context of vv. 21 and 22 to say that God's forbearance and tolerance reveal—or that they function as a sign of—his righteousness. How can one invisible attribute of God *reveal* another? But read in dependence on the forgiveness of sins, the phrase makes good sense in context: God is tolerant precisely in his deliverance from sins, and it is this act that ultimately demonstrates his righteousness.[1] So the section's διά phrase functions semantically exactly where it is placed, and, while this blurs the elegance of the construction, it is still permissible—and perhaps a witness to Paul's lack of full rhetorical training.

The interpretative effects of the arrangement of vv. 25c-26c in an isocolic reduplication will be assessed in the conclusion, when the

---

1. Given that the phrase functions significantly where it is placed, and not parenthetically, its retrospective importance must nevertheless still be noted. For although Christ is not specifically mentioned, the phrase presupposes the previous characterization of his life and death with its reference to release and forgiveness. And its repetition of διά, although not absolutely parallel, is nevertheless a muted signal. Thus, it would seem that the passage as a whole defies neat rhetorical boundaries (as if vv. 22b-24a did not suggest this already!), allowing a residue of one structure to spill over into a following unit, weaving them together. This cross-hatching of prepositional phrases can also be seen in the overlapping repetition of short ἐν clauses:

> διὰ τῆς ἀπολυτρώσεως
> τῆς ἐν Χριστῷ Ἰησοῦ[. . .]
> διὰ τῆς πίστεως
> ἐν τῷ αὐτοῦ αἵματι . . .
> διὰ τὴν πάρεσιν τῶν προγεγονότων ἁμαρτημάτων
> ἐν τῇ ἀνοχῇ θεοῦ . . .
> ἐν τῷ νῦν καιρῷ.

Thus, repeated prepositional phrases (four διά and four ἐν phrases) knit the anaphoric and isocolic units within the passage into an overarching stylistic unity.

passage as a whole is interpreted, but the suggestion of parallelism, both within the sub-section and with the opening subject and verb of the section as a whole, is fairly clear.

Rom. 3.21-26 concludes with the compact phrase εἰς τὸ εἶναι αὐτὸν δίκαιον καὶ δικαιοῦντα τὸν ἐκ πίστεως Ἰησοῦ. Here it may suffice to note that it was customary in ancient rhetoric to pay particular attention to the close of periods and sections, and sometimes to cap them with an especially striking phrase (the clausula). Cicero says, 'as the ends of the sentences show up and are noticed, they must be varied, in order not to be turned down by the critical faculty or by a feeling of surfeit in the ear'.[1] And Quintilian says that 'the beginnings and conclusions of periods, where the sense begins or ends, are the most important'.[2] Similarly, in a good summation concerning the period, Cicero says:

> The arrangement of words in the sentence has three ends in view: 1. that final syllables may fit the following initial syllables as neatly as possible, and that the words may have the most agreeable sounds; 2. that the very form and symmetry of the words may produce their own rounded period; 3. that the period may have an appropriate rhythmical cadence.[3]

Paul's final clause does constitute a ringing conclusion to a remarkable passage. Its opening εἰς seems a deliberate parallel to the purposive or teleological εἰς (and πρός) of v. 25b (cf. Rom. 1.1, 5, 11, 16; 2.4; 3.7, 22), thereby completing a succession of three final purposive phrases: εἰς, πρός, εἰς (a deliberate chiasm?). The articular infinitive construction is quite common in Romans, and a third use of αὐτός echoes the two preceding occurrences of the pronoun in the isocolic reduplication. But since we have already considered the meaning of the phrase ἐκ πίστεως, and because the remaining issues concern righteousness terminology, a full discussion of this statement will be postponed until later in our study when we will address the meaning of Paul's righteousness terminology in more detail.

To draw this part of our discussion to a close, our syntactical hypothesis that Paul has inserted a parenthesis into the epanaphoric central section of an extended periodic sentence not only resolves the

---

1. *On the Orator* 3.49.192.
2. Quintilian does not want the middle neglected, *Institutes* 9.4.67. Hence periods often end with a 'clausula', that is, a pithy maxim or saying.
3. *Orator* 149.

immediate problems in vv. 22b-24b, but greatly clarifies the entire syntax of Rom. 3.21-26.[1] The section can now be seen to constitute a single periodic sentence that is wrapped around an inserted remark, with every part of the sentence exhibiting some debt to rhetorical syntactical devices (and we have not reckoned the full extent of this debt yet[2]). The main subject and verb are initially flanked by an antithesis. Then an epanaphoric central section begins, which is structured with a repeated διά with the genitive, and into which a retrospective parenthesis breaks, itself structured antithetically. This anaphoric central section is followed by a *conduplicatio*, and then the sentence ends, as rhetorical theory dictates, with a ringing concluding *clausula* that draws together various motifs from the preceding clauses and phrases. The complete sentence (and the sentence-within-a-sentence) reads:

21   νυνὶ δὲ χωρὶς νόμου
       δικαιοσύνη θεοῦ πεφανέρωται
                μαρτυρουμένη ὑπὸ τοῦ νόμου καὶ τῶν προφητῶν,
22   δικαιοσύνη δὲ θεοῦ

---

1.   Paul's use of cases also integrates with this reading. The passage begins, of course, with a nominative subject and a verb. In v. 22b a shift back to the nominative takes place. But 3.22b-24 is, as we have seen, a parenthesis. As such it is, in terms of grammar, a self-contained period in its own right: οὐ γάρ ἐστιν διαστολή—πάντες γὰρ ἥμαρτον καὶ ὑστεροῦνται τῆς δόξης τοῦ θεοῦ, δικαιούμενοι δωρεὰν τῇ αὐτοῦ χάριτι (in English, the statement would probably be enclosed within dash marks or bracketed). Thus, a switch back to the nominative case is completely acceptable. In addition to this, as Moule observes, such case shifts are not an infrequent phenomenon in the NT—and of his 14 examples, over half are from Paul (2 Cor. 1.7; 9.1; Eph. 3.17, 18; 4.1-3; Phil. 1.29-30; Col. 2.2; 3.16; 4.11). Finally, BDF notes that *both* πᾶς and coordinating participles are prone to attraction. In particular, attraction tends to cluster around introductory participles that are usually in the nominative (BDF, pp. 243-44, §466; cf. 2 Cor. 12.17). This is exactly the situation in v. 24. Given, therefore, that Paul is prone to nominative oscillations, and especially around πᾶς and coordinating participles, the change in case at Rom. 3.22b is not a particularly difficult problem for our reading of the syntax. But, with the conclusion of the aside, the interrupted sentence resumes, continuing through to the end of v. 26 with a series of genitive and accusative prepositional phrases (with the important exception of v. 25a).

2.   The passage also uses hyperbaton, asyndeton, and more paronomasia or transplacement.

διὰ πίστεως Ἰησοῦ Χριστοῦ
εἰς πάντας τοὺς πιστεύοντας

(οὐ γάρ ἐστιν διαστολή,
23   πάντες γὰρ ἥμαρτον καὶ ὑστεροῦνται τῆς δόξης τοῦ θεοῦ
24   δικαιούμενοι δωρεὰν τῇ αὐτοῦ χάριτι)

διὰ τῆς ἀπολυτρώσεως τῆς ἐν Χριστῷ Ἰησοῦ
25   ὃν προέθετο ὁ θεὸς ἱλαστήριον
διὰ τῆς πίστεως ἐν τῷ αὐτοῦ αἵματι

εἰς ἔνδειξιν τῆς δικαιοσύνης αὐτοῦ
διὰ τὴν πάρεσιν τῶν προγεγονότων ἁμαρτημάτων
26   ἐν τῇ ἀνοχῇ τοῦ θεοῦ
πρὸς τὴν ἔνδειξιν τῆς δικαιοσύνης αὐτοῦ
ἐν τῷ νῦν καιρῷ

εἰς τὸ εἶναι αὐτὸν δίκαιον καὶ δικαιοῦντα
τὸν ἐκ πίστεως Ἰησοῦ.

With the syntax of Rom. 3.21-26 clarified and the mutual relationships and basic function of its clauses determined, only two questions remain to be answered before the passage can be interpreted as a whole, and both are lexical: (1) the question of the meaning of Paul's atonement terms, namely, ἀπολύτρωσις, ἱλαστήριον and αἷμα, and (2) the meaning of Paul's righteousness terminology, and especially of the key phrase δικαιοσύνη θεοῦ. These hotly contested issues are addressed in the following chapters.

Chapter 3

THE MEANING OF PAUL'S ATONEMENT TERMINOLOGY

1. Previous Analyses of Paul's Atonement Terminology

The three atonement terms in Rom. 3.21-26 have traditionally been analysed in isolation, etymologically, with particular attention being paid to ἀπολύτρωσις and ἱλαστήριον. A survey of these studies should therefore establish a range of possible meanings for the words we are interested in.

a. The ἀπολύτρωσις Debate

B.B. Warfield's studies of redemption terminology, although often overlooked, are an excellent point of departure for the debate, particularly because he meticulously analyses the relevant data almost in their entirety,[1] addressing five areas of linguistic evidence:[2] (1) extra-biblical and pseudepigraphal usage,[3] (2) contemporary

---

1. B.B. Warfield, ' "Redeemer" and "Redemption" ', *Princeton Theological Review* 14 (1916), pp. 177-201; *idem*, 'The New Testament Terminology of "Redemption" ', *Princeton Theological Review* 15 (1917), pp. 201-49. The former is a sermon that sets forth the broad sense of the dispute, while the latter contains his detailed linguistic analysis.

2. This data pool should probably be supplemented with the relevant rabbinic material and a greater attention to the MT; the evidence from Qumran (clearly not available to Warfield); and the NT's use of purchase terminology, which Warfield disregards under (4). For studies of the Jewish materials, cf. Procksch, *TDNT*, I, pp. 124-28; V, pp. 335-56; D. Daube, 'Redemption', *The New Testament and Rabbinic Judaism* (London: The Athlone Press, University of London, 1956), pp. 268-78; C. Brown, *NIDNTT*, III, pp. 177-223; and D. Hill, *Greek Words and Hebrew Meanings: Studies in the Semantics of Soteriological Terms* (Cambridge: Cambridge University Press, 1967), p. 58.

3. In his examination of extra-biblical usage, Warfield suggests that the λυτρ-word group originated specifically to preserve the occasional connotation of ransom

inscriptions,[1] (3) the LXX,[2] (4) NT usage,[3] and (5) the Church Fathers and Apologists.[4] Warfield's discussion also clearly delineates the main

in the broad verb λύω (a common verb with the various nuanced meanings within the broad rubric of release; however, it often carried the specific sense of release procured by the payment of a ransom: cf. LSJ, p. 1068). Consequently, in the classical and extra-biblical texts, insofar as the fairly rare words occur, the group invariably bears the sense of release by ransom, or a reference substantively to the ransom itself (specific references are cited in Warfield, 'Terminology', pp. 202-14—the only exception to the rule Warfield notes is ἐκλυτροῦσθαι, found in a scholium on Homer *Odyssey* 4.34: cf. 'Terminology', p. 215 n. 43).

1. Warfield does not stress the popular use of ransom terminology in manumissary procedures as Deissmann and Zahn do, but he notes the similarity between this use of the word and the earlier literary references. Consequently, he suggests that the use of ransom terminology in various inscriptions was simply part of a more general employment. Certainly the ransom connotation remains present (cf. G.A. Deissmann, *Light from the Ancient East* [trans. L.R.M. Strachan; London: Hodder & Stoughton, 2nd edn, 1910 (1908)], pp. 324-25, 331 n. 4; also LSJ, p. 1067).

2. The LXX uses eight of the classical forms in the λυτρ- word group, but only the verb λυτρόω with any frequency (105 instances, rendering *g'l* 45 times, and *pdh* 42). Here Warfield admits that the word's usage shifts away from the uniform classical sense; however, he argues that 27 instances of the verb retain the connotation of a ransom (e.g., Exod. 13.13; Lev.19.20; Num. 18.15-17—this sense occurs in Exodus 6 times, Leviticus 18 times, and Numbers 3 times, but not outside the Pentateuch). The word is often reminiscent of the original great deliverance of Israel in the Exodus, or of subsequent liberations, whether from the Babylonian captivity, or from individual quandaries. Thus, depending on the context, the verb varies from eschatological deliverance to redemption by payment of a sum of money, and no single meaning seems to dominate the word group.

3. In assessing the NT data, Warfield states perceptively that the NT usage need not necessarily be 'a continuation of that of the LXX'. The NT may be utilizing a single strand in the LXX spectrum of meanings, thereby diverging from its configuration of usage ('Terminology', p. 228: cf. his later statement, 'The simple fact. . . is that the characteristic terminology in the two sets of writings is different' [p. 229]). *Prima facie* evidence for this is the use of the compound noun ἀπολύτρωσις ten times in the NT (Lk. 21.28; Rom. 3.24; 8.23; 1 Cor. 1.30; Eph. 1.7, 14; 4.30; Col. 1.14; Heb. 9.15; 11.35—note the predominance of the term in the Pauline corpus), when it occurs only once in the LXX. Similarly, the characteristic LXX verb, λυτρόω, occurs only three times in the NT (Lk. 24.21; Tit. 2.14; 1 Pet. 1.18). Somewhat inconsistently, Warfield goes on to argue that a ransom connotation is present 'in every instance' of the NT occurrences, whether overtly or implicitly.

4. Warfield's consideration of the early Church Fathers and Apologists is interesting really only in that it demonstrates how quickly use of the terminology faded. In these writings, λύτρον occurs twice (*Barn.* 19.10 and *Diogn.* 9.2), λύτρωσις

interpretative choices with which subsequent debate has concerned itself. Warfield himself is reacting against two trends. On the one hand, he objects to the contemporary, predominantly German, interpretation of λυτρ- terminology in the NT as basically synonymous with deliverance or liberation.[1] He thinks that this reading unjustifiably strips the traditional sense of a ransom from the word group. On the other hand, he argues that Adolf Deissmann's suggestion to read the words specifically in terms of manumissary procedures for slaves is also incorrect.[2] This, he argues, overly constricts a broader

twice (*1 Clem.* 12.7; *Did.* 4.6), and λυτροῦσθαι nine times (*1 Clem.* 55.2; *Herm. Mand.* 8.10; *Herm. Vis.* 4.1, 7; Ign. *Phld.* 2.1; *Barn.* 14.4-8; 19.2; *2 Clem.* 17.4). The word's use is invariably broad, although in *1 Clem.* 12.7 blood and redemption intersect. Among the later Apologists the word group only occurs in Justin's *Dialogue with Trypho* (λυτροῦσθαι seven times; λύτρωσις, ἀπολύτρωσις and λυτρωτής once each). And even here, while ten occurrences seems initially impressive, six are in the context of OT quotations (19.6; 26.3; 34.5; 109.3; 26.4; 24.3). Apart from these, the deliverance from Egypt is meant twice (131.3 and 86.1), one reference seems to allude to Ps. 110 (111).1 (83.3), and the remaining usage is general (86.6). This 'semantic fading' is an embarrassment for the contemporary manumissary argument, because the full local relevance of the metaphor had obviously not abated, yet its use died out—the terminology does become more frequent in some of the later Church Fathers, but the NT itself is probably the main reason for this.

   1.   He cites Ewald, Zahn, Seeberg, Hollmann, Oltramare, Kaftan and Ritschl (where *Erlösung* has replaced *Loskaufung* or its equivalent), but attributes the trend originally to the influence of Schleiermacher. An example of the approach in English-speaking scholarship contemporary with Warfield is T.K. Abbott's interpretation of ἀπολύτρωσις in Eph. 1.7 (*A Critical and Exegetical Commentary on the Epistles to the Ephesians and to the Colossians* [Edinburgh: T. & T. Clark, 1897], pp. 11-13, 23-24). The main problem for Abbott with the traditional interpretation is the theological 'grotesqueness' of paying a ransom either to God or to the Devil: 'Here is an insuperable difficulty... To whom is the ransom paid?' (p. 13). Consequently, he interprets the word as 'liberation'.

   2.   Deissmann, *Light*, pp. 322-34. Deissmann notes several inscriptions that record the legal procedure for emancipation from slavery by means of the legal fiction of sale to a god. Significantly, in these procedures ransom terminology is closely combined with the passing from slavery to freedom and this, Deissmann observes, resonates with certain Pauline passages (e.g. Rom. 6–8; Gal. 3–4; etc.). Deissmann cites Delphic inscriptions (cf. *Light*, pp. 325-26, esp. p. 324 n. 2), particularly those in the temple of Apollo, but he also notes the records of analogous transactions discovered at many other sites. He therefore concludes that the practice was

meaning widely attested in classical texts.[1]

In the decades following Warfield's study, the debate has continued to revolve around the meanings he laid out. Thus, it is usually argued that λυτρ- terminology in the NT means one of the following:

1. Deliverance, broadly conceived, and often on analogy to the Exodus or the return from the Babylonian Exile. This interpretation is also susceptible to an eschatological emphasis.

2. The ransoming of a captive by the payment of an exchange price; in the case of slaves or prisoners of war, money, and in the case of Christians in the NT, Christ's blood. Note that the price must be paid to someone (or something), and hence the difficulties with its theological application.[2]

3. The ransom is conceived specifically in terms of manumissary procedures in the Graeco-Roman world. Paul is therefore thinking of a contemporary legal procedure that has no LXX or OT associations (except by coincidence).

Although his reconstruction of the NT position has been disputed, it remains true, in terms of the basic data and interpretative options, that subsequent studies have added little to Warfield's original investigation. Leon Morris echoed his arguments in 1955,[3] countering the broader

widespread, even among Jews (Panticapaeum and Gorgippia are Jewish sites with appropriate inscriptions).

1. Cf. LSJ, p. 1067. Warfield contends that the best evidence for the uniform classical sense of payment is that his opponents can cite no evidence to the contrary ('Terminology', pp. 208-209). Zahn cites only Plato *Theaetetus* 165e; Polybius 18.16.1; and Plutarch *Cimon* 9 [*Aratus* 11?], 'all of which [Warfield claims] expressly intimate a ransom-price as paid' ('Terminology', pp. 208-209 n. 27).

2. Some scholars attempt to avoid these, while still retaining some connection with the idea of ransom, by muting the notion of price to costliness: see, e.g., I.H. Marshall, 'The Development of the Concept of Redemption in the New Testament', in *Reconciliation and Hope* (ed. R. Banks; Grand Rapids: Eerdmans, 1974), pp. 153-69, esp. 153-54 n. 4.

3. L. Morris, *The Apostolic Preaching of the Cross* (London: Tyndale, 1955), pp. 11-64. At certain points Morris provides an important supplement to Warfield: 1. he broadens Warfield's survey of the data, for example, noting the additional occurrence of ἀπολύτρωσις within extra-biblical Greek in Diodorus Siculus, *Fragments* 37.5.3; Philo, *Congr.* 109; Josephus, *Ant.* 12.27; and in a Scholiast on Lucian (cf. *Scholia in Lucianum* 20). 2. Morris also examines the Hebrew words underlying the LXX usage carefully, noting in particular the *kpr* cluster. 3. He introduces 'purchase'

reading of redemption, which had not subsided in the interim.[1] And in 1967 David Hill opposed Warfield's and Morris's reading with yet another exhaustive linguistic survey in favour of the wider meaning.[2] The repetition in these studies suggests that the parameters for the discussion were firmly established by Warfield, and subsequent investigations were only really able to repackage his findings. Further advances in the debate will therefore have to arise from new methodological and interpretative perspectives on the same pool of data.[3]

The NT meaning of ἀπολύτρωσις, however, including Rom. 3.24, remains something of a puzzle. Is it reminiscent of the literal sense of a ransom comprehensible to Graeco-Roman culture and, in certain contexts, to Judaism (but repugnant in relation to human sacrifice)?

terminology into the analysis of the NT data (specifically, ἀγοράζω, ἐξαγοράζω, and περιποούμενοι). While the similarity between the two word groups is not immediately apparent, Morris points out that τιμή, which is associated closely with ἀγοράζω in 1 Cor. 6.19-20 and 7.22-23 (and with λυτρόω in 1 Pet. 1.18-19), is also commonplace in contemporary manumissary procedures. In view of this, and also of the common themes of Sonship, obedience, slavery and freedom, the 'purchase' texts would seem to be closely related to the 'ransom' texts. And when considered as such, a common theme of price and substitution is easily discernible (a similar conjunction may be seen in Rev. 1.5; 5.9; and 14.3, 4). Consequently, he rejects Büchsel's verdict in *TDNT* of a 'watered down' classical usage (*Apostolic Preaching*, pp. 47-48; cf. F. Büchsel, *TDNT*, IV, pp. 328-45, 351-56).

1.   Dodd may be taken as exemplary. In his commentary on Romans (published in 1932), Dodd states of ἀπολύτρωσις in 3.24 that 'Paul's term is not concrete, as the English word *ransom* suggests, but abstract (= the act of redeeming). Further, it can be used without any explicit reference to the payment of money, as a simple equivalent of "emancipation" (ἀπελευθέρωσις)' (*Romans*, pp. 77-78).

2.   Hill, *Greek Words*, pp. 49-81. Hill gives due consideration to the LXX material, as well as to the evidence from Qumran and Philo. He is less optimistic than Morris regarding the preservation of a sense of ransom in the LXX use of the word group, although he admits that it is present relatively frequently (he notes that 28 times λυτρόω clearly suggests a ransom price in the LXX). Philo uses λυτρ- terminology, but, typically, spiritualizes its meaning: *Sacr.* 114 (cf. *Rer. Div. Her.* 186), 117-18 (cf. *Rer. Div. Her.* 124), *Spec. Leg.* 1.77; 2.116, 121, 122. In addition to his careful survey, Hill seems particularly aware of diachronic fluctuation, that is, of shifts in the meaning of words over time (presumably because of Barr). But when he approaches the NT, Hill perceives a sense of ransom only in 1 Pet. 1.18-19 (where it is unavoidable) and in Mk 10.45.

3.   Cf. esp. Marshall, 'The Development of the Concept of Redemption in the New Testament', pp. 153-69.

Or is it rather a subtle transformation of the distinctive notion of deliverance found frequently in the LXX, but usually expressed with the verb? Or does it perhaps have some specific (and more or less obscure) technical origin, such as contemporary manumissary procedures? We will turn to the evaluation of these alternatives in specific relation to Rom. 3.21-26 shortly.

b. *The* ἱλαστήριον *Debate*

Like the redemption debate, the translation of ἱλαστήριον and its cognates in the NT turns on a small range of hotly debated connotations. One such dispute, but of a more preliminary nature, concerns the appropriateness of 'propitiation' vis-à-vis 'expiation' as a general translation of atonement words in the Bible.[1] C.H. Dodd has been the champion of expiation, arguing that the God spoken of in the LXX and NT is never appropriately described as wrathful or angry, and that any atoning action is consequently directed only against sin itself.[2] But he has been challenged by many scholars who seem to regard this thesis as a rather scandalous dilution of the biblical principle of the wrath of God.[3]

---

1. Much ink has been spilled over the difference between 'expiation' and 'propitiation' (for an excellent discussion of the difference between these two terms, see Hill, *Greek Words*, p. 23). To summarize Hill's definitions, expiation is an action oriented towards sin, while propitiation is an action oriented towards a person, whether an offended human being or God. 'Propitiation' and 'expiation', however, may be such archaic terms that they have lost all usefulness: equivalent terms clearer to modern ears are, for 'propitiation', placating, soothing, pacifying or appeasing, and for 'expiation', cleansing, wiping or washing.

2. His arguments were first published in *JTS* 32 (1930–31), pp. 352-60; then reprinted without major alteration in *The Bible and the Greeks* (London: Hodder & Stoughton, 1935), pp. 82-95. He had many followers: cf. C.F.D. Moule, 'The Sacrifice of the People of God (1)', *The Parish Communion Today* (ed. D.M. Paton; London: SCPK, 1962), pp. 78-93: 'It is utterly unthinkable that sacrifice viewed as "bribery" should any longer be contemplated. With the notion of propitiation there disappears also the crude notion of buying off the deity's wrath by sacrifice' (p. 82). Nicole notes that Dodd's hypothesis was also endorsed by, among others, 'such leading authorities as V. Taylor, D.M. Baillie, J. Knox, and T.W. Manson' (R. Nicole, 'C.H. Dodd and the Doctrine of Propitiation', *WTJ* 17 [1954–55], p. 126).

3. Nicole, 'C.H. Dodd and the Doctrine of Propitiation', pp. 117-47; L. Morris, 'The Use of ἱλάσκεσθαι etc. in Biblical Greek', *ExpTim* 62 (1950–51),

Much of this debate, however, can be safely set aside given the focus of the present study[1]—and it is doubtful in any case that this essentially theological issue could be decided here with purely lexical evidence and rendered by one word in isolation. Hence I will speak in what follows in terms of 'means of atonement'.

With respect to the meaning of the word ἱλαστήριον, which occurs in Rom. 3.25, three main interpretative choices are usually argued. ἱλαστήριον means: (1) a means of atonement (or 'a propitiatory'[2]); (2) *the* means of atonement; or (3) the mercy-seat (that is, the *kprt*).

Once again, little fundamental progress in the debate has taken place beyond its definitive statement at the turn of the century. We will consider the prevailing orthodoxy first, namely, the third reading of ἱλαστήριον as 'mercy-seat'.

There is a long tradition which understands ἱλαστήριον in Rom. 3.25 as 'mercy-seat', that is, as a reference to the golden lid of the Ark of the Covenant which figured so centrally in the ceremonies of the Day of Atonement[3] (this meaning is undisputed in Heb. 9.5, the only other NT occurrence of the word).

---

pp. 227-33; reproduced in *The Apostolic Preaching of the Cross*, pp. 144-213. Cf. also the more recent studies by N. Young, ' "*Hilaskesthai*" and Related Words in the New Testament', *EvQ* 55 (1983), pp. 169-76; T.C.G. Thornton, 'Propitiation or Expiation?: 'Ιλαστήριον and ἱλασμός in Romans and 1 John', *ExpTim* 80 (1968–69), pp. 53-55; and P. Garnet, 'Atonement Constructions in the Old Testament and the Qumran Scrolls', *EvQ* 46 (1974), pp. 131-63. The later studies indicate that the question of atonement terminology in the OT is an extremely complex one, involving not merely lexical investigation but, at a bare minimum, a corresponding source analysis of the Pentateuch. They also tend to suggest that Dodd's reconstruction is an oversimplification, as are (perhaps to a lesser extent) the early rebuttals, for example, that of Morris.

1. The question of whether appeasement or merely cleansing is the appropriate connotation of ἱλαστήριον in Rom. 3.25a is one best left for the assessment of the entire section, and of its function in the context of the argument of Romans (particularly chs. 1–4), which takes place later.

2. This refers equally to pagan sacrificial objects, where the gods are (often) angry, and therefore appeasement is an appropriate connotation.

3. The Greek Church Fathers interpret it thus unanimously—a trend which continued through many of the Reformation commentators. But Calvin, while personally favouring an allusion to the *kprt*, stated 'the opinion of anyone who prefers to take it more simply cannot be rejected'. Parker notes that even then the word was extremely troublesome to various commentators (Parker, *Commentaries*, p. 152).

At first glance, statistics certainly seem to favour this view. The word occurs 27 times in the LXX,[1] 21 times translating *kprt*, while *kprt* itself is rendered on only one other occasion by a different word (ἐξιλασμός, in 2 Chron. 28.11).[2] Thus the equation of ἱλαστήριον and *kprt* would seem to be fairly obvious, and many commentators have been so persuaded.[3]

In 1895, however, Adolf Deissmann raised a protest against this traditional translation of ἱλαστήριον as 'mercy-seat'—a protest which was repeated in 1901 and 1903.[4] Deissmann's protest essentially consists of four counter-arguments:

1. ἱλαστήριον always occurs with an article in the LXX, thus the phrase is τὸ ἱλαστήριον, and not the anarthrous and more general ἱλαστήριον that occurs at Rom. 3.25.

2. The first occurrence of the word in the LXX at Exod. 25.16 (17) is the only exception to this rule, reading ἱλαστήριον ἐπίθεμα, but here ἐπίθεμα clearly translates the physical object *kprt* as 'lid', while ἱλαστήριον seems to function as an adjective that qualifies the denoted physical object theologically. To have both words referring to the same object is clearly redundant.[5]

1. Rendering *kprt*: Exod. 25.16, 17, 18, 19, 20, 21; 31.7; 35.11; 37 (38).5, 7, 7, 8; Lev. 16.2, 2, 13, 14, 14, 15 15; Num. 7.89 (and four times *kprt* is not translated: Exod. 30.6; 37.7; 39.35; 40.20 [Job 33.24?]); rendering *zrh*: Ezek. 43.14 (3×), 17, 20; and it also occurs in *4 Macc.* 17.22.

2. The rendering of Exod. 26.34 by καταπέτασμα seems based on a misreading of *kprt* as *pkrt* (cf. G.A. Deissmann, *Bible Studies* [trans. A. Grieve; Edinburgh: T. & T. Clark, 1901 (1895)], p.127).

3. The foremost representative of the position is T.W. Manson ('ΙΛΑΣΤΗΡΙΟΝ', *JTS* [1945], pp. 1-10), who combines the reading with an imaginative proposal that Paul wrote Romans under the influence of the *Yom Kippur* festival, just as 1 Corinthians was written under the influence of the Passover, and 2 Corinthians in context of the Feast of Tabernacles. Hill thinks Tabernacles and *Yom Kippur* are too close, and so amends the festal influence on Romans to a celebration of the Maccabaean martyrs, probably performed at Hanukkah (*Greek Words*, pp. 43-47).

4. Deissmann, *Bible Studies*, pp. 124-35; *idem*, 'Mercy Seat', *Encyclopedia Biblica*, III, pp. 3027-35; *idem*, 'ἱλαστήριος und ἱλαστήριον: Eine lexikalische Studie', *ZNW* 4 (1903), pp. 193-211.

5. A gloss on the basis of the MSS readings does not seem likely, *contra* Manson ('ΙΛΑΣΤΗΡΙΟΝ', p. 3). W.D. Davies accepts this suggestion (*Paul and Rabbinic Judaism*, p. 240), but Morris rejects it (*Apostolic Preaching*, p. 188),

3. In Ezekiel, the same phrase renders '*zrh* five times (not *kprt*), that is, the ledge (or possibly two ledges) on Ezekiel's envisioned Great Altar.[1] The implications of this lesser but still significant cluster are seldom weighed sufficiently by advocates of the mercy-seat translation.

4. Extra-biblical Greek, where the rare term appears, consistently employs it to denote a propitiatory object (whether a monument, a sacrifice, an action or some similar object).[2] Here the testimony of Philo seems particularly significant. Philo refers to the *kprt* as ἐπίθεμα τῆς κιβωτοῦ, but glosses this designation with the comment that in the Scriptures it is called τὸ ἱλαστήριον.[3] (Josephus also uses the word ἱλαστήριον, but not to describe the *kprt*; it is an adjective describing a propitiatory monument of white stone.[4]) A final significant instance is in *4 Macc.* 17.22,[5] a passage very

stating observantly: 'In view of the absence of ἐπίθεμα everywhere else, it is difficult to see how the great majority of the MSS should support the longer text unless it be original'. Besides, as Morris goes on, other equally convincing explanations can be given which do not depend on excising the awkward word from the text.

1. '*zrh* is also rendered by αὐλή at 2 Chron. 4.9 and 6.13, and by τὸ ἱερόν at Ezek. 45.19.

2. The four examples of substantives (excluding three occurrences in Philo: *Vit. Mos.* 3.8; *Fuga* 19; and *Cher.* 8—*Rer. Div. Her.* 166.5 quotes Exod. 25.21) are no. 337 in *Fayum Towns and their Papyri* (ed. B.P. Grenfell, A.S. Hunt and D.G. Hogarth; London, 1900), p. 313; *4 Macc.* 17.22; Josephus, *Ant.* 16.182; and Niceph. Antioch., 'Vita Symeon. Stylit.', in *Act Sanctorum Maii* 5.337.17. There are five examples of the adjective; no. 81 [an inscription from Cos, set up to Augustus] *The Inscriptions of Cos* (ed. W.R. Paton and E.L. Hicks; Oxford: Clarendon Press, 1891), p. 126; *ibid.*, §347; Dio Chrysostom, *Oratoria* 11.355 [10.121.6?]; and Symmachus (twice) in his translation of Gen. 6.16 (15). The TLG also notes a reference in the second-century Herodianus, *De prosodia Catholica* 365.24.

3. *Vit. Mos.* 3.8; *Fuga.* 19; cf. *Cher.* 8.

4. *Ant.* 16.7: ἱλαστήριον μνῆμα λευκῆς πέτρας. It may also be significant that Symmachus describes Noah's Ark as a ἱλαστήριον.

5. As Stuhlmacher notes, the text is disputed, but the variants are seldom critically discussed ('Recent Exegesis of Romans 3.24-26', p. 101). S favours a longer reading: τοῦ ἱλαστηρίου τοῦ θανάτου, while A gives τοῦ ἱλαστηρίου θανάτου. The dispute over the readings seems a little puzzling, in that on either construction the word ἱλαστήριος seems to be functioning as an attributive adjec-

similar to Rom. 3.21-26, where Deissmann states that a reference specifically to the mercy-seat seems unlikely.[1]

Some of Deissmann's arguments of unequal weight,[2] but he also offers an alternative explanation of the puzzling lexical configuration in the LXX.[3] He argues that the LXX translation of *kprt* is not directly reproductive of the Hebrew, but a theologically slanted rendering in terms of *function*. That is, in the LXX *kprt* is translated, not so much in terms of what it is, but of what it does. It is 'the propitiatory'—a rendering made clear by the explanatory gloss in its first citation at Exod. 26.11 (a statement almost identical to Philo's explanation).

tive. That S favours a substantive reading—as Stuhlmacher argues—is not necessary in terms of general grammatical usage, although it is possible. The best explanation for the variation is probably the dropping of the redundant article by A, at the cost of disrupting the stylistic repetition. So S probably does preserve the earlier reading, but one wonders if this helps Stuhlmacher's case very much.

1. This point is often overstated. It should be noted that the first of the martyrs is Eliezar, a saintly man and also a priest. Thus, *4 Macc.* 17.22 could be alluding to the replacement, or at least to the analogy, of temple sacrifice, and therefore be moving in circles of sacrificial and festival imagery.

2. For example, his contention from the lack of a definite article in Rom. 3.25a is not strong, namely, that Rom. 3.25 does not use the definite article, and therefore a more general meaning is being signalled. This is to confuse English with Greek grammar. The notion of supreme and singular atonement is contained in the word ἱλαστήριον itself because of its frequent LXX rendering of *kprt*, and not in the article. Besides, the absence or presence of the article in Paul is an extremely suspect indicator of significance. Stuhlmacher notes further: 'Since the article is not normally used in New Testament formulas, in definitions, and with predicate nouns (cf., for example, Rom. 1.16-17; 3.20; 4.25; 8.3-4; 2 Cor. 5.21; Col. 1.15, 20b, etc.), the absence of the article before *hilasterion* in Rom. 3.25b is no longer surprising, for the word stands here as the predicate' ('Recent Exegesis', pp. 99, 107 n. 38). Cf. BDF §§252.2 and 258.2, and Davies, *Paul and Rabbinic Judaism*, pp. 239-40—who seems particularly concerned with this problem; Fryer concurs in 'The Meaning and Translation of *Hilasterion* in Romans 3.25', *EvQ* 59 (1987), pp. 99-116, esp. p. 108. As D. Seeley notes, this has been disputed by Friedrich (*The Noble Death: Graeco-Roman Martyrology and Paul's Concept of Salvation* [JSNTSup, 28; Sheffield: JSOT Press, 1990], p. 21). It seems best to let the whole contention drop as unprovable and indecisive.

3. He is more or less followed by Bruce, *Romans*, p. 101, Cranfield, *Romans*, I, p. 216, Hill, *Greek Words*, pp. 38-48; Lohse, *Märtyrer und Gottesknecht*, pp. 147-61; Morris, *Apostolic Preaching*; and Sanday and Headlam, *Romans*, pp. 87-88 n. 72. Lohse and Hill nuance this position in terms of martyr theology.

The LXX's singular designation may also be stressed at this point. Greek-speaking Jews knew, of course, of pagan propitiatory rites and objects that could be called ἱλαστήρια, that is, propitiations. But in the context of the law, the Ark of the Covenant on the Day of Atonement was the only place so called, because it was the supreme site of atonement. For the Jew there was no other *legitimate* propitiatory (although, given the hypothetical nature of Ezekiel's visionary cultus, the ledges of the Great Altar that performed the same function could also be designated by the phrase). In short, the *kprt* was *the* propiatory (hence the consistent use of the article?).

Deissmann's explanation gives a convincing account of all, rather than merely the majority of, the LXX references. And this is done in the context of extra-biblical usage. Consequently, it must be favoured over the traditional reading of mercy-seat unless proponents of that view can also explain the LXX irregularities in terms of their own theory.[1]

His case is made even more convincing when the specific implications of a translation in terms of 'mercy-seat' are traced out in detail. If Christ is being described as 'the mercy-seat' in 3.25, then Paul would be making a typological comparison between his death and this item of temple furniture. Such a typological comparison would be unusual for Paul.[2] More importantly, one wonders if such a comparison would even make sense in context.

Few commentators actually grasp this point. If ἱλαστήριον means, literally, the mercy-seat, then Christ's death is being compared (somewhat incongruously) with this specific object. What most commentators find most meaningful in the comparison, however, is not the *kprt* itself, but its role as the site of sacrificial propitiation on the Day of Atonement. Thus, the point of the metaphor derives from the sacrificial associations *that surround the kprt, and not the kprt itself.*

---

1. This, to my knowledge, has never been done. Manson, as we have seen, argues that Exod. 25.16 (17) is possibly a gloss; however, the MS evidence is against him. He does not really address the problematic designation of Ezekiel's propitiatory ledges as ἱλαστήρια, although he appreciates their analogous function in the visionary cultus to the levitical mercy-seat. This point does not strengthen, but, in fact, weakens his own theory ('ΙΛΑΣΤΗΡΙΟΝ', pp. 2-3).

2. He uses allegory in Gal. 4.21-31, 1 Cor. 10.4, and (arguably) in 1 Cor. 9.9, but nowhere else. And note, typology is a more extreme variant of allegory. Within Romans itself, not one of its other approximately 60 OT references seems comparable.

In short, the most meaningful reading of the metaphor does not actually identify Christ directly with the *kprt* at all—such a reading really proves too much, since its proponents cannot use the related but distinct sacrificial metaphor.[1] As a result of this, Deissmann's functional, and hence more metaphorical (as Bruce observes precisely, the relationship is metonymic), interpretation of ἱλαστήριον clearly seems superior to a strictly typological reading and this accords with the functional use of the word in the LXX. But it should be noted that Deissmann's arguments must still be nuanced with respect to Rom. 3.21-26, since it has not been established whether Paul's functional reference in 3.25 is to Jewish concepts, or simply to broader Graeco-Roman usage (as Deissmann himself thinks).

c. *The* αἷμα *Debate*

The controversy over the meaning of αἷμα in the NT, and in particular its use in Rom. 3.25, is both simpler and more one-sided than the two preceding debates. As James Denney has said, the argument to the effect that shed blood signifies the release of life rather than death is a 'strange caprice', and 'a more groundless fancy never haunted and troubled the interpretation of any part of Scripture'.[2] Nevertheless, a significant number of predominantly English-speaking scholars have, in fact, argued that the release of blood in sacrifice is the equivalent of offering or presenting life to God.[3] And they have been duly opposed

---

1.   If it is objected that this is hair-splitting, it may be replied that the distinction is crucial. If the metaphor is applied more loosely in terms of *Yom Kippur*, we have moved away from the LXX usage that supposedly undergirds the translation, as τὸ ἱλαστήριον never means 'the atonement of *Yom Kippur*' in the LXX. In addition to this, we have covertly adopted a functional reading of the terminology, because it is not the site, but the event and operation of the comparison that has become important. Fryer illustrates this well. He states categorically that Christ is being typologically compared to the mercy-seat in Rom. 3.25, but then goes on to say (quoting Hunter): 'What was symbolically figured forth on the Day of Atonement has been fulfilled in Christ' (p. 107). These are not the same thing, and this is *not* a typological comparison, but a broader, metaphorical allusion different from the LXX's strict usage of the word—it is interesting to note Fryer's later qualifications: 'it is not the Apostle's aim to identify Christ with the *kapporeth* in a strict sense. . . [T]he Apostle does not envisage identity between Christ and the *kapporeth*' (p. 108).

2.   *The Death of Christ* (London: Hodder & Stoughton, 1951), p. 149.

3.   So, e.g., H.C. Trumbull, *The Blood Covenant: A Primitive Rite and its*

by an equally prestigious group of scholars and studies.[1] The debate, however, has largely subsided, perhaps because the evidence is so strongly in favour of the interpretation of blood as 'death'. So at this point the controversy need only be noted in passing, and Leon Morris's analysis provides an excellent summary of the relevant texts and arguments.[2] Morris concludes, concerning the suggestion that

---

Bearing on Scripture (Philadelphia: Wattles, 2nd edn, 1885), pp. 99-206; B.F. Westcott, *Saint Paul's Epistle to the Ephesians: The Greek Text with Notes and Addenda* (London: Macmillan, 1906), pp. 11-12; W. Robertson Smith, *Lectures on the Religion of the Semites: The Fundamental Institutions* (London: A. & C. Black, 3rd edn, 1927 [1888–89]), pp. 312-52; C.H. Dodd, *The Meaning of Paul for Today* (London: George Allen & Unwin, 1920), p. 109; *idem, Paul's Epistle to the Romans* (London: John Murray, 1933), p. 79; *idem, The Bible and the Greeks*; W.O.E. Oesterley, *Sacrifices in Ancient Israel: Their Origin, Purposes, and Development* (New York: Macmillan, 1935); P.T. Forsyth, *The Work of Christ* (London: Independent, 1938), pp. 155-56; *idem, The Cruciality of the Cross* (London: Independent, 1948), pp. 85-104; F.C.N. Hicks, *The Fullness of Sacrifice: An Essay in Reconciliation* (London: Macmillan, 2nd edn, 1938 [1930]), pp. 12-13, 34-37, 113-15, 119, 206-11, 141-48; Vincent Taylor, *Forgiveness and Reconciliation: A Study in New Testament Theology* (London: Macmillan, 1941), pp. 46-47; *idem, The Atonement in New Testament Teaching* (London: Epworth Press, 1958), pp. 92-93; and Davies, *Paul and Rabbinic Judaism*, p. 234.

1.   So, e.g., G.F. Moore, 'Sacrifice', *Encyclopaedia Biblica*, II, cols. 4138-4233, esp. cols. 4217-21 (Moore explicitly disavows the 'life' theory in n. 4, col. 4221); J. Denney, *The Death of Christ* (London: Hodder & Stoughton, 1951 [1901]); *idem, The Christian Doctrine of Reconciliation* (London: Hodder & Stoughton, 1917); J. Armitage Robinson, *St Paul's Epistle to the Ephesians* (London: Macmillan, 1922), pp. 29-30; James Moffatt, *A Critical and Exegetical Commentary on the Epistle to the Hebrews* (Edinburgh: T. & T. Clark, 1924), pp. 112-34, esp. 130; C.A.A. Scott, *Christianity According to St Paul* (Cambridge: Cambridge University Press, 1932), pp. 85-97 (who denies any sacrificial associations, but interprets blood as 'death'); F.W. Dillistone, *The Significance of the Cross* (Philadelphia: Westminster Press, 1946), p. 88; and Alan M. Stibbs, *The Meaning of the Word 'Blood' in Scripture* (London: Tyndale, 1947). For more detailed references here, and in the preceding note, see my 'Rhetoric of Righteousness in Romans 3.21-26', pp. 241-43 nn. 74-75.

2.   *Apostolic Preaching*, pp. 112-28. Note, for this particular dispute the OT is a more than adequate lexical resource, since 'blood' occurs there some 362 times. Of these, 203 usages explicitly refer to death, usually by violence; 103 denote sacrificial blood-shedding; 32 are miscellaneous (and often metaphorical); 17 refer to the eating of blood; and approximately 7 may be construed as suggesting the release of life

sacrificial blood is the offering of life to God: 'the whole idea is dubious to say the least',[1] and his evaluation will be assumed here. But this decision still leaves the more specific sense of the word in Rom. 3.25b unspecified, since the basic parameter of 'death' is fairly broad. Does blood evoke sacrifice or merely death?—or is there a muted reference to the Eucharist? Once again, these specific meanings will have to be addressed more carefully in the context of Rom. 3.21-26.

At this point it can be seen that certain interpretative options have been either established or curtailed for the three atonement terms that concern us. ἀπολύτρωσις may mean liberation, or it may connote price, or a release from slavery—and it perhaps has more than one connotation present simultaneously. ἱλαστήριον probably takes either a general Graeco-Roman, or a more specific Jewish cultic meaning, but a literal reference to the mercy-seat seems unlikely. Moreover, αἷμα almost certainly means death, not life, although the precise connotation of that death is as yet undetermined. With these broad parameters in place, we may turn to Rom. 3.21-26 itself in order to determine the meaning of Paul's atonement words more precisely.

(including Lev. 17.11). Thus, at the purely statistical level, a reading in terms of death would seem to be dominant. But Morris also aligns four arguments against the interpretation that blood means 'the release of life': (1) this position usually reads the key passages in an overly literal fashion, which cannot be maintained consistently for the numerous other references (e.g. 2 Sam. 23.17); (2) *nphsh* is not to be equated precisely with the English word 'life', since in various contexts it can also suggest life yielded up, that is, terminated, in death (cf. Gen. 37.21; Num. 35.11; Jer. 40.14; Exod. 4.19; Ps. 35.4; 1 Sam. 28.9; Prov. 1.18; Num. 31.19; Ezek. 13.19; 18.4; Jon. 1.14; 2 Sam. 14.7); (3) such a reading ignores Hebrew anthropology and its strongly unified conception of the person (over against Greek conceptions that were largely dualist and would suit this reading)—the doctrine of the resurrection of the body, developed later in Judaism, is an important correlative at this point (*Apostolic Preaching*, pp. 117-18: studies of Pauline anthropology also corroborate this, e.g. J.A.T. Robinson, *The Body: A Study in Pauline Theology* [London: SCM Press, 1952], esp. pp. 11-33); and (4) atonement, blood and death, are explicitly connected in certain passages (for example, Exod. 32.30, 32; Num. 25.13; 35.33; 2 Sam. 21.3-4; Deut. 21.1-9). For other summaries, cf. J. Behm, 'αἷμα', *TDNT*, I, pp. 172-77; and F. Laubach and G.R. Beasley-Murray, '"αἷμα" and "ῥαντίζω"', *NIDNTT*, I, pp. 222-25.

1. *Apostolic Preaching*, p. 127.

2. A Stylistic Analysis of Paul's Atonement Terminology

In this section the attempt will be made to determine more precisely the meaning of the atonement words in Rom. 3.21-26, beginning the investigation with the immediate context of the words in order to emphasize the information given within their syntactical correlation. This information then functions as a control over the range of meanings suggested by previous investigations, indicating which are appropriate in this specific occurrence, and which inappropriate.

a. The Implications of the Epanaphora

As we have earlier determined, the sub-section within which the atonement terms in Rom. 3.21-26 occur is dominated by the rhetorical technique of epanaphora, in this case, the repetition of a preposition at the beginning of successive phrases. Paul actually arranges five phrases after three occurrences of διά with the genitive in the central part of Rom. 3.21-26:

> διὰ πίστεως Ἰησοῦ Χριστοῦ
> εἰς πάντας τοὺς πιστεύοντας
> διὰ τῆς ἀπολυτρώσεως τῆς ἐν Χριστῷ Ἰησοῦ
> ὃν προέθετο ὁ θεὸς ἱλαστήριον
> διὰ τῆς πίστεως ἐν τῷ αὐτοῦ αἵματι

The direct implication of this syntactical arrangement is that the successive statements are functioning in parallel—one might say that the technique syntactically superimposes the three units. They must therefore be interpreted in parallel if we are to determine Paul's full meaning, but the section requires some further clarification.

In the first διά unit we have already seen that Paul plays on the word πίστις, using it with reference to Christ in the first phrase, and to the individual's saving faith in the second. But as a result of this wordplay Paul shifts away from his main semantic thrust in the second member of the unit, for the saving faith of 'everyone who is believing' does not reveal righteousness of God as the faithfulness of Christ does (and we have seen how Paul continues to deviate along this essentially secondary semantic trail through vv. 22d, 23 and 24a). This deviation within the second member of the first διά unit raises the possibility that the second member of the second διά unit may also be something of a deviation, and that both statements may perhaps actually blur a more succinct instance of epanaphora. Several internal indications reinforce this suspicion. It is significant that Paul returns to the nominative case in v. 25a (ὁ θεός), just as he does within the parenthesis of v. 23. This could well suggest that v. 25a is another aside, stylistically balancing v. 22c, but functioning parenthetically in terms of meaning. The clause fits quite well into its context if it is read in this way: 'The righteousness of God has been set forth by means of the redemption that is in Christ Jesus (whom God intended to function as a *hilasterion*); by means of the faithfulness in his blood...'

Furthermore, the introduction of ἱλαστήριον after ἀπολύτρωσις automatically suggests qualification of an idea already introduced, and hence subordination. Paul is presumably not introducing a completely different concept or metaphor within a relative construction. It is more likely that, having described Christ's death as a redemption, Paul is clarifying the meaning of this word by adding ἱλαστήριον in a subordinate clause.[1] It may be helpful at this point to set out what would be the primary anaphoric statements separately:

δικαιοσύνη θεοῦ πεφανέρωται

διὰ πίστεως Ἰησοῦ Χριστοῦ
διὰ τῆς ἀπολυτρώσεως τῆς ἐν Χριστῷ Ἰησοῦ
διὰ τῆς πίστεως ἐν τῷ αὐτοῦ αἵματι

The remarkable correlation between these statements is a further consideration in support of the disposition suggested above. All three

---

1.   The principle of redundancy also suggests that ἱλαστήριον is probably nuancing a meaning already given, and not functioning as a dominant motif in its own right. The principle of redundancy derives from an observation made particularly by communication theorists that messages are transmitted against a background of 'noise' or interference. Consequently, all human communications tend to incorporate a high measure of redundancy, to ensure that the basic message is understood in spite of any background clutter. The principle of redundancy suggests that many words, including rare ones, often simply nuance or repeat a message stated more clearly elsewhere. Thus, in ambiguous messages—which may result from the use of rare or unknown words—it should be assumed initially that the contribution of any disputed word to the passage's overall meaning is minimal: see M. Silva, *Biblical Words and their Meaning: An Introduction to Lexical Semantics* (Grand Rapids: Zondervan, 1983), pp. 153-55. A very accessible application of redundancy theory is found in E. Leach, *Genesis as Myth and other Essays* (London: Cape, 1969), with a brief theoretical discussion on p. 8.

statements focus on Christ, are of roughly equal length, and are tightly coordinated substantively (were it not for the strongly Pauline motifs of πίστις and a repeated use of ἐν, particularly within the phrase ἐν τῷ Χριστῷ Ἰησοῦ, the presence of early church confessional material would be almost undeniable).

The nature and construction of v. 25a, however, are in sharp contrast to these characteristics. The statement ὃν προέθετο ὁ θεὸς ἱλαστήριον is theocentric and emphasizes a verb. The christological term has dropped from a uniform position immediately after an opening preposition back to the end of the clause, while a verb directly follows the coordinating relative pronoun instead of a preposition (apparently shifted there for emphasis—the rhetorical technique of *hyperbaton*). Thus, the structure of the clause is fundamentally different from that of its three associates, strengthening our suspicion that it is not an integral part of the epanaphoric arrangement.

In sum, on grounds of (1) a possible parallel (subordinate) function like v. 22c, (2) the precedence of ἀπολύτρωσις, (3) the apparent function of the clause as an aside or parenthesis (especially in view of its case); and (4) its radically different construction (possibly supported by [5] the principle of redundancy?), I suggest that v. 25a is not part of the main epanaphoric arrangement in vv. 22-25, and that ἱλαστήριον is therefore best interpreted as an expansion on, and clarification of, the meaning of ἀπολύτρωσις.

One consequence of this arrangement is that ἀπολύτρωσις, πίστις and αἷμα are the three dominant atoning motifs in the passage. Here the initial focus must therefore be on the basic cluster of ἀπολύτρωσις, πίστις and αἷμα, bearing in mind its qualification in the immediate context by ἱλαστήριον. There is also, however, a second, critical qualification that must not be overlooked: διὰ τὴν πάρεσιν τῶν προγεγονότων ἁμαρτημάτων in v. 25d. This phrase supplies the important information that the cluster functions to effect a release from previously committed sins. This cluster of atonement words and phrases may now be addressed in more detail.

b. *The Meaning of Paul's Primary Atonement Words*

It is already established for the present purposes that αἷμα probably means 'death' rather than 'the release of life'.

The meaning of ἀπολύτρωσις, however, is a more difficult issue.

1. *Some preliminary considerations.* Before addressing this question directly, however, three preliminary points must be made in view of the various studies of this word already undertaken and their specific relation to the context of Rom. 3.21-26:

a. ἀπολύτρωσις in Rom. 3.24 is almost certainly not primarily conditioned by the LXX (as, e.g., Hill tends to argue).[1] The word only occurs there once (Dan. 4.34), the Septuagintal theme of redemption being rendered primarily by the verb λυτρόω.[2] If, then, Paul sought to evoke a Septuagintal theme at 3.24 in his letter, he chose a very obscure linguistic signal. Conversely, ἀπολύτρωσις, when it occurs in extra-biblical Greek (which is not often),[3] is used, with one exception,[4] in the context of slavery and its termination. The context for the word ἀπολύτρωσις, therefore, is almost certainly (Deissmann has suggested)[5] slavery.[6]

b. It needs to be borne in mind that Paul is using a metaphor. He is clearly neither stating that Jesus was a sum of money, nor that all Christians were literally and legally slaves. Thus, his language is metaphorical, and he is seeking to elucidate something by generating overlap in terms of meaning between Christ and an evocative and

---

1. Hill, *Greek Words*, pp. 66-81 (he also emphasizes a martyrological influence: for my indirect critique of this, see Appendix 3). Thus, meaning one favoured by the studies surveyed previously may be temporarily set aside.

2. The are 105 occurrences (cf. Warfield, 'Terminology of "Redemption"', pp. 219-28). Even Warfield admits that only about a quarter of these instances retain any clear sense of a ransom payment (p. 227).

3. There are 19 references in total: seven in the Pauline letters (Rom. 3.24, 8.23; 1 Cor. 1.30; Eph. 1.7, 14; 4.30; Col. 1.14), three further references in the NT (Lk. 21.28; Heb. 9.15; 11.35), and one in the OT. This only leaves seven outside the Bible: *Ep. Arist.* 12.33; Josephus, *Ant.* 12.27; Philo, *Congr.* 109; *Prob.* 2.463; Plutarch, *Pompey* 24.5; Diodorus Siculus, *Fragments* 37.5.3; and an inscription from Cos (*Inscr. Cos*, no. 29 [p. 52]).

4. Philo, *Congr.* 109.

5. *Light from the Ancient East*, pp. 319-30. Deissmann has often been misrepresented here: he emphasizes the idea of deliverance, and rather mutes any sense of price or payment (cf. esp. p. 330).

6. This observation does not exclude the LXX from an indirect but significant influence on Paul's understanding of redemption at a broader level. It is just that it does not seem to function at the level of the marker ἀπολύτρωσις (see below).

pervasive social custom of his day—an overlap mediated linguistically. This raises acute questions concerning the extent and nature of this 'semantic overlapping': questions as to which connotations apply (which do not), and to what extent.

c. Much previous debate, at this point, seems artificially polarized—and, hence, also rather inflexible. It tends to swing between two semantic alternatives: either the word (together with its associated terms) means 'liberation'—end of story—or they mean 'ransom payment'.[1] But, even granting the above observation that Paul's usage is governed by the general context of slavery, this seems an oversimplification. Slavery was a complicated social practice, and could have served as a linguistic reservoir for both these notions, and several more besides. Ten different connotations spring to mind almost immediately as possibly important.[2]

> (1) the (usually undesirable!) state of slavery itself: one of captivity, oppression, often also of helplessness (that is, of passivity), but also of hope for release;[3]
> (2) the act of someone (sometimes oneself, but often a benefactor) to free the people in question from their enslaved state. This act involves, at minimum, the exertion of an effort, often in combination with a quality like mercy[4] (and, intriguingly, its 'demonstration');[5]
> (3) a consequent release from slavery,[6] into
> (4) the exhilarating state of freedom (and one of gratitude, if a benefactor was involved); this is a clear passage from one state to another—
> (5) often, however, the new state involves a paradoxical combination of freedom, and service (to one's new master), i.e., a new slavery;[7]

---

1.   Meanings two and three in the summary of debate given in the previous section.

2.   This list is meant neither to be exhaustive, nor in any way definitive of slavery in the ancient world.

3.   Cf. Rom. 8.17-25.

4.   It is this act on the part of God that may be construed as 'costly' but not as 'paying' for a deliverance (cf. esp. Marshall, 'The Concept of Redemption', pp. 153-54 n. 4).

5.   Cf. *Ep. Arist.* 15, 16, 19, 21, 43.

6.   Meaning three, in the previous section. In many cases, of course, this hoped-for, and even anticipated, release never took place (cf. the instances described in Philo, *Prob.*, and Diodorus Siculus, above).

7.   A point emphasised by Deissmann in general terms (see *Light from the*

(6) an act of payment, usually money, or its equivalent, almost always triggers this change: first the amount is gathered;

(7) then it takes the place of the slave(s),

(8) functioning in an exchange that exactly parallels any other purchase of goods or services;[1]

(9) some accompanying process of witnessing and documentary evidence (whether a letter of request, a receipt, etc.), is often involved;

(10) and possibly an act, or acts, of sacrifice are also present, whether as part of a manumissary procedure involving sale to gods, or simply in thanksgiving.

Some, or all, of these connotations may be relevant to Paul's use of ἀπολύτρωσις in Rom. 3.24.

The meaning of ἀπολύτρωσις must now be addressed, first in the specific context of Rom. 3.21-26, and then in the wider contexts of the letter as a whole, and Paul's other writings.

2. *The immediate context (Romans 3.21-26)*. In the immediate context of Rom. 3.21-26, and bearing in mind the syntactical arrangement argued for earlier, three points should again be made:

a. Overall, the passage is dominated by the idea of the revelation of God's eschatological salvation in Christ—something definitively emphasized by the fourfold instance of δικαισούνη θεοῦ (or its equivalent).[2] ἀπολύτρωσις is connected with this idea instrumentally by my resolution of the section's syntax. Consequently, ἀπολύτρωσις must function, as its διά with the genitive suggests, to effect a definitive revelation of this salvation.

This suggests, at the very least, a strong sense of liberation in the word ἀπολύτρωσις. The word may mean more than this, but it means at least this. Furthermore, a reading of the word primarily in terms of liberation integrates the section perfectly: God's eschatological salvation has been revealed through the liberation effected by

Ancient East, pp. 323-37), and Daube with specific reference to the OT and rabbinic developments ('Redemption', pp. 272-84).

1. Meaning two in the previous section.

2. I am forced to anticipate my later discussion of Paul's δικ- terminology here (see Chapter 4, esp. section 2).

means of Christ. The one liberation corresponds to the other, and hence functions as its revelation.[1]

It should also be noted that, if ἀπολύτρωσις is pushed further than this to some sense of 'ransom payment' or its equivalent, the section loses this integration and tends towards dissonance, and even ambiguity. The eschatological salvation of God has now been revealed by a ransom payment. But how does a payment function to reveal God's salvation? It may *effect* a salvation, but it does not actually *reveal* one until it is placed in a broader context. It reveals primarily, as we would expect of any payment, a transaction. This is not an insurmountable difficulty for the reading, but one simply in terms of liberation is clearly more straightforward.

There are, of course, the further complications of who stands to receive the payment when God pays the ransom price,[2] and why God should have to pay a price at all.[3] If God pays the price to himself, then the payment must reveal God's justice as much as his desire to save (and some have read δικαιοσύνη in this way). But if δικαιοσύνη is more akin simply to salvation, then the payment is an ambiguous, and even contradictory, revelation. There is, however, really no other candidate for payment in the context besides God.

At this point the ransom metaphor becomes further strained (connotation eight), because nowhere in the extra-biblical references (or in general), do we find slave-owners paying money to themselves (!)—and the characterization of God as a slave-owner (in the sense of an oppressive one) is also more than a little awkward. Moreover, in the broader context of Paul's depiction of God in Romans, it is difficult to find the notion of any constraint of payment laid on God, even by himself. Rom. 8.28b-30 grounds justification (an act referred to twice in 3.21-26) purely in God's choice and purpose. And chs. 9–11 may be read as an extended justification of God's absolute freedom.[4]

---

1. Specifically, connotations one to four above seem present.
2. See the direct challenge of Abbott: 'Here there is an insuperable difficulty. . . To whom is the ransom paid? We were not in slavery to God. . .' (*Epistles to the Ephesians and to the Colossians*, p. 13).
3. As the author of Second Isaiah knows: cf. 52.3-6, but also 43.3-7.
4. Cf. J. Piper, *The Justification of God: An Exegetical and Theological Study of Romans 9.1-23* (Grand Rapids: Baker, 1983)—although I will argue that there are problems when this argument is imported wholesale into Rom. 3.21-26.

b. Rom. 3.21-26 also co-ordinates ἀπολύτρωσις tightly with πίστις and with blood. These three elements function in parallel to reveal God's righteousness. But how are they related to each other? and do these relationships shed any light on the meaning of ἀπολύτρωσις?

Christ's πίστις is combined with blood in v. 25, and so can only really refer to his faithful obedience through the event of Calvary. One can detect sacrificial nuances in the word αἷμα (particularly with ἱλαστήριον so close by), but it basically means just 'death', as 5.9-10 suggests conclusively, with its clear parallelism between αἷμα and θάνατος. And in view of the epexegetical genitive in 1.5 (supported by 16.26),[1] πίστις itself may also be at least partially explicated by ὑπακοή. πίστις and blood consequently suggest that Christ's faithful submission to death somehow reveals God's salvation. But how is this notion to be co-ordinated with ἀπολύτρωσις?

If the slavery of humanity can be equated with death—and Rom. 1.32, 5.6 and 6.23 suggest that for Paul it can be—then it is possible to understand Christ's entry into death, which πίστις and blood attest, as part of a redemptive act that sets humanity free by some sort of substitution (connotation seven). Christ 'takes our place',[2] just as the payments in a sense used to take the place of slaves, when they were liberated. ἀπολύτρωσις may therefore denote, in addition to the idea of liberation from enslavement, the catalysis of that deliverance by a substitutionary act. In short, the metaphor may suggest deliverance through a substitutionary atonement. But can the sense of the word be pushed further to the idea that this substitution functions as a payment (connotation eight)? Once again, at this point the metaphor seems to run into difficulties. There are two:

1. A passage that seems genuinely Pauline, but out of place: 𝔓[46] suggests 15.33, and, on internal grounds, this seems a reasonable suggestion.

2. And this idea resonates with many other Pauline passages, both in Romans, and elsewhere in his letters: e.g. Rom. 5.6-8; 8.1-4; 2 Cor. 5.14-15, 21; Gal. 2.19-20; 3.13; 4.3-5. This last is particularly important (along with Rom. 8), because the passages and contexts speak explicitly of slavery; a state into which Christ enters (being 'sent') so that humanity might be freed into sonship. This does not prove directly that the word ἀπολύτρωσις means 'substitutionary redemption', because it is not used in these passages. But it does prove that Paul understood the atonement in just this 'substitutionary' sense, and that sense does fit his use of ἀπολύτρωσις in Rom. 3.24.

1. It is hard to understand how the faithful death of Christ functions as a payment or price. Such an understanding would mean that his acceptance of Calvary and endurance of the Cross could somehow be quantified (!). Perhaps this is a marginally easier equation if the price is simply Christ's blood (since liquid is quantifiable, to put it crudely, although not usually in the sense of payment). But Paul's repeated use of πίστις, once in close connection with blood, shows that he is not speaking of blood *per se*. He is speaking more broadly of the whole event of the Cross. That this event could function as a payment seems metaphorically incomprehensible—does an 'atoning value' become assigned to Christ's life and death? and how are the two aspects of the event related? (Is Christ's life worth more, less, or the same as his death?). The metaphor simply seems absurd. This difficulty is made more acute by the observation that nowhere in the parallel ἀπολύτρωσις texts is payment ever in anything but money.[1] Thus, to suggest that Christ's death functions as a payment is to move well beyond the extra-biblical evidence. Some contextual support would have to be supplied to justify such a move. But nowhere in Rom. 3.21-26, or its context, does one find additional metaphors of payment and quantification.

2. A second related problem, pointed out by Hill,[2] is that διά with the genitive is unattested as a way of signifying payment or price. Again, the other redemption texts illustrate this point, for where price is mentioned, it is never in such a construction.[3]

---

1. In Philo's *Congr.* 109, there is really no sense of payment at all.
2. *Greek Words*, p. 70 n. 2, and p. 73; and support for this may be found in Deissmann's collection of data on the manumission of slavery, which nowhere contains price or payment in such a construction—except in much later Christian manumissary documents that cite the NT (!) (*Light from the Ancient East*, pp. 319-30, esp. p. 324 n. 2; cf. also pp. 330-34). The usual construction is a simple genitive. 1 Pet. 1.18-19 may give pause here, but is the dative construction one of price, or simply of instrumentality?
3. Paul uses a different, attested formula for price in 1 Cor. 6.20, 7.23.

These difficulties suggest that, as it attempts to complete the overarching sense of the passage, ἀπολύτρωσις may take a substitutionary connotation but, again, not a sense of payment.

c. The third semantic correlation that can be made with ἀπολύτρωσις from within the passage is with πάρεσις. It has already been suggested that the word means either 'release' or 'remission', in its very rare extra-biblical occurrences. But the former reading can now be seen to integrate perfectly with a reading of ἀπολύτρωσις in terms of 'deliverance'.

If πάρεσις is translated as release, and the phrase in which it occurs as 'the release (or deliverance) from previously-committed sins',[1] then the section in which it stands precisely recapitulates the passage's opening and dominant idea. Verses 21-25b state that 'the saving righteousness of God has been made known through the faithful submission to death of Christ; through that (universal) deliverance. . .' Verses 25c-26c now repeat that idea: 'Christ functions as the (definitive) sign of God's righteousness, because of the release from previously-committed sins [effected by him]. . .' The two sub-sections and ideas are perfectly integrated.

If, conversely, πάρεσις is rendered as 'forgiveness', then the two sub-sections do not reproduce each other in such a symmetrical fashion. The idea of forgiveness may be loosely correlated with the idea of deliverance through Christ's faithfulness and death,[2] but the question is still posed as to how they relate specifically, that is, how this deliverance and death actually effects the forgiveness of sins.[3] It is also worth noting at this point that forgiveness is not really a salient theme for Paul in Romans,[4] whereas deliverance, or some equivalent

1. Note, the genitive should be understood as one of separation (cf. BDF, p. 97, §180).

2. It could be objected at this point that the forgiveness relates primarily to the sacrificial metaphor, ἱλαστήριον, and is quite acceptable in this connection. But it has already been shown how ἱλαστήριον is not nearly the dominant image that traditional interpretation has suggested, functioning rather as an explanatory gloss on ἀπολύτρωσις (and the word's precise function here will be addressed shortly).

3. An idea which seems to lead inexorably back to a 'quantitative' reading of the section—a reading that has already led to considerable difficulties.

4. Is it an important theme for Paul at all? ἄφεσις does not occur in Romans (Paul uses it infrequently in any case, as has already been shown; notably in

idea, clearly is. Thus, the broader context of Romans does not support this second alternative, but rather the first.

The integration facilitated by a reading of both words in terms of release and deliverance is not definitive evidence that they should be read this way, but it favours such a reading.

At this point, primarily on grounds of immediate context, it can be seen that some conclusions can be reached concerning the meaning of ἀπολύτρωσις in v. 24. The accumulation of arguments seems to suggest reasonably clearly that the word means a deliverance, in the specific sense of a liberation from an enslaved condition, by an act of God (connotations one to three above). The word also probably carries (at least, at times) the connotation that this liberation is effected by some sort of substitutionary act (connotation seven). But that it suggests an actual payment (connotation eight), gives rise to a series of difficulties—some of them apparently quite insuperable.

3. *The Context of the Letter as a Whole, and Other Pauline Instances.* The previous argument has already spilled over at times into a consideration of evidence from the rest of Romans, where that seemed necessary. One important piece of evidence from outside the immediate context of 3.21-26 remains to be considered, however: the evidence of 8.23, where ἀπολύτρωσις occurs again. But it is not necessary to spend much time in reflection on this evidence. Clearly the word as used in this passage denotes a deliverance—specifically an eschatological one—and the context is strongly imbued with further imagery drawn from slavery and its termination.

Verses 20-21 are particularly clear—although most translations somewhat obscure the references in the Greek to slavery: 'For the creation was subjected to frustration, not by its own choice, but by the will of the one who subjected it, in hope that the creation itself will be liberated from its bondage to decay and brought into the glorious freedom of the children of God' (NIV). The two key verbs used here

Eph. 1.7 and Col. 1.14), and ἀφίημι occurs in 1.27, and 4.7, the second instance in the context of a quote from Ps. 32. Elsewhere in Paul it only occurs in 1 Cor. 7.11, 12 and 13, where clearly it does not mean forgive. Furthermore, it seems that ἄφεσις in these other contexts may just as happily be rendered by 'release from' as by 'forgiveness of'.

are ὑποτάσσω and ἐλευθερόω; both are commonplace in the usual descriptions of enslavement and its reversal. And the 'bondage' spoken of is a rendering of δουλεία,[1] which may be translated more literally simply as 'slavery'. There are also references to the characteristic hope of release, and to the new state hoped for under a new master, God (vv. 15-17, 20b-21, 23b-25). Thus, connotations one to five from the metaphorical cluster associated with slavery are present in this passage.

Given that the context of Paul's use of ἀπολύτρωσις is undeniably one of slavery and deliverance from it, the word simply cannot, however, take the further connotation of a ransom payment. It refers to a future event in the life of the Christian community, for which it waits expectantly in the midst of travail, namely, the eschatological deliverance of the groaning body, along with the deliverance of the groaning cosmos. Moreover, the event is precisely equivalent to the receipt of sonship. Thus, the passage clearly suggests that ἀπολύτρωσις is an event accomplished in the lives of Christians because of the work of Christ: not a reference to the specific function of that work itself. This can only mean that the word carries the primary notion of a deliverance from slavery—this time in the future—with its accompanying connotations of release from travail, the presence of hope, and the expectation of a kinder, gentler lordship, all of which nevertheless stop short of the idea of a literal payment.

Defenders of the ransom connotation can only object at this point that the two usages in Romans are different—and this is always possible.[2] But how likely is it that Paul would vary his use of such a rare word? More importantly, and given the ambiguity of its occurrence in 3.24, what grounds do we have for ignoring a second usage in the same letter, and favouring a sense (supposedly) found in much more distant literature? If the ransom reading cannot be established on grounds given in the immediate context of 3.21-26, then one has little reason for ignoring the implications of 8.23.

---

1. It also occurs in v. 15, accompanied by φόβος, the characteristic fear of the slave.

2. Conversely, they may suggest that the section 'presupposes' the ransom effected by Christ's death—but it does not presuppose it, in this direct sense (so Warfield and Morris). Various scholars have pointed out the rather desperate nature of the arguments made in favour of a ransom reading here by its defenders (so, e.g., Hill, *Greek Words*, pp. 72-73, esp. p. 73 n. 1).

The further, unambiguously eschatological, instances of ἀπολύτρωσις in the Pauline corpus only reinforce this conclusion. This evidence is admittedly weakened if Ephesians and Colossians are not accepted as Pauline—but the evidence is only weakened, and not rendered irrelevant. Furthermore, this case has yet to be made, to my mind, conclusively.[1] Within these disputed letters, the occurrence of ἀπολύτρωσις in Eph. 4.30 is clearly an identical usage to Rom. 8.23. Eph. 1.14 also seems similar.[2] And further compounding the difficulty of the ransom connotation is the presence in these texts of the Spirit, who functions in an equivalent position to Christ's blood in Rom. 3.24 and Eph. 1.7. If ἀπολύτρωσις denotes ransom payment, the payment is no longer Christ's blood but the Spirit—there seems to have been an unaccountable change in currency! And who, in any case, argues that the Spirit has paid for our sins as a ransom?[3]

Thus, on grounds of Pauline evidence alone,[4] and emphasizing the

1.   Cf. K. Neumann, *The Authenticity of the Pauline Epistles in the Light of Stylostatistical Analysis*.

2.   Some difficulty attaches to the meaning of the genitive phrase τῆς περιποιήσεως. But this is probably best referred to the Christian community as God's possession, which he will eschatologically redeem (cf. Marshall, 'The Development of the Concept of Redemption', pp. 161-62).

3.   Eph. 1.7 and Col. 1.14 are almost identical texts to Rom. 3.24, where ἀπολύτρωσις is closely related to a 'release from sins', and also to Christ's blood (v. 7 in Ephesians; v. 20 in Colossians).

4.   The instance in 1 Cor. 1.30 can only be addressed briefly here in passing. In this letter, ἀπολύτρωσις occurs in a very compact statement, which has consequently often attracted the designation (like Rom. 3.24-26) of an early church credal statement or confession. In this statement, ἀπολύτρωσις occurs in close relation to δικαιοσύνη and ἁγιασμός. The immediate context simply does not give sufficient evidence to allow a decision about the meaning of ἀπολύτρωσις on local grounds alone. But it is worth noting a strangely symmetrical statement that Paul makes in 1 Cor. 6.11, this time using verbs instead of substantives, while the rest of his statement is almost exactly the same (especially the recapitulated motif of ἐν Χριστῷ). Corresponding to the three earlier nouns are three apparently equivalent verbs: δικαιόω, ἁγιάζω and ἀπολύω. ἀπολύω, of course, simply means release, and carries little, if any, sense of a ransom—although it is a commonplace in discussions of slavery. If Paul regards ἀπολύω as the verbal equivalent of ἀπολύτρωσις, then clearly the note of deliverance in the substantive prevails, and any sense of ransom is almost completely submerged. In support of this, the verb also occurs in the contexts of discussions of slavery and emancipation, and as an apparent verbal equivalent to ἀπολύτρωσις, in *Ep. Arist.* 14, 17, 19, 20, 22, 24; and in Josephus, *Ant.* 12.17,

information given in the immediate context of the word's occurrence in Romans, first in 3.21-26, and then in ch. 8, a fairly clear picture of the word's meaning emerges.[1] ἀπολύτρωσις is a word coloured by the context of slavery. It denotes, primarily, deliverance from that slavery—and hence means more than merely 'freedom' or even 'liberation'. It is freedom *from* an oppressive, enslaved state. ἀπολύτρωσις also suggests at times, however, that this freedom from slavery has been effected by a substitutionary act. Just as slaves were freed by the substitution of money, which, in a sense, takes their place, so Christians have been freed as Christ has entered into their state on their behalf. This act of identification and entry into our condition is both a connotation distinct from that of payment, and one quite important to Paul elsewhere in his letters, not to mention the remainder of the NT.[2] Consequently, the word may also signify a deliverance from

21, 26 (narrations of the same events—Josephus uses *Ep. Arist.* as a source). Philo tends to use ἐλευθερόω and ἐλευθερία, but it is also interesting to note an instance of ἄφεσις, in the sense of 'release', in the immediate context of ἀπολύτρωσις in *Congr.* 109.

1. This conclusion will only be strengthened by any detailed survey of the extra-Pauline occurrences, however. Of the 12 remaining instances of ἀπολύτρωσις, four suggest 'deliverance from slavery', and *cannot* be read in terms of a ransom payment (Lk. 21.28; Heb. 11.35; Dan. 4.34; and Philo, *Congr.* 109). Three further instances should probably be translated, on grounds of context, in terms simply of 'release' (Heb. 9.15; and *Ep. Arist.* 12, 33). The remaining five can all take the meaning 'release from slavery', but are indecisive in that they can also take the meaning 'ransom' (Josephus, *Ant.* 12.27; Philo, *Prob.* 2.463; Plutarch, *Pompey* 24.5; Diodorus Siculus, *Fragments* 37.5.2; and the inscription from Cos). Any such survey should also probably be broadened to include λύτρωσις. This word also occurs in Luke and Hebrews in the NT (Lk. 1.71; 2.38; Heb. 9.12). The Lukan instances support the rendering 'deliver'—the meaning is basically equivalent to salvation. Heb. 9.12 is arguable either way, but on grounds of sacrificial procedure, not redemption from slavery (cf. Büchsel, *TDNT*, IV, p. 351 nn. 1 and 2; for an accurate evaluation of the 10 LXX instances, cf. Warfield, 'The NT Terminology of Redemption', p. 219).

2. It is easy to detect at this level the theological influence of the LXX and the whole Jewish tradition, which viewed God consistently as a Redeemer in just these terms. This influence is not apparent at the lexical level, when Paul uses ἀπολύτρωσις, because the word is drawn, as has already been stated, from the specific, local context of slavery. But the LXX may still have functioned at an earlier and broader level in the process that eventually gave rise to the word and its associated ideas, by creating the theological framework within which this specific 'secular'

an enslaved condition effected by a substitutionary act. It does not, however, seem to go further than this to the suggestion that this substitution functions as a payment. Such a reading tends to generate metaphorical and contextual contortions, to put it mildly.

These conclusions might be summarized in theological terms as follows: ἀπολύτρωσις speaks of a vicarious and substitutionary deliverance, but not of a penal substitution and consequent deliverance. 'Redemption', understood in these terms, is a satisfactory (!) rendering of ἀπολύτρωσις as it occurs in Rom. 3.24 (and 8.23). 'Deliverance' is also an adequate rendering. 'Freedom' and 'liberation' have a tendency to be too general, and to lose the key connotations of slavery and substitution. They may be acceptable if these associations are made clear from the context, and a clear emphasis is placed on the notion of freedom *from* (an enslaved condition). In what follows, I will speak primarily of deliverance and redemption.

c. *The Meaning of* ἱλαστήριον
It now remains only to address the meaning of ἱλαστήριον in greater detail. Here the range of possible meanings established in the preceding section for this much-disputed word may be taken up again and evaluated in context.

As we have already seen, Manson and his supporters have suggested a reading dependent on the LXX translation of *kprt* by ἱλαστήριον, namely, 'the mercy-seat'—and this is probably the dominant reading today. But Deissmann has subjected this essentially typological reading to a searching critique, and his reformulation of this position is better, namely, that ἱλαστήριον is a more functional reference to atonement, and, therefore, possibly to the atoning ritual central to the Jewish feast of atonement, *Yom Kippur*. This possibility is the main alternative to a more general understanding of ἱλαστήριον in terms of general Greek usage, which is advocated by Leon Morris (among others), hence, 'means of propitiation'. Is ἱλαστήριον a Jewish cultic metaphor? Or, is it a more general allusion to propitiatory sacrifices familiar to pagans?

appropriation could take place. Unfortunately, this function cannot be explored further here (but cf. esp. Daube, 'Redemption', pp. 268-84; and Hill, *Greek Words*, pp. 53-66).

Before attempting a decision here, the fairly extensive area of overlap between these two alternatives should be noted. Whatever its precise shading, the word suggests that the deliverance effected through Christ's death is not merely analogous to a commercial transaction, but something sacrificially atoning. In short, the death of Christ is a sacrifice for sin, as well as a deliverance from it. But can we say more than this? Three observations suggest that the more specific Jewish reading is the correct one:

1. *Yom Kippur* was perhaps one of the two highest points of the Jewish calendar (along with Passover), and it was certainly the absolutely central ritual of atonement for any pious Jew.[1] In view of this, it seems more appropriate that, when he speaks of God's final act of salvation in Christ, Paul evokes the singular and supremely atoning resonance of *Yom Kippur*, rather than the much more general, pagan idea of propitiatory sacrifice which was repetitive. God's eschatological salvation is by definition singular and supreme, and this is echoed in 3.21a-c. Such ideas are present in the Jewish festival metaphor, but they would not be suggested by the generalized pagan usage.

In addition to this, *Yom Kippur* was, for the Jew, the divinely prescribed festival of atonement; that is, it was the sole legitimate means of removing sin. Once again, while it is not absolutely necessary for Paul to be suggesting this, it integrates well with the basic thrust of the section to adopt the Jewish reading. Christ would therefore be, by analogy, the atonement divinely prescribed and set forth by God.

2. Moreover, Paul states that the present, definitive revelation of God's salvation is in continuity with the Scriptures (v. 21d). Admittedly, he may not be referring specifically to the word ἱλαστήριον here, but a Jewish reading of the word *does* maintain continuity with the Scriptures—while a pagan reading cannot create such an association, but rather violates it: a pagan atonement would be *un*scriptural.

---

1.   The Mishnah records that three passages were read publicly on the festival of *Yom Kippur*: Lev. 16, Lev. 23.26-32 and Num. 29.7-11. In these texts the word ἱλαστήριον occurs seven times (only in Lev. 16). Thus it seems likely that most pious Jews would have recognized the word and associated it with the atoning rituals of *Yom Kippur*—if the Mishnah accurately reflects earlier practice (Stuhlmacher correctly emphasizes this point, 'Recent Exegesis', p. 107 n. 37; cf. also Hermann and Büchsel [independently], *TDNT*, III, pp. 308-309, 316-17).

3. Such a reading also integrates with the somewhat muted strand of Levitical imagery that I have previously argued is running through Romans. A reference to *Yom Kippur* in 3.25a would integrate with this theme perfectly.[1]

We have already noted that Romans often uses specifically sacrificial and priestly motifs, along with broader cultic allusions. In particular, Christ is often depicted in priestly and cultic terms. In 5.2 he obtains 'access' (προσαγωγή) for the believer into the presence of God.[2] In 8.3 his death is described as περὶ ἁμαρτίας, the standard LXX rendering of 'sin-offering' (*hatta't*).[3] In 8.34, he fulfills the priestly function of interceding for his people at the right hand of God,[4] and the ascription to him of the role of διάκονος at 15.8 may also align with these priestly terms.[5] A depiction of Christ's death in 3.25a in terms of *Yom Kippur*, therefore, correlates nicely with this tendency to depict him in terms of cultic function and imagery elsewhere in the letter.

The main objection to this argument (and to the previous two) can only really be that Paul's Gentile audience would not have understood such subtle Levitical allusions.[6] But it has been argued elsewhere at

---

1.   *Contra* Morris, 'The Meaning of ΊΛΑΣΤΗΡΙΟΝ in Romans III.25', *NTS* 2 (1955–56), pp. 33-43; cf. Stuhlmacher, 'Recent Exegesis', p. 99; and M. Hengel, *The Atonement* (trans. John Bowden; London: SCM Press, 1976), pp. 45-46.

2.   Cf. Eph. 2.18; 3.2; Heb. 4.16; and 1 Pet. 3.18. In view of these references, Dunn's objection seems forced (*Romans 1–8*, p. 248).

3.   Cf. 1 Jn 2.2; 4.10, where περὶ ἁμαρτίας is combined with ἱλασμός. Cf. also Lev. 5.6-7, 11; 16.3, 5, 9; Num. 6.16; 7.16; 2 Chron. 29.23-24; Neh. 10.33 [2 Esd. 20.34 LXX]; Ezek. 42.13; 43.19. Dunn cites Wright, Wilckens, Denney and Michel here *contra* Lagrange, Lietzmann, Barrett, Murray, Black, Cranfield and Zeller (*Romans 1–8*, p. 422). He himself finds a sacrificial reference 'wholly natural and unremarkable in a first-century context'. We regard this view as particularly strong because the actual phrase περὶ ἁμαρτίας is awkward in context, and seems deliberately added as an explanatory gloss or metaphor.

4.   A muted reference to Ps. 110?

5.   Cf. BAGD, pp. 184-85. The word can mean simply 'helper' but, particularly in view of the foregoing (and 15.16), it is better rendered by 'deacon', with the attendant connotations of priestly ministry and officiation (cf. also Paul's self-reference at 11.13, which is also cultically reinforced by 15.16).

6.   Other objections are usually made on grounds like the word's anarthrous occurrence (which has already been addressed in section 1), the awkwardness of the image (which is only true of a literal correlation with the mercy-seat that has already

some length that the recipients of Romans included at least a significant proportion of Jewish Christians.[1] Such allusions would have been
quite comprehensible to this group.[2]

Thus, in my opinion, Paul's use of ἱλαστήριον in Rom. 3.25a is
neither an explicit reference to the *kprt*, nor a vague reference to
propitiation in general, but a metaphorical description of Christ's
death as the supreme, divinely-ordained sacrifice for sin, in analogy to
the great Jewish festival of atonement, *Yom Kippur*.[3]

---

been discarded above), the hiddenness of the mercy-seat versus the public nature of
Christ's death underlined in Rom. 3.21-26 (see the next section, but note, προέθετο
does not have to be read this way), and Paul's failure to use this image anywhere else
(apart from begging the question, this ignores the particularity—indeed, the pecu-
liarity—of Romans): cf. J.S. Pobee, *Persecution and Martyrdom in the Theology of
Paul* (JSNTSup, 6; Sheffield: JSOT Press, 1985), pp. 62-63, and Seeley, *The
Noble Death*, pp. 19-27.

   1. Cf. Introduction: (1) Paul's occasional direct admonitions and remarks to
Jews (cf. 1.14, 16; 2.17-24; 4.1; 7.1); (2) the greetings to Jewish Christians in
ch. 16, including several probable leaders within the community—if ch. 16 is an
integral part of Romans; (3) the constant interaction with Jewish concerns and themes
(not merely of interest to Jews, but some of them only *comprehensible* to Jews)
within which we isolated particularly Paul's constant use of Scripture (usually a
signal that the Church has had Jewish training; cf. the Corinthian correspondence and
Galatians); and the series of Levitical allusions and metaphors throughout the letter
summarized just previously.

   Note, we are not thereby denying any Gentile presence among the addressees, but
merely stating that some Jews were present. As extensive a case can be made for
Gentile addressees as for Jews, prompting the frequent observation that the Church
at Rome was a collection of Jewish and Gentile Christian congregations (perhaps a
group of house-churches varying in composition): cf. 1.6, 13; 11.13-32; 15.7-12,
15-16.

   2. Cf. Fryer, 'The Meaning and Translation of *Hilasterion* in Romans 3.25',
p. 105. It might perhaps still be objected at this point that any Gentile readers would
still interpret the word more generally. But it is hard to imagine a Gentile readership
rejecting a typological or metaphorical reading of Christ based on the Scriptures,
once they were aware of it—do Gentiles today reject the reading as uninteresting?
(cf. KJV).

   3. This is also probably the meaning of the term in Heb. 9.5 and *4 Macc.* 17.22.
In *4 Maccabees*, the point is that the supreme atoning (that is, propitiating) sacrifice
has been made. And while it has been customary to read Heb. 9.5 as a specific reference to the *kprt*, Deissmann's reading is also acceptable there.

d. *The Meaning of* προτίθημι

With the function of the three atonement terms clarified, it should also be possible to investigate the meaning of the troublesome verb in v. 25a more successfully.

Scholars have followed one of two interpretative options at this point: (1) the verb takes the meaning of its two other Pauline occurrences (Rom. 1.13; Eph. 1.9), namely, 'purposed', 'designed', or 'intended'; or (2) it takes its extra-biblically attested sense of 'set forward', or 'put forward publicly', in continuity with φανερόω in v. 21—generally speaking, option (2) has been favoured.

These alternatives are finely balanced, and a conclusive interpretative decision may ultimately prove impossible. It is important to note, however, that given the cogency of the syntactical argument and the reading of v. 25a above, the verb does not function in alignment with the overarching sense of the passage so much as in its immediate context, where its clause is an expansion of v. 24b. Here Paul seems to be clarifying with v. 25a how the ἀπολύτρωσις in Christ Jesus functions, namely, as a ἱλαστήριον. If this explanatory function of v. 25a is accepted, then the meaning 'purposed' seems marginally more integrated into the context. Paul would be saying that Christ's deliverance was *intended* to function as a ἱλαστήριον, that is, as a final *Yom Kippur*. In this reading, the relative clause would be tightly correlated with its preceding, more dominant, phrase, explaining and qualifying its meaning.

Such a qualification also makes thematic sense. The notion of a human sacrifice somehow dealing with sin was almost certainly repugnant to most Jews at this time.[1] So the statement 'Christ's blood

---

1.   Cf. R. de Vaux, *Ancient Israel: Its Life and Institutions* (trans. J. McHugh; London: McGraw–Hill, 1961), pp. 441-46; and Hengel, *The Atonement*, pp. 6-9 (who cites Deut. 24.16; Jer. 38.20; Ezek. 3.18-19; 8.4-5; and Ps. 106 [?]). This is not to deny that late Second Temple Judaism could accept certain positive aspects in the death of a righteous person, and so the trajectory of martyrological theology (cf. B.W. Bacon, 'The Festival of Lives Given for the Nation in Jewish and Christian Faith', *HibJ* 15 [1916–17], pp. 256-78; J. Downing, 'Jesus and Martyrdom', *JTS* 14 [1963], pp. 279-93; H.A. Fischel, 'Martyr and Prophet', *JQR* 37 [1947], pp. 265-80; W.H.C. Frend, *Martyrdom and Persecution in the Early Church: A Study of Conflict from the Maccabees to Donatus* [Oxford: Basil Blackwell, 1965]). But the association of vicarious atoning power with human death has never been, to my knowledge, conclusively demonstrated as a Jewish *theologoumenon* at this time.

has delivered you from your sins' would be somewhat provocative theology. But Paul is committed to making some sense of the Cross for his Jewish audience—it could hardly be avoided. His qualification of the bald idea of a human atonement with the associations of *Yom Kippur*, therefore, goes a long way towards making Jesus' death more palatable. In effect, it baptizes the idea into the more legitimate—and powerful—Jewish associations of the great feast of atonement. The deliverance in Christ is, like *Yom Kippur*, divinely prescribed and presented, underwritten by the Scriptures, and singularly and supremely effective.[1]

A reading in terms of 'purposed' also enjoys the advantage that it takes the verb in the sense in which Paul uses it elsewhere (and he is the only NT author to use it), particularly since it occurs in Rom. 1.13. Paul is, of course, not obliged to maintain the same sense for his words, and he often varies his meaning from instance to instance. But perhaps the contextual considerations in 3.21-26 are simply too evenly balanced to justify a shift away from Paul's earlier usage in this particular instance.[2]

Lohse, Seeley and Hengel (among others) have attempted to make such a case, but they have been convincingly critiqued by S.K. Williams (specifically Lohse, but Williams's arguments are fatal to all such attempts: cf. Lohse, *Märtyrer und Gottesknecht*; Hengel, *The Atonement*; Seeley, *The Noble Death*; and S.K. Williams, *Jesus' Death as Saving Event: The Background and Origin of a Concept* [Missoula, MT: Scholars Press, 1975]). Williams himself endorses the theory, but on the sole evidence of *4 Maccabees*. Needless to say, for Williams's case to hold, *4 Maccabees* must be pre-Christian (or, at the least, roughly contemporary), but I hold his early dating of the text (which relies on an argument by E. Bickermann, *Studies in Jewish and Christian History* [Leiden: Brill, 1976], I, pp. 275-81) to be invalid (see Appendix 2), placing the document in the second century—and probably the latter half. In view of this, somewhat reluctantly, I exclude any link with developed martyrological theology and *4 Maccabees* from the analysis of Rom. 3.21-26.

1.   Unfortunately, it is impossible to tell from the present context whether this association (broadly speaking) was a Jewish, a Christian or a Pauline development.

2.   In Eph. 1.9, the only other occurrence of the word, there is a rather striking accumulation of motifs either similar to, or identical with, Rom. 3.21-26. God is making known the riches of his grace, echoing the two themes of revelation and grace in Rom. 3.21-26. Three of the four critical atonement motifs are repeated: ἀπολύτρωσις, αἷμα and forgiveness (Christ is also called ὁ ἠγαπημένος in 1.6, the beloved, an expression very closely linked with Sonship [cf. Gen. 22.2; 2 Sam.

If the verb is read as 'displayed' or 'set forward', however, the tight connection between vv. 24b and 25a is loosened. The clause's meaning shifts away from an explanation of the atoning function of Christ to the notion of display, which is more in accordance with the broader context of the passage.[1] Consequently, the clause no longer seems to function parenthetically or in a subordinate sense: 'The righteousness of God has been revealed... by means of the redemption that is in Christ Jesus, whom God set forth as a ἱλαστήριον'—and its position consequently seems a little peculiar. Furthermore, the thematic development of ἀπολύτρωσις in terms of *Yom Kippur* is lost: there is now no strong association between these terms, beyond a simple juxtaposition.[2]

Against this, however, it might be argued that Paul is introducing a different thematic development, namely, that the hidden act of propitiation which took place in the Holy of Holies once a year has now been brought out into the open for all to see. This is an appealing notion—despite the fact that it seems to be suggested as much by Mt. 27.51a and the theology of Hebrews (both of which were written significantly later)—as by Romans itself—and it integrates, as we have seen, very well with the main verb in the section, a contention supported by the principle of redundancy.

In conclusion, a decision between these two readings seems impossible—the evidence is too finely balanced, and both readings yield an excellent sense. Perhaps Paul intended both (once again, paronomasia), and perhaps an interpreter would be forgiven for utilizing

7.15], and hence probably to πίστις in the sense of *ᵉmûnâ*). And the verb προτίθημι is also present, and very clearly in the sense of 'purposed', or 'intended'. If there is a recapitulation of common theology by Paul in this passage (or even, perhaps, by one of his disciples, assuming that the teaching of the master has not been lost), then προτίθημι seems to be used in the sense of intention, in relation to God's provision of his Son as an atoning sacrifice; Christ is the perfect expression, not so much of the Father's display, as of his will.

1.   To argue that Paul is here evoking the rather rare, cultic meaning of προτίθημι in the Pentateuch, where it is used of the sacred bread in the tabernacle (cf. Exod. 29.23; 40.23; and Lev. 24.8), would be to torture any sacrificial metaphor: is Jesus' death simultaneously the bread of the presence displayed in the Holy Place, *and* the atoning lid of the ark, hidden in the Holy of Holies?— C.K. Barrett (*A Commentary on the Epistle to the Romans* [London: Adam & Charles Black, 1962], p. 77) and Ziesler (*Romans*, p. 112) still prefer it.

2.   προτίθημι, significantly, does not occur in Lev. 16–17.

both, in view of the difficulty of choosing between them. προτίθημι in Rom. 3.25a seems a genuine instance of polysemy.[1]

e. *The Meaning of the Cluster as a Whole*
The complex of atonement terms in Rom. 3.24-25 may now be summarized. The basic conception seems to be that of an atoning death, denoted by ἀπολύτρωσις in conjunction with αἷμα (and also by Paul's later statement in v. 25d that a release from sins has been effected: διὰ τὴν πάρεσιν τῶν προγεγονότων ἁμαρτημάτων). ἀπολύτρωσις also introduces the notion of a deliverance, achieved by a costly act of substitution.

ἀπολύτρωσις is immediately qualified by the word ἱλαστήριον, which probably links the deliverance to the Jewish festival of *Yom Kippur*. As a result of this association, Christ's death is semantically overlaid with the rich associations of the Jewish Day of Atonement— that is, with its legitimacy, its singularity and its forgiveness. There may even be an eschatological connotation present (cf. 11QMelch), but it is hard to be sure of this. Thus, the possibly pagan and rather abhorrent notion of a human sacrifice is baptized into the Jewish tradition—although it is impossible to be certain whether Paul is also suggesting here that the traditionally hidden central ritual of atonement has been brought out and displayed for all to see in the Cross of Christ, as suggested by one reading of προτίθημι. This would be a (partial) reversal of the Day of Atonement metaphor, and is also appropriate in this eschatological context.

With the meaning of these words established (as far as possible!), the only significant component in Rom. 3.21-26 that still requires investigation prior to an interpretation of the passage as a whole is its righteousness terminology. This controversial and difficult word group is addressed in the next part of the study.

---

1. The major interpretative mistake that can be made here would therefore seem to be that of choosing one alternative too boldly.

Chapter 4

RIGHTEOUSNESS TERMINOLOGY IN ROMANS 3.21-26

1. A Brief History of the Righteousness Debate

It is standard practice to begin any discussion of Paul's righteousness terminology (that is, words formed from the stem δικ-)[1] with the disclaimer that the debate is so widespread and complex it defies any exhaustive analysis.[2] The uncontrollable nature of the discussion is, at least partially, a result of the role of righteousness terminology in the Reformation. Since Luther's 'great awakening', the 'righteousness of God' in Paul has become something of a clarion call for Christian

---

1. Namely, δικαιοσύνη, δίκαιος, δικαιόω, and the less frequent δικαίωμα, δικαίωσις, and δικαίως (perhaps also relevant here, δίκη, δικαιοκρισία, ἄδικος and ἀδικία). Debate has particularly focused on the meaning of the noun δικαιοσύνη, the verb δικαιόω, and the noun phrase that is so significant in Romans, δικαιοσύνη θεοῦ.

2. Good bibliographies can be found in E. Achtemeier, *IDB*, IV, p. 85; P. Achtemeier, *IDB*, IV, p. 99; C. Brown, *NIDNTT* III, pp. 374-76; Cranfield, *Romans*, I, pp. 92-93; Dunn, *Romans 1-8*, pp. 36-37; G. Klein, *IDBSup*, p. 752; A. Schweitzer, *Paul and his Interpreters* (trans. W. Montgomery; New York: Schocken, 1964 [1912]), pp. 15-21 (esp. the notes); Schrenk, *TDNT*, II, pp. 174, 192; Wilckens, *Römer*, pp. 202-203; and J.A.T. Ziesler, *The Meaning of Righteousness in Paul* (Cambridge: Cambridge University Press, 1972), pp. 217-30. Surveys of the history of the debate, with particular attention to the twentieth-century discussions in biblical scholarship, can also be found in M.T. Brauch, ' "God's Righteousness" in Recent German Discussion', in E.P. Sanders, *Paul and Palestinian Judaism* (Philadelphia: Fortress Press, 1977), pp. 523-42; J. Reumann, *Righteousness in the New Testament* (Philadelphia: Fortress Press, 1982); and V. Taylor, *Forgiveness and Reconciliation*, pp. 29-69. A broader overview may be found in H.G. Anderson, T.A. Murphy and J.A. Burgess (eds.), *Justification by Faith: Lutherans and Catholics in Dialogue VII* (Minneapolis: Augsburg, 1985).

theology.[1] The battle for its meaning is seen to be the battle for Paul, and hence, indirectly, for the Scriptures and for salvation itself. But the ironic result of this attention may have been the obscuring of Paul's meaning, since various words in the δικ- group—as overburdened and bludgeoned as Balaam's ass—have often been forced to go on semantic paths where they should not be travelling.

The 'battle' has frequently been characterized as a conflict between a Protestant forensic emphasis and a Catholic emphasis on the ethical,[2] but this dichotomy—perhaps predictably—is oversimplified. Certainly δικαιοσύνη θεοῦ was generally read up to the Reformation as *iustitia distributiva*. But there were important exceptions to this trend, notably Augustine, who argued for an additional soteriological component in the righteousness of God,[3] as well as for the sufficiency of grace.[4] Wilckens claims that this theme continued to be central in all subsequent Catholic scholarship, so it is not entirely fair to characterize the Catholic perspective as purely ethical.[5] Nor did the Council of Trent abandon the idea of grace or that of an eschatological declaration of righteousness (i.e. the forensic dimension). It merely tended to emphasize the future nature of this declaration.[6]

Just as Catholicism's position has been nuanced, so too Protestantism's forensic emphasis has been constantly interwoven with ethical ideas, and it remained itself in a somewhat fluid state, even within the Book

---

1. Certainly it seems to have created 'a Lutheran agenda' and, as Sanders notes, German Lutheranism constitutes the single largest and most influential body of Pauline scholarship today (*Paul and Palestinian Judaism*, p. 434).

2. So, e.g., Taylor, *Forgiveness and Reconciliation*, pp. 29-69; Ziesler, *The Meaning of Righteousness*, pp. 1-14; and J. Plevnik, *What Are They Saying About Paul?* (New York: Paulist Press, 1986), pp. 55-57 (esp. 57).

3. Also Ambrosiaster (cf. Wilckens, *Römer*, pp. 224-26).

4. Anderson *et al.*, *Justification by Faith VII*, pp. 17-22.

5. Wilckens, *Römer*, p. 225. It was precisely the reconciliation of God's salvific action with his ethical nature that precipitated the problem of theodicy and the atonement, and which led to Anselm's famous theory. The Council of Trent also spoke of 'the righteousness of God—not that whereby God is righteous, but that whereby he makes us righteous' (Anderson *et al.*, *Justification by Faith VII*, p. 34).

6. Cf. Anderson *et al.*, *Justification by Faith VII*, pp. 33-36.

of Concord itself.[1] In fact, seventeenth- and eighteenth-century Protestant Pietism probably stressed inner transformation more strongly than Trent.[2] In view of this, to characterize the origins of the dispute as Catholic ethicism versus Protestant judicialism is somewhat inaccurate. It is perhaps better simply to state that interpretation of the δικ- word group in Paul has usually ranged between ethical and forensic emphases.

Ethicism holds that Paul assumes some transformation of the Christian's being when he uses righteousness terms, so that good works become at least theoretically possible, and even necessary, if only as proof of that inner transformation. Here metaphors of communication, infusion and substantial change are appropriate.[3] The forensic reading of the word group is more relational, and therefore prefers a judicial metaphor in which the accused is declared in the right and hence acquitted, whether or not a substantial change has in fact taken place[4]—the accused is 'in the right' even though not necessarily 'being' so or remaining so, although the acquittal is no less real for that.[5] Thus, at the lexical level, the dispute has essentially revolved

---

1. Cf. J. Reumann, *Righteousness*, pp. 3-10, and Anderson *et al.*, *Justification by Faith VII*, pp. 36-38. This is also apparent in the divergence between the early and the late Luther, and between Lutheranism and Calvinism, the latter evidencing a quite different, although thoroughly Protestant, centre of gravity (cf. K. Barth's comments, *Church Dogmatics* [trans. G.W. Bromiley; Edinburgh: T. & T. Clark, 1956], IV.1, pp. 514-642).

2. Anderson *et al.*, *Justification by Faith VII*, p. 40.

3. So the Council of Trent used Aristotelean and Augustinian verbs like 'poured', 'inhered', 'received', 'engrafted', 'infused', 'added', 'unites', 'makes one a living member', and so on (Anderson *et al.*, *Justification by Faith VII*, p. 35).

4. This emphasis also relies heavily on ch. 4's explication of 3.21-26 in terms of λογίζομαι or 'crediting' in Romans. This commercial metaphor, it is argued, suggests a judicial and declarative reading, rather than a substantial or ethical one. Certainly it integrated smoothly with Mediaeval concepts of merit and imputation; cf. the wording of the Augsburg Confession and the following Apology (Anderson *et al.*, *Justification by Faith VII*, pp. 28-29).

5. This overarching difference in emphasis also often combined with subordinate antitheses, for example, a subjective versus an objective reading of δικαιοσύνη θεοῦ in Romans. The subjective reading emphasizes that the righteousness is God's, hence (supposedly) de-emphasizing the anthropological theme in justification. Conversely, the objective reading stresses the transformation of man, and correspondingly re-weights the anthropological perspective.

around which set of metaphors and images is the most appropriate for understanding Paul's terminology.[1]

While it is probably fair to say that the forensic reading of the terms (i.e. the 'Lutheran agenda') has enjoyed a certain dominance historically—perhaps testified to by various quite recent Catholic endorsements of the reading[2]—the twentieth century has seen a number of devastating scholarly volleys levelled against that position (often by Lutherans!). I will distinguish three main counter-blasts in what follows: (1) dissent within turn-of-the-century Pauline scholarship; (2) Ernst Käsemann's celebrated analysis of 'the righteousness of God' (which broke away from the more traditional Protestant position of his teacher, Rudolph Bultmann), and (3) the ongoing analysis of righteousness words in terms of their Jewish background.

a. *Dissent within Early Pauline Scholarship*
At the turn of the century, a number of Pauline scholars urged the wholesale abandonment of justification by faith, along with its associated terminology, as the centre of Paul's theology. Three now-famous

---

1. But this critical distinction also tends itself to disintegrate on closer analysis. If good behaviour is ethical, it also clearly functions relationally (what virtue doesn't?). But is this ethical or forensic?—really righteous? or merely declarable as righteous? or both? Fundamentally, ethical behaviour *is* relational behaviour, and if relational change is present, then it is difficult to deny the presence of an ethical presupposition.

2. This seems to have been largely a product of the ecumenical dialogue: cf. H. Küng, *Justification: The Doctrine of Karl Barth and a Catholic Reflection* (trans. T. Collins, E.E. Tolk and D. Granskou; New York: Nelson, 1964)—for Barth's comments, see pp. xix-xxii; H. McSorley, *Luther, Right or Wrong?: An Ecumenical-Theological Study of Luther's Major Work, the Bondage of the Will* (London: Augsburg, 1969); the Catholic biblical scholars (all of whom have written commentaries on Romans) Kuss, Kertelge and Wilckens; and esp. J. Reumann, *Righteousness in the New Testament* (Philadelphia: Fortress Press, 1982), a transcript of the proceedings of the U.S. Lutheran–Catholic dialogue on justification. The book includes responses by Catholic scholars J.A. Fitzmyer and J.D. Quinn (although most of the analysis is by Reumann). Fitzmyer's position on justification has shifted (largely because of the ecumenical conference); compare his 'Pauline Theology', *JBC*, pp. 800-27, esp. p. 817, §§94-97, with his stance in 'The Gospel in the Theology of Paul' and 'Reconciliation in Pauline Theology', in *To Advance the Gospel: New Testament Essays* (New York: Crossroad, 1981), pp. 149-85.

exponents of this position were G. Adolf Deissmann, Albert Schweitzer, and William Wrede.[1] These scholars argued for a relocation of the heart of Paul's thought elsewhere, whether in 'Christ-mysticism' or apocalyptic eschatology. Such redefinitions effectively displaced justification by faith to the periphery of Paul's theology. Two significant implications for the righteousness debate were generated by this new perspective: (1) Paul's righteousness terminology was subjected simultaneously to a powerful negative critique, especially from Schweitzer. Justification was, to use his famous metaphor, 'a subsidiary crater, which has formed within the rim of the main crater' of Paul's thought—it was only a 'fragment of the doctrine of redemption'.[2] And (2), with the role of the word group so curtailed, the question of its meaning also became far less significant. Once it was no longer considered necessary to find Paul's distinctive contribution to Christian theology within its terminology (or, perhaps more significantly, to protect the legacy of the Reformation at this point), scholars felt free to interpret justification terminology on the basis of Paul's background.[3] It was thus happily conceded that Paul was not saying anything new in speaking of justification. He was merely appropriating familiar Jewish terms. As Deissmann observes, justification was broad soteriological language, which functioned interchangeably with other generalized metaphors, like reconciliation:

> The countless statements about Christ made by the letter-writer in unsystematic sequence do not represent a diversity of many objects but a diversity in the psychological reflection of the *one* object of piety to which St Paul bears testimony in figurative expressions with constantly new variations of kindred meanings. . .
>
> All these 'concepts' of justification, reconciliation, forgiveness, redemption, adoption, are not distinguishable from one another like the acts of a drama, but are synonymous forms of expression for one single thing. . . We shall not comprehend St Paul until we have heard all these

---

1.   G.A. Deissmann, *St Paul: A Study in Social and Religious History* (trans. L.R.M. Strachan; London: Hodder & Stoughton, 1912), pp. 139-47; A. Schweitzer, *The Mysticism of Paul the Apostle* (trans. W. Montgomery; New York: Seabury, 1968), pp. 205-206; W. Wrede, *Paul* (trans. E. Lummis; London: Philip Greer, 1907), pp. 122-42.

2.   *Mysticism*, pp. 225, 226.

3.   Variously conceived as rabbinic, diaspora, mystical or apocalyptic, but, essentially (within this group of scholars), as Jewish.

various testimonies concerning salvation sounding together in harmony like the notes of a single chord.[1]

Thus, since the late nineteenth century, a significant enclave within Pauline scholarship has dissented from the traditional Lutheran interpretation of Paul's righteousness terminology. This group's modern descendants continue to include many distinguished representatives, a surprisingly large proportion of which are Lutherans, for example, Johannes Munck, Krister Stendahl, Nils Dahl, E.P. Sanders and Hans Joachim Schoeps, among others.[2] These scholars—even more impressively when taken together—continue to suggest (usually on slightly different grounds) that justification is a notion shared with Judaism, and that it consequently only functions in Paul's letters when the status and calling of Jews and Gentiles are being considered.[3] It seems plausible that Paul would employ shared terminology when discussing such an agenda with other (predominantly Jewish) church leaders and congregations. Hence, in these discussions the terminology itself is not in dispute (which would seem a little confusing): it is the theological implications of the gospel that are unclear.[4] This reading of

1.   *St Paul*, pp. 144, 153-54.
2.   Cf. J. Munck, *Paul and the Salvation of Mankind* (trans F. Clarke; London: SCM Press, 1959); K. Stendahl, *Paul among Jews and Gentiles* (Philadelphia: Fortress Press, 1976); H.J. Schoeps, *Paul: The Theology of the Apostle in the Light of Jewish Religious History* (trans. H. Knight; Philadelphia: Westminster Press, 1961), pp. 200-12; and Sanders, *Paul*, pp. 434-41, 470-72, 491-95, 502-508, 515-18 and 544-46.
3.   Schoeps broadens the scope of this shared terminology to include faith—after all, the Scriptural citations Paul uses to prove the need for faith are drawn from the OT! It is not faith that changes, but its *object*: 'We shall only be able to elucidate this matter if we break through the terminological nominalism. . . The Pauline faith is not trust in the Biblical God, but is faith in the sacral event. . . of Christ-soteriology. . . With Paul the faith of the pious believer (in the Messianic status of Christ) replaces the Jew's fidelity to the law' (*Paul*, pp. 204-205: cf. also Philo, *Rer. Div. Her.* 93–95).
4.   So H.D. Betz characterizes Gal. 2.15-16 as a presupposition shared with Jerusalem apostles—and that is certainly how it seems to read: ἡμεῖς. . . εἰδότες. . . καὶ ἡμεῖς. . . ἐπιστεύσαμεν. It is the consequences of this position for mosaic torah-observance in Galatia that Paul wishes to spell out (*Galatians* [Philadelphia: Fortress Press, 1979], pp. 114, 115, 119): 'Justification by faith is part of a Jewish-Christian theology. . . [T]he disagreement [between Paul and his opponents] does not pertain to the doctrine of justification by faith for Jewish

justification terminology in Paul, if it is sound, drives the question of its meaning irresistably back to its Jewish precursors.

b. *The Bultmann–Käsemann Debate in Post-War Germany*

A particularly important episode within this history of dissent erupted after World War II in Germany. As with so many hypotheses in NT scholarship, Rudolph Bultmann was probably the most eloquent post-war exponent of an anthropological reading of Paul's righteousness terminology—a reading that was still quite prominent in Germany in his day, despite the protestations of the dissenters.[1] Bultmann's studies updated, but essentially recapitulated the traditional, anthropological, Lutheran reading.[2] But Ernst Käsemann opposed this reading in a celebrated paper (presented in 1961 at an Oxford Congress) entitled

---

Christians, but as to the implications of that doctrine for Gentile Christians' (cf. Reumann, *Righteousness*, pp. 42-43). Note, we may agree with Betz's assessment, while not necessarily endorsing his reasoning that this section is a *propositio*, and therefore builds from shared ideas.

1. See his *Theology of the New Testament*, I, pp. 270-85. Bultmann made four main points about righteousness terminology in Paul: (1) it functions as the presupposition for the life and salvation of the believer, and therefore is *not* functionally synonymous with these word groups; (2) it is occasionally ethical, but only in a relational sense (cf. Rom. 5.19; 2 Cor. 5.21), and otherwise it is forensic and eschatological (cf. Rom. 2.13; Gal. 5.5)—it is never analogous to distributive justice; (3) δικαιοσύνη θεοῦ is often best rendered as a genitive of origin (cf. Rom. 10.3; Phil. 3.9), referring to humanity's receipt of the gift of righteousness from God (Bultmann must be clearly understood at this point: he did not advocate a unilateral *genitivus auctoris* reading of δικαιοσύνη θεοῦ, as his later article makes clear—he accepts, e.g., a subjective genitive reading at Rom. 3.5; Jas 1.20 and 2 Pet. 1.1 were also conceded to be [ethical] subjective genitives); and (4) Paul's distinctive point is to make righteousness and justification rest on faith. The two were indissolubly fused in his theology, in opposition to Jewish works-righteousness and boasting. Bultmann defended this position later against Käsemann in 'ΔΙΚΑΙΟΣΥΝΗ ΘΕΟΥ', *JBL* 83 (1964), pp. 12-16.

2. Bultmann's position was supported by two of his pupils, G. Bornkamm (*Paul* [trans. D.M.G. Stalker; New York: Harper & Row, 1971 (1969)], pp. 135-56), and H. Conzelmann ('Paul's Doctrine of Justification: Theology or Anthropology?', in *Theology of the Liberating Word* [ed. F. Herzog; Nashville: Abingdon Press, 1971 (1968)], pp. 108-23). Jewett also notes the support of Schlier and Fuchs ('Major Impulses in the Theological Interpretation of Romans since Barth', *Int* 34 [1980], p. 25).

'The New Testament Today'.[1] In this address Käsemann clearly attempted to shift the emphasis in the doctrine of justification away from an appropriated and past event in the believer, as the traditional reading understood it, to some notion with an ongoing claim for discipleship and obedience.[2]

The key to Käsemann's specific proposal for the word-group is an ingenious power–gift synthesis, a conception which he claims is rooted in Jewish apocalyptic literature and the OT. While the believer certainly receives righteousness as a gift from God,[3] Käsemann argues that this is also a participation in a sphere of power, so that the gift remains inseparable from the lordship of the giver.[4] Where the gift is, an ongoing relationship is simultaneously present. Consequently, the

1.   Published as 'The Righteousness of God in Paul', in *New Testament Questions of Today* (trans. W.J. Montague; London: SCM Press, 1969 [1965]), pp. 168-93. See also his 'Justification and Salvation History in the Epistle to the Romans' and 'The Faith of Abraham in Romans 4', in *idem, Perspectives on Paul* (trans. Margaret Kohl; London SCM Press, 1971), pp. 60-101; and his commentary, *Romans*, pp. 23-30.

2.   Käsemann's pastoral motivations are clear at various points. Here he wishes to overcome the traditional conundrum in justification of ethical passivity. Later he also wishes to oppose the importance of salvation-history in Paul, because it is susceptible to Nazi abuse in terms of historicism ('Justification and Salvation History', p. 64).

3.   Käsemann never denies this, and in many respects his analysis remains quite anthropological.

4.   Käsemann was preceded in this by J. Drummond, 'On the Meaning of the Righteousness of God in the Theology of St Paul', *HibJ* 1 (1902), pp. 83-95; and 2 (1903), pp. 272-93. Although Drummond usually prefers different imagery (that is, Platonic essences or forms), the conception is the same, and, on one occasion, identical:

> He [Paul] would regard righteousness not as the mere mode of some individual, but as an eternal essence by participation in which particular men become righteous. This essence would necessarily have its seat in God, and be a form of His unchangeable being, in other words, it would be an attribute or predicate of God. Thus it would both reside *in* God and flow forth *from* Him; and its flow into any particular mind might be conditioned by that mind's faith. . . [If] an eternal essence flowing forth from the depth of the divine nature take complete possession of them and fill them. . . it glows in their eyes, vibrates in their speech, and pours its beneficent power through their deeds (p. 275). It is no judicial figment, *but a true, Divine power* into which we enter when we commit ourselves in faith to God (p. 284, emphasis added).

plaguing dichotomies between the forensic and the ethical, the indicative and imperative, subjective and objective, future and present, and justification and sanctification, are collapsed in favor of a dynamic, relational conception that encompasses both. In short, Käsemann's dialectical conception overcomes the traditional polarities. Käsemann also interprets the gift not merely in covenantal terms, but as a cosmic claim and vindication by God. Thus, in sum, Käsemann's analysis preserves justification as central to Paul, but redefines it with new breadth, and in terms of a more dynamic function:[1]

> All we have been saying amounts to this: δικαιοσύνη θεοῦ is for Paul God's sovereignty over the world revealing itself eschatologically in Jesus. And, remembering the Greek root, we may also say that it is the rightful power with which God makes his cause to triumph in the world which has fallen away from him and which yet, as creation, is his inviolable possession.[2]

It is a brilliant theory, for which Käsemann can gather wide support in Paul,[3] and somewhat less extensive Jewish evidence,[4] and it stirred a generation of supporters.[5] It may be that Käsemann himself was

---

1. It was also significant that Käsemann separated the doctrine of justification from the question of the noun phrase δικαιοσύνη θεοῦ. The argument that this last phrase is a fixed technical term in Jewish apocalyptic has found less acceptance, but it is not crucial to his basic thesis.

2. 'Righteousness of God', p. 180.

3. Käsemann draws an analogy between righteousness in Paul and the Spirit, grace, peace, love, the gospel and Christ's body. All of these also partake of the character of both gift and power, that is, at times Paul speaks of them as a possession, and at times as a Lord or power: cf. 1 Cor. 9.9-10; Phil. 1.11; Gal. 5.5 against Gal. 3.6; Rom. 4; and Phil. 3.12. Käsemann cites of righteousness: Rom. 1.17; 3.21; 5.21; 6.13, 18-19; 10.3, 6; 1 Cor. 1.30; 2 Cor. 3.7; 5.21; 6.7; Gal. 2.20; of ἀγάπη: Rom. 5.5; 8.39; and of the gospel: Rom. 1.16; 1 Cor. 9.19; 2 Cor. 2.14-15.

4. Deut. 33.21; *T. Dan.* 6.10; 1QS 11.12. Cf. K. Berger, 'Neues Material zur "Gerechtigkeit Gottes"', *ZNW* 68 (1977), pp. 266-75, for an only partially successful attempt to broaden the lexical base for Käsemann's analysis.

5. Notably C. Müller, *Gottes Gerechtigkeit und Gottes Volk: Eine Untersuchung zu Römer 9–11* (Göttingen: Vandenhoeck & Ruprecht, 1964); P. Stuhlmacher, *Gerechtigkeit Gottes bei Paulus* (Göttingen: Vandenhoeck & Ruprecht, 1966); K. Kertelge, *'Rechtfertigung' bei Paulus* (Münster: Aschendorff, 1967); and Markus Barth, *Justification: Pauline Texts Interpreted in the Light of the Old and New Testaments* (trans. A.M. Woodruff; Grand Rapids: Eerdmans, 1971).

unable to transcend his Lutheran legacy completely, in that justification, suitably redefined, remains central to the thought of Paul, and
strong forensic and relational notes continue to prevail—humanity is
never actually changed, but is merely placed in a relationship under a
new Lord that compels obedience.[1] Nevertheless, the way was made
clear for further advances by his pupils and followers against the
more traditional Lutheran position.[2] After Käsemann's address it
became acceptable in Germany for Pauline scholars to argue that the
righteousness of God is a power that actively embraces the believer,
creating salvation, and that it is also a power which places the recipient in a new, ongoing, relationship of obedience. Further impetus was
also given to analysis of the phrase and the word-group in terms of
their cultural background.

c. *The Analysis of the Terms against their Jewish Background*
This tradition of dissent has steadily increased the importance of the
investigations of righteousness terminology in terms of its general
cultural background[3]—and in particular, its Jewish background—

Käsemann himself was significantly influenced by A. Oepke, 'Δικαιοσύνη Θεοῦ
bei Paulus in neuer Beleuchtung', *TLZ* 78 (1953), pp. 257-64.

1. Ironically, in this Käsemann seems to have broken with his own eschatological agenda, since he stops short of inaugurating righteousness in the believer. But
this is surely the creative act of God on the Last Day. And, even more significantly,
the figure of Christ remains peripheral—unless he constitutes the new Lord, but one
suspects that this must be God the Father who is the origin of the eschatological
righteousness. Participatory categories would complete Käsemann's analysis in both
these respects, in direct continuity with his presuppositions. This would mean capitu-
lation, however, in one sector of his 'war on two fronts'; a price he seems unwilling
to pay.

2. Cf. particularly Stuhlmacher, who has modified his earlier thesis: 'The
Apostle Paul's View of Righteousness', in *Reconciliation, Law, and Righteousness*,
pp. 68-93. Stuhlmacher comments on his shift in pp. 91-92 n. 16, and there
endorses the work of Kertelge, Reventlow and Wilckens.

3. In the mid-nineteenth century, the German scholar Kautzsch suggested that
the heart of the δικ- word group was the concept of 'norm', 'canon' or 'rule', primarily on the basis of an analysis of the Greek root: cf. E. Kautzsch, *Über die
Derivate des Stammes TSDQ im alttestamentlichen Sprachgebrauch* (Tübingen: Mohr
[Paul Siebeck], 1881); cf. also *TDNT*, II, pp. 193, 195; and Drummond, 'On the
Meaning of the Righteousness of God', p. 85. The reading enjoyed a brief vogue;
however, it was vulnerable to criticism in terms of its singular derivation from Greek

which were being undertaken concurrently with the debate within Pauline scholarship.[1] The ground-breaking study was submitted by Herbert Cremer in 1899.[2] He suggested that righteousness must be understood within the cultural and religious framework of the OT, that is, as a relational concept.[3] For the Hebrew, he argued, righteousness denoted fidelity to the demands of a relationship, whether with a spouse, neighbour, tribe, nation or God.[4] This fundamental insight has

philosophy and culture, and its reliance on etymology.

1.   But while the Hebrew provenance for the terminology must certainly be given priority, the Greek sense of 'norm' should not be abandoned in a flush of semitic enthusiasm. This normative nuance was clear to the LXX translators, who still used the word group with remarkable consistency to render *tsdq* terminology from the MT. Ziesler states that, of 504 words in the MT formed from the root *tsdq*, only 50 (approximately 10%) are *not* rendered by δικ- terms. Substantive terminology is so rendered from the MT 449 out of 481 times (*Righteousness*, pp. 18, 52-69). And certain modern commentators (e.g. D. Hill) have consequently maintained at least some sense of normativity in the word group (*Greek Words*, p. 83). Ziesler rejects this meaning as fundamental because only 14 OT occurrences are susceptible of it (*Righteousness*, pp. 31-32). But pause should also perhaps be given by Schmid's observation that in 1Q27, the eschatological dawning of God's righteousness is also rendered in term of 'norm' or 'canon' (cited by P. Stuhlmacher, *Reconciliation, Law, and Righteousness*, p. 92 n. 17). Criticisms of an approach via the Greek background may also tend to exaggerate the difference between the two cultures. δικ- terms were relational and social in the context of the Greek πόλις, as Ziesler shows (against Dodd and Snaith: Ziesler, *Righteousness*, pp. 47-51; cf. C.H. Dodd, 'Righteousness, Mercy and Truth', in *idem, The Bible and the Greeks*, pp. 42-59). Consequently, it is better to maintain that the LXX translators and the NT writers were aware of the ethical dimension in the words and happy to retain it, rather than that they misunderstood the subtleties of the Hebrew.

2.   H. Cremer, *Die paulinische Rechtfertigungslehre im Zusammenhange ihrer geschichtlichen Voraussetzungen* (Gütersloh: Bertelsmann, 2nd edn, 1900).

3.   A brief summary of this position is given by E. Achtemeier ('Righteousness in the Old Testament', *IDB*, IV, pp. 80-85) and is applied to the NT by P. Achtemeier ('Righteousness in the New Testament', *IDB*, IV, pp. 91-99).

4.   Thus, the specific content of the righteousness varied, depending on the particular relationship at issue. There are 504 occurrences of the terms based on *tsdq* in the OT; 41 instances of the verb, and 481 instances of substantives (Ziesler, *Righteousness*, p. 18-36—I am not sure why Ziesler's figures do not add up). Reumann observes that Koch's figures differ only slightly (Reumann, *Righteousness*, p. 13). Statistically, the words are most frequent in the Psalms, Proverbs, Isaiah and Ezekiel (over two-thirds). For broad surveys of the OT usage, see Cremer, *Die paulinische Rechtfertigungslehre*; Dodd, 'Righteousness, Mercy and

been presupposed by all subsequent analyses, although it is developed somewhat divergently.

One influential school associates righteousness with the relationship *par excellence* in the OT (namely, the covenant), following the thesis of Walther Eichrodt that the covenant underlies all of the OT.[1] Von Rad went so far as to argue on this basis that δικ- language was always salvific, because wrath would constitute an irreconcilable contradiction of the covenant.[2] This covenantal association has continued through into much NT analysis by scholars such as David Hill and James Dunn,[3] who relate the words almost presuppositionally to the covenantal God of Israel—although such a position is not without its problems.[4]

Truth', pp. 42-95; W. Eichrodt, *Theology of the Old Testament* (trans. J.A. Baker; Philadelphia: Fortress Press, 6th edn, 1961, 1967); E. Achtemeier, 'Righteousness in the Old Testament', *IDB*, IV, pp. 80-85; Reumann, *Righteousness*, pp. 12-22; and Ziesler, *Righteousness*, pp. 17-46, 52-69.

1. W. Eichrodt, *Theology of the Old Testament*, II, pp. 36-69, 178-288, 457-511, II, pp. 231-529; cf. G. Quell, *TDNT*, II, p. 195.

2. G. von Rad, *Old Testament Theology* (trans. D.M.G. Stalker; Edinburgh: Oliver & Boyd, 1962), I, pp. 370-76.

3. Cf. Dunn, *Romans 1–8*, where the righteousness of God is 'the power of God put forth to effect his part in his covenant relation with Israel, that is, particularly his saving actions, his power put forth to restore Israel to and sustain Israel within its covenant relationship with God' (p. 47—the detailed justification is given for this on p. 41).

4. This attractive interpretation may be flawed for two reasons. First, the OT data do not specifically suggest a covenantal presupposition in many of the usages. Admittedly, the emphasis is present at times, but not universally, or even very frequently. Thus the notion of covenant must be imported on an *a priori* basis into many of the occurrences as the necessary presupposition of the entire OT. Secondly, that covenant *is* the centre of the OT is disputed. Certainly it is significant, but it is absent from vast tracts of OT material—particularly the Wisdom Literature (see W.R. Roehrs's attempt to deal with this: 'Covenant and Justification in the Old Testament', *CTM* 35 [1964], pp. 583-602; it may be countered that the Wisdom Literature can be interpreted on a covenantal basis, but such analyses lead us far from the present task into detailed considerations of the OT, and so cannot be discussed here). Against this, the debate over the centre of the OT, and whether it even has a centre, is extremely complex and far from resolved (cf. H. Graf Reventlow, *Problems of Old Testament Theology in the Twentieth Century* [Philadelphia: Fortress Press, 1985], esp. pp. 134-86). And while a canonical reading may strengthen the hand of those arguing for the covenant's centrality (first century

When one surveys the OT data, however, overly specific readings of the terminology tend to become awkward. Von Rad's exclusion of wrath from the terms (Lam. 1.18 and Isa. 19.22 notwithstanding) seems to misconstrue a relationship that could legitimately issue in anger and wrath in the case of covenant violation.[1] Similarly, a monolithic reading in terms of salvation, premised primarily on Second Isaiah and certain Psalms, oversimplifies a relationship that could certainly restore the covenant people from Exile, but that also maintains them in faithfulness, protects them, vindicates them in battle, and rescues them at the End of the Age. In fact, it seems that any interpretation which reduces righteousness terminology to a single, specific stratum of meaning within the broad notion of appropriate relational behaviour, seems doomed to founder on the actual diversity of usage.[2]

A second important source for the meaning of Paul's righteousness terminology, and one not available to the early investigators, is the Qumran scrolls. The appearance of terminology and theology in the scrolls uncannily similar to Paul's has led to considerable discussion and disagreement.[3] Scholars have (correctly) pointed out that Paul's

---

Judaism—and earlier forms—heavily emphasized the Pentateuch and the Psalms; both of these sections of the OT where righteousness terminology is reasonably common [cf. the pattern of citations in Hebrews]), the lack of emphasis in many of the relevant Psalms remains embarrassing. But if this interpretation is incorrect in the narrow sense, broadly conceived the point is less easily refuted. The covenant(s?) with Israel reveals the relational nature of God particularly clearly, thus it seems fair to claim that this sense does underpin most occurrences of righteousness terminology in the OT. That is, while the covenant *per se* may not be obvious, *the God revealed in the covenant is*, namely, an electing and sustaining Deity. So, correctly understood, covenant may still be employed as a useful category for understanding righteousness in the OT.

1. Cf. J.A. Bollier, 'The Righteousness of God: A Word Study', *Int* 8 (1954), pp. 405-406.

2. The opposite error is to broaden the word group into the centre of the entire OT, as done, for example, by H.H. Schmid (*Gerechtikeit als Weltordnung* [Tübingen: Mohr (Siebeck), 1968]) and H. Graf Reventlow (*Rechtfertigung im Horizont des Alten Testaments* [Munich: Kaiser, 1971]).

3. Cf., e.g., P. Benoit, 'Qumran and the New Testament', in *Paul and Qumran: Studies in New Testament Exegesis* (ed. J. Murphy-O'Connor; London: Chapman, 1968), pp. 1-30; N. Dahl, 'The Doctrine of Justification: Its Social Function and Implications', in *Studies in Paul: Theology for the Early Christian Mission*

doctrine of 'justification by faith' is not found at Qumran.[1] But we must carefully distinguish the theology or soteriology of 'righteousness by faith' from the lexical question of what righteousness terminology itself means, and at this lexical level the two sets of writings evidence an almost identical use of righteousness terminology.[2]

It is fairly clear that *ṣdq* and *ṣdqh*, as they occur in the scrolls, function analogously to lovingkindness, mercy, goodness and truth. These qualities effect salvation, which is variously characterized as *mšpṭ*, drawing near, being judged (righteous), being pardoned, being atoned for, and cleansing.[3] Sherman Johnson even goes so far as to claim that if it is never actually said that the covenanter is made righteous, this is plainly what happens (at least in an inaugurated sense).[4]

This usage is in fundamental accord with the OT, although it also incorporates a postexilic sense of human sinfulness and inadequacy

(Minneapolis; Augsburg, 1977), pp. 95-120; P. Garnet, 'Qumran Light on Pauline Soteriology', in *Pauline Studies: Essays Presented to F.F. Bruce on his 70th Birthday* (ed. D.A. Hagner and M.J. Harris; Exeter: Paternoster Press, 1980), pp. 19-32; W. Grundmann, 'The Teacher of Righteousness of Qumran and the Question of Justification by Faith in the Theology of the Apostle Paul', in *Paul and Qumran*, pp. 85-114; Käsemann, *Romans*, pp. 25-30; S. Johnson, 'Paul and 1QS', *HTR* 118 (1955), pp. 157-65; and Sanders, *Paul*, pp. 305-12.

1. Observing that this doctrine is not found at Qumran is tantamount to saying that the Qumran covenanters were not Christians, which seems gratuitous. Nevertheless, such an observation is made by Grundmann ('The Teacher of Righteousness', p. 100) and Sanders (*Paul*, pp. 308-309, 494-95).

2. So Dahl, 'The Doctrine of Justification', pp. 96-100; Käsemann, *Romans*, pp. 22, 25-26, 27, 29-30; and Wilckens, *Römer*, pp. 214-17; 'That the Pauline teaching concerning justification was very closely connected with the Essene is undeniable...Paul concurs with Qumran' (*Römer*, p. 221). Sanders also notes Burrows, Black, Stendahl and Schulz in support of this position (*Paul*, pp. 305-306). Sanders defines Qumran's righteousness terminology as follows: 'The two most striking and characteristic usages of ts-d-q in connection with God...are the assertions of his righteousness in contrast to man's sinfulness and inadequacy and the statements of God's righteousness as approximately equivalent to his grace... The word is [also] occasionally clearly used of distributive justice [1QM 11.14; 1QH 9.9; 14.15; 9.33; 1.26]...On the other hand, it is a characteristic assertion of the hodayot that no one can be righteous (*yitsdaq*) in God's judgment (1QH 9.14f.)' (pp. 310-11).

3. Cf. 1QS 10.11; 11.2-15; 1QH 4.36-37; 5.6; 6.9; 9.14-15, 34; 11.29-30 (cf. also 1QS 1.21–2.4; 10.23; and 1QH 1.26; 4.29-31; 7.28; 12.19, 30-31; 13.16; and 16.11). For discussion see Sanders, *Paul*, pp. 308-309.

4. S. Johnson, 'Paul and 1QS'.

(and hence the saving element in the covenantal relationship), perhaps compounded by the idealism of a small, zealous group of adherents.[1] But the usage is also strikingly similar to Paul (and to other NT authors[2].) Thus, it seems almost impossible to escape Dahl's conclusion:

> The Old Testament idea of God's righteousness was alive in Judaism at the time of the New Testament, at least in certain circles and in some connections: God's *sedaka* is not a revenging or distributive justice, but the saving righteousness he shows in his treatment of his chosen ones. It is not necessary to suppose that the Pauline terminology is directly taken over from circles in Qumran or related groups. At the same time, however, it is obvious that we no longer stand before the alternative that the terminology of justification is either shaped in opposition to the Pharisaic doctrine or taken over from the Septuagint: it has a positive connection to a religious language still existing in Judaism... [T]hese expressions appear in a new context marked by a deep sense of the sinfulness of man, a mood of penance and practice of piety, and, moreover, a personal hope for salvation... The similarity with Paul's doctrine of justification through the saving righteousness of God is truly remarkable.[3]

A third area of Jewish material that merits consideration is the intertestamental literature,[4] and, not surprisingly, many of these documents continue the emphases found in the OT and parallel those apparent at Qumran.[5] In *4 Ezra* we read that people are sinful and

---

1. So P. Garnet, 'Qumran Light on Pauline Soteriology', pp. 20-21 (cf. *idem*, *Salvation and Atonement* [Tübingen: Mohr, 1977], *passim*), and M. McNamara, *Intertestamental Literature* (Wilmington, DE: Glazier, 1983), pp. 165-86, who cites Sir. 36.1-17; Dan. 9.4-19; *2 Apoc. Bar.*, 1.14–3.8; Dan. 3.26-45 (LXX); *Jub.* 9; *Pr. Man.*, Est. 13.14 (LXX); *3 Macc.* 3.2-20; 6.2-15.

2. Cf. D. Flusser, 'The Dead Sea Sect and Pre-Pauline Christianity', *Scripta Hierosolymitana* 4 (1958), pp. 215-66.

3. N. Dahl, 'The Doctrine of Justification', pp. 99-100.

4. The rabbinic development of the terminology (some of which was no doubt much later) adds little to our discussion, because the words seem to have been partially displaced. They were interpreted in terms of *zkt* and focused on concrete ethical actions like almsgiving. For discussions see Sanders, *Paul*, pp. 142-47, 198-212; and Ziesler, *Righteousness*, pp. 112-27 (Sanders initially approved of Ziesler's analysis—cf. 'Patterns of Religion in Paul and Rabbinic Judaism', *HTR* 66 [1973], pp. 470-72; but he later criticized it in *Paul*, pp. 184-85).

5. For discussions of *1 Enoch*, *Jubilees*, and the *Psalms of Solomon*, see Sanders, *Paul*, pp. 329-428, esp. pp. 380-83 and 398-409; also Brown, *NIDNTT*, III, p. 358.

unrighteous, but God is able, by his grace, to cleanse and to save them.[1] This salvific sense of righteousness must be conditioned, however, by the strongly ethical sense the word group often carries, for example, in many of the *Psalms of Solomon*. Here God's righteousness frequently denotes his somewhat harsh judgment, which is just (even against Israel) in that it punishes the wicked and vindicates the oppressed righteous.[2] Moreover, while the hypothesis that the Psalms are Pharisaic is unproven,[3] the temper of the Odes is nevertheless very close to much of Paul's argumentation in Romans.[4] Thus, in the intertestamental literature, the salvific sense of righteousness, attested to so clearly at Qumran and in *4 Ezra*, seems to be accompanied by an ethical and even wrathful dimension as evidenced by the *Psalms of Solomon*—apparently Second Temple Judaism did not find these two connotations incompatible.[5]

The interpretation of Paul's terminology in Romans against this OT and Jewish background has been widespread, particularly in English-speaking scholarship, where 'an Anglo-apologetic consensus' of sorts is apparent.[6] The interpretation of δικαιοσύνη θεοῦ as an essentially salvific phrase is particularly characteristic of this school, with the genitive relationship usually being interpreted either in terms of Hebraic action concepts, or in terms of God's inscrutable action in

---

1. Cf. *4 Ezra* 3.7-8, 12, 20-22; 4.12; 5.11; 7.46, 60 (self-referential), 68-69, 72, 77, 83, 94 (?), 105, esp. 116-40; 8.12, esp. 31-36, 45, 48-60; 9.32-37.

2. Cf. *Pss. Sol.* 1.1; 2.10-13, 15-18, 32-36; 3.3-12, 23-25; 5.1-19; 6.6; 7.1-10; 8.6-17, 23-34; 9.1-11; 10.1-8; 13.7-12; 14.1-10; 15.6, 13; 16.15; 17.10, 22-23, 26, 32, 40; 18.7-8. The two senses do still intermingle, with 'ethical' usages appearing in *4 Ezra*, and 'salvific' and 'forensic' occurrences in the *Psalms of Solomon*.

3. Cf. McNamara, *Intertestamental Literature*, pp. 185-88; and Sanders, *Paul*, p. 388, esp. nn. 4 and 5.

4. Cf., e.g., the theme of impartiality; so J. Bassler, *Divine Impartiality; Paul and a Theological Axiom* (Chico, CA: Scholars Press, 1982), pp. 31-35; and *idem*, 'Divine Impartiality in Paul's Letter to the Romans', *NovT* 26 (1984), pp. 43-58.

5. Cf. Sanders's comments on Qumran in *Paul*, pp. 282, 312; and also S. Schechter, *Some Aspects of Rabbinic Judaism* (New York: Schocken Books, 1961 [1909]), pp. 13-17.

6. See Chapter 1, part 1 (although 'Anglo-Franco-American. . .' would perhaps be more accurate). It is applicable to the analyses of Dodd, Leenhardt, Hill, Barrett, Best, V. Taylor, Beare, Bruce, Nygren, Sanday and Headlam, Dunn, Ziesler and so on. Dissenting are Cranfield, Knox, O'Neill and Ridderbos, who opt for a strongly objective genitive reading of δικαιοσύνη θεοῦ.

Christ breaking down 'Western' subject/object distinctions.[1] Here, whether the interpreter opts for a subjective genitive or a genitive of author, the meaning is fundamentally the same: the righteousness of God designates a saving quality which originates from God and also actively embraces the believer. Sanday and Headlam illustrate what remains a very persuasive reasoning:

> The righteousness of which the Apostle is speaking not only proceeds from God but *is* the righteousness of God Himself: it is this, however, not as inherent in the Divine Essence but as going forth and embracing the personalities of men. It is righteousness active and energizing; the right-eousness of the Divine Will as it were projected and enclosing and gather-ing into itself human wills... God attributes righteousness to the believer because He is Himself righteous. The whole scheme of things by which he gathers to Himself a righteous people is the direct and spontaneous expression of His own inherent righteousness; a necessity of His own Nature impels Him to make them like Himself.[2]

It is probably fair to state that the analysis of righteousness termi-nology in terms of its OT background and various Jewish parallels has largely carried the day in English-speaking scholarship (although the specifics of such analyses vary)—and it also seems decidedly ascendant on the Continent. In particular, the phrase δικαιοσύνη θεοῦ is gen-erally interpreted as the saving power of God,[3] with various

---

1. This results in Käsemann's partially justified complaint that meaning is obscured behind the 'fog' of grammar; 'Grammatical distinctions merely label and abridge what is perceived to be a material problem without finally clarifying it... [E]veryone conceals his own opinion behind this grammatical cipher [a genitive of author]. In a technical age, rules of language often wrap material prob-lems in a thick fog and make it possible for opposing views to achieve an easy peace' (*Romans*, pp. 26, 28).

2. Sanday and Headlam, *Romans*, p. 25, also pp. 34-39. Sanday and Headlam were in the forefront of this 'new' interpretation, attributing the initial interpretation to Barmby and A. Robertson—although the view was 'beginning to attract some attention in Germany' (*Romans*, p. 24). Dodd's later commentary (1932) evidences an essentially unchanged position (*Romans*, p. 38). And Dunn's position (1988), although stated more carefully, is basically the same.

3. A few commentators prefer to strengthen the effect of righteousness and its objective state, and so speak of a righteousness *before* God in the sense that Luther did. Here God as origin is somewhat obscured behind God as judge. This alternative is somewhat archaic, however, and is usually found in Mediaeval and Reformation commentators, although it has a few modern representatives, notably Cranfield,

creational or covenantal associations sometimes being added depending on the implications of the immediate context.[1] A Protestant reading also probably dominates interpretation of the rest of the word group (a reading now endorsed, as we have seen, by a number of Catholic scholars), although here a broader relational reading seems more important than a strictly judicial one. Consequently, Paul's various δικ- words are usually translated in terms of the restoration of a relationship or of status, perhaps with a judicial connotation if the context supports it. Hence, δικαιόω is generally referred to acquittal and vindication before God, and δίκαιος and δικαιοσύνη to the condition of being in a right relationship with him. But it is only fair to note that the interpretative consensus here is considerably more fragile than that surrounding the phrase δικαιοσύνη θεοῦ.

d. *Final Observations concerning the Debate*

Before we turn to the text we are specifically interested in, a number of final observations may be made on the righteousness debate.

1. While analyses of the previous use of δικ- words can sketch out broad landscapes of potential meaning, it is important to note that the specific nuancing of the critical words and phrases must still be left for the immediate context to decide. That is, there is still sufficient play in the previous usage of the various words to give (as always) a pre-eminent interpretative role to the context of their further usage—in our case

---

O'Neill and Ridderbos (*Paul: An Outline of his Theology* [trans. J.R. DeWitt; Grand Rapids: Eerdmans, 1975], pp. 159-81). Bultmann's reading also stands somewhat against this tide of opinion, and he is followed, as we have seen, by Bornkamm and Conzelmann. They would not, however, dispute all occurrences of δικαιοσύνη θεοῦ in this sense, but only some. The objection is particularly hard to sustain in Rom. 3.21-22—and Bultmann agrees with a subjective genitive reading at Rom. 3.5.

1. Note, an analysis of the OT reveals a broader range of possible nuances than Käsemann's simple dichotomy in terms of power and gift (or trichotomy, adding source) would suggest. Within the broadly relational conception, specific notions of power, normativity, saving grace, wrath, glorification (whether of self or of Israel), judgment, covenant-fidelity and so on, may be detected, depending on the context. Thus it can be seen that any one of a dozen different loci and modalities are possible within this basic relational and salvific framework.

the section 3.21-26, and then the surrounding chapters of Romans.

2. Any agreement on the meaning of δικαιοσύνη θεοῦ does not necessarily generate firm consequences for the meaning of the δικ- word group as a whole. It does not follow that the individual words will semantically correlate with this phrase, and, furthermore, the phrase's apparent meaning (which amounts to 'the salvation of God') is too broad to allow much determination beyond the general (and obvious) point that the group is coloured by the idea of salvation. Thus, the relative consensus on the meaning of δικαιοσύνη θεοῦ does not really carry over into any discussion of Paul's other δικ- words and phrases, both for methodological and substantive reasons.

3. It is also important to note, when interpreting δικαιόω and δικαιοσύνη, that Paul's Christian nuancing of these words may have shifted them markedly away from what we would expect, given an analysis of their background usage. Since they summarize the effect of Christ on the believer, it is possible that they have been redefined by the newness and dynamism of this event. Putting it more succinctly, the new context of the gospel may have had a marked impact over time on the meaning of the δικ- word group. Previous investigations of the word-group have not, despite the warnings of James Barr, been particularly sensitive to this methodological consideration.

2. *The Meaning of* δικαιοσύνη θεοῦ *in Romans 3.21-26*

At the risk of appearing somewhat mechanical, five specific arguments will be made here in support of reading δικαιοσύνη θεοῦ in Rom. 3.21-26 in terms of the prevailing consensus, that is, as a subjective genitive phrase, understood in an active relational sense, which bears the OT and Jewish meaning of salvation. The emphasis within the genitive is on God's possession of righteousness, and the particular connotation of that righteousness in Rom. 3.21-26 is God's saving purpose and activity which proceeds outwards and enfolds wayward humanity.

a. *The Relationship between Verses 25-26 and Verses 21-22*

The most significant indicator of the meaning of δικαιοσύνη θεοῦ in vv. 21-22 is the pronominal qualification of the two later uses of δικαιοσύνη in vv. 25-26. There commentators unanimously attribute the reference of the pronoun to God, and no other subject is really possible.[1] But these two later phrases seem constructed in a deliberate stylistic parallelism to the earlier statements of vv. 21-22. The direct implication of this is the attribution of righteousness in vv. 21-22 to God. If the two relevant semantic units are separated out from the text and juxtaposed, their symmetry becomes even clearer:

$$\text{νυνὶ δὲ}$$
$$\text{δικαιοσύνη θεοῦ πεφανέρωται. . .}$$
$$\text{δικαιοσύνη θεοῦ [πεφανέρωται]. . .}$$

εἰς   ἔνδειξιν τῆς δικαιοσύνης αὐτοῦ. . .
πρὸς τὴν   ἔνδειξιν τῆς δικαιοσύνης αὐτοῦ. . .
             ἐν τῷ νῦν καιρῷ

Not only is the noun phrase repeated in almost identical genitive constructions, but the verb corresponds semantically to the later nouns. φανερόω and ἔνδειξις, while not identical, exhibit a considerable area

---

1.   The clearest indicator for this attribution is the repetition of the pronoun in the concluding clause of v. 26b: εἰς τὸ εἶναι αὐτὸν δίκαιον καὶ δικαιοῦντα τὸν ἐκ πίστεως Ἰησοῦ. Here both Jesus and humankind function as objects, therefore the subject must be God. This clause is set in a deliberate stylistic parallel to the two preceding δικαιοσύνη clauses, as the opening εἰς indicates (which reiterates the preceding εἰς and πρός; cf. also the continued use of δικ- terminology). Reinforcing this suggestion are the implications of the subordinate διά and ἐν clauses in vv. 25b and 26a. In v. 25b the demonstration of 'his' righteousness is 'because of the release from previously committed sins, in the forbearance of God'. Here the forbearance of God is stated to be the basis of the release from sins, thus the deliverance is God's. And the release from sins is, in turn, the ground of the revelation of 'his' righteousness, thus, the righteousness must also be God's. The verse as a whole consequently states that God's forbearance leads to his deliverance (in Christ), which demonstrates his righteousness—a clear enough meaning. Similarly, in v. 26a 'his' righteousness is demonstrated in the present (literally, 'now') time. This would be tautological if applied to Christ—his righteousness could hardly be demonstrated prior to his birth. But interpreted in parallel with v. 25b, and with reference to God, it makes good sense. The righteousness of God has been specifically and clearly demonstrated in the Christ-event which has just taken place, that is, 'now'. Thus, several local stylistic indicators anchor the righteousness of vv. 25-26, and its demonstration, firmly to God.

of semantic overlap in the sense of 'manifestation', 'revelation' or 'demonstration'.[1] It is therefore hard to avoid the conclusion that Paul is lexically nuancing the same point, namely, that God's righteousness is being set forth in a tangible and observable fashion.[2] A third stylistic indicator is the repeated νῦν that qualifies both sets of phrases. In both instances, the demonstration is taking place 'now'—the stylistic connections could hardly be clearer.[3] That righteousness also does not seem to be hypostasized or separate from God in any sense, as the successive possessive pronouns emphasize. It describes God's character as it is revealed in the Christ-event. Thus, on a relational spectrum of meaning, the phrase is positioned at the subjective end of the scale. It is 'God's righteousness'.[4]

We have already observed that the central thrust of Rom. 3.21-26 is the present revelation of God's righteousness, and that this revelation is elaborated through the text's central section in terms of various aspects of the Christ-event. Furthermore, we have since largely determined the meaning of the terminology which is used with reference to Christ in the central section.[5] As a result, it is both possible and logically permissible to work 'backwards', that is, to infer from Paul's characterization of Christ in 3.21-26 what that revelation itself is[6] (in formal terms: if A is equivalent to B, than by knowing B, we can infer A). In other words, if God's demonstrated righteousness is equivalent to Christ, then by investigating Paul's portrait of Christ, we can infer what his understanding of righteousness is.

Christ is characterized within 3.22-25 via a tight conjunction of two sets of metaphors, the one referring to a sacrificial deliverance, and

1. BAGD, pp. 262, 852-53.
2. The precise nuance is not that important at this stage. A broad similarity of meaning is sufficient to establish that the two clusters of δικαιοσύνη phrases are functioning in parallel.
3. So J.H. Ropes, '"Righteousness" and "The Righteousness of God" in the Old Testament and in St Paul', *JBL* 22 (1903), p. 223 n. 19.
4. Although this 'attribute' must, of course, be understood in an active, relational, Hebraic sense.
5. So Chapter 1, section 3, and chapter 3.
6. This is working in the opposite direction to the passage's readers, who would no doubt have understood what the righteousness of God meant, and therefore would have known how Christ was to function! But a time lapse in interpretation of two thousand years creates such anomalies.

the other to faithfulness, or obedience. Uniting these two perspectives (Christ's atoning death and his perfect obedience), it can be seen that Christ functions in essence (and as we would expect) to save humanity from every possible dimension of oppression and disobedience. He atones for sin, and, as Paul explains later (5.14-21), he also replaces its very basis in Adam. In short, he functions as God's complete salvation.

This suggests rather strongly that δικαιοσύνη should be understood in salvific terms. Christ reveals God's righteousness and is basically salvation personified; therefore, God's righteousness is also clearly salvific. Such a nuance is hardly surprising, given the context of the early church. As Stuhlmacher observes,

> Since the understanding of righteousness in the community's texts is oriented totally toward Jesus' mission and atoning death, the righteousness of God appears in them primarily in the light of salvation: God does not want to be simply the judge of unrighteousness but in Jesus Christ the creator and Lord of the world who brings his creatures to life, justifies and saves them.[1]

Connotations of power and triumph are also not out of place at this point: Christ is God's complete and final solution to the human condition. Thus, Christ's role also suggests an eschatological dimension within God's righteousness—and this seems particularly evocative of the righteousness language of Isaiah.[2] Consequently, the coordination of God's righteousness with Christ in 3.21-26 strongly suggests a salvific reading of the phrase, nuanced with eschatological connotations of triumph and completeness.

At this point it can be seen that, on the internal grounds alone, the nature of the genitive and the specific nuancing of the critical phrase διακαιοσύνη θεοῦ in 3.21-26 can be largely determined. Further

---

1. P. Stuhlmacher, 'The Apostle Paul's View of Righteousness', in *idem*, *Reconciliation, Law, and Righteousness* (trans. E. Kalin; Philadelphia: Fortress Press, 1986), p. 83.

2. Cf. Isa. 5.16; 9.7; 11.5; 16.5; 29.9; 32.16, 17; 33.5, 6; 41.2; 42.6, 7; 45.8, 13, 24; 46.12, 13; 51.5, 6, 8; 56.1; 59.11, 14, 17; 61.10, 11; 62.1, 2; 63.1. 'Eschatology' is a much-abused word, but it is used here in the sense of the following studies: J.C. Beker, *Paul the Apostle* (Philadelphia: Fortress Press, 1980), pp. xiii-xxi [introduction to the paperback edn], 17-19; Byrne, *Reckoning*, pp. 22-25; and D.S. Russell, *The Method and Message of Jewish Apocalyptic* (Philadelphia: Westminster Press, 1964), pp. 205-390, esp. pp. 263-84.

support for this position, however, can be found within the rest of the letter—evidence that lies beyond the text under discussion, but still within the boundaries of its literary and argumentative unit.

b. *A Comparison with Romans 1.16-18*

Rom. 1.16-18 is a clear anticipation of 3.21-26, repeating key words, themes and even phrases, and so the former should be carefully considered for the light it sheds on the latter.[1] This section strongly reinforces just the two senses we have argued for in 3.21-26. The two genitive phrases that bracket δικαιοσύνη θεοῦ are both subjective, that is, both 'power' in v. 16 and 'wrath' in v. 18 are clearly God's. So for Paul to shift to a different genitive relationship in mid-stride, while not impossible, would be awkward—and perhaps even clumsy, because the parallelism throughout the section would be disturbed[2] (the signal from the repeated γάρ should also not be overlooked[3]).

The presence of σωτηρία in v. 16 also clearly nuances δικαιοσύνη θεοῦ in a soteriological sense—in fact, in v. 16 Paul specifically states that the purpose of the gospel is the salvation of everyone who believes. Thus the righteousness of God, whatever its genitive relation, must be salvific. This clearly reinforces the salvific connotation in the phrase already suggested by the christology of 3.21-26.

---

1.   It is perhaps more accurate to say that 3.21-26 is a deliberate resumption and expansion of 1.16-17. In either event, however, the stylistic parallelism still holds.

2.   Against this fairly consistent evidence, supporters of a genitive of author or object usually appeal to the sense of v. 17 and the role of faith. Cranfield, for example, proposes four considerations in favour of an objective reading, the first of which we may set aside, viz., that various Pauline cross-references confirm his usage here (Rom. 5.17; 10.3; 1 Cor. 1.30; 2 Cor. 5.21; Phil. 3.9). Where these are not ambiguous or disputed, they are nevertheless not necessarily determinative for 1.17. All three remaining arguments depend heavily on the πίστις language in the passage. Cranfield argues (1) that ἐκ πίστεως εἰς πίστιν cannot be reconciled with God's activity; (2) Hab. 2.4 focuses on human responses to God; and (3) Hab. 2.4 also suggests an overarching argumentative structure in Romans, in which the first four chapters describe ὁ δίκαιος ἐκ πίστεως (*Romans*, I, p. 98). Thus, the role of πίστις as believing faith focuses the section, for Cranfield, on the *receipt* of the gift of righteousness, and hence δικαιοσύνη θεοῦ is best read as an objective genitive. But a christological reading of πίστις renders all these contentions, if not necessarily false, certainly questionable, and one may also dispute the theology (and methodology) of interpreting δικαιοσύνη θεοῦ with reference to πίστις.

3.   Cf. Cranfield, *Romans*, I, p. 96.

c. *The Significance of Romans 3.1-8*

Rom. 3.1-8 has attracted considerable attention of late as a significant but oftentimes puzzling passage.[1] We are only concerned, however, with the incontestable occurrence of δικαιοσύνη θεοῦ as a subjective genitive at 3.5. Here, 16 verses before his next usage, Paul clearly uses a subjective genitive construction. He is not for that reason bound to it, but strong reasons should be given if a departure is advocated.

It is also worth observing that the phrase is co-ordinated with both the faithfulness (3.3) and the wrath of God (3.5: μὴ ἄδικος ὁ θεὸς ὁ ἐπιφέρων τὴν ὀργήν;).[2] Both of these links are far from simple correlations, and a detailed analysis of the passage would be necessary if they were to be described precisely (which is beyond the limits of the present study). Nevertheless, the different associations show that Paul's uses of δικαιοσύνη vary, and in similar ways to the OT data. Different types of behaviour within a relationship, whether the righteousness of wrath or the righteousness of faithfulness, may still be appropriate, and hence characterized as righteous.

d. *The Implications of Romans 9.30–10.10*

The remaining section in Romans where δικαιοσύνη θεοῦ occurs is 9.30–10.10, in the context of Paul's discussion of Israel's response to the gospel. Here δικαιοσύνη occurs 11 times, twice in a form close to its earlier genitive construction.[3] This is a complex section in a complex passage, so suffice it to say that, without a detailed analysis, it is again difficult to state with certainty what the precise reference of the phrase is.[4] (In fact, δικαιοσύνη seems to shift subtly in meaning

---

1.   So W.S. Campbell, 'Romans 3 as a Key to the Structure and Thought of the Letter', *NovT* 23 (1981), pp. 22-40; N.A. Dahl, 'Romans 3.9: Text and Meaning', in *Paul and Paulinism* (ed. M.D. Hooker and S.G. Wilson; London: SPCK, 1982), pp. 184-204; R.B. Hays, 'Psalm 143 and the Logic of Romans 3', *JBL* 99 (1980), pp. 107-15; J. Piper, 'The Righteousness of God in Romans 3.1-8', *TZ* 36 (1980), pp. 3-16; and S.K. Stowers, 'Paul's Dialogue with a Fellow Jew in Romans 3.1-9', *CBQ* 46 (1984), pp. 707-22 (for a comprehensive bibliography, see Dunn, *Romans 1–8*, pp. 128, 144).

2.   Cf. also 1.16-17.

3.   τὴν τοῦ θεοῦ δικαιοσύνην (10.2); τῇ δικαιοσύνῃ τοῦ θεοῦ (10.3).

4.   Cranfield's confidence seems unjustified (*Romans*, I, p. 97). For more detailed analyses with specific reference to Rom. 9–11, see K. Kertelge, *Rechtfertigung bei Paulus* (Münster: Aschendorff, 2nd edn, 1971); G.P. Richardson,

throughout this section.)[1] But while the passage cannot help us with the genitive relation,[2] it is almost incontestable that it gives the phrase a salvific sense.

In 10.1, Paul states that his prayer on behalf of his brothers is εἰς σωτηρίαν. Then in v. 4 he states εἰς δικαιοσύνην παντὶ τῷ πιστεύοντι. Here δικαιοσύνη replaces σωτηρία after the purposive preposition εἰς (cf. v. 1). δικαιοσύνη also seems to replace σωτηρία within the programmatic statement Paul made much earlier, in 1.16. In 10.4, εἰς σωτηρίαν παντὶ τῷ πιστεύοντι has become εἰς δικαιοσύνην παντὶ τῷ πιστεύοντι, suggesting a very close relationship between God's righteousness and salvation in Romans. Furthermore, in 10.9 the argument also clearly refers to the salvation available through confession and belief in the gospel (Paul's final word is σωθήσῃ). Finally, in v. 10 a Hebraic parallelism aligns δικαιοσύνη and σωτηρία precisely alongside one another:

> καρδίᾳ γὰρ πιστεύεται εἰς δικαιοσύνην
> στόματι δὲ ὁμολογεῖται εἰς σωτηρίαν.

Thus, δικαιοσύνη and σωτηρία are at times practically synonymous for Paul in Romans. Christ, proclaimed in the gospel, is a saving righteousness, whether that righteousness is God's, is present in Christ, lives in humanity, or combines all three.

e. *Intertextual Considerations*

As mentioned earlier, Paul states in 3.21 that Christ's revelation is testified to by the Scriptures (cf. 1.2). A handful of scholars have

---

Israel in the Apostolic Church (Cambridge: Cambridge University Press, 1969); and J. Piper, *The Justification of God: An Exegetical and Theological Study of Romans 9.1-23* (Grand Rapids: Baker, 1983).

1.   Once again we may note that a christological reading is possible alongside the traditional anthropological and theocentric alternatives, since Paul states in 10.4, obviously detailing the righteousness that the Jews have not submitted to, τέλος γὰρ νόμου Χριστός.

2.   Drummond, however, notes that an objective relation is unlikely in 10.3: How can one submit to one's own (gift of) righteousness? Submission implies externality, and hence power—although it might be vested in Christ ('On the Meaning of the Righteousness of God in the Theology of St Paul', *HibJ* 2 [1903], p. 273).

noted the implications of this statement for the interpretation of δικαιοσύνη θεοῦ.[1]

Although the direct meaning of the statement is that the testimony of the Scriptures is christocentric, implicit is the point that they also testify to the righteousness that God reveals.[2] Thus, one would expect Paul's use of δικαιοσύνη θεοῦ to correlate, at least in broad terms, with the testimony of the OT.[3]

The actual phrase δικαιοσύνη θεοῦ only really occurs in the OT at Deut. 22.31. But there, and in many closely related places (e.g. Ps. 143.1!), δικαιοσύνη is clearly oriented towards God. This subjective genitive reading is confirmed by the evidence from Qumran, where the phrase occurs in Hebrew at 1QS 10.25-26; 11.12; 1QM 4.6. It is also supported by certain apocalyptic texts such as *T. Dan* 6.10, and *1 En.* 71.14; 99.10; 101.3, which at least confirm that the phrase was in use and comprehensible within late Second Temple Judaism. Conversely, an objective genitive reading is not really attested in the writings of the period, that is, a righteousness before God. But the testimony of the Scriptures may be even more specific than this general witness.

In 3.20 Paul concludes a long exposé of sin by citing Ps. 142.2b [LXX] (suitably modified)[4] after inserting an anticipatory parenthesis.[5]

1.   Notably J.H. Ropes, '"Righteousness"', pp. 213, 225; W.H. Cadman, 'Δικαιοσύνη in Romans 3,21-26', in *Studia Evangelica* (ed. F.L. Cross; Berlin: Akademie, 1964), pp. 532-34.

2.   If something shows that y is revealed definitively by z, it *must* describe y as well as z, so that its possession allows the correlation to be fully understood. For if it spoke only of z, one might know what z was (in this case, the Messiah), but one would not know that z corresponded to y. Yet this correspondence is precisely Paul's point in 3.21-26.

3.   As we have seen, this still leaves a fair semantic range of meaning undetermined. But it should be assumed that Paul's usage will *not depart radically* from the range of meaning that is established by the OT. To do so would be to undermine the principle that he himself has just stated, and his argument would thereby become confusing, to say the least.

4.   Cf. E.E. Ellis, *Paul's Use of the Old Testament* (Grand Rapids: Eerdmans, 1957), pp. 12, 14-15.

5.   A frequent feature of Romans—in this case the phrase is διὰ γὰρ νόμου ἐπίγνωσις ἁμαρτίας; cf. Chapter 2.

This quotation effectively concludes his argument of 1.18–3.20.[1] Paul's citations can often be fragmentary and (to us) even contextually violent, but to deny him any knowledge of context on that ground would be a *non sequitur*. Here the context of his citation is striking:

κύριε, εἰσάκουσον τῆς προσευχῆς μου,
ἐνώτισαι τὴν δέησίν μου ἐν τῇ ἀληθείᾳ σου,
ἐπάκουσόν μου ἐν τῇ δικαιοσύνῃ σου,
καὶ μὴ εἰσέλθῃς εἰς κρίσιν μετὰ τοῦ δούλου σου,
ὅτι οὐ δικαιωθήσεται ἐνώπιόν σου πᾶς ζῶν.

If Paul had the opening verses of Psalm 142 [LXX] in mind when he moved on from 3.20 to 3.21, this would also serve to draw his reference to δικαιοσύνη there into the circle of God's salvation. In support of this association we may note, over and above the linguistic similarity between the passages and the Psalm's citation in the immediate context, both Psalm 142 and Romans presuppose broad situations of human need and sin. The psalmist is throwing himself on God's mercy, and the same action is certainly required by Paul's argument in 1.18–3.20. Thus, not only does his citation give a scriptural warrant for the fact that no one is righteous, but it also indirectly emphasizes Paul's more fundamental point that salvation is by dependence on God's grace.[2]

It is always difficult to prove an intertextual reference or allusion beyond reasonable doubt. The case for an association is certainly

---

1. That this is a citation seems confirmed by its identical occurrence in Gal. 2.16.

2. It may be surmised that Ps. 142 was a standard text within Jewish Christianity (cf. C.H. Dodd, *According to the Scriptures* [London: Collins, 1952]). This may perhaps be indicated by Paul's citation of the Psalm in the context of the Antioch confrontation, described in Galatians. In 2.15-16 Paul seems to be establishing shared theological principles, prior to drawing out their implications for the Galatian church (so H.D. Betz, *Galatians* [Philadelphia: Fortress Press, 1979], pp. 114, 115, 119; also Reumann, *Righteousness*, pp. 42-43). Paul's quotation of Ps. 142 in this context may therefore simply be an allusion to a text already well known within the early church (cf. another possible allusion in 1 Cor. 4.4). In effect, Paul would be arguing, 'We all know that we are justified by faith in the faithful one—as our constant use of Ps. 142 [LXX] indicates'. And as in Galatians, Paul uses a third-person plural verb in Rom. 3.19-20 that suggests inclusiveness: οἴδαμεν (cf. ἡμεῖς . . . εἰδότες. . . καὶ ἡμεῖς. . . ἐπιστεύσαμεν, ἵνα δικαιωθῶμεν. . . : Gal. 2.15-16).

stronger for 3.20-21 than it is for an allusion to Psalm 97 in Rom. 1.16,[1] and although this still falls short of absolute demonstration, it seems a tantalizing possibility.[2] Certainly, if Paul does not have this specific text in mind, the Psalm does serve to strengthen our observation that the OT knows only of a subjective sense to δικαιοσύνη θεοῦ.

In sum, Paul seems to be using δικαιοσύνη θεοῦ in what was probably a standard Jewish sense to denote the salvation of God. But because of the frequent eschatological associations of this phrase and, more importantly, the eschatological function of Christ, the basic meaning of salvation is probably overlaid with eschatological connotations of triumph, power, finality and vindication. Fundamentally, however, the phrase denotes God's powerful will to save—a purpose that fulfils his promises to Israel and is therefore characterizable as righteous.

The phrase does not seem in Rom. 3.21-26 to carry overt associations of the covenant (beyond the association with God's promises), or of wisdom or creation. God and salvation seem to be its primary content, supplemented by various clustering secondary associations with eschatology, faithfulness, and perhaps wrath.

---

1.   Barmby and (less enthusiastically) Cranfield note that Ps. 97.2 [LXX] is very close to Paul's wording in 1.16-17. The relevant verses in the Psalm read:

ἐγνώρισεν κύριος τὸ σωτήριον αὐτοῦ,
ἐναντίον τῶν ἐθνῶν ἀπεκάλυψεν τὴν δικαιοσύνην αὐτοῦ
ἐμνήσθη τοῦ ἐλέους αὐτοῦ τῷ Ἰακώβ
καὶ τῆς ἀληθείας αὐτοῦ τῷ οἴκῳ Ἰσραήλ.

What makes this allusion particularly attractive is the clear reference of the psalmist to the salvation of the Gentiles alongside the salvation of Israel. This integrates perfectly with Paul's statement in 1.16b that the gospel is intended for the salvation of everyone who believes, Ἰουδαίῳ τε πρῶτον καὶ Ἕλληνι, and reinforces the shared use of δικαιοσύνη, σωτηρία, and ἀποκαλύπτω. The phrase ἀπεκάλυψεν τὴν δικαιοσύνην αὐτοῦ is close to δικαιοσύνη...θεοῦ...ἀποκαλύπτεται, but in Romans the possessive pronoun has become a definite noun (to parallel δύναμις θεοῦ), the verb has shifted from aorist to present, and the order has been reversed. Such rearrangement is moving beyond quotation to allusion, and, in the absence of a common phraseology, rather than merely a shared vocabulary, it is impossible to claim more than an allusion here for Paul—it is also perhaps significant that in the closely parallel 3.21-26, the verb changes and σωτηρία drops out of direct sight.

2.   Dunn favours it (*Romans 1–8*, p. 158).

3. The Meaning of δικαιόω in Romans 3.21-26

Here I will again present a series of arguments in support of a basic thesis, namely, that Paul's use of the verb δικαιόω in Rom. 3.21-26 (appearing as two participles in vv. 24 and 26d) is strangely active, and even 'transformational', in meaning. Hence the word is strongly conditioned by its Christian usage, although its meaning remains in continuity with its wider, extra-ecclesial use. The function of v. 26b must first be analysed, however, before these considerations can be addressed in detail.

a. *Preliminary Interpretative Questions in Verse 26b*
Paul's conclusion to Rom. 3.21-26 reads, εἰς τὸ εἶναι αὐτὸν δίκαιον καὶ δικαιοῦντα τὸν ἐκ πίστεως Ἰησοῦ.[1] Two difficulties within this clause must be dealt with before its meaning as a whole can be understood, and the meaning of δικαιόω derived: (1) the sense of δίκαιος must be determined, and (2) the function of καί must be specified.

(1) In Romans, Paul generally uses δίκαιος in an absolute ethical sense, for example, to denote an idealized good person (2.13; 5.7), God (here in 3.26), or the law (7.12).[2] All of these things are axiomatically good.[3] Consequently, in v. 26d Paul is probably making

---

1. Piper (following Cranfield, *Romans*, I, p. 213) argues that v. 26d comprises a significant shift because the sense of demonstration (ἔνδειξις) is replaced by the verb εἶναι (*The Justification of God*, pp. 123, 129). But in view of the preposition εἰς, which parallels εἰς in v. 25b and semantically reproduces πρός in v. 26a (this could be a deliberate chiasm: εἰς. . . πρός. . . εἰς), one must question whether Paul is stating something substantially different from what has preceded, rather than nuancing a basic position. The repeated pronoun reinforces the similarity with what has preceded (although it is no longer possessive). Moreover, the function of the clause as a conclusion to the whole section of six verses speaks strongly in favour of some continuity. Paul is probably not introducing a new point at this stage, although this conclusion does not solve the problem of the clause's precise meaning.

2. Cf. *TDNT*, II, p. 190.

3. Such an ethical sense should not be understood statically, since personal goodness always involves fulfilment of the demands of relationship. This much is clear from the various background studies. Ziesler in particular shows how δίκαιος refers not merely to intact relationships, but to conduct that preserves and restores them. Cf. also P.J. Achtemeier, 'Righteousness in the New Testament', *IDB*, IV,

the eminently unremarkable statement that God is 'good' or 'right'.[1] No one would object to this, but the specific connotation of that rightness has yet to be determined since the word itself, standing in isolation, does not really supply it.

(2) Our understanding of δίκαιος is intimately related to the function of καί in the clause, which links it with another phrase. This word has traditionally been read, as we have seen,[2] against a backdrop of theodicy. That is, a specific question tends to dominate the mind of the reader at this point: How can God forgive sins without impugning his justice?[3] The response is ingenious and, assuming certain translations, not particularly unfaithful to the text. For God simply to ignore sins would not be just. For him to punish them immediately, however, would mean the destruction of the sinner. But the sinner is preserved *and* God's justice is maintained if judgment is postponed throughout an earlier age, and then exhausted in Christ's sacrifice of himself on the Cross. Thus, the theory explains both an earlier age of forbearance, of which Paul seems to speak in v. 25d, and the present age of vicarious punishment, that is, the Cross, which seems to be spoken of in Paul's series of atonement terms, ἀπολύτρωσις, ἱλαστήριον, and αἷμα. These words suggest that Jesus' death is the point where God's justice is satisfied as the consequences of sin are atoned for in a bloody payment. In short, God's justice and his saving purpose, conceived essentially antithetically, have both been maintained intact by a theory of sacrificial atonement. Rom. 3.24-26 seems to presuppose this theology, while v. 26d seems to summarize it.[4]

---

pp. 91-99. δίκαιος in 3.26 must therefore be understood in active terms, as indeed Jesus was ὁ δίκαιος because he was obedient to God's call and accepted his humiliating death (cf. Rom. 1.3-4; 8.3-4; and esp. Phil. 2.5-11). This is not passive goodness, but an active fulfilment of the demands of the relationship between God and humanity.

1. Cf. Deut. 32.4; 1 Kgs 2.2; 2 Esdr. 9.15; Tob. 3.2; 114.5; Ps. 144.17; 1 Jn 1.9; Rev. 16.5, 7; 15.3; 19.2; Josephus, *Ant.* 2.108; 11.55 (cf. 7.269; 8.23), *War* 7.323; and Philo, *Somn.* 2.194; *Vit. Mos.* 2.279 (cf. *Fuga* 82).

2. See Chapter 1, section 1.

3. This issue is raised by v. 25b, where διὰ τὴν πάρεσιν τῶν προγεγονότων ἁμαρτημάτων is usually translated 'because of the passing over of sins previously committed'. This automatically generates the theological problems of why God passed over previous sins, and what he plans to do about them now.

4. This is, of course, a brief paraphrase of Anselm's famous theory, elaborated in *Cur Deus Homo*, which Kümmel attacks, and Piper defends in relation to this

In alignment with this reading, the conjunction καί in v. 26d tends to be read with an emphasis on the incongruity of the co-ordinated ideas, that is, in a contrasting sense: 'in order that he should be [*both*] just *and* the one who justifies the one [who lives] out of the faith of Jesus'.[1] Here the καί is understood to link thoughts that are essentially different, but which Paul has united theologically by means of his theory of the atonement.

Many have felt, however, that this reading presupposes a rather anachronistic theology—the idea seems more Christian than Pauline.[2] But, while Paul may perhaps be forgiven such theology, the reading may also violate the basic sense of the text. Primarily, it has been shown to misunderstand πάρεσις. Kümmel has demonstrated that contextual considerations allow 'forgiveness' rather than 'pass over' for πάρεσις,[3] and the meaning 'release' is even surer: this lexical change reorients the entire clause. It now refers, not to the past with its troublesome overlooking of sin, but to the present and to the atoning work of Christ: *sins* committed beforehand are *now* neutralized (πάρεσις) because of the Cross. Thus, the problem of theodicy disappears (since there is no troublesome 'overlooking' of sin in the past), and the meaning of the clause now appears much more straightforward. Previously God was angry with sins (1.18–3.20), but now he releases us from them out of his forbearance.[4]

---

particular text. Cf. also the commentators listed in Chapter 1, section 1.

1. Cf. BAGD, p. 393, meaning II.3.

2. One such early objector was G.A. Frick, who protested that the reading was inaccurate in his *Der Paulinische Grundbegriff der Δικαιοσύνη Θεοῦ*, published in 1888 (cited by W.F. Lofthouse, 'The Righteousness of God', *ExpTim* 50 [1938–39], p. 445 n. 2).

3. W.G. Kümmel, 'Πάρεσις und ἔνδειξις: Ein Beitrag zum Verständnis der paulinischen Rechfertigungslehre', *ZTK* 49 (1952), pp. 154-67.

4. Broader studies of the Jewish background to the NT also suggest that theodicy does not seem to have been a primary preoccupation in the OT or at Qumran when δικ- terminology is used. The careful reconciliation of justice and mercy is very seldom prominent in the sources, with the customary understanding being uncritically synthetic, reading δικ- words in association with mercy, faithfulness, salvation and (occasionally) wrath. Thus, it seems doubly unlikely that the καί should be read in adversative terms in v. 26d. The rabbis did discuss this question (cf. *TDNT*, II, pp. 197-98), but it seems to have been a post-destruction development (cf. J.H. Ropes, '"The Righteousness of God" in the Old Testament and in St Paul', pp. 217 n. 11). It may be objected to this that the passage still supports a

Consequently, it is unnecessary and probably incorrect to read καί in v. 26d in the light of a theodicy. Instead, the preceding section of ἔνδειξις phrases may be given its proper weight, and the conjunction in v. 26b maybe interpreted in terms of its immediate context. This suggests a simple connective sense with no sense of contrast. God is δίκαιον 'and' δικαιοῦντα κτλ. If the καί in v. 26b is read as a simple connective, however, the two components in the clausula are clearly unbalanced. δίκαιος faces an entire phrase, which not only outnumbers it but incorporates a key theme from the preceding section—and it becomes itself rather redundant. But this asymmetry is overcome if the καί is read in an explicative or adverbial sense, within which the final phrase functions specifically to develop the meaning of the term δίκαιος.[1] Given this reading, the entire clause operates in a significant and integrated fashion:[2] the καί links the two δικ- words suggesting that God is δίκαιος *even as he* δικαιοῦντα τὸν ἐκ πίστεως 'Ιησοῦ. Hence, in this reading, δικαιόω and its associated phrase specifically develop Paul's use of δίκαιος, and this interpretation is favoured by a number of commentators.[3] Such an interpretation subtly changes the thrust of Paul's final clause. Paul's final phrase is dependent grammatically on the participle for its integration into the sentence, as a more literal rendering of the Greek suggests: 'in order that he might be righteous and rightwizing-the-one-out-of-the-faithfulness-of-Christ'. Thus, it should not be read with a general reference to the rest of the clause, as is often done. This violates the specific implications of the participial construction. It is a

theology of atonement, but this reading now rests entirely on the individual sacrificial words Paul uses: ἀπολύτρωσις, ἱλαστήριον and αἷμα. It finds no argumentative development within the section, and Paul's main concern seems to be something different. In short, the theology of atonement has become a minor and rather muted theme.

1. Cf. BAGD, p. 393, meaning I.3—there seems little semantic difference between this adverbial sense and the previous explicative sense of the connective use.

2. Cf. BAGD, p. 393, meaning II.2, citing C. Blackman, 'Romans 3.26b: A Question of Translation', *JBL* 87 (1968), pp. 203-204. I would, in fact, oppose Blackman's suggestion of an intensive use (and it is interesting to note that, in part, he continues to interpret the passage as a theodicy, citing Ps. 3.9 as a parallel).

3. For example, Blackman ('Romans 3.26b'); Cranfield (*Romans*, I, p. 213), Dodd (*Romans*, p. 82), Käsemann (*Romans*, p. 101), Sanday and Headlam (*Romans*, p. 91), and S.K. Williams, 'The "Righteousness of God" in Romans', *JBL* 99 (1980), p. 277.

specific development of Paul's use of δίκαιος. In sum, the two δικ-words do not function best alongside one another in a simple associated sense. The second, along with its dependent phrase, is better read as an explanation of the first. Paul is stating that God is right *within the very act* of rightwizing the one who lives out of the faith of Christ.[1]

The overall effect of this reading is to suggest that the revelation of God's righteousness in Christ is not simply some passive form of display—it is not a revelation that floats with impressive objectivity in history. God reaches out through it *to draw the believer into its sphere*.[2] Thus the rightwizing of the believer is the completion of the revelation of God's righteousness in Christ.[3] God reveals his salvation in order that he might actually save—and such a statement seems a fitting finale to the passage.

b. δικαιοῦν *and the Completion of the Setting (3.21-26)*

The specific meaning of δικαιόω must now be addressed within the broader semantic framework already established. We have seen that the dominant concept in the section, righteousness, means God's salvation. In particular, it means his dawning, eschatological salvation, made public and effective through Christ. It is also undeniable that Paul is still speaking of salvation in Christ in v. 26d.[4] Thus δικαιοῦντα must mean, broadly speaking, 'saves'.

This consideration alone suggests that a forensic or declaratory translation of δικαιόω like 'declared right' is too weak, and that, at

---

1.   This also seems the best reading of εἶναι. It suggests that God is 'being' right insofar as he rightwizes. Thus, it functions to connect the two δικ- terms in the clausula, and does not have semantic consequences much beyond this point (*contra* Piper).

2.   As Ropes says, 'Paul is saying that God has given his Son in order to show his "vindicative" and redeeming righteousness, that he might be both vindicative and vindicator (redeemer and justifier) of him who has faith in Jesus' ('"Righteousness" and "The Righteousness of God"', p. 226).

3.   And Käsemann's characterization of God's righteousness as a power seems doubly appropriate, since it clearly conveys the active and all-embracing sense of God's righteousness that Paul presupposes throughout the section.

4.   The shift in meaning is not away from salvation, but towards the active sense in which God effects salvation in the believer by means of Christ, rather than merely having his own saving purpose revealed historically in Christ.

the least, the more active 'set right' must be supplied. God is actively involved, by means of Christ, to save the believer. He accomplishes the action. He does not just acknowledge it. Thus, we would render v. 26d: 'so that he might be right even in the act of saving (or 'setting right') the one who lives out of the faithfulness of Jesus'.

This interpretation also fits well into v. 24a. Here God is actively correcting a fallen condition, described in some detail in the previous section (1.18–3.20), and alluded to and summarized in v. 23. But in v. 24a, the gift of God's grace freely rightwizes the fallen and sinful, that is, it precisely overcomes and reverses it, as its antithetical syntactical placement suggests. Consequently, 'set right' or 'saves' is a very appropriate rendering: '—for all sinned and are fallen short of the glory of God, being saved, as a gift, by his grace'.

This rendering of 'set right', or, more appropriately (because it is a little less awkward and uncolloquial) 'saved', is a translation of the participial form of δικαιόω that can be fairly well-established for Rom. 3.21-26—and it should be noted that the strongly salvific and eschatological thrust of the section, with its fourfold δικαιοσύνη θεοῦ, seems to carry little additional sense of a forensic or judicial dimension. The basic meaning seems to be simply salvation, in a general sense, from a many-faceted plight.

c. *Some Further Implications from the Parenthesis (3.22-24a)*
The first member of the antithesis in vv. 23-24a may, however, contain an additional implication for our discussion. In it Paul states that all fall short τῆς δόξης τοῦ θεοῦ. This phrase is almost certainly a subjective genitive,[1] although it is to be expected that God's glory also functions like a power for Paul, dialectically enfolding object within subject.[2] Thus, at its simplest level, the phrase suggests that humanity has fallen short of (or 'lacks'[3]) God's presence, his and her derived imaging of God, and the realm bathed in God's light, namely, heaven.

This statement accords with Paul's argument elsewhere. He states in 1.23 that humanity ἤλλαξαν τὴν δόξαν τοῦ ἀφθάρτου θεοῦ ἐν

---

1. Cf. 3.7.
2. Cf. Käsemann, 'The Righteousness of God in Paul', pp. 168-82; although Käsemann does not make this point specifically with respect to δόξα.
3. R.L. Scroggs, *Last Adam: A Study in Pauline Anthropology* (Oxford: Basil Blackwell, 1966), p. 73 n. 42.

ὁμοιώματι εἰκόνος φθαρτοῦ ἀνθρώπου κτλ.; in 2.7 that the doer of good works will receive δόξα, along with honour and immortality in the judgment (and also peace: cf. 2.10); and in 5.2 that the right-wized 'boast in the hope of the glory of God'.[1] But it is also possible that Paul is alluding here to Adam.[2]

The rabbinic literature and other contemporary Jewish writings reveal that Adam's Fall was often understood in postexilic times as a loss of glory.[3] Paul himself echoes this theology in 8.19-22, where the creation eagerly awaits the fall's reversal with the revelation of the glory of the sons of God.[4] Paul also considers Adam in detail within his central argumentative unit, in 5.12-21 and 7.7-25. Thus, the association is certainly possible.[5]

---

1. Cf. Dunn, *Romans 1–8*, p. 168: 'Paul's own use of the δόξα motif elsewhere in Romans shows how much he was influenced by the same line of [Jewish] reflection'.

2. So Barrett, *Romans*, p. 74; Cranfield, *Romans*, I, pp. 205-206; W.D. Davies, *Paul and Rabbinic Judaism*, pp. 36-57, esp. p. 46; Dunn, *Romans 1–8*, p. 178; Sanday and Headlam, *Romans*, p. 85; and Scroggs, *Last Adam*, p. 73, esp. n. 42 (in what follows I am largely dependent on Scroggs, who also cites Lietzmann and Bultmann in support of this point). Black (*Romans*, pp. 66-67) and Käsemann (*Romans*, pp. 94-95) are more ambivalent.

3. Part of the general postexilic meditation on sin, which was often closely related to Adam: cf. Sir. 49.16 (Lk. 3.38?), 2 *Enoch* 30.10-18; *T. Mos.* 21.6; *Pesiq. R.* 36b; 115a; *b. B. Bat.* 58a; *Gen. R* 12.6; 20.12; *Lev. R.* 20.2 *Eccl. R.* 8.1, 2; *Tanḥ. B.* 17 (57b) (cf. also Str–B, 4: 887; Davies, *Paul*, p. 46; and Scroggs, *Last Adam*, pp. 26, 35-37, 48-49).

4. For Jewish hope that the end-time would result in a restoration of glory, cf. *T. Moses* 39.2; *1 En.* 50.1; *4 Ezra* 7.122-25; 8.51; *2 Apoc. Bar.* 15.8; 51.1, 3; 54.15, 21; 1QS 4.1-8, 23; CD 3.20; 1QH 17.15; *Gen. R.* 12.6; 14.8; 17.1; 21.1, 7 (cf. Dunn, *Romans 1–8*, p. 168, and Scroggs, *Last Adam*, pp. 26-27, 48, 49, 53-56, 61-72, 91—Scroggs notes that the rabbis emphasized the return of the luminaries, that is, the restoration of the light created on the first day; *Tanḥ.* 9.16b; *Gen. R.* 12.6; 17.5; *Pes. R.* 36.161a-b). For Paul, cf. Rom. 2.10; 5.2; 8.17; 9.23; 1 Cor. 15.43, 50; 2 Cor. 3.18; 4.17; Phil. 3.21; and Col. 3.4 for the future (and present) glory of the believer, and Rom. 8.17; 2 Cor. 3.7–4.6; Phil. 3.20 for the glory of Christ (Scroggs, *Last Adam*, pp. 64-65, 71-72, 95-96).

5. Admittedly, the idea of lost glory also suggests Paul's earlier characterization of Gentile sin (1.21, 23), and, as we have seen, it is a theme he uses throughout the letter. But these themes are not necessarily mutually exclusive. It does not seem unreasonable that universal human sin, which results in a loss of glory, and the fall of Adam, which also resulted in a loss of glory, should be intermingled in Paul's

Furthermore, a stylistic clue suggests the presence of this theme specifically at 3.23. The clause begins πάντες [γὰρ] ἥμαρτον, in a summary of the theological theme of universality that is constantly repeated through the first chapters of Romans.[1] But what is seldom noticed is that this precise clause recurs in 5.12 in the context of Paul's discussion of the origin of sin through Adam:[2]

διὰ τοῦτο ὥσπερ δι' ἑνὸς ἀνθρώπου ἡ ἁμαρτία εἰς τὸν κόσμον εἰσῆλθεν καὶ διὰ τῆς ἁμαρτίας ὁ θάνατος, καὶ οὕτως εἰς πάντας ἀνθρώπους ὁ θάνατος διῆλθεν ἐφ' ᾧ **πάντες ἥμαρτον**.

This precise recapitulation of 3.23 in 5.12 is almost certainly more than coincidental. It would seem that, as for much of Judaism, Adam and the universality of sin were ideas linked together closely in Paul's mind. Consequently, within a brief retrospective aside concerning the theme of universal sin and culpability, he makes an allusion to Adam in elliptical form.

Given this allusion to Adam at 3.23, it follows that the participle in v. 24 refers, at least on one level, to the restoration of the lost Adamic image and glory. Here the second member of the antithesis precisely counterbalances the first, so, opposing 'sinned' and 'fallen short of the image of God' (or 'lacking the image of God') is some

---

thought—they seem to be so intertwined in 5.12-14 (assuming that this earlier allusion resolves some of the ambiguity attendant on 5.12 and its notorious ἐφ' ᾧ: cf. Scroggs, *Last Adam*, pp. 77-82), and in the detailed argument of 7.7-25 (assuming a 'gnomic' reading: so—to my mind convincingly—W.G. Kümmel, *Römer 7 und die Bekehrung des Paulus* [Leipzig: Hinrichs, 1929]; and R.N. Longenecker, *Paul, Apostle of Liberty* [New York: Harper & Row, 1964], pp. 86-97; bibliography in Dunn, *Romans 1–8*, pp. 374-75). It may even be that the Genesis narrative underlies 1.18ff. In addition to this, as *4 Ezra* and *2 Baruch* show, free will and determinism were not contradictory ideas in broader Jewish reflection (cf. *4 Ezra* 3.7, 26; 4.30; 7.92, 118; *2 Bar.* 54.15, 19; Sir. 15.11-15). Furthermore, Scroggs notes that such speculations frequently took place with reference to Adam (*Last Adam*, p. 36, 41-42, 73). Consequently, a possible allusion to Adam in 3.23 cannot be excluded on the grounds that it contradicts Paul's earlier emphasis on universal culpability, or his use of a more widespread theme of lost glory. Far from being mutually exclusive, these themes seem to have been intermingled within Second Temple Judaism.

1. Cf. πάντες in 1.5, 16; 2.9, 10; 3.4, 9, 12, 19, 20.

2. ἁμαρτάνω only occurs in Romans in 2.12 (twice); 3.23; 5.12, 14, 16; and 6.15; cf. Cranfield, *Romans*, I, p. 279.

countervailing sense of 'being rightwized'. It may be conceded that this process is only inaugurated, nevertheless it has begun—it is part of Paul's eschatological anthropology.[1]

The critical point to note is that for Paul, as for much of Judaism, this restoration of Adam's lost image was conceived of as a new creation[2] (hence, possibly, the frequency of creation imagery in Paul's writings).[3] The participle in v. 24 may, therefore, if it really speaks of the reversal of this situation, be translated legitimately in strong, restorative terms, which must almost certainly include some idea of transformation or recreation: the Adamic image, originally unsullied and glorious, but corrupted by sin, is being restored by God's gift and grace in Christ.[4] If this admittedly somewhat speculative line of reasoning is correct, then when we read 'set right' or 'saves' in v. 24a (and in v. 26d), a connotation of recreation and transformation should be recognized as present. Humanity is being reshaped relation-ally *and* ethically through a salvation that essentially transcends both these dimensions within a completely new creation and image: 'all sinned and are fallen short of the glory of God, being set right freely by his grace'—that is, declared right and even made right in the sense that all are recreated.[5]

---

1.   Note, a purely Protestant reading is even quite awkward here since a relational restoration would set humanity in a right relationship with humanity's lost image—the idea doesn't really make sense. A declaratory verdict mixes the metaphors even further, by declaring everyone right before the bar of divine justice, when they have just fallen from the glory of paradise and their created image! Conversely, a creative sense in δικαιούμενοι restores the lost image of Adam, in perfect continuity and symmetry with the stated problem (cf. Scroggs, *Last Adam*, p. xxii).

2.   Cf. Isa. 11.6; 65.25; *4 Ezra* 7.29, 32 (cf. also Davies, *Paul and Rabbinic Judaism*, pp. 37, 39-41; Scroggs, *Last Adam*, pp. 21, 23, 35.

3.   Cf. Rom. 8.22, 23, 26; 2 Cor. 4.6; 5.17; and Gal. 6.15.

4.   Scroggs says, '[Paul] does not intend to separate man's eschatological humanity from the ethical quality this humanity is to demonstrate. The new nature is not an ineradicable gift, independent of the believer's quality of life. But it *is* a gift, given prior to man's achievement and out of which his achievement comes. The *extra nos* of the Christ event is not simply the reconciliation of the Cross; it is also the life of the resurrection through the Spirit. . . the statements centring about the eschato-logical humanity of the last Adam tend to speak of the new nature more than the new obedience' (*Last Adam*, p. 61; cf. also pp. 55 and 61).

5.   It has been observed previously that Paul's δικ- terminology often evidences

We may now conclude our discussion of Paul's righteousness terminology, as it occurs in Rom. 3.21-26.

When Paul uses δικαιοσύνη θεοῦ, or its equivalent, he seems to be drawing the phrase from his Jewish heritage (as close analogies at Qumran show clearly), and it has the appearance of standard Jewish religious terminology. As such, it may still carry specific connotations within quite a range of meaning depending upon the context, but it is almost invariably active, theocentric and relational. With respect to Rom. 3.21-26, it has been argued that the phrase is clearly a subjective genitive, with God's righteousness acting specifically as his saving purpose and power. It does not seem covenantal (although it is related to God's 'words' and promises), juridical or creational, but is basically salvific with eschatological connotations of triumph and finality. And for Paul, the phrase now has a specifically christological

a baptismal setting, as indeed it seems to at Qumran: so N. Dahl, 'The Doctrine of Justification', esp. pp. 100-105 (who cites E. Löhse, 'Taufe und Rechtfertigung bei Paulus', in *Die Einheit des Neuen Testaments* [Göttingen: Vandenhoeck & Ruprecht, 1973], pp. 228-44); cf. also F. Hahn, 'Taufe und Rechtfertigung: Ein Beitrag zur paulinische Theologie in ihrer Vor- und Nachgeschichte', in *Rechtfertigung* (ed. J. Friedrich, W. Pöhlmann, and P. Stuhlmacher; Göttingen: Vandenhoeck & Ruprecht, 1976), pp. 95-124. If indeed δικαιόω is contextualized in Paul's thought within baptismal theology, which in turn relates it to Christ's death and resurrection, the full implications of these associations for its meaning should be appreciated— although few have followed them through. Scroggs makes several pointed observations in this connection (*Last Adam*, pp. 109-12, esp. n. 44), as does Reumann (*Righteousness*, p. 32, esp. n. 46) and Ziesler (*Righteousness*, pp. 156-58). More extensive discussions may be found in L. de Lorenzi (ed.), *Battesimo e Giustizia in Rom 6 e 8* (Rome: Abbazi S. Paolo fuori le mura, 1974); and A.J.M. Wedderburn, *Baptism and Resurrection* (Tübingen: Mohr, 1987), which is in part a critique of R.C. Tannehill's use of the Mystery religions to describe Baptism in his influential *Dying and Rising with Christ: A Study in Pauline Theology* (Berlin: Töpelmann, 1967). Corroboration for this may be found particularly in Rom. 6.7, which is very closely paralleled by 1 Cor. 6.11, and more distantly by Rom. 1.3-4 and 4.25; (cf. 1 Tim. 3.16b; Tit. 3.4-7). A close correlation between baptism, the gift of the Spirit and the resurrection, is apparent in these texts. This correlation would further support a strongly 'transformational' reading of the verb—and would also explain why it may be veering away from customary, extra-ecclesial usage; it would be part of Christian, 'in-house' jargon. Paul is still aware, however, of a forensic (and eschatological) use, as Rom. 2.13 and 8.30-34 conclusively demonstrate. These instances must caution a unilateral 'baptismal' or 'transformational' reading of the verb (although the latter reading seems more appropriate for Rom. 3.21-26).

fulfilment,[1] as he brings δικαιοσύνη θεοῦ into association with Christ's life and death. This interpretation of the phrase integrates with, and smoothly completes the sense of, the passage as a whole, in addition to satisfying its stylistic connections with 1.16-17, 3.1-9, and 9.30–10.10. Intertextual allusions were more difficult to demonstrate (although I cautiously favour an allusion to Ps. 142 [LXX]), but the stylistic evidence seemed sufficient to support the above position, which is at any rate that of the majority of scholars, and, in particular, of the 'Anglo-apologetic consensus'.

With respect to δικαιόω, which appears twice in the passage (vv. 24 and 26d), it was argued that the word should be read (at least) in a strongly salvific sense, particularly since it punctuates and concludes a passage that speaks so emphatically of God's eschatological salvation in Christ.

The allusion in v. 23 to the restoration of Adam's lost glory, however, suggested the possibility (and it is no more than this) of an even stronger, 'transformational' reading, which would derive from the idea of the recreation of the believer in Christ, which was understood by Paul to be the (inaugurated) restoration of Adam's corrupted and lost imaging of God (a notion possibly related in turn to the receipt of the Spirit, to the resurrection and to baptism). Here both forensic and ethical connotations would be appropriate, within a broader and rather striking reference to ontological transformation. This meaning is an exciting possibility for δικαιόω, but it remains a less substantiated one, at least insofar as the above investigation of Rom. 3.21-26 is concerned.

The only remaining instance of δικ- terminology in the passage is δίκαιος, which occurs in v. 26d. This term is much less controversial in its meaning than the verb—although it is dominated in its context by δικαιοῦντα and its associated phrase. Paul's use here seems unremarkable, and the adjective, especially in this context, merely takes on the meaning of the noun.

1. Not 'meaning'.

Conclusion

A SUGGESTED READING OF ROMANS 3.21-26

It is now possible to attempt an interpretation of Rom. 3.21-26 as a whole—although it is only suggested as one among many possible readings. I hold that Rom. 3.21-26 makes one central point that receives several closely-related semantic developments. This fundamental meaning is partially obscured, however, by the accretion of two incidental and retrospective points, which probably owe their development to the oral dimension in the text's original production. While these asides enrich the section's argument, they do so at the price of partially obscuring its meaning. But if they are identified and stripped away, the primary semantic structure of the passage is clearly revealed. The above analysis suggests that there are two such secondary points that we may address initially within Rom. 3.21-26: (1) Paul's two antithetical comments about 'the law' in v. 21; and (2) the parenthesis of vv. 22d-24a.

1. *The Antithesis in Verse 21*

Verse 21b states that the revelation of God's saving righteousness is χωρὶς νόμου, which is the first member of a twofold statement whose antithetical structure we have discussed. This phrase is clearly very close to certain other phrases in Romans, namely, χωρὶς ἔργων νόμου (3.28), and χωρὶς ἔργων (4.6).[1] Consequently, it seems likely

---

1. χωρίς is an adverb (taking the genitive), which simply means 'apart from', 'separate from', or 'outside of'. Paul uses it in this sense throughout Romans: 3.21, 28; 4.6; 7.8, 9; 10.14 (it appears on nine other occasions in the Pauline corpus: 1 Cor. 4.8; 11.11; 2 Cor. 11.28; 12.3; Eph. 2.12; Phil. 2.14; 1 Tim. 2.8; 5.21; Phlm. 14; cf. also BAGD, pp. 890-91). A close relationship between νόμος and ἔργον is also suggested by Paul's questions in 3.27 that immediately follow 3.21-26: διὰ ποίου νόμου; τῶν ἔργων; Verse 21 also follows the statement ἐξ ἔργων νόμου in 3.20.

that the specific phrase χωρὶς νόμου is simply a paradigmatic variation of the basic statement 'apart from works of law', and that the notion of works is unstated but understood as present in v. 21 (a possible instance of ellipsis).[1]

A brace of grammatical, historical and theological problems are implicit within this statement,[2] but the phrase is really too brief to permit or even to suggest any detailed reconstruction of Paul's understanding of the law at this point.[3] Indeed, the phrase is not functioning as a positive statement of Paul's attitude to the law at all. Here the meaning of the adverb χωρὶς must be fully appreciated. χωρὶς νόμου is a general, negative statement. It states that, whatever Paul's precise understanding of the role of the law, the righteousness of God has been revealed independently of it.[4]

1. So Cranfield, *Romans*, I, p. 201; and Dunn, *Romans 1–8*, p. 165. Paul uses the comparable phrase οὐχ ἔργων νόμου in Gal. 2.16 and Eph. 2.9.

2. Grammatically, the genitive relation is (although often unnoticed) problematic; (cf. L. Gaston, 'Works of Law as a Subjective Genitive', in *idem, Paul and the Torah* [Vancouver: University of British Columbia Press, 1987], pp. 100-106, who discusses an important, earlier analysis by Lohmeyer). Historically, interpreters have been puzzled by the apparent lack of parallels for the phrase in contemporary Jewish literature (so M. Barth, *Ephesians* [Garden City, NY: Doubleday, 1974], pp. 244-28; but cf. Jas 1.25). Theologically, scholars have puzzled over the soteriology the phrase presupposes.

3. Any evaluation of Paul's understanding of the law is unfortunately beyond the limits of this study, being essentially separate from the argument of Rom. 3.21-26. But it is important to note that the contemporary re-evaluation of Judaism in Pauline (and NT) scholarship has shown that it is no longer necessary to understand this phrase in a narrowly legalistic sense. 'Works' arose from various, often exalted, motives, and Paul could be presupposing one of a number of nomistic soteriologies at this point, whether covenantal nomist, legalistic or something else (cf. Davies, *Paul and Rabbinic Judaism*, pp. vii-xxxviii, 1-16; Longenecker, *Paul, Apostle of Liberty*, pp. 65-85; Sanders, *Paul and Palestinian Judaism*, pp. 270-321, 382-83, 395, 409, 418; and Gaston, *Paul and the Torah*). Which precise understanding is at issue is impossible to say without an analysis of his discussion of the law later in the letter (5.21; 7.1-25), and throughout the Pauline corpus.

4. The absence of the word ἔργον at v. 21 opens up the possibility that Paul is saying something subtly different, namely, that salvation is revealed apart from Torah *per se*, and not merely separately from works of law. But in view of v. 20 and the immediate resumption of the theme of works in v. 27, it seems more likely that ἔργον should be understood as present semantically at v. 21. Besides, 'apart from Torah' makes less sense in v. 21 than works, if Torah is understood to mean

Admittedly, a revolutionary notion is implicit within this general statement (and Paul was no doubt aware of this), namely, that the focal point of salvation has shifted away from the Torah to the messiah. But this idea's radical implications remain undeveloped at this point in the letter. Paul's earlier argument is summarized,[1] and later ideas are hinted at, but the law in the sense of works disappears

the 'boundary-marker' of the people of God (cf. Dunn), because Paul believes that Jesus came within (and even 'under') the law, that is, Jesus was a Jew (cf. 15.8). And the gospel was, and is, preached to Israel (cf. 10.18-21). If Torah is understood more broadly as Scripture, its integration into the section becomes still more awkward. In what sense is it actually meaningful to speak of God's salvation coming 'separate from Torah' in view of v. 21b? But understood as a religious system, that is, as 'works of Torah' (whether covenantal nomist or legalist), the phrase integrates smoothly into the sense of the clause. Paul is stating that the revelation of the salvation of God by means of Christ constitutes a mode of relating to God that is distinct and separate from Torah-obedience, however this last phrase is construed.

1. Paul has previously addressed the law, particularly in 2.6-29 and 3.19-20. His argumentation in these sections is clearly related to his use of χωρὶς νόμου in v. 21, but it is also hotly disputed—not least because his attitude to the law in these sections seems to be so different from his evaluations elsewhere in Romans and in his other letters. The main problem seems to be that here Paul presupposes a some-what crass 'legalistic' use of the law within which salvation is earned by works (so 2.6)—a rather biased understanding, compared with the statements of the Judaism of Paul's time, and with his own statements elsewhere: cf. 2 Cor. 3, Phil. 3.6b-7a, etc.: cf. also Dunn (*Romans 1–8*, pp. 85, 86, 93, 104-107), Byrne (*Reckoning*, p. 65), K.R. Snodgrass, 'Justification by Grace—to the Doers: An Analysis of the Place of Romans Two in the Theology of Paul', *NTS* 32 (1986), pp. 72-92, and E.P. Sanders, *Paul, the Law, and the Jewish People* (Philadelphia: Fortress Press, 1983), pp. 123-35. But Paul's earlier argument concerning the law in these chapters is also, I would suggest, perfectly logical (even if it is unfair): Paul states that perfect, ethical righteousness is required for salvation (2.5b-11), but he observes that those possessing the law do not in fact have such perfect righteousness, whether Israel, who possesses the written code, or the Gentiles, with a law written on the heart (2.1-5a, 17–3.20). Therefore, not only are Israel and the Gentiles not saved, but it can be seen that mere possession of (and the attempt to keep) the law does not save. It is the direct corollary of this conclusion that salvation, when it comes, *must* be separate from the law. The law's prior failure makes this inevitable. So Paul's comment χωρὶς νόμου in 3.21 functions as a reminder of this previous sweep of reasoning: it evokes this prior discussion—but *only* this discussion. Presumably, other functions of the law which Paul has not described or criticized in Rom. 1.18–3.20 are not necessarily included within the rejection of v. 21.

from the present section after this opening remark.

Paul's second incidental point is that the Scriptures, here referred to as 'the law and the prophets',[1] testify to God's saving righteousness—something axiomatic for a Jew of Paul's time and training.[2] This statement is also consistent both with Paul's earlier comment in 1.2 that the gospel προεπηγγείλατο διὰ τῶν προφητῶν αὐτοῦ ἐν γραφαῖς ἁγίαις, and with his practice, frequent throughout Romans, of citing scriptural texts in support of his argument.[3] Once again, however, 3.21-26 contains little development of the idea: it does not seem to incorporate a specific Scriptural attestation to God's saving righteousness (excepting possible allusions to Hab. 2.4 and to Gen. 3). It only states that the Scriptures do so testify. Thus, while Paul sets something of a challenge for later interpreters at this point,[4] his present intention again seems distinct from the idea of Scriptural witness.[5]

With respect to the meaning of the antithesis as a whole, most interpreters seem to have grasped Paul's point (as noted in Chapter 1, section 1), namely, that Paul's statements amount to a deliberate contrast between different functions of the same body of writings—a contrast made possible by wordplay on the signifier νόμος. As part of a soteriological condition or response, the Torah now seems defunct for

---

1. Despite the fact that the assertion does not occur in this particular form elsewhere in Paul (who rarely speaks of the Prophets, but cf. 1.2 and 16.26). Cf. Mt. 5.17; 7.12 11.13 [Lk. 16.16]; 22.40; Lk. 24.44; Jn 1.45; Acts 13.15; 24.14; 28.23, and also Sirach, prologue, 2 Macc. 15.9; and *4 Macc.* 18.19.

2. That the Scriptures testify to the saving acts of God would have been (and is) perfectly acceptable to Judaism: it is the *particular* testimony Paul has in mind that Jews would (and often still do) find objectionable.

3. Cf. up to 3.21; 1.17; 2.24 and 3.10-18. Romans is, of course, the most citation-packed of Paul's letters. Nestle–Aland lists 64 quotations, and this does not take allusions into account, of which there are many (cf. 3.20).

4. Gen. 15.6 and Hab. 2.4 seem particularly good candidates, along with Ps. 142 [LXX], but Paul probably has a more widespread witness in mind at this point.

5. On this important topic in Paul, cf. C.H. Dodd, *According to the Scriptures* (London: Nisbet, 1952 [Fontana, 1965]); E.E. Ellis, *Paul's Use of the Old Testament* (London: Oliver & Boyd, 1957); A.T. Hanson, *Studies in Paul's Technique and Theology* (Grand Rapids: Eerdmans, 1974); B. Lindars, *New Testament Apologetic: The Doctrinal Significance of the Old Testament Quotations* (London: SCM Press, 1961); R.N. Longenecker, *Biblical Exegesis in the Apostolic Period* (Grand Rapids: Eerdmans, 1975), pp. 104-32; R.B. Hays, *Echoes of Scripture in the Letters of Paul* (New Haven, CT: Yale University Press, 1989).

Paul, but as an inspired and authoritative testimony to the acts of God, the writings still serve their appointed function—although they suggest (again, for Paul) the rather surprising 'act' of Jesus Christ.[1]

As a result of this careful opposition, the antithesis actually allows Paul to sugar a very bitter pill for the devout Jew. He has just launched a severe attack on the law, and has indeed stated the soteriological scandal that salvation now comes 'apart from' the law within his gospel. But by claiming that the Scriptures, which are the vehicle of the law as a soteriological system, still testify to God's salvation—albeit in its startling new form—Paul maintains at least some continuity with the traditional positions of Judaism. Paul himself also continues to bear at least some of the hallmarks of the devout Jew. The law may no longer save, but it is certainly still important and even sacred, if only to point beyond itself.

But as we have already noted, the full theological implications of Paul's statements are not spelled out within this specific section, and we should probably not overload Paul's abbreviated phrases with theological meaning at this point. This is not to say that Paul is not committed to the positions they indicate, but in this section the phrases are more allusive than argumentatively explicit.[2]

Thus, it can be seen that the two opening qualifications in v. 21 (concerning the law and Scripture) make significant points, but more by way of allusion and summation than by explicit reasoning. Certainly, they do not function essentially within Paul's present argument, appearing more as a theological vestibule to Paul's main point. After this initial appearance, both themes drop out of sight completely. The antithesis therefore integrates the section with the preceding and following argument in the letter, but it is only after these comments that Paul moves on to his central concern, reiterating the

---

1. One can also almost certainly detect an element of 'reasoning backwards' here, that is, the law cannot save for Paul, because he is convinced that now salvation comes through Christ (cf. Sanders, *Paul and Palestinian Judaism*). Thus, the phrases have a negative content, rather than a purely positive one: they suggest that to be involved with 'works of law' is to be 'not in Christ' as much as anything else (and vice versa): cf. my 'The Meaning of ΠΙΣΤΙΣ and ΝΟΜΟΣ in Paul: A Linguistic and Structural Perspective', *JBL* (forthcoming).

2. He both constantly cites Scripture as a support for his positions (as earlier stated), and argues at length for the supercession of the law (particularly in 7.1–8.17; cf. also 10.4).

critical governing phrase for the section, δικαιοσύνη θεοῦ in v. 22a (an instance of *repetitio*—and possibly of ellipsis, with the absence of the verb). The repetition serves both to indicate that Paul's present concern is something different, and to emphasize it. Paul now wishes to address the eschatological salvation of God. But before addressing this subject ourselves, Paul's second incidental statement in 3.21-26 must be identified and separated from his main theme.

2. The Parenthesis in Verses 23-24a

Paul's second, more incidental, statement begins in v. 22d and extends to v. 24a. This is the critical parenthesis that (as I have argued) interrupts his central argumentative unit, prompted by the occurrence of πάντας in the preceding clause:

> διὰ πίστεως Ἰησοῦ Χριστοῦ
> εἰς πάντας τοὺς πιστεύοντας,
>
> (οὐ γάρ ἐστιν διαστολή·
> πάντες γὰρ ἥμαρτον καὶ ὑστεροῦνται τῆς δόξης τοῦ θεοῦ
> δικαιούμενοι δωρεὰν τῇ αὐτοῦ χάριτι).

Here Paul cannot resist elaborating on the theme of universality, which he has been describing in terms of sinfulness from 1.18 to 3.20. He does this by making a retrospective aside which is incomplete in itself and so must be followed with a more detailed antithesis. The initial comment states boldly that 'there is no difference'. But this is a puzzling statement, in that Paul's repeated use of the phrase 'Jew first and Greek' in his earlier chapters suggests distinction. And much of his argument assumes a significant ethnic differentiation between Jew and Gentile as a Gentile protagonist alternately outrages and shames an archtypal Jew (cf. 1.18–2.29). So Paul must precisely specify the lack of distinction which he has in mind.

It was argued earlier that the first member of the antithesis is probably an elliptical reference to the loss of the original image and glory of Adam. Given this allusion, Paul's point is that all are descendants of Adam, and consequently have lost Adam's glory and, like their common forefather, now live in exclusion from paradise and from the presence of God. Thus, in this sense there is no distinction between Jew and Gentile—perhaps surprising, but an irrefutable point.

Such a statement supports Paul's claim in v. 22d that all are saved

by faith—since there is no distinction in the basic problem, by implication there is also none in the proposed solution: corresponding to
the universal fall from paradise, stated in v. 23, stands the assertion in
v. 24 that God's grace acts on humanity to restore the lost created
condition. Paul thereby balances sin and lost glory against grace and
restored glory (and this encourages a rendering of δικαιόω in strong,
restorative terms along the lines of 'set right' and 'saved': the word
refers to God's gracious reversal and recreation of humanity's fallen
condition in all its various corrupt and darkened aspects).

Aside from its theological force, the counter-balancing statement in
the second member of the antithesis also allows Paul to return neatly
to his present argument concerning the revelation of the salvation of
God, which he has strayed from, prompted by an ever-tempting πᾶς
in v. 22c. Consequently, while the theology of the parenthesis is again
laden with theological significance, it does not function as an integral
part of Paul's present argument. It is a summary of 1.18–3.20 and an
anticipation of positions developed later in the letter (cf. 5.12-14; 7.7-
25). As a result of this, we should note its implications, but we are
essentially free to set it to one side for the purposes of exegeting 3.21-
26, along with the νόμος antithesis in v. 21.

With Paul's essentially secondary statements identified (in terms of
the argument in 3.21-26), the main components of the passage can be
considered in isolation. The reconstructed text reads:

21   νυνὶ δὲ . . .
     δικαιοσύνη θεοῦ πεφανέρωται. . .
22   (. . . δικαιοσύνη δὲ θεοῦ)
        διὰ πίστεως Ἰησοῦ Χριστοῦ
        εἰς πάντας τοὺς πιστεύοντας . . .
24b   διὰ τῆς ἀπολυτρώσεως τῆς ἐν Χριστῷ Ἰησοῦ
25   ὃν προέθετο ὁ θεὸς ἱλαστήριον
     διὰ τῆς πίστεως ἐν τῷ αὐτοῦ αἵματι
     εἰς ἔνδειξιν τῆς δικαιοσύνης αὐτοῦ
        διὰ τὴν πάρεσιν τῶν προγεγονότων ἁμαρτημάτων
26   ἐν τῇ ἀνοχῇ τοῦ θεοῦ
     πρὸς τὴν ἔνδειξιν τῆς δικαιοσύνης αὐτοῦ
        ἐν τῷ νῦν καιρῷ
     εἰς τὸ εἶναι αὐτὸν δίκαιον
        καὶ δικαιοῦντα τὸν ἐκ πίστεως Ἰησοῦ.

3. *The Main Point of Romans 3.21-26*

The passage is clearly dominated grammatically, and hence thematically, by its subject, δικαιοσύνη θεοῦ, and the verb φανερόω, both of which are introduced in v. 21. Since the entire section is one sentence (with the exception of parentheses), these words function as the semantic spine of the text. Paul cannot and does not move away from this opening idea. The subsequent prepositional phrases, while they constitute a critical development of this central statement, nevertheless remain dependent on it.

With the use of the phrase δικαιοσύνη θεοῦ, it would seem that Paul is deliberately echoing religious phraseology widely comprehensible within late Second Temple Judaism. It is hard to imagine today the chord that such language must have struck in the hearts of his listeners, as Paul assured them that God's long-awaited salvation was finally at hand. It should also be noted that the Jewish understanding of God and of his righteousness entails that this dawning salvation is not merely apparent or visible, but an active force, legitimately likened to a power expanding and exerting itself over Israel and over the world. It is the final revelation and appearance of this salvation that Paul is referring to in Rom. 3.21-26.

But Paul does not just begin the section with a twofold evocation of this idea. Its centrality is strongly reinforced by its twofold repetition at the end of the sentence, which suggests that the sentence itself is basically chiastic in structure. Verses 21-22 find an answering echo in the repeated ἔνδειξις τῆς δικαιοσύνης αὐτοῦ of vv. 25c and 26b. With the introduction of ἔνδειξις and its associated phrases, however, certain difficult problems that have traditionally accompanied their interpretation are raised, notably, the precise meaning of ἔνδειξις, and the meaning of the accusative with διά in v. 25d (and its following phrase). I will address these in detail in a later section. It should suffice here to note that Paul's main point is clearly the revelation of the final salvation of God.

4. *The Development of the Main Theme in Verses 22b-c and 24b-25b*

The paralysing scandal of Rom. 3.21-26 lies in Paul's prepositional phrases which develop this fundamentally Jewish notion. The central part of the section goes on to state that the specific point of revelation of God's salvation is Christ Jesus. That is, God's saving purpose and activity have now been made concrete, objective and manifest, the vehicle of that manifestation being Christ.[1] Paul goes on to describe the particular manner in which Christ represents God's salvation, but these are mere nuances of the primary statement that 'God's saving righteousness has now been revealed by means of Christ'. It is this surprisingly simple and clear proposition that must govern all subsequent interpretation of the section, and that also determines the section's function within the broader argument of the letter as a whole—and while we may think the proposition a somewhat obvious one (looking back from two millennia of familiarization), yet for Paul's readers, and for Paul himself at one point, this was no doubt a startling statement.

This basic proposition is developed by Paul within the rest of the section in terms of one major and one minor theme. The major theme comprises his detailed development of the manner and mode of Christ's revelation, which occupies most of the text (vv. 22b-25a). Then Paul gives this theme an added twist in the colon of v. 26d. Paul's christological revelation of God's salvation itself takes place in two stages. First, in the section's central portion of three instrumental διά phrases (vv. 22b-25a), Paul describes the specific aspects of Christ that comprise the revelation of the salvation of God. Then, secondly, in two parallel ἔνδειξις phrases (vv. 25b-26a), he emphasizes Christ's function as the singular eschatological sign or emblem of God's saving righteousness. I will discuss these last two points in turn.

As seen above, Paul brings together two groups of metaphors within the section's three central διά phrases, namely, the faithfulness of Christ, and his death as the final atoning sacrifice for sin. Both ideas occupy one διά unit, then they are combined together in a third summarizing phrase:

---

1.   The revelation is termed νῦν, because, from the perspective of salvation-history, it has taken place in the present, although technically Christ died and was raised in the immediate past. For Paul, the revelation of Christ's death and resurrection certainly also continues into the present whenever the gospel is preached and the Spirit of the Lord is present within and among his people.

διά πίστεως Ἰησοῦ Χριστοῦ
    εἰς πάντας τοὺς πιστεύοντας
διὰ τῆς ἀπολυτρώσεως τῆς ἐν Χριστῷ Ἰησοῦ
    ὃν προέθετο ὁ θεὸς ἱλαστήριον
διὰ τῆς πίστεως ἐν τῷ αὐτοῦ αἵματι.

Paul's use of πίστις here in relation to Christ is probably determined by, among other considerations, his messianic reading of Hab. 2.4 (which was cited at 1.17). πίστις no doubt describes Christ's obedience or faithfulness. Paul is also probably utilizing a dyad of atonement terms in vv. 24b-25a, namely, ἀπολύτρωσις and αἷμα, but these words are glossed metaphorically in context by the term ἱλαστήριον. This shifts the slightly ambiguous terminology of a redeeming death, possibly influenced by Graeco-Roman religion or simply commercial circles, towards the distinctively Jewish notion of supreme atonement, comprehensible in terms of *Yom Kippur*.[1] After this, Paul draws the two perspectives together and fuses them within v. 25b.

As a result, the central descriptive section raises the delicate question of how these two sets of metaphors are to be coordinated—if indeed they can and should be. Certainly, the third διά unit in v. 25b suggests some sort of correlation, since it boldly states that Christ's faithfulness is ἐν τῷ αὐτοῦ αἵματι. This presumably refers to the faithfulness demonstrated by his death. Thus it may be argued that throughout 3.21-26 πίστις refers to the faithfulness displayed as Christ accepted and endured the Cross.

Such an interpretation is reinforced by Paul's statement in v. 25d that the release from sins made possible by the Cross reveals the salvation of God. Here Paul's focus again seems to be on Calvary—and Phil. 2.5-11 may be cited as a precise Pauline analogue, although this evidence is weakened by its occurrence in a different (and possibly much later) letter.[2]

While this reading accords well, however, with the third διά unit of v. 25 and with v. 25d, it does not integrate so smoothly with the

---

1. It also seems impossible to determine precisely whether προέθετο means 'displayed [as]. . .' or 'intended [to be]. . .' a ἱλαστήριον. I would perhaps favour the latter, but not on any conclusive grounds (cf. Rom. 1.13, and Eph. 1.9 and context).

2. So Dunn *et al.* I would argue for a fairly short interval between the writing of Romans and of Philippians (approximately one year).

phrase τὸν ἐκ πίστεως Ἰησοῦ in v. 26. Here the believer lives 'out of', or 'on the basis of', the faithfulness of Christ. It may be countered that this statement is functioning metonymically to denote the basis of the believer's life in the atonement of Calvary, or, that the believer exists on the basis of, and within, the perfect obedience of Christ that led to and through death.

But at this point the importance of Christ's obedience within the rest of the letter should not be forgotten, particularly as it is described at 5.15-21 and 8.3-4. There, the two christological themes of 3.21-26 resurface as nodal points in God's salvation of humanity, although with slightly different metaphorical contexts and emphases. In ch. 8, Christ's obedience clearly suggests the condemnation of sin in the Cross (v. 3), but v. 4 also speaks of walking in the obedience of the Spirit: ἵνα τὸ δικαίωμα τοῦ νόμου πληρωθῇ ἐν ἡμῖν. This is a positive dimension of obedience that extends beyond the atonement of the Cross, but which must nevertheless be grounded in Christ himself.

Similarly, 5.19 states that διὰ τῆς ὑπακοῆς τοῦ ἑνὸς δίκαιοι κατασταθήσονται οἱ πολλοί. This may refer primarily to the one obedient act of the Cross, but such a reference is not certain. It could equally well denote a pervasive righteousness and obedience within Christ's entire life and ministry which reverses the disobedience of Adam.

Thus, while the dominant sense of πίστις in 3.21-26 seems to be the obedience of Christ in accepting and going to the Cross (so for v. 25a, b and d, and in precise analogy to Phil. 2.5-11), a broader sense of obedience cannot be excluded from vv. 22b and 26d. In these last statements Christ's πίστις may primarily suggest the faithfulness apparent in Calvary, but his entire life also functions as a revelation of God's saving purpose and activity. Both perspectives reveal God's will to save, and it is probably unnecessary to distinguish the one from the other too sharply.[1]

In sum, within the central section of διά phrases Paul describes the

---

1. Here a balance comparable with the Gospels is perhaps apparent, where the death of Christ is strongly emphasized, but an account of his ministry, however abbreviated, is always included. The Gospels are not truncated passion narratives, but passion accounts *with an introduction*, and so it is with Paul in Rom. 3.21-26. The Cross is dominant, but Jesus' life is also discernible as a revelation in its own right.

means by which God's saving purpose and activity is revealed. He primarily emphasizes Christ's death on the Cross as an atoning sacrifice that functions to deliver from sins, and within which Christ's steadfast obedience is also a singular testimony to God's desire to save humanity. But the faithfulness and obedience of the life of Jesus of Nazareth as a whole also seems implicit as a secondary and supporting revelation of God's salvation.

We might also note at this stage that, within the section of Rom. 3.21-26, God's atoning action in Christ is clearly expiatory, rather than propitiatory. All three of Christ's adjectives of atonement, along with their associated phrase, suggest the expunging of sins and transgressions—they are said to be redeemed, and atoned for sacrificially on analogy to *Yom Kippur* (although these two notions should probably not be separated too far from each other). This expiatory orientation of Paul's atonement terminology is reinforced by the dominant sense that God is actively saving believers through Christ: his activity throughout the passage is operative within this salvific mode. Thus, a theme of propitiation can only be introduced into Paul's words and understanding on the grounds that either the words themselves demand it (which seems dubious), or the surrounding context in Romans does.

The latter contention raises issues that extend far beyond our present purview. But we may perhaps note in passing that, while ὀργή is a distinct theme within 1.18–3.20 (cf. 1.18, 32; 2.5-10), hence justifying some reference in 3.21-26 to the assuaging of divine anger, the critical presupposition in this argument is that 3.21-26 is precisely correlated to 1.18–3.20 (much as 'solution' to 'problem').[1] The majority of commentators have of course assumed as much, but this correlation is not at all a simple one, and a case can be made for a rather different relationship between 3.21-26 and Paul's preceding arguments, which would undermine this contention fundamentally.[2]

---

1.   That is, in Rom. 1.18–3.20 Paul is understood to be 'setting the scene' for the proclamation of the gospel, by first establishing the universal culpability of humanity on independent grounds. After this somewhat depressing context has been established, Paul goes on in 3.21-26 to introduce the gospel and its offer of salvation, which is now perceived as necessary, and so will probably be accepted. So, argumentatively, the first section serves to drive the listener into the arms of the second.

2.   Cf. my 'Covenant and Contract in Rom. 1–4', as yet unpublished.

So suffice it at this point to note that any reading of Paul's atonement terms in 3.21-26 in a propitiatory sense depends on the importing of some notion of God's wrath into the section, on the basis of a traditional reading of 1.18–3.20.[1]

After describing the means by which God's salvation is revealed through Christ in this central cluster of διά phrases, Paul then concludes the sentence with three successive πρός/εἰς phrases, the first two of which repeat each other in an isocolic reduplication. This prepositional repetition comprises Paul's second development of his christological theme:

εἰς   ἔνδειξιν τῆς δικαιοσύνης αὐτοῦ
     διὰ τὴν πάρεσιν τῶν προγεγονότων ἁμαρτημάτων
     ἐν τῇ ἀνοχῇ τοῦ θεοῦ

πρὸς τὴν ἔνδειξιν τῆς δικαιοσύνης αὐτοῦ
     ἐν τῷ νῦν καιρῷ.

We must now turn to address the difficult problems asociated with this section, addressing first the meaning of the word ἔνδειξις.

5. The Isocolic Reduplication in Verses 25c-26c

In his significant analysis of πάρεσις, Werner Georg Kümmel also analysed ἔνδειξις.[2] He began by noting that the word (like πάρεσις) could take two closely related meanings: 'proof', or '(rational) demonstration' (*Beweis*—and Kümmel notes the large number of scholars who follow it, usually along with a reading of πάρεσις in terms of 'overlook'[3]); or 'demonstration', or 'show' (*Kundwerden,*

---

1.   Needless to say, such a move should also be supported by a broader analysis of the relationship between divine wrath and salvation in Paul. If the latter is more fundamental than the former, then any introduction of propitiatory connotations into a context dominated by expiation and salvation must be problematic.

2.   W.G. Kümmel, 'Πάρεσις und ἔνδειξις', pp. 154-67.

3.   'Πάρεσις und ἔνδειξις', p. 260 n. 1; namely, Zahn, Althaus, Dodd, Haering, Bardenhewer, Brunner, Gaugler, Wizsäcker and Albrecht, Moffatt, Holtzmann, Feine, Bultmann, BAGD, Teiger, Karner and V. Taylor.

Hinweis).[1] The difference between these two ideas is certainly difficult to address, because the semantic distance between 'demonstrate' and 'prove' is so slight (particularly in English, where a demonstration may be either a logical or rational proof, or an exhibition: cf. the German *Beweis* and *Erweis*). The point of contention in Rom. 3.25-26, according to Kümmel, is whether God is being described as either rationally (or forensically) 'proving' himself, as against merely demonstrating or exhibiting his nature in Christ.

Kümmel observes in his survey of the word's general usage that the noun is extremely rare,[2] but it is interesting to note the close use of the verb, which opens up a wider range of evidence.[3] Paul himself uses the noun in two places in addition to Rom. 3.25-26: in Phil. 1.28, probably in accordance with the meaning 'sign, index' (cf. LSJ, *s.v.* πάρεσις), which doesn't help us much, and in 2 Cor. 8.24, again in conjunction with the verb: τὴν οὖν ἔνδειξιν τῆς ἀγάπης ὑμῶν καὶ ἡμῶν καυχήσεως ὑπὲρ ὑμῶν εἰς αὐτοὺς ἐνδεικνύμενοι εἰς πρόσωπον τῶν ἐκκλησιῶν. Here 'demonstrate' and 'prove' (or both) seem possible meanings.[4]

---

1. He cites as authoritative forbears the Vulgate and Luther (*WA*, 7.39); also C.A.A. Scott, H. Lietzmann, W. Mundl, K. Barth, H.D. Wendland, E. Stauffer and A. Nygren [this last citation is questionable].

2. It does not occur in the LXX or papyri, according to Kümmel, 'Πάρεσις und ἔνδειξις', p. 263 n. 16. In extra-biblical sources, Kümmel cites Aeschines, *Epistles* 3.219, ἀπηνέχθη γὰρ ἡ κατὰ τοῦδε τοῦ ψηφίσματος γραφή, ἣν οὐχ ὑπὲρ τῆς πόλεως, ἀλλ' ὑπὲρ τῆς πρὸς Ἀλεξάνδρον ἐνδείξεώς με φῆς ἀπενεγκεῖν. πῶς ἂν οὖν ἐγὼ προενδεικνύμην Ἀλεξάνδρῳ. Here, 'demonstration' seems a likely translation.

3. In the following extra-biblical texts 'demonstrate' seems the best interpretation: Thucydides 4.126: τὸ εὔψυχον ἐν τῷ ἀσφαλεῖ ὀξεῖς ἐνδείκνυνται; Aristophanes, *Plutos* 785: ἐνδεικνύμενος ἕκαστος εὔνοιάν τινα; Demosthenes 21.145: τῷ σώματι τὴν εὔνοιαν οὐ χρήμασι οὐδὲ λόγοις ἐνεδείξατο τῇ πατρίδι; Herodianus, *Ab excessu divi Marci* 2.10.9 (63): πᾶσαν ἐνεδείκνυντο προθυμίαν καὶ σπουδήν; and POxy. 3.494.9: εὐνοούσῃ μοι καὶ πᾶσαν πίστιν μοι ἐνδεικνυμένῃ. Cf. BAGD's citation (p. 262) of evidence from the verb for the meaning 'prove': Polybius 3.38.5; Philo, *Op. Mund.* 45; 87; Plutarch, *Pericles* 31. 1.

4. 'Demonstrate' seems the best translation for the verb in Rom. 2.15; 9.17 (Exod. 9.16), 22; and Eph. 2.7. Cf. also 1 Tim. 1.16; Tit. 2.10 and 3.2, where it occurs in conjunction with μακροθυμία, ἐπιεικεῖς, πραΰτης, and ἀμάχος. Cf. Heb. 6.10, 11. 2 Tim. 4.14 is best understood neither as 'prove' nor 'demonstrate',

Thus, while Kümmel himself favours the rendering 'demonstrate',[1] it can be seen that his array of linguistic evidence is (and he admits this) rather inconclusive. We may certainly dismiss a crude sense of 'proof' as unlikely, but we are unable to distinguish between more nuanced readings of the same position. Depending on the interpretation of ἔνδειξις, two rather different readings are still possible for this particular unit and, consequently, for the final statements of 3.21-26.

On the one hand, Paul could be saying that the righteousness of God has been revealed for the purpose simply of displaying his righteousness. In other words, God's final justification is himself, as John Piper argues.[2] On the other hand, Paul might be stating that Christ and the Cross function as a sign or emblem of God's desire to save. Thus, Christ is the focal point of God's righteousness.

but LSJ's 'indictment' (p. 558: I, 2 and the examples there). The evidence from δείκνυμι also suggests 'demonstrate', where 22 occurrences suggest 'point out, show', and only two (Mt. 16.21, Acts 10.28) suggest 'prove' (BAGD, p. 172). Paul himself seems to prefer ἐνδείκνυμι, since he only uses δείκνυμι at 1 Cor. 12.31, but has nine out of the twelve NT uses of ἐνδείκνυμι, and the only four instances of the noun.

It is also interesting to note that ἔνδειξις often occurs in conjunction with a 'quality' which is being demonstrated: in 2 Corinthians Paul asks for a demonstration specifically of ἀγάπη, although in the extra-biblical texts the quality is often εὔνοια (Aristophanes, Demosthenes and the POxy.). In the biblical references, the verb is often associated with μακροθυμία, πραΰτης, ἐπιείκεια, and ἀμάχος. Interestingly, μακροθυμία occurs alongside χρηστότης and ἀνοχή in Rom. 2.4. The implication of these combinations is that when ἔνδειξις occurs, ἀνοχή is one of a cluster of several possible words that one would expect to occur in the context, as a designation of the particular (virtuous) quality being demonstrated. Rom. 3.25b-26 is just such an instance, where ἀνοχή explicates both πάρεσις and the demonstration of God's righteousness.

1.   Kümmel also reasons from the immediate context that the translation of ἔνδειξις by 'proof' in vv. 25-26 is awkward, not merely in the passage itself, but within the whole framework of NT (and biblical) theology. God is never, Kümmel argues, really required to 'prove' himself to anyone; he acts sovereignly out of grace. Thus, although both the meanings 'demonstrate' and '(rationally) prove' are formally possible on extra-biblical grounds, the argument from Pauline and NT usage suggests that 'demonstration' is to be preferred.

2.   'The Demonstration of the Righteousness of God in Romans 3.24-26', *JSNT* 7 (1980), pp. 2-32; *idem, The Justification of God: An Exegetical and Theological Study of Romans 9.1-23* (Grand Rapids: Baker, 1983).

These readings are far from being compatible, since they involve quite significant differences of emphasis. Yet their semantic integration with the section is so tight that it is almost impossible to decide between them. At this point we must therefore carefully address the immediate context of the word's twofold occurrence in Rom. 3.21-26 in an attempt to resolve its meaning. I wish to argue that, on balance, the 'christological' reading should be preferred over the more theocentric reading—but this conclusion is based on delicate grounds, to say the least. I will evaluate the more theocentric reading suggested by Piper first.

A theocentric understanding reads the two ἔνδειξις units in dependence primarily on Paul's opening statement, δικαιοσύνη θεοῦ πεφανέρωται, assuming that the intervening section of διά units is a largely self-contained and separate development of the section's subject. It interprets the prepositions εἰς and πρός in a purposive or goal-oriented sense. As a result, the passage is understood to state that the revelation of God's righteousness (so v. 21) has the purpose, or goal, of a display of his righteousness. To paraphrase: 'The righteousness of God has been made known (by means of Christ), for the purpose of a display of his righteousness'.

This might initially appear tautologous—that God's righteousness has been revealed to make known his righteousness—but ἔνδειξις develops the verb φανερόω in a specific sense. The revelation of God's righteousness is not simply a making known *per se*, but a vindication, and a certainly deliberate display or placarding of his will and power. It is therefore not a proof, as if God had to justify himself to humanity. Nor is it ostentatious, as if God were vainly exhibiting his character. It is an assertion that God's revelation is ultimately intended to result in a (legitimate) glorification of himself.[1]

This reading has the advantage of integrating with Paul's theology elsewhere,[2] and with his use of the verb ἐνδείκνυμι in Rom. 9.17 (a quotation of Exod. 9.16) and, perhaps less obviously, with its occurrence in 9.22. Admittedly, the function of the verb need not help our reading of the noun but, as we have seen, the noun itself is so scarce in

---

1.   This is an interpretation that Kümmel seems to have overlooked in his discussion of two main interpretative alternatives for the word, namely, *Hinweis* or *Beweis*.

2.   Cf. Eph. 1.13-14; 2.4-7.

both Paul and extra-biblical writings, and the verb is so closely linked to the noun by Paul in 2 Cor. 8.24, that this argument carries more weight than might otherwise be the case.

It is also grammatically permissible for the prepositional phrases to reach back and to modify the opening noun and verb in the passage.[1] Paul often utilizes a broadly chiastic pattern when arguing, returning to his main theme after an intervening discussion. Thus, the pattern of 3.21-26 could well be the typically Semitic one of A–B–A, with v. 21 constituting the dominant subject, the διά units of vv. 22-25a the intervening discussion, and vv. 25b-26 a resumption of the main theme. In short, it could be an *inclusio*.

Furthermore, a theocentric reading is reasonably integrated with the preceding argument. Paul has just stated that all of humanity, including Israel, is under sin, and is therefore doomed to condemnation and punishment on the Last Day. Especially in view of the apparent ineffectiveness of circumcision and the law, this whole scenario might be seen seriously to question God's essential goodness and his desire to save. But in 3.21-26 Paul responds to this implicit objection with the assertion that God has made his salvation known, and that this salvation is not grounded in humanity or Israel, but in God's right to demonstrate, display and glorify his own character. Thus, the anthropocentric objection to God's judgment is doubly undermined. Not only is God, in fact, a saving God, but salvation arises from the nature of his own character and not the plaintive demands of a corrupt humanity.

The only real stylistic problem with this interpretation concerns the διά phrase that begins in v. 25b: διὰ τὴν πάρεσιν τῶν προγεγονότων ἁμαρτημάτων ἐν τῇ ἀνοχῇ τοῦ θεοῦ. This statement is hard to integrate smoothly into a theocentric reading. It is axiomatic that the preposition should be interpreted, if at all possible, in its standard *Koine* sense, in this instance, 'because of'.[2] Failing this, resort can be

---

1. A formal grammatical analysis of the prepositions is of little help here in view of their characteristic fluidity of meaning and flexible function (cf. BAGD, pp. 228-30, 709-11; Moule, *Idiom Book*, p. 48).

2. More fully, 'because of', 'on account of', 'inasmuch as', 'since' (BAGD [p. 181] is a little confusing here, lumping purposive and causal meanings together, and suggesting a possible instrumental sense). The instrumental sense is almost unattested—or, at least, the occurrences are disputable—relying primarily on Rev. 12.11 and 13.14 (cf. Moule, *Idiom Book*, pp. 54-55). It is used as something

made to the far less commonly attested purposive sense, 'for the sake of' or 'with a view to', which is used occasionally by Paul.[1] The so-called instrumental sense, borrowed from the genitive with διά, seems dubious, and particularly so in the present context (if Paul intended a genitive meaning, why did he not just use that case—as he has three times immediately previously?).

It remains true, no matter how this range of possible prepositional meanings is combined with the various readings of πάρεσις argued by Käsemann and Kümmel, that the clause proves awkward for Piper's overarching interpretation. In effect, the preposition asks for God's πάρεσις and ἀνοχή to function either as a cause (on a causal reading), or as a purpose or goal (the less well-attested purposive sense). Either of these alternatives, however, contradicts the theocentric motivation for God's display that Piper sees in the passage, since both supply additional causes or motives for the revelation of God's righteousness.

The full force of the preposition must be appreciated at this point, that is, the idea of causality. It makes little sense to say that God displays his saving power *because of* a deliverance from sins, or, in other words, that a deliverance from sins *causes* God's display of righteousness. Read literally, this is nonsense. Alternatively, assuming that a purpose or intention to redeem from sins is the cause, it undermines the motivation just given, namely, that God's righteousness has originally been made known *because of* God's wish to display himself—a genitive with διά would be much more comprehensible at this point, but Paul does not use one.

---

of an escape-hatch for the present passage (for example, by Käsemann), and should only be resorted to when all else fails.

1. Suggested by D.S. Sharp, 'For our Justification', *ExpTim* 39 (1927–28), pp. 87-90; see criticism by V. Taylor, 'Great Texts Reconsidered', *ExpTim* 50 (1938–39), pp. 295-300. H.G. Meecham's demonstration of the extreme rarity of the construction in classical and Hellenistic Greek attempts to curtail this possibility ('Romans iii, 25f., iv, 25—The Meaning of διά with the Accusative', *ExpTim* 50 [1938–39], p. 564). His case is weakened, however, by occurrence of διά in Rom. 4.23, 24, and 25, where no other sense seems possible. Hence 3.25d, on analogy and in context, could well be rendered 'for the sake of the forgiveness of previously committed transgressions' (cf. also Mk 11.27), and it would seem that the well-attested modern Greek prospective sense was already germinating in the first century (so Moule, *Idiom Book*, p. 55).

Instead of emphasizing the notion of display in ἔνδειξις, however, and so relating the units to the passage's governing phrase δικαιοσύνη θεοῦ πεφανέρωται, ἔνδειξις may be read to mean sign or index, and the *reduplicatio* related to the immediately preceding section where Christ functions as the means by which God's revelation has been made known. For this reading, vv. 25b-26a continue to describe the *means* by which God's righteousness has been revealed, that is, Christ, and not its overarching *purpose*. By introducing the motif of ἔνδειξις, Paul would be stressing that Christ's revelation functions as a sign of God's righteousness. Thus, the overall point of the passage is not so much that God's righteousness has been manifested for the purpose of display, but that Christ is the definitive means and vehicle of its revelation. To paraphrase: 'Now God's saving righteousness has been made known by means of Jesus Christ. . ., for a (tangible) sign of his saving righteousness. . ., so that (he might be) *the* sign of his saving righteousness'.

It is the particular advantage of this reading that the causal meaning of διά can be given its full weight. The clause states that Christ functions as the sign of God's saving righteousness *because* in his atoning death on the Cross, and in the deliverance it procures, God's saving intention is made plain. In short, the Cross makes the saving purpose of God apparent. Its public redemption causes the revelation of God's salvation (and not the salvation itself).

Hence, the causality of v. 25b consists in the Cross causing the sign to function as an effective revelation, and it is the emphasis on Christ as sign, rather than the broader idea of God's purpose of display, that allows this smoother reading. Liberation from sins can function as the cause of a sign's effectiveness when that sign reveals a saving will, but it cannot function as the cause of a display of God's righteousness or as the cause of a revelation. Neither is an ultimate concern for deliverance compatible with an ultimately theocentric ground of action.

This reading in terms of Christ as the definitive sign of God's righteousness also enjoys a series of related semantic advantages, which although rather fragile in their own right, nevertheless serve to strengthen the above contention. Such a reading accords precisely with Paul's use of the noun elsewhere. In 2 Cor. 8.24 and Phil. 1.28, ἔνδειξις means the visible evidence of a hidden quality. In the case of the Corinthians, a generous contribution to the collection will be a concrete manifestation of their love for Paul. At Philippi, the fearlessness of the believers and their unity is a present, visible sign of the coming judgment on their persecutors. Here in Rom. 3.25-26, Christ is the objective, physical manifestation of God's hidden saving purpose and power. He is the visible point at which that invisible quality has been made known.

The reading also integrates more smoothly with the following phrase, ἐν τῇ ἀνοχῇ τοῦ θεοῦ. If it is emphasized in v. 25b that a display of God's righteousness is taking place, then the stress on God throughout makes the reintroduction of θεός at v. 26 somewhat redundant. It is not for this reason impermissible, but it is stylistically a little rough.[1] If the unit is read with an emphasis on Christ as the sign of God's saving righteousness, however, then the reaffirmation that this visible index is ultimately grounded in the grace and forbearance of God appears as a significant and fully integrated statement. It returns the emphasis in the section from Christ to God: '[Christ functions] as the sign of his saving righteousness, because of the deliverance from sins previously committed, in the forbearance of God'.

The christological reading also takes προγίνομαι where it stands, that is, as modifying ἁμαρτημάτων, and the participle does not need to be wrenched out of its immediate context in an attempt to focus the whole phrase on the past (as, for example, Käsemann's interpretation demands).

Finally, such a reading also seems superior in terms of linearity (although this principle should be used with caution). One cannot help suspecting that Piper's affirmation of the theocentric nature of 3.21-26 depends heavily on his reading of the theocentric argumentation in 9.6-23 (the subject of his monograph). But this is to use argumentation that comes considerably later on in the letter from 3.21-26, and one may question how closely connected the two sections are. From the perspective of the writer, the reader and the listener, it is better to look to the *preceding* argument, before later considerations are mobilized.[2] And in terms of preceding material, the christological reading

1.   It reads: 'God's righteousness has been revealed. . .for a display of his (i.e. God's) saving righteousness, (comprehensible) because of the deliverance from sins committed previously, in the forbearance of God'. A second use of αὐτοῦ would perhaps be better.

2.   This is not to deny that Paul thinks ahead when he writes his letters! But to use later material as an interpretative control is methodologically difficult in that evidence must be given for the relevance of a particular section. Theoretically, the entire

is argumentatively more integrated than the theocentric reading.

The earlier discussion in Romans, while strongly theocentric, does not suggest the elements of vindication, self-glorification and display that are so apparent in ch. 9. Rather, the first part of Romans speaks of the need of humanity and of Israel for salvation apart from the traditionally trusted vehicles of covenant, circumcision and law. In 3.21, Paul then makes the revolutionary statement that God's eschatological saving righteousness has now been made known by means of Christ, and it seems more consistent with this theme that vv. 25-26 should continue to speak of Christ's concretization of that salvation, rather than that Paul should turn to speak of God's self-glorification through it. Both readings are theologically acceptable and argumentatively possible, but a christological reading is more continuous with what precedes. Over against the failure of circumcision and the law to produce righteousness (with the consequent threat to the whole notion of a covenantal God), in 3.21 Paul states:

> But now, the saving righteousness of God has been made known by means of Christ. . . who is *the sign* of his salvation, because of the deliverance procured by means of the Cross, which is grounded in the forbearance and grace of God; he is *the sign* of his saving righteousness in the present time. . .

To summarize our findings concerning the isocolic reduplication in vv. 25c-26c: the accusative with διά functions in its usual causal sense, and the reduplication as a whole states that Christ and his Cross function as the definitive sign and manifestation of God's righteousness *because* the deliverance effected by the atonement makes God's saving purpose clear.

6. *The* Clausula *in Verse 26d*

It now remains only to assess the importance and function of the section's clausula. In v. 26d Paul gives his main theme a final departing twist. Whereas throughout most of the section Paul has been concentrating on the revelation of God's salvation in Christ, he goes

---

letter can be used to elucidate earlier statements. And one may question why Rom. 9 is more relevant to 3.21-26 than, for example, 10.1-10 (which uses δικαιοσύνη θεοῦ far more), or ch. 14 (which speaks of certain ethical consequences from Christ's death; cf. esp. vv. 9 and 15).

on to say that the ultimate purpose of this revelation is that God might actively rightwize the individual by means of it. In short, having set forth the Cross, God reaches out through it to make the believer righteous.

This is an important theological addition to the passage's main point because Christ is thereby defined, not as an end in himself, but as the means to an end. He is a focal point without which all else is impossible, but he is not an endpoint. The Cross therefore remains a mediation, incomplete in itself. At the end of his exalted presentation of Christ and his Cross, Paul seems deliberately to prevent the revelation of God's saving righteousness from becoming a mere artifact or a sterile dogma. It functions within the broader goal of the salvation of humanity.[1]

7. Some Final Observations

As a result of this, it can be seen that buried underneath the elegant metaphors and constructions of Rom. 3.21-26 is a theology of the Cross.[2] This theme certainly resonates with other Pauline writings[3] (although such links do not themselves constitute evidence for the presence of the motif in Rom. 3.21-26). But Paul's understanding of Christ's revelatory function in Rom. 3.21-26 is unmistakable. His primary focus is on the events leading up to and through the death of Christ. Consequently, the Cross constitutes the eschatological revelation of the saving righteousness of God (subject to the qualifier noted previously, that Christ's life is also significant, although in a subordinate sense).

But the very indirection of Paul's introduction of this stock motif raises a significant question. Why is Paul's presentation of this theme in Rom. 3.21-26 so unusually elliptical, metaphorical and crafted? In short, why is Paul being so indirect? A possible explanation for his measured presentation in Rom. 3.21-26 may lie in the nature of his audience. Boasting and disorder and, in particular an aggressive

---

1.   Cf. 1.16: δύναμις. . . θεοῦ ἐστιν εἰς σωτηρίαν παντὶ τῷ πιστεύοντι.

2.   Using 'the Cross' as a summary phrase for a cluster of essentially theological ideas in Paul, and not as a specific reference to Paul's own use of σταυρός.

3.   Notably 1 Cor. 1.17–2.8; 2 Corinthians *passim*, esp. 13.4; and Gal. 2.20; 6.12, 14.

intellectualism, at Corinth—a church also within Paul's apostolic jurisdiction (as he defines it)—demanded an abrupt response couched in terms of σταυρός and its reversal of worldly values such as wisdom. Similarly, the undermining of Paul's mission in Galatia sparked a heated and polemical response: 'circumcision or crucifixion'! But the Jewish-Christian leadership at Rome (and, it may be surmised, simply the Jews), no doubt required a more sensitive approach. The slogans of the Galatian and Corinthian correspondence would have been far too abrasive and offensive in this context, and a crucified messiah a major stumbling-block to Paul's presentation of his gospel.

Consequently, Paul still glories in the Cross in Rom. 3.21-26, but it is a scandal presented eloquently and carefully in terms of its fulfilment of Scripture, its analogy to *Yom Kippur*, and the supreme faithfulness and obedience of its messianic protagonist. It is a *theologia crucis* redefined. Here, in fact, the Cross seems less of a scandal than a final consummation of God's saving purposes. To be sure, the tragedy and horror of the crucifixion can still be seen within Paul's rhetoric. But the humiliating life and death of Jesus are still presented in almost poetic form as a symbol worthy of their role as the manifestation of God's eschatological salvation.

Closely related to this observation that a submerged theology of the Cross seems to be operative in 3.21-26, is the perception that Paul's depiction is decidedly Jewish.[1] His universalist theme is confined strictly to the parenthesis of vv. 22b-24a, which we have already separated from the text's main thrust as something of a retrospective interruption. But even here it should be noted that Paul's argument in terms of the eschatological restoration of Adam's lost glory is a theme only comprehensible to Jews. And the two remaining secondary points are strongly Jewish in their allusions to works of Torah and to the testimony of the OT.

In addition to this, the ideas and metaphors of Paul's main semantic structure are again thoroughly Jewish in tone. The governing phrase in the passage, δικαιοσύνη θεοῦ, seems deliberately chosen to

---

1. A point noted by Kertelge, although in his commentary the Jewishness consists specifically of covenant-theology (and this notion is grounded in a reading of πάρεσις as 'pass over', *The Epistle to the Romans* [trans. F. McDonagh; New York: Herder & Herder, 1972], p. 48).

resonate against the backdrop of the Jewish Scriptures and contemporary Jewish religious discussions. The repeated references to Christ's faithfulness are comprehensible within the understanding of the righteous person prevalent within late Second Temple Judaism, a notion strongly conditioned by martyrology and the value it placed on suffering on behalf of God and the *torah*—and Paul's precise wording here may only be illuminated completely by the scriptural text of Hab. 2.4. The metaphors of atonement are explained in terms of the Jewish feast of *Yom Kippur*. Finally, the broader ideas of the dawning *eschaton* and its salvation are only really coherent within a Jewish theological and historical framework. In short, Rom. 3.21-26 is a mosaic of Jewish themes.

We may therefore conclude that Rom. 3.21-26 depicts, in remarkably elegant and balanced terms, a theology of the Cross. The dawning of God's salvation coincides with Calvary and the suffering of its victim. But Paul's presentation of this powerful and disturbing image utilizes distinctly Jewish metaphors and allusions. It would seem therefore that in Rom. 3.21-26 Paul has crafted an apologetic and Jewish theology of the Cross.

Having presented this suggested reading of the text, the analysis is nevertheless not complete without some indication, however brief, of its implications. I venture to submit at this point discussions of three notions that are *not* found within Rom. 3.21-26:

1. Rom. 3.21-26 is often read, as we have previously noted, in terms of a theodicy of atonement. According to this reading, the section describes the reconciliation effected between the justice and the mercy of God by means of Christ's atoning death. Within the Cross, the apparent tolerance of sin in the past is smoothly combined with a just judgment on it in the present *and* with the salvation of the actual sinner.

But our reading suggests that such a theodicy is not the primary semantic thrust of Rom. 3.21-26. Paul is presenting Christ as the focal point of God's eschatological salvation, with the ultimate purpose of saving the (perhaps generic) individual who lives out of his faithfulness. It must be noted, however, that this present focus does not *exclude* such a theology from Paul. It merely removes this particular text from its orbit. It is probably fair to claim that a theology of the atonement is present within the section, that is, specifically within its atonement terminology and within the subordinate statement of v. 25d. But the crucial point to note is that, while this theology is discernible, *Paul himself is not at present occupied with it.* That is, the text's present focus is something different, namely, that the atoning function of the Cross *reveals God's desire to save.* Consequently, any interpretation which emphasizes a theodicy of the atonement in Rom. 3.21-26 really mistakes a secondary and largely unstated consideration for the text's primary meaning. Such an interpretation, therefore, simply misses the point.[1]

2. A second implication within the suggested reading is that Rom. 3.21-26 is an authentic expression of Paul's theology. More precisely, Rom. 3.21-26 does not quote or cite early church material. Certainly, principles and individual terms from the early church are apparent (particularly in Paul's atonement terms), but this is true of a great deal of Paul's discourse, and it would be foolish—and unnecessary— to deny this. Rom. 3.21-26, however, has often been read as so strongly influenced by such material that Paul's *syntax* and *argument* are conditioned by it. That is, whole phrases and clauses have been assumed to be incorporated within his argument. This is untenable, however. The integrated stylistic form of the entire section is disrupted if any part of it (with the exception of its parentheses) is removed. Thus, either *the entire section* is an early church confession (minus the asides), or none of it is.[2] On balance, I would suggest the origin of the passage within Paul rather than within the early church,

---

1. One cannot help noting in passing the possible origin of this reading in a theological agenda. If the text is read from an anthropological and soteriological perspective, then this sense, which responds to such an agenda, no doubt seems the most important within the text. Moreover, an apologetic desire to resolve the apparent contradiction between God's mercy and his justice can only strengthen such a reading.

2. I have already discussed this possibility briefly in Chapters 1 and 2. There we noted that it is an automatic concomitant of such a position that all the material within the section has to be grounded within the early church, and not within Paul. This includes the verb and concept of φανερόω, the phrase ἐν Χριστῷ Ἰησοῦ of v. 24b, the eschatological emphasis on νῦν in vv. 21 and 26, the verbal form εἰς τὸ εἶναι... and the terms and notions of δίκαιος and δικαιόω, not to mention δικαιοσύνη θεοῦ. Such a relocation of theology and terminology is certainly possible, but in view of the large number of clearly Pauline themes, it seems unlikely.

if 'origin' is understood in terms of syntactical and theological shaping. We cannot penetrate further than this into the question of the text's origin within Paul.

3. It may also be noted briefly that the doctrine of universal justification by faith is not really present within the passage. Certain elements from this theory are present, but even then only as secondary ideas. The specific theme of universality, while a legitimate argumentative emphasis within the letter as a whole, is limited to Paul's parenthesis, and hence is retrospective and secondary within 3.21-26. Similarly, the individual believer's faith is present only at v. 22b, in Paul's favoured εἰς construction (cf. 1.16b)[1]—Paul's use of πίστις is really dominated by Christ's faithfulness, which is mentioned three times in the passage. Finally, justification, in the sense of a forensic declaration of righteousness before God, is not really present within the section either. Paul's use of δικαιόω is really stronger and broader than this, being completely dominated in context by the ideas of eschatology and salvation. And possibly there is also a notion implicit within it that the believer has been transformed, on analogy to (and by incorporation within) the resurrected Christ, by means of baptismal participation. Certainly, forensic emphases and images are entirely absent: they must be found (if they are to be found) within the immediate connotations of the words themselves.

In sum, my reading of Rom. 3.21-26 suggests that universality is a minor, retrospective theme in it; that believing faith (on the part of the Christian) is a muted theme; and that justification and the doctrine of justification by faith are not present there at all. It now remains only to note briefly the function of Rom. 3.21-26 within its broader argumentative context,[2] where the starting point must again be the interpretative conclusions reached concerning Rom. 3.21-26 based on its lexical, stylistic and contextual dimensions.

As we have seen, Rom. 3.21-26 makes the essentially simple point

---

1. This allusory presence need not be taken as implying any lack of approval. It may simply have been assumed by Paul (as by much of the early church and contemporary Judaism).

2. This question can only be addressed superficially here, because a complete answer would require a detailed exegesis of the section's context as a whole—a task that clearly lies beyond the bounds of the present study.

that Christ, and above all his death, is the definitive eschatological revelation of the saving righteousness of God. This point responds to Paul's previous argument that all of humanity, including Israel, stands in need of salvation. Therefore, where law, circumcision and good works have failed, the vehicle of salvation for both Jew and Greek is Christ and the Cross. Humanity has not been abandoned, and neither has God's obligation to Israel been overlooked. In his own time God has stretched out his arm to save.

As such, although the section makes an *important* point, and makes it with unusual elegance, it would be exaggerating to say that it makes *the dominant point* within Paul's entire letter. That Christ saves can hardly be regarded as the heart of Romans, since presumably most of the Roman Christians already knew this. Thus, Rom. 3.21-26 is probably neither the thesis paragraph of the letter, nor even perhaps a programmatic statement of Paul's gospel.[1] It is a carefully crafted step in the first broad stage of his argument—a 'hinge' rather than a 'fulcrum'.[2] In it Paul presents a theology of the Cross in essentially Jewish terms, stating that God's eschatological salvation is found in Christ and Calvary. Rom. 3.21-26 offers an elegant and poignant statement of this point, and our understanding of Paul's letter to the Romans will be considerably increased if this simple but significant assertion concerning the gospel is kept in mind when reading it.

I would translate the passage as follows:

> But now the final saving righteousness of God has been revealed (apart from the works of law, although witnessed to by the law and the prophets): a righteousness of God revealed through the faithfulness of Jesus Christ, for everyone who believes (for there is no difference: everyone sinned and lacks the glorious image of God, being saved by his grace as a gift); revealed through the redemption which is in Christ Jesus, whom God intended to be a supremely atoning sacrifice for sin; revealed through the faithfulness in his bloody death; so that he, Christ, might be the sign of his saving righteousness, because of the release from sins committed beforehand, in God's mercy; so he might be the sign of his saving righteousness in the present time; so that he (that is, God) might be right in the very act of setting right the one who lives out of the faithfulness of Jesus.

---

1. If the six verses in Rom. 3.21-26 are Paul's gospel, then a lot is unexplained!
2. Byrne, *Reckoning*, p. 78.

Appendix 1

THE SIGNIFICANCE OF HABAKKUK 2.4 FOR
τὸν ἐκ πιστέως Ἰησοῦ

A further argument in favour of a subjective genitive reading of πίστεως Ἰησοῦ Χριστοῦ derives from the observation that the meaning of the phrase τὸν ἐκ πίστεως Ἰησοῦ in Rom. 3.26 may be controlled by Paul's reading of Hab. 2.4, as cited in 1.17. This would in turn influence the interpretation of the two earlier occurrences of πίστις in the passage at vv. 22 and 25.[1]

It is seldom noted that the πίστις Χριστοῦ genitive phrases in the Pauline corpus have an unusually striking configuration. Paul only uses ἐκ πίστεως in those letters that also quote Hab. 2.4 (that is, Galatians and Romans). But in those letters where πίστις is such a significant motif, this specific construction occurs some 21 times. In the same letters it also occurs in a clear stylistic parallel to the phrase διὰ πίστεως Ἰησοῦ Χριστοῦ or its equivalent (cf. Rom. 3.22-26, esp. 3.30; Gal. 2.16; 3.12-14; and possibly Phil. 3.9). It therefore seems possible that Paul's use of Hab. 2.4 underlies, or at least is significantly related to, many of his problematic πίστις genitives. His reading of Hab. 2.4, particularly at Rom. 1.17, may even comprise the semantic cornerstone for his entire network of πίστις Χριστοῦ expressions.[2] So Paul's specific understanding of Hab. 2.4 may shed considerable light on the entire dispute, if it can be ascertained.[3]

The critical section of text for our present purposes is Rom. 1.16-18, where Paul quotes Hab. 2.4. In these three verses we find an intricate web of semantic relationships. Most importantly, the quotation of Hab. 2.4 in v. 17b is prefigured by the occurrence of the phrase ἐκ πίστεως in 17a, allowing the investigation of the same phrase from two different perspectives. But certain contextual features must be noted here before the disputed πίστις phrases are examined:

1. Paul has inserted a theological summary into his epistolary prologue (vv. 1-4): εὐαγγέλιον θεοῦ ὃ προεπηγγείλατο διὰ τῶν προφητῶν αὐτοῦ ἐν γραφαῖς ἁγίαις, περὶ τοῦ υἱοῦ αὐτοῦ κτλ.; a summary further reinforced by the parenthesis

---

1. Because Hab. 2.4 is quoted at the beginning of the letter, not because 3.26 is retroactive!

2. Cf. my 'The Meaning of ΠΙΣΤΙΣ and ΝΟΜΟΣ in Paul: A Linguistic and Structural Perspective', *JBL* (forthcoming).

3. With respect to the meaning of 3.26, it is only necessary to consider whether ἐκ πίστεως in 1.17 refers to the believer or to Christ, since the phrase in 3.26 clearly precludes a reference to God—τὸν ἐκ πίστεως Ἰησοῦ can only mean the believer's faith in Jesus, or one who lives 'out of' Jesus' own faith.

of v. 9: θεός—ᾧ λατρεύω ἐν τῷ πνεύματί μου ἐν τῷ εὐαγγελίῳ τοῦ υἱοῦ αὐτοῦ. This clearly establishes the gospel as the central theme in the proem (vv. 1-17), and the Son as the content of the gospel. One would expect this theme to be maintained in some sense through vv. 16b-17, unless it is otherwise indicated.

Verse 16b does, in fact, continue this theme. It states that the gospel is the power of God, effecting as its goal the salvation of everyone who believes (whether Jew or Greek). This pattern of a statement concerning substance being followed by a statement concerning purpose is also significant for v. 17.

2. Verse 17a is constructed in a close stylistic parallel to 16b with a subject in the form of a compound genitive using θεοῦ, a post-positive γάρ, and a final purposive clause beginning with εἰς. But what is seldom noticed at this point is that two translations of this critical opening clause are initially possible. The sentence reads δικαιοσύνη γὰρ θεοῦ ἐν αὐτῷ ἀποκαλύπτεται κτλ. This may be read, on the one hand (paraphrasing): 'the righteousness of God, which is in the gospel, is being revealed. . .' Here ἐν αὐτῷ is read almost parenthetically, and the stress is placed on the present revelation of God's righteousness. On the other hand, the phrase may be read: 'the righteousness of God is being revealed within the gospel. . .' Here the stress is placed on ἐν αὐτῷ, and the clause emphasizes the gospel, at this point stating that it reveals God's righteousness (in the former, the prepositional phrase functions adjectivally; in the latter, as an agent or instrument of the verb).

In view of the first two points made above, the latter certainly seems the better reading. It continues the proem's emphasis on the gospel, and it parallels the strong emphasis of v. 16 on what the gospel *is*.[1] Thus, v. 17a is best read as a statement that the gospel contains a revelation of the righteousness of God, just as v. 16 states that the gospel is a power intended to save the believer.

3. Paul's use of ἐκ πίστεως in 17a is also a clear stylistic anticipation of his quotation of Hab. 2.4 in 17b. So any explanation of the section must interpret the two phrases in parallel, in a manner that also makes sense of the later quotation from Scripture. The alternative possibility—of explaining how they differ—is a difficult position to argue.

The occurrence of ἐκ πίστεως in v. 17a is discussed first. There are three possible references for ἐκ πίστεως in v. 17a. (1) It may refer to the faithfulness of God, and so the sentence would read, 'the righteousness of God is being revealed in the gospel, [that event springing] from the faithfulness of God'. Here a presuppositional or causal ἐκ reads better than an instrumental sense, and the phrase signifies that the revelation of God's righteousness arises out of his faithfulness.[2] (2) It may refer to the faithfulness of Christ: 'the righteousness of God is being revealed in the

---

1. On either reading, the concluding purposive εἰς clauses should be read in parallel and with reference to the believer. So in both verses Paul states clearly that the goal of the gospel is found in the belief of the individual (at this point, probably a generic figure)—it is also interesting to note that here a participial phrase in v. 16 is reproduced by a substantive phrase in v. 17a; thus Paul can use both πιστεύω and πίστις to refer to the faith of the believer.

2. As already pointed out, however, this option need not be considered with respect to Rom. 3.21-26.

gospel, by means of the faithfulness of Christ, for the believer'. Here the phrase signifies that Christ's faithfulness constitutes the concrete revelation of God's righteousness in the gospel. The ἐκ is instrumental and the sentence remains focused on the substance of the gospel. (3) It may refer to the faith of the believer: 'the righteousness of God is revealed in the gospel, by means of the faith of the believer and for that faith'. This last interpretation must now be explored further.

It is crucial to grasp the exact function of the disputed phrase in the third reading. Faith is best understood here as the means by which the believer appropriates the revelation of God's righteousness in the gospel. In short, it is instrumental, and so the sentence as a whole reads: 'the righteousness of God is revealed in the gospel, being understood by means of faith, and with the goal of faith'. But this reading generates certain problems.

The comment shifts the focus of the discussion away from the gospel itself to its means of appropriation. This is not an incidental shift—the appropriation of the gospel would constitute the crowning point of the proem. But the proem has not previously been particularly concerned with appropriation. It has focused emphatically on the content of the gospel itself. In vv. 2-4 Paul interrupted his epistolary opening to specify its content with what is probably a solemn liturgical statement, repeating the point parenthetically in v. 9. He did the same in v. 16 and v. 17a, where the gospel was characterized as a power effecting salvation and as a revelation of God's righteousness.

Individual appropriation is admittedly present in the proem—but only as a minor theme, occurring in vv. 5 and 12 (in v. 5 it is once again the goal or end of the gospel). In short, the whole context of v. 17a seems to stand against this reading of ἐκ πίστεως. Both immediately, in the proem, and with respect to the letter as a whole,[1] the theme seems incongruous.

---

1. It may be argued that it contradicts the theocentric and apocalyptic tone of the entire letter. Throughout Romans Paul's perspective is almost invariably theocentric, as against anthropological or even christological (cf. 1.1-4, 16, 18; 3.1-9; 3.21; 4.20-25; 5.5, 8, 15-16; 8.3-4, 29-39; 9.6-29; 11.1-36; 16.25-27). The only broad exception to this trend is the discussion of chs. 6–7, which are some distance both stylistically and thematically from 1.17. Not surprisingly, this theocentric focus is accompanied by emphases on God's sovereignty and his apocalyptic revelation within the present (and both these themes figure in the proem; cf. κλητός in v. 1; the eschatological tone of ὁρισθέντος υἱοῦ θεοῦ ἐν δυνάμει κατὰ πνεῦμα ἁγιωσύνης in v. 4; Paul's apostolic commission in v. 5, ἐλάβομεν χάριν καὶ ἀποστολήν; Paul's entreaty of v. 10, δεόμενος εἴ πως ἤδη ποτὲ εὐοδωθήσομαι ἐν τῷ θελήματι τοῦ θεοῦ . . .; εἰμὶ ὀφειλέτης in v. 14; δύναμις θεοῦ in v. 16; and ἀποκαλύπτεται in v. 17). But this overarching soteriology is almost diametrically opposed to a stress on individual appropriation. One suspects, at the level of fundamental theology, that for Paul this would be a scandalous undermining of God's sovereignty. The gospel is given by God as and to whom he wills (cf. 1.1), and, while its reception may be conditioned by faith in individual instances, the cosmic revelation of the gospel itself, which is the subject of Rom. 1.16-17, is not dependent on faith. It is given by God at a specific time and to specific people, out of his graceful will and purpose. To condition the saving power of God in the gospel by individual choice seems suspiciously modern. Cf. also Gal. 1.1, 11-12, 15-16; 2.7-8; 4.4-7; Eph. 1.3-14; 2.4-10; 3.5-12.

In addition to the problem of context, the phrase seems internally jumbled in terms of causality. Paul would then be saying that the righteousness of God is revealed with the ultimate goal of faith (vv. 16b, 17a), and by means of the believer's faith. Thus, the believer's faith functions as both means and goal. This seems unusual, and even contradictory, for if faith is the goal, how can it be a means?—can it function before it is created? But if faith is the means, why then is it also the goal? Has it not already been introduced? Thus the phrase's causality seems fundamentally disjointed.[1]

The causal confusion may be avoided by a smoother translation, for example, 'by faith from first to last'.[2] Such readings, however, although favoured by most commentators, are little more than paraphrases. They also create a redundancy. It seems odd that Paul uses two phrases, when one would have been sufficient. The statement seems a little gratuitous.

Finally, and most significantly, if we follow the most probable rendering of ἀποκαλύπτω, the reading does not really make sense. If Paul is stating in v. 17a that 'the eschatological saving righteousness of God is being revealed (now) within the gospel...', then it is difficult to imagine how the believer's faith could have anything to do with this sovereign and cosmic process. Believing faith receives the gospel, but it does not pour God's eschatological salvation into it in the first place!

These accumulating problems suggest that reading ἐκ πίστεως in v. 17a as the believer's faith is unlikely. Certain phrases and themes must be presupposed, tensions are generated at every contextual level, and if an 'apocalyptic' understanding of v. 17a is adopted, it verges on the impossible.

At this point it does at least seem clear that in v. 17a Paul is referring to an instrumental entity within the salvific process, in a sense continuous with Hab. 2.4, that creates believing faith as its end-product. If a reading in terms of Christ's faithfulness (our second reading) is able to fulfil this agenda in addition to avoiding contextual tensions, then it should probably be preferred over the third reading.[3]

---

1. One possible resolution of this difficulty is to allow Paul a nuancing of the word πίστις, so that in its first occurrence it refers to the initial saving response of faith, and in the second to the ongoing life of obedient faithfulness in the life of the believer (cf. 1.5, 12). This shift is certainly acceptable at the lexical level, but it violates the parallelism between 1.17b and 17a. In 17a the εἰς phrase clearly designates saving faith: εἰς σωτηρίαν παντὶ τῷ πιστεύοντι. According to this reading, however, εἰς πίστιν in 17b must be read as obedience. This is possible, but it seems more likely that the two phrases are deliberate parallelisms, and that both refer to believing faith.

2. See Cranfield for eight alternatives (*Romans*, I, p. 99). All these alternatives, however, suffer from the disadvantage that they paraphrase the disputed expressions, presupposing unstated concepts. Or they use the prepositions in a sense that loyalty to their normal meaning will not permit. For example, how can ἐκ πίστεως εἰς πίστιν possibly mean 'from the faith of the OT to the faith of the NT'? And a reading in terms of 'faith alone' is just as embarrassing, because εἰς πίστιν, against its meaning in v. 16, now seems to mean 'sola' as in 'sola fide'—hardly a literal rendering!

3. As said earlier, the first reading is not being emphasized in this discussion (that the faith refers to God); however, it is interesting to note that, although its problems are not as extensive as those caused by the third reading, it is nevertheless not as smooth as the second reading. If a theocentric reading is employed, once again the discussion shifts away from a focus on the gospel, in this case to an emphasis on the ground of the gospel in God's faithfulness. But this statement

When ἐκ πίστεως in 17a is read with reference to the faithfulness of Christ, any shift in the overall focus of the discussion disappears. The sentence smoothly continues the sense of v. 16 (and that of the rest of the section), in stating that the faithfulness of Christ is the means by which God's righteousness is revealed in the gospel. Thus the focus of the discussion remains on the substance of the gospel. Furthermore, the overarching apocalyptic and theocentric soteriology of Romans is strengthened, and the verse continues smoothly to v. 18 as well.[1] Most significantly, however, the statement is in complete contextual agreement with Paul's previous statements in vv. 2-4 and v. 9 concerning the content of the gospel. In both these earlier comments Paul states that the gospel 'concerns the son' (περὶ τοῦ υἱοῦ αὐτοῦ in v. 2; τῷ εὐαγγελίῳ τοῦ υἱοῦ αὐτοῦ in v. 9). Verse 17, therefore, simply elaborates that the faithfulness of the son is at the centre of the gospel.[2] Moreover, any temporal confusion is replaced by a smooth progression from the righteousness of God, through the faithfulness of the son, to the faith of the believer.[3] Finally, whatever redundancy has been perceived in the clause is eliminated.

For these reasons it would seem that the second reading set out above is superior to the third reading, and that ἐκ πίστεως in Rom. 1.17a should be translated 'by means of the faithful one' (or words to that effect). This reading highlights the proem's emphasis on the gospel, and gives a clearer transition in Paul's use of

---

also seems peculiarly superfluous—or, perhaps, convoluted. Does God's righteousness arise from God's faithfulness? They seem almost synonymous (as noted by Käsemann, 'Zum Verständnis', p. 98). In addition to this, Hab. 2.4 must then be read as a statement concerning God's faithfulness. Again this seems odd and superfluous. Surely it was assumed that humanity lived on the basis of God's faithfulness. It seems even more puzzling in view of the textual variant Paul uses. If Paul wished to emphasize God's faithfulness, the use of a pronoun by certain variants would have made this clear, yet he failed to select one (e.g. B or S). Finally, Paul's later employment of the phrase ἐκ πίστεως, e.g., at 3.26, must be unmotivated as well as awkward, because it shifts away from the meaning the phrase takes in 1.17. The critique here is in no sense to be taken as disparaging the concept of the faithfulness of God, which is important to Paul (cf. esp. Rom. 3.3). But I argue that it is difficult to sustain as the interpretation of ἐκ πίστεως at 1.16, or as an interpretation of this phrase anywhere in Paul.

1. In vv. 18-32 Paul is describing the concrete manifestation of the wrath of God in various paradigmatic Gentile sins such as idolatry, sexual immorality, violence and so on (in other words, the standard indictments of the Jewish propaganda literature; cf. Wisdom of Solomon, esp. chs. 13–14). Thus, while v. 18 describes a wrathful power emanating from heaven, the following argument concretizes that power in specific forms and manifestations. This sense is continuous with the idea that Christ is the specific manifestation of the righteousness of God ἐκ πίστεως, although a reading in terms of God's faithfulness is also continuous with v. 18.

2. For obedience as an important part of the Semitic conception of Sonship, see O. Cullmann, *The Christology of the New Testament* (trans. S.C. Guthrie and C.A.M. Hall; Philadelphia: Westminster Press, 1959 [1957]), pp. 270-305; R.N. Longenecker, *The Christology of Early Jewish Christianity* (London: SCM Press, 1970), pp. 93-99; and B. Byrne, *'Sons of God'-'Seed of Abraham'* (Rome: Biblical Institute, 1979).

3. Thus an archetypal pattern of the Son's mediation of the Father's will and power to the lost believer is precisely set forth (cf. 3.21-26; 5.6-11; 5.15-19; 8.3-4; 10.3-4).

πίστις. In sum, it seems best to read ἐκ πίστεως in 1.17a as a reference to the faithfulness of Christ. But this position may also be argued on the basis of the phrase's second occurrence in v. 17b. Here several features of Paul's citation imply a messianic reference for the text, and hence a reading of πίστις with respect to Christ.[1]

1. Paul's use of δίκαιος elsewhere also suggests a reading of ὁ δίκαιος in Hab. 2.4 in terms of either God or the messiah, but not humanity. The evidence is complicated by Paul's occasional use of δίκαιος to denote simply a 'good' or 'upright' person, often in a legal context, over against 'righteous'[2] as a divine attribute that approaches perfection.[3] Careful attention to context, however, allows this distinction to be clearly made in the Pauline occurrences.

Of the 17 instances of δίκαιος in Paul, seven are in Romans. Here Paul uses the term twice of the generic good person (2.13; 5.7[4]), once of the law (7.12), and in 3.26 it is God who is δίκαιος. Most significantly, in 3.10 'no one' is righteous. This is confirmed by one of Paul's rare uses of ἄδικος, in 3.5, where God is not ἄδικος but humanity is.[5] Finally, in 5.19 the many are made δίκαιοι, but only διὰ τῆς ὑπακοῆς τοῦ ἑνός—that is, by the obedience of Christ. It is also important that the mitigated legal and human use of the term occurs rarely in Romans, and then in a carefully defined context.

Essentially the same configuration is found in the term's use outside Romans. δίκαιος occurs with a human reference in Eph. 6.1,[6] Phil. 1.7,[7] Col. 4.1[8] (cf. 1 Tim. 1.9,[9] and Tit. 1.8[10]). In Phil. 4.8, however, it denotes 'whatever' is good generically, and in 2 Thess. 1.5, 6 it refers to the judgment of God (cf. Rom. 2.5:

---

1. There has been considerable conflict over the rather subtle question of whether ἐκ πίστεως modifies the subject or the verb, assuming in both cases that the individual believer is the reference of the citation (cf. H.C.C. Cavallin for a full documentation of the dispute and its effect on various Bible-translations: ' "The Righteous Shall Live by Faith": A Decisive Argument for the Traditional Interpretation', *ST* 32 [1978], pp. 33-44, esp. pp. 33-35, although the confidence of the title is perhaps unjustified).

2. It is probably less confusing if 'righteous' is consistently used for δίκαιος, which allows 'righteousness' to be used for δικαιοσύνη.

3. BAGD, pp. 195-96. For the 'good' man, cf. Mt. 1.19, 1 Jn 3.7 and Rev. 22.11. This shift in usage has been noted by, e.g., G. Schrenk, *TDNT*, II, pp. 182-91.

4. Note Paul's careful equation in the second text of δίκαιος with ἀγαθός, thus approaching the legal sense of the word—although one wonders if Paul believes in these 'men' as little more than ethical possibilities, only concretely fulfilled in Christ.

5. See 1 Cor. 6.1, 9. Cf. also the related ἀδικία; Rom. 1.18, 29; 2.8; 3.5; 6.13; 9.14 (BAGD, pp. 17-18), which really strengthens the point, since all the references are to human beings in their corruption and sinfulness (except 9.14, where a reference to God is once again strenuously denied by Paul).

6. As children rightly obeying their parents.

7. Where it is 'right' for Paul to feel intensely protective about the Philippians.

8. Where slave owners should give their slaves what is 'right' (and ἰσότης).

9. Where the law is not for the 'righteous', meaning τις αὐτῷ νομίμως χρῆται.

10. A quality of ἐπισκοποί and πρεσβύτεροι, along with monogamy, temperance, hospitality, self-control and so on.

δικαιοκρισίας).[1] From this brief survey it can be seen that where Paul uses δίκαιος in what we may call his 'absolute' sense (i.e. apart from generic references), it never refers to humanity, but only to God, to Christ or to the law. The evidence is complicated by Paul's 'double' use. But references to a less elevated, legal or human rightness are once again clearly denoted by context.[2]

In sum, for ὁ δίκαιος to refer to a just person in Rom. 1.17 would be to cut across Paul's use of δίκαιος everywhere. In addition to this, it would contradict his explicit statements in Romans that humanity is not righteous, but ἄδικος and guilty of ἀδικία.[3] Given Paul's usual deployment of δίκαιος, therefore, Hab. 2.4 should be read as a reference to Christ.[4]

2. Over and above this basic meaning, δίκαιος may be functioning in the Hab. 2.4 quotation as a stereotyped titular reference to Christ. The phrase ὁ δίκαιος was an early Jewish-Christian christological title, which is fairly frequently attested in the NT.[5] The Jewish nature of (at least some of) the letter's recipients, who would be familiar with such a usage, lends credence to the title's presence here. More importantly, Paul's tendency to use articular substantives as titles for Christ also supports a titular use of δίκαιος.[6] Thus, for ὁ δίκαιος to refer to Christ in

---

1. In 2 Tim. 4.8 it denotes Christ as the righteous judge, in a pointed parallel to Hab. 2.4: ὁ κύριος. . . ὁ δίκαιος κριτής.

2. This may seem initially like begging the question, but it must be noted that if Paul's 'legal' or 'human' usage is introduced to Hab. 2.4, it undermines his doctrine of justification, because a person is merely 'good' by faith. Furthermore, πίστις is *never* mentioned in relation to these usages elsewhere. δίκαιος always refers to 'works-righteousness', or to good ethical behaviour.

3. It may be argued that 5.19 supplies such a warrant for applying 1.17 to humankind. The context of 5.19, however, establishes clearly that humanity apart from Christ is in Adam, and that all the blessings of God's salvation are premised on the obedience of the one man, in whom the many become righteous. This text, in fact, suggests more a messianic reading of Hab. 2.4 than anything else, since Christ's mediation and achievement of righteousness are so prominent.

4. Or to God, but this second reference is again rather more difficult in context.

5. See Acts 3.14, 7.52, and, most significantly, 22.14, where Luke places it on the lips of Paul (although its use is ascribed to Ananias). If Luke can be trusted, Paul was obviously familiar with it. The title also occurs in Jas 5.6, anarthrously in 1 Pet. 3.18, 1 Jn 2.1, and possibly at 2 Tim. 4.8. It is also possibly in *1 En.* 38.2 and 53.6, but the *Similitudes* cannot be dated with complete certainty to pre-Christian times, and a possible occurrence in the Qumran literature is ambiguous. Similarly, the significance of the phrase's occurrence in Isa. 53.11 is debatable. Despite the problems associated with the title's pre-Christian use, however, the association of rightness with the Messiah is certainly attested in Jewish circles, and as such the title ὁ δίκαιος would admirably suited to a Jewish-Christian apologetic (see R.N. Longenecker, *Christology*, pp. 46-47).

6. This stylistic tendency may be evident in Rom. 6, where Paul discusses the relation between Christ's death, Christian baptism and sin. R. Scroggs argues that here ὁ ἀποθανών refers to Christ ('Rom. 6.7 ὁ γὰρ ἀποθανὼν δεδικαίωται ἀπὸ τῆς ἁμαρτίας', *NTS* 10 [1963], p. 104-108), and such a reading would certainly eliminate a number of redundancies in the text, while integrating Paul's first- and second-person constructions smoothly into the argument (as against leaving a rather confusing series of grammatical shifts in person unresolved). Confirmation for a christological reading here would seem to be found in Paul's later statement in 8.34, Χριστὸς Ἰησοῦς ὁ ἀποθανών, μᾶλλον δὲ ἐγερθείς, ὅς καί ἐστιν ἐν δεξιᾷ τοῦ θεοῦ, ὅς καὶ ἐντυγχάνει ὑπὲρ ἡμῶν (cf. also 14.9). Similarly, Paul's tendency to describe Christ in terms of articular substantives

Rom. 1.17 would be consistent not only with Jewish-Christian messianic conventions generally, but also with Paul's stylistic tendencies in particular.

3. In close relation to the foregoing, a fairly strong case can be made for the use of Hab. 2.4 in the early church as part of a messianic testimonium.[1] The practice of collating testimonia was widespread in the early church.[2] The actual text of Hab. 2.4 was used in *pesher* exegesis at Qumran,[3] and, most significantly, it is also cited in the NT as a messianic proof (although this is not its argumentative function in context) at Heb. 10.37-38.[4] Thus, it seems a reasonable inference that Hab. 2.4 functioned as an early church messianic testimonium, and this naturally suggests that the reference of ἐκ πίστεως is to the faith of the messiah.[5]

4. Finally, the MS variant employed by Paul may support this contention. It is commonly stated that Paul, in quoting Hab. 2.4, is following no known text.[6] Our interest at this point, however, is in the stylistic function of the citation. The absence of the pronoun specifically liberates the meaning of πίστις from precise reference

---

is apparent elsewhere in the letter, for example, ὁ υἱός (Rom. 1.3, 4, 9; 5.10; 8.3, 29, 32), ὁ Χριστός (Rom. 9.3, 5, 14.18; 15.3, 7, 19; 16.16), ὁ εἷς (Rom. 5.15, 17, 18, 19), and so on (ὁ πιστός?—cf. 1 Thess. 5.24; 2 Thess. 3.3. This may also perhaps be apparent in an inverse form in 2 Thess. 2.3 and 8, where the Antichrist is described as ὁ ἄνθρωπος τῆς ἀνομίας, ὁ υἱὸς τῆς ἀπωλείας, and ὁ ἄνομος).

1. So C.H. Dodd, *According to the Scriptures*, p. 51; and A.T. Hanson, *Studies in Paul's Technique and Theology* (Grand Rapids: Eerdmans, 1974), pp. 39-45; endorsed by R.B. Hays, *Faith of Jesus Christ*, pp. 150-57. Cf. also T.W. Manson, 'The Argument from Prophecy', *JTS* 46 (1945), pp. 129-36; J.A. Sanders, 'Habakkuk in Qumran, Paul, and the Old Testament', *JR* 39 (1959), p. 233; and B. Lindars, *New Testament Apologetic: The Doctrinal Significance of the Old Testament Quotations* (London: SCM Press, 1961), pp. 230-32.

2. See Dodd, *According to the Scriptures*.

3. Cf. W.H. Brownlee, 'Messianic Motifs of Qumran and the New Testament', *NTS* 3 (1956–57), p. 209; and J.A. Fitzmyer, 'Habakkuk 2:3-4 and the New Testament', in *idem, To Advance the Gospel*, pp. 236-46.

4. Cf. Hanson, *Studies in Paul*, pp. 44-45. Note, while it is a different MS variation, this does not prevent the text from being used as a testimonium. The reading of A actually strengthens the messianic reference of the text—ὁ ἐρχόμενος. . . ὁ . . . δίκαιός μου.

5. Even granting Paul's distinctive interpretation of the verse, the text may still have circulated in the early church as a messianic reference (so Heb. 10.35-37, a letter written to Rome?). Thus, if Paul wished ὁ δίκαιος to refer to the justified believer, he would be significantly altering a text without explanation, a text that had perhaps already been presented to the Roman Christians from a different perspective. This would be confusing, and therefore seems unlikely. Consequently, in the absence of any clear explanatory gloss in the context, Paul's reading of the text should be assumed to be that of the rest of the early church, which was probably messianic.

6. It is unwise to suggest immediately that he is modifying the verse, because Paul's exegesis is relatively conservative, and our knowledge of textual variants is extremely poor (cf. R.N. Longenecker, *Biblical Exegesis*, pp. 104-32, esp. comments at 105 and 132-33). In fact, Paul's quotation is reproduced by W, which is a good source for Habakkuk, being third-century (the Freer MS, Washington; cf. LXX, ed. A. Rahlfs). The apparatus suggests, however, that this reading is a later correction. But whether Paul deliberately omitted the pronoun—or simply chose a variant that omitted it (i.e. W)—is somewhat beside the point. It is the interpretative effect of the omission that is significant.

either to God's faithfulness (as in the LXX according to B and S), or to humanity's (as in the MT). Two conclusions are possible: (1) Paul intended the phrase to include all three possible objects (God, Christ and a human being), or at least two of these three;[1] or (2) Paul intended the phrase to refer specifically to Christ, in which case the pronouns would also have had to be omitted.[2] But the former option has already been rendered problematic by contextual and terminological difficulties, and seems doubly unlikely in view of the precise correlation between ἐκ πίστεως and the citation of Hab. 2.4 in Paul's letters. Consequently, Paul's choice of textual variants is best explained if he intended the text to refer primarily to the faithfulness of the messiah.[3]

In view of the above four arguments, it seems a reasonable hypothesis that Paul quotes Hab. 2.4 at Rom. 1.17 with reference to the faith of Christ. Such a quotation would attest scripturally to his presentation of the gospel of Christ as God's eschatological salvation, and would also bring the christological emphasis in the proem to a fitting climax. This conclusion regarding v. 17b is further strengthened by the above analysis of v. 17a and the phrase ἐκ πίστεως εἰς πίστιν, where ἐκ πίστεως also reads more smoothly if it refers to Christ. Moreover, in view of the remarkable correlation between Hab. 2.4 and phrase ἐκ πίστεως in Paul's letters, it is perhaps not unreasonable to assume that the phrase ἐκ πίστεως is strongly coloured by Paul's messianic use of Hab. 2.4. And so the final πίστις phrase of 3.21-26 should be read as a reference to the messianic faith of Christ. But, as we have seen, Paul uses διὰ πίστεως Χριστοῦ as a stylistic parallel to ἐκ πίστεως, and in 3.21-26 the three phrases are particularly closely aligned. Thus, the messianic reference of ἐκ πίστεως in 3.26d also draws the interpretation of the two previous διά phrases into its orbit. In sum, Paul's statement in 1.17a that the righteousness of God is revealed in the gospel ἐκ πίστεως εἰς πίστιν, and his citation of Hab. 2.4 in v. 17b, set in motion a chain of associations around the phrase ἐκ πίστεως that evoke messianic

---

1. So Hays, but with the primary emphasis on Christ (*Faith of Christ*, pp. 156-57).

2. If Paul intended a primary reference to God, it seems strange that he did not use a text (namely, B or S), that makes this explicit. And if he wished to emphasize the believer's faith, why did he not simply use the version that makes the aspect specific—namely, the MT, which supplies a pronoun to designate the faith as belonging to ὁ δίκαιος (cf. Dunn, *Romans 1-8*, p. 44). A messianic reading is perhaps favoured by A and C, which read ὁ δίκαιός μου (and so the author of Hebrews), but this is not necessarily more messianic than the simple construction ὁ δίκαιος that Paul uses, which has a titular resonance. Moreover, if Paul wishes to utilize the critical phrase ἐκ πίστεως repeatedly as something of a catch-phrase or slogan within his later arguments, the presence of the pronoun would be extremely clumsy, if not incomprehensible; cf. ὁ θεὸς δικαιωθήσεται ἐξ ἔργων νόμου ἢ ἐκ πίστεώς μου, ἢ ἐκ πιστέως αὐτοῦ? (!).

3. An argument is sometimes made against this position from 2 Cor. 2.16. This verse essentially supports the idea of a particular quality moving actively from God to humanity (in this case life and death). Its relevance to Rom. 1.17, however, is sharply limited by the fact that the parallelism there is conditioned not by stylistic considerations but by the quotation of Hab. 2.4. It also seems unlikely that ἐκ in Rom. 1.17b denotes source; it is more likely to denote instrumentality, like the repeated διά in the genitive in 3.21-26 and 3.30-31.

faithfulness. These finally serve to strengthen the reading of the πίστις genitives in 3.21-26 as subjective genitive constructions that refer to the faith or faithfulness of Christ.[1]

1. Although it may seem at times that there are too many steps in the argument for this conclusion to be held firmly, this is, I would suggest, merely the effect of reconstructing Paul's thematic and textual relationships essentially backwards. The influence at the level of the text is really very simple. Paul's quotation of Hab. 2.4 largely controls his use of the phrase ἐκ πίστεως and its equivalents. For him (as for the rest of the early church), the verse refers to the Messiah. I would suggest that it is only our own subsequent exegetical and theological programme that has blinded us to this christological reading of the verse.

Appendix 2

THE OBJECTIVE GENITIVE READINGS OF
πίστις Ἰησοῦ Χριστοῦ

No consideration of the πίστις Χριστοῦ genitive is really complete without some consideration of the evidence for the objective reading,[1] so here we will consider the arguments of Arland J. Hultgren in some detail.[2] Hultgren advances six considerations in support of an objective genitive reading of the disputed phrases (A-F), but all of these may be seriously challenged.

In A, Hultgren contends that Paul *never* uses an article with πίστις in πίστις Χριστοῦ expressions, but *always* in other uses of πίστις with the genitive. These last include clearly subjective constructions; thus, if Paul intended his christological πίστις genitive to be subjective, it is reasonable to expect that he would use the articular phrase ἡ πίστις τοῦ Χριστοῦ—which does not occur.

This is perhaps Hultgren's best argument, but several considerations undermine its initially engaging hypothesis:

1. One wonders why the presence or absence of an article is significant for controlling the interpretation of a genitive relationship—there seems to be, initially, no obvious causal relationship between the two grammatical phenomena.[3]

2. One such alternative explanation is that Paul's problematic christological πίστις genitives usually function instrumentally in his sentences, following a genitive with διά or ἐκ. The articular subjective constructions Hultgren considers, however, do not usually function in this way, but are almost always found in the position of subject or object. Thus, syntactical considerations may be what dictates Paul's use of the article.

3. This suspicion is strengthened by the observation that Paul frequently uses anarthrous subjective genitive constructions for combinations of other words, for example: (in Romans alone) υἱοῦ θεοῦ and πνεῦμα

---

1. Although this reading seems to have been assumed for so long that considered statements in its support are rather rare.

2. 'The PISTIS CHRISTOU Formulation in Paul', *NovT* 22 (1980), pp. 248-63. Hultgren has also been challenged by S.K. Williams, 'Again *Pistis Christou*', *CBQ* 49 (1987), pp. 431-37.

3. The apparent correlation could be a spurious, or disguised, relationship, that is, one in which the two phenomena are caused by something else altogether.

ἁγιοσύνης (1.4), νόμου πίστεως (3.27—an exception to A?), and δικαιοσύνη θεοῦ (probably subjective in 1.17; 3.21, 22, and certainly in 3.5). This last phrase is particularly interesting because it occurs both with and without the article, without changing the nature of its genitive relation overmuch (1.17; 3.5, 21 and 22, are anarthrous; 3.25, 26 and 10.3 are articular).

4. In addition to the problems caused by a comparison with other genitives, it may be queried whether Hultgren's survey of πίστις genitives is too abbreviated. He considers evidence from seven letters within the Pauline corpus, and, while many scholars work within these boundaries, such a restriction does have the added convenience of excluding some extremely awkward pieces of evidence—for example, Eph. 3.12: διὰ τοῦ πίστεως αὐτοῦ (in context this can only be Christ's faith); 2 Thess. 1.4: ὑπὲρ τοῦ ὑπομονῆς ὑμῶν καὶ πίστεως (an anarthrous subjective genitive not referring to Christ).[1]

5. In addition to these problematic exclusions (which Hultgren even cites on occasion as 'non-Pauline' evidence), he fails to note that *all* the non-christological πίστις genitive constructions are subjective, irrespective of their precise grammatical make-up, as Howard has pointed out. This weakens his contention that it is the presence or absence of the article that is critical.

6. Even granting Hultgren a seven-letter canon, certain instances clearly strain his rule, for example Rom. 3.25b, where what is probably an articular πίστις phrase clearly parallels an anarthrous πίστις genitive in 3.22, which I contend is subjective. Most significantly, however, the correlation between τὸν ἐκ πίστεως Ἰησοῦ in 3.26 and τῷ ἐκ πίστεως Ἀβραάμ in 4.16 is very difficult for Hultgren's thesis,[2] as is 4.12 (which he seems to overlook). Gal. 2.20 is also problematic: ἐν πίστει ζῶ τῇ τοῦ υἱοῦ τοῦ θεοῦ. If this is subjective—and according to Hultgren's article rule it should be—it seems a clear exception.[3] Thus it would seem that Hultgren's promising distinction fails to withstand closer scrutiny.

---

1. Cf. also 1 Tim. 3.13: ἐν πίστει τῇ ἐν Χριστῷ Ἰησοῦ (a possible, articular, christological genitive); 2 Tim. 1.13: ἐν πίστει καὶ ἀγάπη τῇ ἐν Χριστῷ Ἰησοῦ (almost certainly a reference to the faithfulness of Christ); and 3.15: διὰ πίστεως τῆς ἐν Χριστῷ Ἰησοῦ (again an articular genitive that seems subjective). Is it really credible that all these 'Pauline imitators' have completely misconstrued and misrepresented Paul's original use of the construction?

2. On the one hand, if Hultgren classifies Rom. 4.16 as an articular subjective πίστις genitive construction, then his contention that such constructions never occur with respect to Christ is undermined, because of 3.26, On the other hand, if he denies it is an articular construction with specific respect to πίστις (and, strictly speaking, it isn't), then his assertion that subjective πίστις genitive constructions are invariably articular when they do not refer to Christ is refuted—an unenviable dilemma.

3. Cf. also Gal. 3.26: διὰ τῆς πίστεως ἐν Χριστῷ Ἰησοῦ.

7. Finally, and in support particularly of points 2 and 3, we may note Stuhlmacher's observation concerning ἱλαστήριον, that predicate nouns in Paul often lack the definite article. This general tendency must encompass the disputed πίστις Χριστοῦ genitives, which are all prepositional constructions and therefore automatically part of the predicate.[1]

Argument B considers the possibility of an assumed preposition intervening between the two members of the genitive. Hultgren claims that where other NT writers use πίστις ἐν, Paul uses πίστεως without a preposition, suggesting the believer's faith in both cases—in fact, for Hultgren, πίστις ἐν 'is not a Pauline idiom', because for the objective relation Paul simply uses a genitive construction.

As Hultgren knows, however, Paul does use πίστις with this preposition, for example, in 1 Cor. 2.5 (cf. the use of πίστις with the closely related πρός in 1 Thess. 1.18 and Phlm. 5, and the dative in Gal. 3.6). Moreover, one wonders how Hultgren can assume equivalence between Paul's πίστις genitives and various πίστις ἐν constructions elsewhere in the NT, and also how convincing it is to argue that πίστις ἐν is not Pauline, in view of Paul's fondness for the preposition. Most importantly, however, Gal. 3.26 (perhaps supported by 2.20) and Rom. 4.12 are clear refutations of this entire contention. If these are references to the faithfulness of Christ, they are expressed in genitive ἐν constructions (and with articles!)—embarrassing statements for Hultgren, to say the least.[2]

In argument C, Hultgren asserts that Gal. 2.16 'confirms' that πίστις Χριστοῦ is equivalent to πιστεύειν εἰς Χριστόν. But this also begs the question, rejoicing in a triple redundancy of πίστις phrases within the verse. Hultgren seems unaware that this verse does not define διὰ πίστεως Χριστοῦ Ἰησοῦ as an objective genitive, but rather discredits the reading, since Paul seems to make the same point three times consecutively. The critical third clause is also rather difficult to read as a parenthesis as Hultgren suggests: it is followed by a dependent ἵνα clause, and so most scholars interpret this clause as the main subject and predicate of the sentence!

In argument D, Hultgren observes that Paul uses both subjective and objective genitive constructions in similar prepositional formulations based on διά, ἐκ and ἐν, so the observation, as he concedes, adds little to the debate. But we may note that all the constructions surveyed are anarthrous (Rom. 10.17; 2 Cor. 2.10; 4.6; Gal. 1.6, 12), whether subjective or objective, which seems something of a problem for Hultgren's argument in A.

Argument E suggests that Paul seldom follows such prepositions in any case with a genitive combining πίστις and another substantive. Hultgren overlooks a few exceptions (e.g. Gal. 2.20), and does not consider genitives with πίστις in the second, rather than in the first, position (Rom. 1.5; 3.7; 4.13; 16.26; Gal. 3.2, 5). But it does not follow that, as Hultgren contends, such constructions are the same as

---

1. Stuhlmacher, 'Recent Exegesis', pp. 99, 107 n. 38 (citing BDF §§252.2 and 258.2 in support—but note esp. §§254, 255 and 259).

2. He simply denies that the references are to the faith of Christ in the Galatians references—rather a blatant instance of begging the question—and he seems to overlook Rom. 4.12.

Paul's simpler constructions that have no combined substantive. Against him, it must be emphasized that the addition of Χριστός is a rather significant one, and its meaning is precisely the point at issue—if it was the same as his simple πίστις statements, why did Paul bother to add the word? And, as Hultgren is well aware, Rom. 4.16 is a thorn in the flesh for this argument, since it seems a clear instance of a subjective genitive construction, but one structured extremely closely to the christological genitives. In fact, such is the awkwardness of 4.16 that Hultgren devotes an entire argument to its redefinition (F).

He contends that the phrase is governed by a 'Semitic syntax', where the governing noun is determined by, as much as it determines, the associated genitive. Such a construction—a genitive of quality—also often lacks the article. Hence the phrase in 4.16 means not 'the faith of Abraham', but 'an Abraham-like faith'.

But this translation, while perhaps grammatically plausible, is not possible in the context of Romans 4. The specific figure of Abraham is so integral to the argument of ch. 4 that any attempt to displace his centrality is not credible. The stated intention of 4.1, Paul's repeated quotation of Gen. 15.6 with reference to Abraham's faith, the extended phrase τῆς ἐν ἀκροβυστίᾳ πίστεως τοῦ πατρὸς ἡμῶν Ἀβραάμ in 4.12, and ὅς ἐστιν πατὴρ πάντων ἡμῶν in 4.16, all stand against Hultgren's reading.

In addition to this, Hultgren overlooks that a Hebrew could shift with great ease between individual and corporate considerations (cf. Paul's discussion of Adam in 5.12-14 and 7.7-25). Thus, a corporate meaning or application in 4.16 does not preclude an individual reference as well.

Hultgren's 'Semitic syntax', in fact, proves to be something of a two-edged sword for his basic contention. If Ἰησοῦ or Χριστοῦ is taken to modify πίστεως, because of the Semitic genitive of quality, then Hultgren has proved too much and the phrase can no longer be translated as the objective genitive statement of 'faith in Jesus Christ'. It must be rendered 'a Christ-like faith' (on analogy to the 'Abraham-like faith' of 4.16). Even more significantly, Hultgren has himself explained the anarthrous incidence of πίστις that has been so important in his previous arguments against a subjective reading: 'The governing noun in construct state consistently lacks the definite article'.[1] Thus, the christological πίστις with the genitive constructions may have dropped the article under the influence of the Semitic genitive of quality (and this certainly accords with anarthrous genitives elsewhere in Paul). In short, Hultgren has strengthened the case for a subjective reading, by explaining one of its anomalies. His argument in F undermines his contention in A.

Hultgren's simultaneous failure to redefine Rom. 4.16 credibly also weakens his contentions in B through E, as does his overlooking of important exceptions to the trends he cites. Thus, it must be concluded that Hultgren's attempt to defend the objective genitive reading of πίστεως Χριστοῦ on grammatical grounds is inadequate.[2]

1. 'The PISTIS CHRISTOU Formulation', p. 257.
2. In addition to the flaws in his argument, a fundamental problem that becomes apparent

In retrospect, however, one suspects that the primary objection to a subjective genitive reading is—despite Hultgren's disavowal[1]—probably not grammatical at all, but theological. That is, the objective reading is held to be theologically significant, whereas the subjective reading is irrelevant and even incomprehensible.

C.F.D. Moule's brief rejoinder to Thomas Torrance's 1957 article illustrates this well.[2] On the one hand, although his grammatical observations are correct, they do not influence the disputed readings. For example, he cites instances of looser, objective genitives in Paul (Rom. 1.5 [sic]; 8.21; 2 Thess. 2.13), and of πίστις where it means the believer's faith (Gal. 3.2, 5; Rom. 10.17). Even conceding these readings, they cannot establish in advance that the genitives in Rom. 3.21-26 are also objective.

But Moule's real motive for opposing Torrance seems to be revealed in his fourth point: 'To throw so much weight upon what God in Christ has done is, in the passages adduced by Professor Torrance, seriously to reduce necessary reference to man's act of will in response to God's approach'.[3] In other words, Torrance's proposal is damaging to Moule's conception of how the individual relates to God.

While such essentially pastoral motivations often underly, and even motivate, biblical exegesis, yet, as evidence for particular readings they count for very little. We cannot dictate to Paul in advance what his theology will be, since to do so would be to lose the only control we have on our modern reconstructions of his thought, namely, the text itself. As argued in Chapter 1, section 3, an accumulation of evidence from the text points towards a subjective reading of the christological πίστις + genitives in Rom. 3.21-26, no matter what the theological consequences (and they are not that bad). Certainly, no rejoinder from the objective genitive camp, including that of Hultgren, has forced an abandonment of that perspective.

during the course of Hultgren's analysis is that no grammatical argument can determine in advance, independently of context and syntax, what a reading of a particular phrase should be.

1.   'The PISTIS CHRISTOU Formulation', pp. 251-53.

2.   As does the third section of Hultgren's article, where he simply repeats the traditional antithesis between justification through works and justification by faith. Hultgren seems incapable of conceiving of the alternative opposition of justification through works versus justification through the faithfulness of Christ ('The PISTIS CHRISTOU Formulation', pp. 258-62).

3.   C.F.D. Moule, 'The Biblical Conception of "Faith"', *ExpTim* 68 (1957), p. 157.

Appendix 3

THE DATE OF *4 MACCABEES*

Several scholars have argued that *4 Macc.* 17.22 constitutes the critical background source for understanding Rom. 3.21-26.[1] There we find, not only a clearly attested statement of the vicarious atoning effect of the (cruel) death of a righteous Jewish man, but a cluster of atonement terms that seems extremely close to that found in Rom. 3.24-25. Attractive as this explanation is, however, I will contend (1) that the terminological correlation is more apparent than real, and (2) that a sober dating of the document pushes it well beyond any possible connection with Romans. In the final analysis it would seem that all we have is a common utilization of a broad linguistic stratum in the Jewish tradition, perhaps reinforced by motifs in Graeco-Roman society relating to religion and sacrifice in general.

1. *The Linguistic Similarities*

In Rom. 3.24-25, as we have seen, Paul correlates three atonement terms with the notion of deliverance from sins: ἀπολύτρωσις, αἷμα and ἱλαστήριον. Remarkably, in *4 Macc.* 17.22 we also find ἱλαστήριον and αἷμα, and also the rare word ἀντίψυχον, with the forgiveness of sins being clearly implied in the context.

The first problem concerns the precise form of ἱλαστήριον in 17.22. Some MSS give an articular form, while others are anarthrous. The issue is seldom discussed in great detail, but Peter Stuhlmacher has argued that the articular reading given by S is more likely to be the earlier one,[2] and I would support this conclusion on two further grounds: (1) it is easier to explain the accidental omission of an article in the very convoluted text, than the reverse phenomenon; and (2) given that the text (like so many Jewish Apocryphal and Pseudepigraphal texts) was preserved by Christian editors and scribes, the text may well have been deliberately harmonized with Paul's usage in Rom. 3.24. But these contentions are, admittedly, finely balanced.[3]

The word is apparently functioning as an adjective in *4 Maccabees*, but we are not

---

1. Among the commentators, Byrne, Wilckens and Ziesler.
2. S is generally superior to A; cf. 'Recent Exegesis', pp. 94-109.
3. Against this it might be argued that (1) the article was added to harmonize the text with standard LXX usage (which is, with one unusual exception, articular); and (2) the text may also have been harmonized with Heb. 9.5, rather than with Paul.

exactly sure how ἱλαστήριον functions in Rom. 3.24. It could be a noun or an adjective—and either reading alters interpretation little in any case. At this point, therefore, any comparison reaches an impasse. The two words could be identical anarthrous substantives or adjectives, but the instance in *4 Maccabees* could also be as different as an articular adjective from an anarthrous substantive. The similar close association of αἷμα is also unhelpful. The word was common enough, and in a sacrificial context is almost to be expected. A marked divergence is apparent, however, in the third term within the two atonement clusters.

I have argued that ἀπολύτρωσις is a term that refers primarily to a release from slavery and bondage. The rare word ἀντίψυχον, however, seems drawn specifically from the Greek text of Leviticus 17, where it combines two words from the oft-quoted v. 11: 'For the life of a creature is in the blood and I have given it to you to make atonement for yourselves on the altar; it is the blood that makes atonement for one's life [αἷμα . . . ἀντὶ . . . ψυχῆς]' (NIV). Thus, *4 Macc.* 17.22 seems to be evoking Jewish sacrificial motifs, and it seems more than coincidental that the Jewish festival of *Yom Kippur* is described in the adjacent Leviticus 16.

At this point it would seem that a good explanation can be formulated for the close terminological similarities between Rom. 3.24-25 and *4 Macc.* 17.22. Any similarity rests on the mutual incidence of ἱλαστήριον, supported by the use of αἷμα in context and the surrounding notions of sacrifice, death and forgiveness—there is no real correlation between ἀπολύτρωσις and ἀντίψυχον except for a very broad sense of vicarious action, and the fact that each constitutes a third important word in its context (and they both begin with 'α'!). The probable cause of this correlation is that both texts seem to be drawing on Jewish sacrificial motifs as they occur in the LXX, and in particular relation to the feast of *Yom Kippur*. This series of allusions reinforces the presentation of the deaths of their respective heroes as vicariously and powerfully atoning. Certainly, any similarities between them are completely accounted for by the access of both authors to the text of Leviticus 16–17, where we find repeated use of ἱλαστήριον and αἷμα, and also strong themes of atonement, sacrifice and forgiveness.

Furthermore, the *differences* between the two texts are also explained. If Paul was directly dependent on *4 Maccabees*, one would also expect the third crucial term to be reproduced, namely, ἀντίψυχον in place of ἀπολύτρωσις (and probably an instance also of θάνατος), but clearly the terms (and even the syntax) are not precisely reproduced. This broadly similar usage, however, conditioned by similar thematic emphases but also divergences and terminological differences, is explained if both authors are dependent on a common source that they both develop in slightly different ways.

As a last resort, it might be claimed that Paul is not directly dependent on *4 Maccabees* itself, but that this last text simply testifies to a common *theologoumenon* and terminology of the time. Against this I would point out that the motif of vicarious human atonement that *4 Maccabees* presupposes is unattested in contemporaneous documents.[1] Furthermore, a late date for the origin of the treatise completely undermines any possibility of arguing that both used a common cultural motif. I turn now to consider this critical question in more detail.

2. *The Case for an Early Date for* 4 Maccabees

The *terminus a quo* of *4 Maccabees* is not really disputed. The comment in 4.1 that Onias held the priesthood for life suggests at least a Hasmonean date, when this principle was abrogated. More certainty, however, is provided by Louis Robert. He notes that θρησκεία was never used in Hellenistic literature until it 'became modish' from Augustus onwards.[2] In addition to this, Eliezar is described as νομικώς, rather than as a γραμματεύς, a scribal designation that was only used in Roman times. Thus, the document is probably post-Augustan, and its earliest possible date of composition would seem to be just before the turn of the century, that is, c. 10 BCE. It is the *terminus ad quem* of the document that is disputed.

The debate concerning the latest possible date for *4 Maccabees* is now governed primarily by the argument of E. Bickermann, who suggested that the author's subtle modification at 4.2 of a statement in 2 Macc. 4.4 betrays an early first-century provenance.[3] In 2 Macc. 4.4, a certain Apollonius is designated τὸν Κοίλης Συρίας καὶ Φοινίκης στρατηγόν. This is an accurate reference to two of the four satrapies created in Southern Syria after the Seleucid victory at the battle of Panium. In *4 Macc.* 4.2 this statement is modified, incredibly, to τὸν Συρίας τε καὶ Φοινίκης καὶ Κιλικίας στρατηγόν. The author thereby redefines the area governed by Apollonius to cover most of the Seleucid empire, that is, all of its western dominions and its heartland around the Orontes.

Bickermann's explanation for this rather astonishing modification is that here the author of *4 Maccabees* is updating his source to conform with contemporary arrangements, specifically, an area defined in terms of Roman provincial boundaries.[4] By including Cilicia among the three regional designations of the province of Syria, the author therefore betrays a provenance when Cilicia was officially conjoined to Syria. This provincial configuration only existed early in the first century,

---

1. As S.K. Williams has shown conclusively in *Jesus' Death as Saving Event: The Background and Origin of a Concept* (Missoula, MT: Scholars Press, 1975). Williams himself favours such a connection between *4 Maccabees* and Paul, but it is a solitary one as he himself fully realizes.

2. *Etudes épigraphiques et philologiques* (Paris: Champion, 1938), pp. 219-35, esp. 226-35.

3. 'The Date of 4 Maccabees', in *Studies in Jewish and Christian History: Part One* (Leiden: Brill, 1976), pp. 275-81. J.J. Collins concurs that Bickermann's arguments still hold the field; cf. *Between Athens and Jerusalem: Jewish Identity in the Hellenistic Diaspora* (New York: Crossroad, 1982), pp. 187-91.

4. Most scholars hold that *4 Maccabees* used 2 Maccabees as a source; cf. Bickermann, 'The Date of Fourth Maccabees', p. 276 n. 8. Bickermann notes that H.W. Surkau holds the contrary position, namely, that 2 Maccabees and *4 Maccabees* both draw on popular oral tradition (a third position being that they both drew on Jason of Cyrene's five-volume history?). The first position generally seems the most cogent.

when the reforms of Germanicus added Cilicia Pedias to Syria, an action independently attested as taking place before 18 CE. The arrangement was abrogated by Vespasian c. 72 CE, although some scholars argue for a separation as early as Nero's reign, hence around 55 CE.[1]

This argument would place *4 Maccabees* firmly within the formative years of the NT, and a fairly direct line could then be drawn from *4 Maccabees* to Paul (or even to Jesus).[2] The apparent objectivity of the position—not to mention the theory's explanatory power—has convinced many scholars.[3] The steps in Bickermann's argument, however, must be carefully noted.

The author of *4 Maccabees* reads the phrase Κοίλη[4] Συρία καὶ Φοινίκη in 2 Macc. 4.4, and then draws an equation in his (or her[5]) mind between this phrase and a provincial arrangement of their own day, namely, the Roman province of Syria. That is, the author must have read these words and taken them to mean 'the province of Syria'.[6] Note, this equation between 2 Macc. 4.4 and Roman provincial

---

1.   Bickermann, 'The Date of Fourth Maccabees', pp. 279-80. Cf. also S.A. Cook, F.E. Adcock and M.P. Charlesworth (eds.), *The Cambridge Ancient History* (Cambridge: Cambridge University Press, 1934), X, *The Augustan Empire: 44 BC–AD 70*, pp. 279-83, 618-21, and XI, *The Imperial Peace: AD 70–192*, pp. 602, 613-26 (which cites Tacitus, *Annals* 6.41, 12.55). Cf. also Gal. 1.21, Acts 15.23, and A.H.M. Jones, *The Cities of the Eastern Roman Provinces* (Oxford: Clarendon Press, 2nd edn, 1971), pp. 191-214, 226-94.

2.   As done by Williams, *Saving Event*, pp. 230-54; J. Downing, 'Jesus and Martyrdom', *JTS* 14 (1963), pp. 279-93; P. Staples, 'The Unused Lever?': a Study of the Possible Literary Influence of the Greek Maccabean Literature in the New Testament', *Modern Churchman* 9 (1965–66), pp. 218-24; and D. Hill, *Greek Words*, pp. 41-47. Hill notes that probably the earliest representative of the opinion is H. Rashdall; cf. his *The Idea of the Atonement in Christian Theology* (London: MacMillan, 1920), p. 132.

3.   For example, Williams, *Saving Event*; Hill, *Greek Words*; M. Hadas, *The Third and Fourth Books of Maccabees* (New York: Segal & Nickelsburg, 1953); H. Anderson, '4 Maccabees: A New Translation and Introduction', in J.H. Charlesworth (ed.), *Old Testament Pseudepigrapha* (2 vols.; New York: Doubleday, 1985), II, pp. 531-64; J.S. Pobee, *Persecution and Martyrdom in the Theology of Paul* (JSNTSup, 6; Sheffield: JSOT Press, 1985); and D. Seeley, *The Noble Death: Graeco-Roman Martyrology and Paul's Concept of Salvation* (JSNTSup, 28; Sheffield: JSOT Press, 1990). This position was anticipated by R.B. Townshend, 'The Fourth Book of Maccabees', in *The Apocrypha and Pseudepigrapha of the Old Testament in English* (ed. R.H. Charles; Oxford: Oxford University Press, 1913), II, p. 654. The most likely place of composition is also usually asserted to be Antioch; cf. M. Hadas, *The Third and Fourth Books of Maccabees*, pp. 109-13, and M. Schatkin, 'The Maccabean Martyrs', *VC* 28 (1974), pp. 97-113.

4.   'Valley'—literally, 'hollow'—Syria, hence inland Syria; cf. LSJ, p. 967. The term could be applied to regions, suggesting a valley, or depression, because of its literal sense of hollow. Cf. also *Odyssey* 4.1; Herodotus 7.129, 8.13; Sophocles, *Oedipus Coloneus* 378, 1387; Euripides, *Iphigenia* 1600; and Polybius 3.18.10 and 1.3.1 (a direct parallel, Κοίλη Συρία). In 2 Macc. 4.4 it denotes the inland area astride the great Syrian valley, running parallel to coastal Phoenicia (hence the logic of governing the two provinces conjointly).

5.   This is less likely, given the predominantly male authorship in ancient times, and also the high level of education presupposed by the author, a level only available as a rule to men.

6.   It may be that the author has no idea what Κοίλη Συρία καὶ Φοινίκη in 2 Macc. 4.4 is referring to (!), and hence the 'redefinition'. For the phrase 'valley-Syria and Phoenicia' to suggest

Syria remains mental and unstated. The author of *4 Maccabees* then verbally describes this updated, contemporary political entity in the appropriate regional terms that include Cilicia, Syria and Phoenicia (*4 Macc.* 4.2). So he describes the content of an envisioned *political* unit with three slightly different, *regional* designations. Bickermann, as we have seen, explains this somewhat astonishing redefinition in terms of the author's desire to update the boundaries of the area in terms of the province of Syria, but this ingenious explanation is neither completely plausible, nor the only one possible.

With respect to plausibility, it needs to be pointed out that we do not know from the text that the author is thinking of the Roman province of Syria when 2 Maccabees is modified; both 2 Maccabees and *4 Maccabees* use *regional* terminology. The only possible inference of a political frame of reference seems to come from Apollonius's designation as a στρατηγός. But this is a broad term, usually employed in the NT to refer to military or legal command or leadership, and never used in the specific sense of 'provincial governor'.[1] Furthermore, a survey of classical usage suggests that the author of *4 Maccabees* is almost certainly using the word in its standard sense of 'general', a usage frequently combined with the areas of command in a genitive (or, less frequently, in a dative, accusative or prepositional) construction. This is exactly the phrase we find in *4 Macc.* 4.2, which would be appropriately rendered by 'Apollonius, the general (or commander) of Syria, Phoenicia and Cilicia'.

If the author intended to designate a Roman province, why did he not also use the appropriate word for a provincial ruler? Furthermore, if the author was thinking of the political province of Syria, why did he not just say 'Συρία', that is, *the name of the province*? For a careful political redefinition, the surrounding terminology seems suspiciously imprecise.

Certain aspects of *4 Maccabees* also suggest a rather cavalier—or at least indifferent—approach on the part of the author. For example, in 4.15 Antiochus Epiphanes is incorrectly called the son of Seleucus IV, not his brother (something Josephus knows; cf. *Ant.* 12.4). Such inaccuracies suggest that the author was not particularly precise and, as J. Collins notes, the treatise is by its own admission a quasi-philosophical tract (Gr. λόγος), arguing for the fulfilment of the law as the

simply 'Syria' to the author of *4 Maccabees*, both the words Κοίλη and Φοινίκη must really be either ignored or completely misunderstood. But would a first-century Jew (living in Antioch, according to some interpreters) have been this uninformed about provincial arrangements under the later Seleucids, which were only abrogated by Augustus and Germanicus at the turn of the century? The greater the distance in time (and space) between the authors of *4* and 2 Maccabees, the more possible this rather ridiculous redefinition becomes, and vice versa.

1. Luke (the only NT author to use the term) refers it to officer(s) of the temple guard and chief magistrates (cf. Lk. 22.4, 52; Acts 4.1; 5.24, 26; 16.20, 22, 35-36, 38). Luke (and other NT authors) of course do refer to 'governors', but they use the term ὁ ἡγεμών (cf. Mt. 10.18; 27.2, 11, 14; Mk 13.9; Lk. 20.20; Acts 23.24; 24.1; 26.30); cf. also Luke's reference to proconsuls in Acts 13.7 and 18.12, using ἀνθύπατος and ἀνθυπατεύω. LNSM comment on στρατηγός that 'in a number of instances στρατηγός may be rendered simply as "the chief of the town" or "the ruler of the city"' (p. 482).

appropriate fulfilment of reason. One would not necessarily expect great historical precision from such a document.

In view of these problems with Bickermann's explanation, it seems even more significant that a quite different interpretation of this critical linguistic datum is possible. It is, in fact, far simpler to assume that the author of *4 Maccabees* is thinking of an entity within the story itself in 4.2, namely, the western part of the Seleucid empire (in general terms), when the crucial redefinition takes place, rather than a contemporary Roman province.[1]

The Seleucid empire included for most of its history the neighbouring region of coastal Cilicia,[2] and 2 Maccabees assumes this to be so (cf. 4.36). The author of *4 Maccabees* could therefore simply be stating that Apollonius's area of control (presumably military) embraced a large area including Syria, Phoenicia and Cilicia, rather than merely Phoenicia and Damascene Syria. This would simply be an instance of *hyperbole*, and one that makes perfect sense in terms of the logic of the story—the villain and enemy of Israel, Apollonius, had vast dominions that stretched around the entire northwestern coast of the Mediterranean—an eminently suitable enemy for Israel heroically to resist.

Our alternative explanation correlates well with the redactor's terminological and historical vagueness that we have noted above. But it also enjoys the advantage that Bickermann's claim, that the author is thinking of Roman provincial Syria, can be eliminated. This is a connection to which we have no direct access (because it is internal to the mind of the author), and for which, therefore, no actual evidence exists. Occam's razor inexorably points to the simpler, two-step reading. This alternative explanation, however, although it seems more consistent with the nature of the story, gives us little direct evidence of when the treatise was written. Its use of ubiquitous regional terms is too vague for a precise dating—although the historical improbability of it all seems broadly suggestive of a considerably later time.

Thus, the central plank in Bickermann's case for an early first-century CE date for *4 Maccabees* may be seriously challenged. But Bickermann also makes a supporting argument for his date, claiming that the treatise plainly presupposes the existence of the temple. Citing 4.20 and 14.9,[3] he states, 'Every unprejudiced reader of

---

1.   Bickermann argues that it was common for authors updating sources to make them comprehensible within the political framework of their own day. But it is unnecessary to update 2 Macc. 4.4 in *political* terms in order to make it currently *comprehensible*. The author's use of regional and ethnic boundaries makes 4.4 perfectly comprehensible in contemporary terms (understandable in all probability for considerably longer than a political revision!). Bickermann's desire to anchor the author's reference in empirical realities (rather than in the story itself) seems a good example of 'the referential fallacy'.

2.   Jones, *Cities*, p. 199. Jones points out that the Ptolemies often made attempts on Cilicia, but in general only managed to control Tracheia, which in any case was particularly valuable to them because it supplied timber for their navy. Its relative inaccessibility also made it easy to defend. On the other hand, apart from small, temporary incursions, Cilicia Pedias remained under Seleucid control.

3.   4.(19-)20 reads, 'In total disregard for the Law, Jason changed the nation's whole mode of life and its polity; [20] not only did he lay out a gymnasium on the citadel of our native Land but he

IV Macc. cannot but be impressed by the fact that the Temple and its service are regarded as existent in the book'.[1] But this is simply not true. The existence of the temple is not plainly attested to by these verses—and 7.4 may indicate just the opposite: 'No city beleaguered by many devices of all kinds has ever offered such resistance as did that perfect saint'. Admittedly this comment could simply be an eloquent figure, like the buffeted vessel of v. 1, or the protruding cliff of v. 5. But it is also possible that the comment represents a subtle expression of anti-Zealot sentiment after the fall of Jerusalem in 70 CE. Many regarded the Zealots' fanaticism as extremely destructive—including many of the surviving Pharisees.[2] The emphases of *4 Maccabees* on a passive resistance to persecution and on the law, as against a violent defense of either the temple or the land, speak in favour of this, since they are suggestive of Pharisaic theological principles. Thus, while the implication of 7.4 is not unequivocal, it is considerably more certain than 4.20 and 14.9. Consequently, the existence of the Temple at the time of writing must be deemed unproven.[3]

3. *Alternative Arguments for the Date of* 4 Maccabees

With the collapse of both Bickermann's arguments into ambiguity, we are left with various alternative approaches to dating. Dupont-Sommer argued originally on the basis of diction and style that the treatise was 'late'.[4] More recently, Urs Breitenstein has undertaken a detailed analysis of the work with particular reference to rhetoric, and, although his statistical analysis must be viewed with some caution, his meticulous stylistic and rhetorical investigation confirms Dupont-Sommer's date: 'The first third of the second century CE'.[5]

These broad stylistic observations may be strengthened by some specific

also rescinded the service of the Temple'; and 14.9 seems completely irrelevant: 'Even now we shudder when we hear of the affliction of those young men; but they, not only looking on with their own eyes, not only hearing the instant threat pronounced against them, but actually suffering the torment, endured to the end, and that in the agonies of burning. . . ' (trans. H. Anderson, *The Old Testament Pseudepigrapha* [ed. J.H. Charlesworth; 2 vols.; New York: Doubleday, 1983, 85], II, pp. 549, 59 [and the immediately following], p. 552).

1. Bickermann, 'The Date of 4 Maccabees', p. 277.
2. Cf. S.D. Cohen, *From the Maccabees to the Mishnah* (Philadelphia: Westminster Press, 1987), p. 216.
3. As Collins concludes (*Between Athens and Jerusalem*, p. 187).
4. A. Dupont-Sommer, *Le Quatrième Livre des Machabées* (Paris: Champion, 1939), pp. 75-85.
5. U. Breitenstein, *Beobachtungen zu Sprache, Stil und Gedankengut des Vierten Makkabäerbuchs* (Basel: Schwabe, 1976), p. 179. Note, Breitenstein rejects by implication many of Williams's arguments (neither scholar seems aware of the other's studies). He denies any connection between *4 Maccabees* and Ignatius, and he carefully confirms the stylistic claims of Dupont-Sommer, which Williams rejects as subjective. Finally, he denies that the rhetorical style is ambiguous, arguing that the diction and syntax place the treatise clearly in the period of Asiatic reassertion over Atticism, which took place in the second century. Features of both schools are apparent, which would probably not be the case in the first century. Admittedly, such stylistic arguments are fragile, but they are not completely lacking in force.

implications in the analysis of Robert Renehan.[1] Renehan is interested in the philosophical training and perspective of the author of *4 Maccabees*. After a careful analysis, he demonstrates that both the author of *4 Maccabees* and Galen seem to be drawing on a philosophical tractate (now lost) of Posidonius. Precise similarity in both phraseology and argumentation suggests the common use of this underlying source. Posidonius lived too early to fix the date of *4 Maccabees* (135–51 BCE?). Implicit in Renehan's analysis, however, is the point that the author of *4 Maccabees* closely shares both syntax and diction with Galen.

This relationship may be illustrated by the rare word τροχαντήρ, which is used in *4 Macc.* 8.13 to designate one of the instruments of torture. In the broadly contemporary literature, τροχαντήρ is only attested in Galen,[2] and in an epigram of Sextus Empiricus.[3] Needless to say, both these are late second-century figures. Granting the partial nature of our literature, this evidence would nevertheless seem to suggest a broadly similar, that is a second-century, date for *4 Maccabees*.

A second support for such a date is the parallel between *4 Maccabees* and other second-century accounts of martyrdom, for example, the execution of certain rabbis by Hadrian, recorded in the Talmud.[4] *4 Maccabees* and the Talmudic accounts do not exhibit a literary dependence, but they do display two rather striking points of contact:

1. In *Ber.* 61b, *'Abod. Zar.* 18a and *Sanh.* 11a, 14a and 110b, like *4 Maccabees*, the external threat is directly against the practice of the law, not against the temple, the land or apostasy in general. This corresponds to the Hadrianic persecution, rather than the first revolt in 66–70 CE.
2. Certain of the Talmudic traditions exhibit the lurid description that is characteristic of *4 Maccabees*, but not of the other texts.[5] For example, Rabbi Akiba's flesh is combed with iron carding instruments (*Ber.* 61b; cf. 'the iron claws' of *4 Macc.* 8.13); Haninah ben Teradyon is burned alive, by being wrapped in a scroll of the Law packed with wet wool

1. 'The Greek Philosophical Background of Fourth Maccabees', *Rheinisches Museum für Philologie* 115 (1972), pp. 223-38.

2. Galen uses the word 40 times (cf. TLG).

3. *Adversos Mathematicos* 316.6; 317.2. There are also three much later references (4th century and beyond), which clearly depend on these preceding usages (cf. TLG).

4. Rabbi Akiba (*Ber.* 61b), Judah ben Baba (*Sanh.* 14a) and Haninah ben Teradyon (*'Abod. Zar.* 18a; cf. also *Ṣem.* 8). These almost certainly historical martyrdoms of Pharisees who defied Hadrian's suppression of the law, recorded in the Talmud, must be distinguished from the legend of the ten martyrs (*'Asarah Haruge Malkut*) preserved in a Midrash (Midrashim *'Asarah Haruge Malkut* and *Eleh Ezkerah*). This last tradition is associated with *Yom Kippur* and also the ninth of Ab, probably in dependence on *Jubilees*, which speaks of the need to atone for the sin of selling Joseph. Consequently, Zeitlin argues that the historical value of the tradition is minimal. It is also too late to be of interest to us (S. Zeitlin, 'The Legend of the Ten Martyrs and its Apocalyptic Origins', *JQR* 36 [1945], pp. 1-17, supplemented by 'A Note on the Legend of the Ten Martyrs', *ibid.*, pp. 209-10)—although the tradition's attestation to both the historical occurrence of martyrdom and to speculation on its rationale should not be overlooked.

5. *4 Maccabees* is a considerable development from 2 Macc. 7.1-13.

('*Abod. Zar.* 18a); and Judah ben Baba is driven through three hundred times with spears so that he looks like a sieve (*Sanh.* 14a). These descriptive details parallel, but do not reproduce, the descriptions in *4 Maccabees.*[1]

Thus, the rather striking points of contact between the two literary traditions suggest a similar point of development in the Jewish presentation of martyrdom. Moreover, it seems probable that the two sets of writings arose out of the same historical context, namely, the Hadrianic persecutions. Hadrian's reign correlates neatly both with the exhortations of *4 Maccabees* to resist passively encroachments on the law, and with the stylistic observations of Dupont-Sommer and Breitenstein.

But *4 Maccabees* is also strikingly similar to various Christian martyrologies.[2] This literary genre makes its first appearance in Christian form during the second century, from which point the accounts proliferate.[3] Many of these texts also exhibit the lurid description characteristic of *4 Maccabees*; for example, Polycarp is burned alive on the Sabbath,[4] and the martyrs at Lyons are scourged, attacked with animals, roasted on a hot griddle, and tossed in a net before a bull.[5] More significant than this generally gruesome similarity, however, is the precise correlation between the tortures of Carpus, Papyius and Agathonice, and those ostensibly performed on the rabbis and on the Maccabean martyrs. Like Akiba, and Eliezer and the seven sons, the Christian martyrs are tortured by combing or scraping (the Latin verb being

---

1.   For a detailed discussion of the development of the martyrological tradition (although we differ over the date of *4 Maccabees*), cf. Pobee, *Persecution and Martyrdom*, esp. pp. 13-46.

2.   Conveniently gathered, with critical introductions and editing, in *The Acts of the Christian Martyrs* (ed. H. Musurillo; Oxford: Clarendon Press, 1972).

3.   Musurillo dates the various accounts as follows: *The Martyrdom of Polycarp* (c. 175-200 CE); *The Acts of Carpus, Papylus and Agathonice* (c. 166); *The Martyrdom of Ptolemaeus and Lucius* (c. 150-60); *The Acts of Justin and Companions* (c. 165); *The Letter of the Churches of Lyons and Vienne* (c. 177-78); *The Acts of the Scillitan Martyrs* (c. 180); *The Martyrdom of Apollonius* (the event took place between 180-85 CE, but this MS is corrupt and probably originates from the 5th or 6th century); and *The Martyrdom of Perpetua and Felicitas* (c. 200) (cf. Musurillo, *Acts*, p. xii-xxvii). T.D. Barnes ('Pre-Decian ACTA MARTYRUM', *JTS* 19 [1968], pp. 509-31) only accepts six of these as pre-Decian, dating them critically as follows: *Polycarp* (156/57), *Ptolemaeus and Lucius* (early 150s), *Justin and his Companions* (162-67), *The Martyrs of Lugdunum* ([Musurillo's *The Letter of the Churches of Lyons and Vienne*] 165-75), *The Scillitan Martyrs* (180), and *Perpetua and Felicitas* (203) .

4.   *Martyrdom of Polycarp*, 8, 11-15.

5.   *The Letter of the Churches of Lyons and Vienne* 56 (also 18, 19, 27 and 28). Barnes also notes the bizarre tortures in *Martyrdom of Potamiaena and Basilides*, stating that 'one must weigh the predilection of hagiographical fiction for refined tortures against the Roman addiction to cruelty' ('ACTA MARTYRUM', pp. 525-26). He adds the comments of Jerome, Tertullian ([the Romans were] *omne ingenium in tormentis: Mart.* 4.2) and Dionysius (bishop of Alexandria during the Decian persecution) on outlandish executions (one young man was covered in honey and then exposed to flies in the mid-day Egyptian sun; two others were dissolved in quicklime). These are, of course, all much later figures and accounts. Barnes believes that *Potamiaena* has been substantially refashioned. If there is a kernel of fact in the document, it relates to the prefect of Egypt from Oct./Nov. 206 until 210-11 CE, Subatianus Aquila ('ACTA MARTYRUM', pp. 526-27).

ungulo, and the Greek ξέω), probably performed with metal combs or carding instruments.[1] This specific parallelism suggests either a similar point of historical development with respect to the technology of torture, or (more probably) a similar stage in literary development, when torture accounts were embellished in these terms. Either way, the association is once again at least in the second century, and possibly even in the third.[2]

Consequently, we conclude that the most likely time of origin for *4 Maccabees* is definitely after 135 CE, and possibly up to a century later. With the adoption of this range of dates as the most probable for the origin of the treatise, any direct influence on Paul's atonement terminology in Rom. 3.21-26 is clearly precluded.[3]

1.   *The Acts of Carpus, Papylus and Agathonice*, 2.23 (l. 25). Barnes dates this document much later than Musurillo, probably in the third century ('ACTA MARTYRUM', pp. 514-15).

2.   The pagan martyrological tradition collated by Musurillo (in *The Acts of the Pagan Martyrs: Acta Alexandrinorum* [Oxford: Clarendon Press, 1954]) is more difficult to date and stylistically less applicable, so it has not been introduced here. Musurillo states in the preface that 'the influence [of the Pagan Acts on the Christian] was indeed slight' (p. v). With respect to date, he speculates that 'various pieces were separately composed and adapted at various dates in the first and second centuries' (p. 274). Such an imprecise collection is not helpful to us at this point.

3.   In no way is this argument to be taken as a diminishment of the influence of a more generalized martyrological tradition on Paul, which I hold to be very significant, particularly for his use of πίστις. I am disputing the more limited point that this tradition generates Paul's atonement terminology and his (or the early churches') corresponding interpretation of the death of Jesus as vicariously atoning.

Appendix 4

THE MEANING OF δικαιοσύνη θεοῦ OUTSIDE ROMANS

There should also probably be a brief discussion of certain arguments that have *not* been made, concerning Paul's δικ- terminology. It is customary to cite evidence from Paul's other letters in support of various positions on δικαιοσύνη θεοῦ in Romans. But a careful examination of that evidence suggests that it would not be very useful. This is because δικαιοσύνη θεοῦ seldom occurs outside Romans, and where δικ- terms in general occur, particularly δικαιοσύνη, they are almost invariably combined with a strong participatory theme.[1] This theme is largely absent from Romans 1–4 (and, to a lesser extent, 9–11), the two argumentative sections where δικαιοσύνη θεοῦ functions in that letter.

In more detail, in 1 Cor. 1.30 the setting is clearly 'in Christ' (cf. 6.11). The critical verse 2 Cor. 5.21 is also strongly participatory in context. Verse 14 reads, εἷς ὑπὲρ πάντων ἀπέθανεν ἄρα οἱ πάντες ἀπέθανον. Similarly, v. 17 states, εἴ τις ἐν Χριστῷ, καινὴ κτίσις. Finally, v. 21 specifically qualifies δικαιοσύνη θεοῦ in participatory terms: τὸν μὴ γνόντα ἁμαρτίαν ὑπὲρ ἡμῶν ἁμαρτίαν ἐποίησεν, ἵνα ἡμεῖς γενώμεθα δικαιοσύνη θεοῦ ἐν αὐτῷ. δικαιοσύνη θεοῦ never receives such qualification in Romans.[2]

In Galatians the genitive phrase does not occur and the argument is dominated by the verb, the isolated noun only appearing in 2.21, 3.6, 21 and 5.5.[3] Alongside 2 Corinthians 5, Philippians offers the closest analogy to the argument in Romans. The critical verse is 3.9 (cf. 1.11 and 3.6), and this is very clearly premised on incorporation in Christ: καὶ εὑρεθῶ ἐν αὐτῷ, μὴ ἔχων ἐμὴν δικαιοσύνην τὴν ἐκ νόμου ἀλλὰ τὴν διὰ πίστεως Χριστοῦ, τὴν ἐκ θεοῦ δικαιοσύνην ἐπὶ τῇ πίστει, (10) τοῦ γνῶναι αὐτόν. . .

Thus, it can be seen that, almost without exception, Paul's use of the word δικαιοσύνη outside Romans, even where it appears in a similar or identical genitive phrase, is heavily conditioned by the participatory notion of life in Christ. While this

---

1. Cf. *TDNT*, II, pp. 208-209.
2. Except perhaps, very indirectly, in Rom. 3.24b. Here, however, the ἐν Χριστῷ motif does seem unremarkable, and it is almost certainly merely instrumental. The occurrences of δικαιοσύνη in Ephesians and the Pastorals also seem mainly 'ethical-participatory' (Eph. 4.24; 5.6; 6.14; 1 Tim. 6.11; 2 Tim. 2.22; 3.16; 4.8; Tit. 3.5), that is, conditional on a recreation in Christ.
3. 2.21 and 3.21 refer to the law; 3.6 quotes Gen. 15.6; and 5.5 is probably eschatological.

position may be the end-point of Paul's argument in Romans, it is certainly illegitimate to import it into any analysis of chs. 1–4. As a result of this, I hold that the external evidence—even if it were directly admissible—is not particularly helpful for deciding the meaning of δικαιοσύνη θεοῦ in Rom. 3.21-26, where the contextual qualification apparent elsewhere is not present.[1]

---

1.   This evidence is more helpful for analysing the terminology in chs. 9–11—and one suspects that, once again, Paul is indulging in paronomasia with the phrase δικαιοσύνη θεοῦ, playing on the ambiguity of the genitive construction. Whereas he begins with the standard Jewish notion of 'the saving righteousness *of* God', during the course of the argument in Romans he redefines and specifies the nature of this saving righteousness (in Christ, of course), so that the same genitive phrase begins to take the meaning later on of 'the saving righteousness *from* God', which is Christ (cf. 1 Cor. 1.30). Thus, Paul again manages to create continuity between Christ and more traditional Jewish theology and expectations—in this instance, the hope for eschatological salvation.

BIBLIOGRAPHY

Primary Sources

Greco-Roman Rhetorical Sources

Aristotle, *Poetics* (trans. W.H. Fyfe; Cambridge, MA: Harvard University Press, 1953).

—*The 'Art' of Rhetoric* (trans. J.H. Freese; Cambridge, MA: Harvard University Press, 1947).

Cicero, *Two Books on Rhetoric, Commonly Called On Invention* (trans. H.M. Hubbell; London: William Heinemann, 1949).

—*On the Orator* (trans. H. Rackham; London: Heinemann, 1968).

—*Brutus* (trans. G.L. Hendrickson; London: Heinemann, 1939).

—*Orator* (trans. H.M. Hubbell; London: Heinemann, 1939).

—*Partitions of Oratory* (trans. H. Rackham; London: Heinemann, 1968).

—*The Best Kind of Orator* (trans. H.M. Hubbell; London: Heinemann, 1949).

—*Topics* (trans. H.M. Hubbell; London: Heinemann, 1949).

Demetrius, *On Style* (trans. W.R. Roberts; Cambridge, MA: Harvard University Press, 1953).

Dionysius of Halicarnassus, *On Literary Composition* (trans. W.R. Roberts; London: Heinemann, 1910).

Hermogenes, *On Stases*, in R. Nadeau (ed. and trans.), 'Hermogenes' *On Stases*: A Translation with an Introduction and Notes', *The Speech Teacher* 31 (1964), pp. 361-424.

Isocrates (trans. G. Norlin [vols. I and II] and L. Van Hook [vol. III]; London: Heinemann, 1928–29, 1945).

Longinus, *On the Sublime* (trans. W.H. Fyfe; Cambridge, MA: Harvard University Press, 1953).

Philodemus, 'Art of Rhetoric', in H.M. Hubbell (trans.), 'The Rhetorica of Philodemus', *Transactions of the Connecticut Academy of Arts and Sciences* 23 (1920), pp. 243-382.

Plato, *Phaedrus* (trans. H.N. Fowler; London: Heinemann, 1971).

—*Gorgias* (trans. W.R.M. Lamb; London: Heinemann, 1983).

Quintilian, *Institutes of Oratory* (trans. H.E. Butler; 4 vols.; London: Heinemann, 1933, 1939, 1943).

Rhetoric to Alexander, in *The Complete Works of Aristotle: Revised Oxford Translation* (ed. J. Barnes; trans. E.S. Forster; 2 vols.; Princeton: Princeton University Press, 1984), II, pp. 2270-315.

Rhetorica ad Herennium (trans. H. Caplan; London: Heinemann, 1954).

Tacitus, 'A Dialogue on Oratory', in *Tacitus* (trans. W. Peterson; rev. M. Winterbottom; London: Heinemann, 1970), pp. 229-347.

Jewish and Christian Primary Sources

The Acts of the Pagan Martyrs (ed. H.A. Musurillo; Oxford: Acta Alexandrinorum, 1954).

The Acts of the Christian Martyrs (ed. H.A. Musurillo; Oxford: Clarendon Press, 1972).

The Apostolic Fathers (ed. K. Lake; 2 vols.; London: Heinemann, 1912–13).

The Babylonian Talmud (ed. I. Epstein; 34 vols.; London: Soncino, 1935–48).

The Dead Sea Scrolls in English (ed. G. Vermes; Harmondsworth: Penguin, 2nd edn, 1975).

Early Christian Writings: The Apostolic Fathers (ed. M. Staniforth; Harmondsworth: Penguin, 1968).

The Mishnah (ed. H. Danby; London: Oxford University Press, 1933).

Josephus (ed. H.S.J. Thackeray; 10 vols.; London: Heinemann, 1926–65).

Novum Testamentum Graecae (ed. E. Nestle, K. Aland *et al.*; Stuttgart: Biblia-Druck, 3rd corr. edn, 1983).

The Old Testament Pseudepigrapha (ed. J.H. Charlesworth; 2 vols.; New York: Doubleday, 1983).

Philo (ed. L. Cohn and P. Wendland; 2 vols.; Berlin: Georgi Reimeri, 1896).

Septuaginta (ed. A. Rahlfs; Stuttgart: Deutsche Bibelgesellschaft, 1979).

The Works of Philo Judaeus, the Contemporary of Josephus (trans. C.D. Yonge; 4 vols.; London: Bohn, 1854–55).

Lexical and Grammatical Reference Works

Bachmann, H., and W.A. Slaby, *Vollständige Konkordanz zum griechischen Neuen Testament* (2 vols.; Berlin: de Gruyter, 1978).

Bauer, W., *A Greek–English Lexicon of the New Testament and Other Early Christian Literature* (rev. and augmented by W.F. Arndt, F.W. Gingrich and F.W. Danker; Chicago: University of Chicago Press, 2nd edn, 1979).

Blass, F., and A. Debrunner, *A Greek Grammar of the New Testament and Other Early Christian Literature* (trans. and rev. by R.W. Funk; Chicago: University of Chicago Press, 1961).

Horsley, G.H.R., *New Documents Illustrating Early Christianity* (5 vols.; Marrickville, N.S.W.: Southwood Press, 1981–89).

Liddell, H.G., and R. Scott, *A Greek–English Lexicon* (rev. and augmented by H.S. Jones, with a supplement; Oxford: Clarendon Press, 1968).

Louw, J.P., E.A. Nida, R.B. Smith, and K.A. Munson, *Greek–English Lexicon of the New Testament Based on Semantic Domains* (2 vols.; New York: United Bible Societies, 2nd edn, 1988, 1989).

Moule, C.F.D., *An Idiom Book of New Testament Greek* (Cambridge: Cambridge University Press, 2nd edn, 1959 [1953]).

Moulton, J.H., and G. Milligan, *The Vocabulary of the Greek New Testament Illustrated from the Papyri and Other Non-Literary Sources* (London: Hodder & Stoughton, 1930).

Moulton, W.F., and A.S. Geden, *A Concordance to the Greek New Testament according to the Texts of Westcott and Hort, Tischendorf and the English Revisers* (Edinburgh: T. & T. Clark, 3rd edn, 1926).

Robertson, A.T., *A Grammar of the Greek New Testament in the Light of Historical Research* (London: Hodder & Stoughton, 1914).

Smith, J.B., *Greek–English Concordance to the New Testament* (Scottsdale, PA: Herald, 1955).

Zerwick, M., and M. Grosvenor, *A Grammatical Analysis of the Greek New Testament* (Rome: Biblical Institute Press, rev. edn, 1981 [1966]).

Secondary Literature

Abbott, T.K., *A Critical and Exegetical Commentary on the Epistles to the Ephesians and to the Colossians* (Edinburgh: T. & T. Clark, 1897).

Achtemeier, E.J., 'Righteousness in the Old Testament', *IDB*, IV, pp. 80-85.

Achtemeier, P.J., 'Righteousness in the New Testament', *IDB*, IV, pp. 91-99.

—*Romans* (Atlanta: John Knox, 1985).

Alonso-Schökel, L., *The Inspired Word: Scripture in the Light of Language and Literature* (trans. F. Martin; New York: Herder & Herder, 1972 [1965]).

Alonso-Schökel, L., and W. Wuellner (eds.), *Narrative Structures in the Book of Judith* (Berkeley, CA: The Center, 1975).

Alter, R., *The Art of Biblical Narrative* (New York: Basic Books, 1981).

—*The Art of Biblical Poetry* (New York: Basic Books, 1985).

Anderson, H.G., T.A. Murphy, and J.A. Burgess (eds.), *Justification by Faith: Lutherans and Catholics in Dialogue VII* (Minneapolis: Augsburg, 1985).

Anderson, H., '4 Maccabees: A New Translation and Introduction', in *Old Testament Pseudepigrapha* (2 vols.; ed. J.H. Charlesworth; New York: Doubleday, 1985), II, pp. 531-64.

Aulén, G., *Christus Victor* (trans. A.G. Herbert; London: SPCK, 1950).

Aune, D.E., Review of *Galatians: A Commentary on Paul's Letter to the Churches of Galatia*, by H.D. Betz, *RelSRev* 7 (1981), pp. 323-28.

—*The New Testament in its Literary Environment* (Philadelphia: Westminster Press, 1987).

Bacon, B.W., 'The Festival of Lives Given for the Nation in Jewish and Christian Faith', *HibJ* 15 (1916–17), pp. 256-78.

Bahr, G.J., 'The Subscriptions in the Pauline Letters', *JBL* 87 (1968), pp. 27-41.

Bailey, R.W., L. Matejka, and P. Steiner, *The Sign: Semiotics around the World* (Ann Arbor, MI: Michigan Slavic Publications, 1978).

Baillie, D.M., *God was in Christ: An Essay on Incarnation and Atonement* (London: Faber & Faber, 1948).

Banks, R. (ed.), *Reconciliation and Hope: New Testament Essays on Atonement and Eschatology Presented to L.L. Morris on his Sixtieth Birthday* (Grand Rapids: Eerdmans, 1974).

Barmby, J., *Romans* (London: Funk & Wagnalls, 1890).

Barnes, T.D., 'Pre-Decian ACTA MARTYRUM', *JTS* 19 (1968), pp. 509-31.

Barr, J., *The Semantics of Biblical Language* (Oxford: Oxford University Press, 1961).

—*Biblical Words for Time* (London: SCM Press, 1962).

—*Comparative Philology and the Text of the Old Testament* (Oxford: Clarendon Press, 1968).

Barrett, C.K., *A Commentary on the Epistle to the Romans* (London: Adam & Charles Black, 1957).

—*From First Adam to Last* (London: Adam & Charles Black, 1962).

—'I am not Ashamed of the Gospel', in *idem, New Testament Essays* (London: SPCK, 1970), pp. 116-43.

Barth, K., *The Epistle to the Romans* (trans. E.C. Hoskyns; London: Oxford University Press, 6th edn, 1952 [1933]).

—*Church Dogmatics* (trans. G.W. Bromiley; 12 vols.; Edinburgh: T. & T. Clark, 1956).

—*Christ and Adam: Man and Humanity in Romans 5* (trans. T.A. Smail; New York: Octagon Books, 1983 [1956]).

Barth, M., 'Jews and Gentiles: The Social Character of Justification in Paul', *JES* 5 (1968), pp. 241-67.

—'The Faith of the Messiah', *HeyJ* 10 (1969), pp. 363-70.

—*Justification: Pauline Texts in the Light of the Old and New Testaments* (trans. A.M. Woodruff; Grand Rapids: Eerdmans, 1971).

—*Ephesians* (2 vols.; Garden City, NY: Doubleday, 1974).

Barthes, R., 'Style and its Image', in *Literary Style: A Symposium* (ed. S. Chapman; New York: Oxford University Press, 1971), pp. 3-15.

—'Myth Today', in *idem, Mythologies* (trans. A. Lavers; New York: Hill & Wang, 1972 [1957]), pp. 109-59.

Bassler, J., *Divine Impartiality: Paul and a Theological Axiom* (Chico, CA: Scholars Press, 1982).

—'Divine Impartiality in Paul's Letter to the Romans', *NovT* 26 (1984), pp. 43-58.

Batey, R., and J.H. Gill, 'Fact, Language, and Hermeneutic: An Interdisciplinary Exploration', *SJT* 23 (1970), pp. 13-26.

Baumgarten, J.M., 'Sacrifice and Worship among the Jewish Sectarians of the Dead Sea (Qumran) Scrolls', *HTR* 46 (1953), pp. 141-59.

Beare, F.W., 'Romans', *IDB*, IV, pp. 112-22.

Beasley-Murray, G.A., and F. Laubach, ' "αἷμα" and "ῥαυτίξω" ', *NIDNTT*, I, pp. 222-25.

Behm, J., 'αἷμα κτλ', *TDNT*, I, pp. 172-77.

Beker, J.C., *Paul the Apostle: The Triumph of God in Life and Thought* (Philadelphia: Fortress Press, 1940).

Bengel, J.A., *Gnomon of the New Testament* (trans. C.T. Lewis and M.R. Vincent; Philadelphia: Perkinpine & Higgins, 1860–62 [1742]).

Benoit, P., 'Qumran and the New Testament', in *Paul and Qumran: Studies in New Testament Exegesis* (ed. J. Murphy-O'Connor; London: Chapman, 1968), pp. 1-30.

Berger, K., 'Neues Material zur "Gerechtigkeit Gottes" ', *ZNW* 68 (1977), pp. 266-75.

Berlin, A., *Poetics and Interpretation of Biblical Narrative* (Sheffield: Almond Press, 1983).

Best, E., *The Letter of Paul to the Romans* (Cambridge: Cambridge University Press, 1967).

Betz, H.D., *Der Apostel Paulus und die sokratische Tradition* (Tübingen: Mohr, 1972).

—'The Literary Composition and Function of Paul's Letter to the Galatians', *NTS* 21 (1974–75), pp. 353-79.

—*Galatians: A Commentary on Paul's Letter to the Churches in Galatia* (Philadelphia: Fortress Press, 1979).

—*Second Corinthians 8 and 9: A Commentary on Two Administrative Letters of the Apostle Paul* (Philadelphia: Fortress Press, 1985).

Bickermann, E., *From Ezra to the Last of the Maccabees: Foundations of Post-Biblical Judaism* (trans. M. Hadas; New York: Schocken, 1962 [1947]).

—'The Date of IV Maccabees', in *idem*, *Studies in Jewish and Christian History: Part One* (Leiden: Brill, 1976), I, pp. 275-81.

Bitzer, L., 'The Rhetorical Situation', *Philosophical Review* (1968), pp. 1-14.

Black, M., 'The Pauline Doctrine of the Second Adam', *SJT* 7 (1954), pp. 170-79.

—*Romans* (London: Marshall, Morgan & Scott, 1973).

Blackman, C., 'Romans 3.26b: A Question of Translation', *JBL* 87 (1968), pp. 203-204.

Blass, F., *Die Rhythmen der asianischen und römischen Kunstprosa* (Hildesheim: Gerstenberg, 1972 [1905]).

J. Bligh, *Galatians in Greek: A Structural Analysis of St Paul's Epistle to the Galatians with Notes on the Greek* (Detroit: University of Detroit Press, 1966).

Bollier, J.A., 'The Righteousness of God: A Word Study', *Int* 8 (1954), pp. 404-13.

Boman, T., *Hebrew Thought Compared with Greek* (trans. J.L. Moreau; New York: Norton, 1970 [1954]).

Booth, W., *The Rhetoric of Fiction* (Chicago: University of Chicago Press, 2nd edn, 1982).

Bornkamm, G., *Paul* (trans. D.M.G. Stalker; New York: Harper & Row, 1971 [1969]).

Bottorff, J.F., 'The Relation of Justification and Ethics in the Pauline Epistles', *SJT* 70 (1973), pp. 421-30.

Bowker, J., *The Targums and Rabbinic Literature: An Introduction to Jewish Interpretations of Scripture* (Cambridge: Cambridge University Press, 1969).

Brandt, W.J., *The Rhetoric of Argumentation* (New York: Bobbs–Merrill, 1970).

Brauch, M.T., ' "God's Righteousness" in Recent German Discussion', in E.P. Sanders, *Paul and Palestinian Judaism* (Philadelphia: Fortress Press, 1977), pp. 532-42.

Breitenstein, U., *Beobachtungen zu Sprache, Stil und Gedankengut des Vierten Makkabäerbuchs* (Basel: Schwabe, 1976).

Bromiley, G.W., 'The Doctrine of Justification in Luther', *EvQ* 24 (1952), pp. 91-110.

Brown, C. (ed. and trans.), *New International Dictionary of New Testament Theology* (Exeter: Paternoster Press; Grand Rapids, MI: Zondervan, 1978 [1971–72]).

Brown, S., *The Origins of Christianity: A Historical Introduction to the New Testament* (Oxford: Oxford University Press, 1984).

—'Reader-Response: Demythologising the Text', *NTS* 34 (1988), pp. 232-37.

Brownlee, W.H., 'Messianic Motifs of Qumran and the New Testament', *NTS* 3 (1956–57), pp. 195-210.

Bruce, F.F., 'Justification by Faith in the Non-Pauline Writings of the New Testament', *EvQ* 24 (1952), pp. 66-77.

—*The Letter of Paul to the Romans: An Introduction and Commentary* (Grand Rapids: Eerdmans, 2nd edn, 1985).

Brunner, E., *The Letter to the Romans: A Commentary* (trans. H.A. Kennedy; Philadelphia: Westminster Press, 1959 [1938]).

Buber, M., *Two Types of Faith* (trans. N.P. Goldhawk; London: Routledge & Kegan Paul, 1951).

Büchler, A., *Studies in Sin and the Atonement in the Rabbinic Literature of the First Century* (New York: Ktav, 1967).

Büchsel, F., 'ἀγοράζω, ἐξαγοράζω', *TDNT*, I, pp. 124-28.

Büchsel, F., and J. Hermann, 'ἵλεως κτλ', *TDNT*, III, pp. 300-23.

Büchsel, F., and O. Procksch, 'λύω κτλ', *TDNT*, IV, pp. 335-56.

Bultmann, R., *Der Stil der paulinische Predigt und die kynisch-stoische Diatribe* (Göttingen: Vandenhoeck & Ruprecht, 1910).

—'Neueste Paulusforschung', *TR* 8 (1936), pp. 11-12.

—'Glossen im Römerbrief', *TLZ* 4 (1947), pp. 197-202.

—*Theology of the New Testament* (trans. K. Grobel; 2 vols.; New York: Scribners, 1951, 1955 [1948]).

—'ΔΙΚΑΙΟΣΥΝΗ ΘΕΟΥ', *JBL* 83 (1964), pp. 12-16.

—'πάρεσις κτλ', *TDNT*, VI, pp. 509-12.

Bultmann, R., and A. Weiser, 'πίστις', *TDNT*, VI, pp. 174-228.

Burney, C.F., 'The Hebrew Word for "Atone" ', *ExpTim* 22 (1910–11), pp. 325-27.

Burton, E. de Witt., *A Critical and Exegetical Commentary on the Epistle to the Galatians* (Edinburgh: T. & T. Clark, 1921).

Byrne, B., *'Sons of God'–'Seed of Abraham': A Study of the Idea of the Sonship of God of All Christians in Paul against the Jewish Background* (Rome: Biblical Institute Press, 1979).

—'Living out the Righteousness of God: The Contribution of Rom. 6.1–8.13 to an Understanding of Paul's Ethical Presuppositions', *CBQ* 43 (1981), pp. 557-81.

—*Reckoning with Romans: A Contemporary Reading of Paul's Gospel* (Wilmington, DE: Michael Glazier, 1986).

Cadman, W.H., 'Δικαιοσύνη in Romans 3,21-26', in *Studia Evangelica* (ed. F.L. Cross; Berlin: Akademie Verlag, 1964), pp. 532-34.

Caird, G.B., *The Language and Imagery of the Bible* (London: Gerald Duckworth, 1980).

Callaway, J.S., 'Paul's Letter to the Galatians and Plato's *Lysias*', *JBL* 67 (1948), pp. 353-56.

Campbell, D.A., 'The Rhetoric of Righteousness in Romans 3.21-26' (PhD dissertation, University of Toronto, 1989).

—'The Meaning of ΠΙΣΤΙΣ and ΝΟΜΟΣ in Paul: A Linguistic and Structural Perspective', *JBL* (forthcoming).

—'Ambiguity and Apocalypse in Hab. 2.4—Rom. 1.17 Revisited', (forthcoming).

Campbell, W.S., 'The Romans Debate', *JSNT* 10 (1981), pp. 19-28.

—'Why Did Paul Write Romans?' *ExpTim* 85 (1973–74), pp. 264-69.

—'Romans III as a Key to the Structure and Thought of the Letter', *NovT* 23 (1981), pp. 22-40.

Cavallin, H.C.C., 'The Righteous Shall Live by Faith', *ST* 32 (1978), pp. 33-43.

Church, F.F., 'Rhetorical Structure and Design in Paul's Letter to Philemon', *HTR* 71 (1978), pp. 17-33.

Cohen, S.D., *From the Maccabees to the Mishnah* (Philadelphia: Westminster Press, 1987).

Collins, J.J., *Between Athens and Jerusalem: Jewish Identity in the Hellenistic Diaspora* (New York: Crossroad, 1982).

—'The Testamentary Literature in Recent Scholarship', in *Early Judaism and its Modern Interpreters* (ed. R.A. Kraft and G.W.E. Nickelsburg; Atlanta: Scholars Press, 1986), pp. 268-85.

Colson, F.H., 'Μετασχημάτισα 1 Cor. iv 6', *JTS* 17 (1915–16), pp. 379-84.

Conzelmann, H., 'Paul's Doctrine of Justification: Theology or Anthropology?', in *Theology of the Liberating Word* (ed. F. Herzog; Nashville: Abingdon Press, 1971 [1968]), pp. 108-23.

Cook, S.A., F.E. Adcock, and M.P. Charlesworth (eds.), *The Cambridge Ancient History*. X. *The Augustan Empire: 44 BC–AD 70*. XI. *The Imperial Peace: AD 70–192* (Cambridge: Cambridge University Press, 1934).

Corbett, E.P.J., *Classical Rhetoric for the Modern Student* (New York: Oxford University Press, 1965).

—(ed.), *Rhetorical Analyses of Literary Works* (New York: Oxford University Press, 1969).

Corsani, B., 'ΕΚ ΠΙΣΤΕΩΣ in the Letters of Paul', in *The New Testament Age: Essays in Honor of Bo Reicke* (ed. W.C. Weinrich; Macon, GA: Mercer University Press, 1984), I, pp. 87-93.

Cosgrove, C.H., 'Arguing like a Mere Human Being: Galatians 3.15-18 in Rhetorical Perspective', *NTS* 34 (1988), pp. 536-49.

Cotterell, P., and M. Turner, *Linguistics and Biblical Interpretation* (London: SPCK, 1989).

Cranfield, C.E.B., *A Critical and Exegetical Commentary on the Epistle to the Romans* (2 vols.; Edinburgh: T. & T. Clark, 1975, 1979).

—'The Significance of διὰ πάντος in Romans 11,10', in *Studia Evangelica* (ed. F.L. Cross; Berlin: Akademie Verlag, 1964), pp. 546-50.

Creed, J.M., 'ΠΑΡΕΣΙΣ in Dionysius of Halicarnassus and in St Paul', *JTS* 41 (1940), pp. 28-30.

Cremer, H., *Die paulinische Rechtfertigungslehre im Zusammenhange ihrer geschichtlichen Voraussetzungen* (Gütersloh: Bertelsmann, 2nd edn, 1900).

Crowther, C., 'Son of God and Sons of God [Rom. 8.29]', *ExpTim* 86 (1974–75), pp. 274-75.

Crüsemann, F., 'Jahwes Gerechtigkeit im Alten Testament', *EvT* 36 (1976), pp. 427-50.

Culler, J., *Saussure* (London: Fontana, 1976).

Cullmann, O., *Christology of the New Testament* (trans. S.C. Guthrie and C.A.M. Hall; London: SCM Press, 1957).

Culpepper, R.H., *Interpreting the Atonement* (Grand Rapids: Eerdmans, 1966).

Daalen, D.H. von, 'The Revelation of God's Righteousness in Romans 1.17', in *Studia Biblica 1978: Papers on Paul and Other New Testament Authors at the Sixth International Congress on Biblical Studies* (ed. E.A. Livingstone; JSNTSup, 3; Sheffield: JSOT Press, 1980), pp. 183-89.

Dabourne, W., 'The Faithfulness of God and the Doctrine of Justification in Romans 1.16–4.25' (unpublished dissertation, University of Cambridge, 1988).

Dahl, N.A., 'Two Notes on Romans 5', *Studia Theologica* 5 (1951–52), pp. 37-48.

—'The Atonement—An Adequate Reward for the Aqedah?', in *Studies in Honour of Matthew Black* (ed. E.E. Ellis and M. Wilcox; Edinburgh: T. & T. Clark, 1969), pp. 15-29.

—*Studies in Paul: Theology for the Early Christian Mission* (Minneapolis: Augsburg, 1977).

—'Romans 3.9: Text and Meaning', in *Paul and Paulinism—Essays in Honour of C.K. Barrett* (ed. M.D. Hooker and S.G. Wilson; London: SPCK, 1982), pp. 15-29.

Daly, R.J., *Christian Sacrifice: The Judaeo-Christian Background before Origen* (Washington, DC: Catholic University of America Press, 1978).

Daube, D., 'Rabbinic Methods of Interpretation and Hellenistic Rhetoric', *HUCA* 22 (1949), pp. 239-64.

—'Redemption', in *idem*, *The New Testament and Rabbinic Judaism* (London: Athlone Press, 1956), pp. 268-78.

Davies, G.N., *Faith and Obedience in Romans: A Study in Romans 1–4* (JSNTSup, 39; Sheffield: JSOT Press, 1990).

Davies, W.D., *Paul and Rabbinic Judaism: Some Rabbinic Elements in Pauline Theology* (London: SPCK, 4th edn, 1980 [1948]).

Deissmann, G.A., *Bible Studies* (trans. A. Grieve; Edinburgh: T. & T. Clark, 1901).

—'ἱλαστήριος und ἱλαστήριον: Eine lexikalische Studie', *ZNW* 4 (1903), pp. 193-212.

—*Light from the Ancient East* (trans. L.R.M. Strachan; London: Hodder & Stoughton, 2nd edn, 1910).

—*St Paul: A Study in Social and Religious History* (trans. L.R.M. Strachan; London: Hodder & Stoughton, 1912).

—'Mercy-Seat', in *Encyclopaedia Biblica*, III, pp. 3027-35.

Delitzsch, F., *Bible Commentary on the Psalms* (trans. F. Bolton; 2 vols.; Edinburgh: T. & T. Clark, 1880).

Denney, J.F., *The Death of Christ* (London: Hodder & Stoughton, 1951 [1902]).

—*The Christian Doctrine of Reconciliation* (London: Hodder & Stoughton, 1917).

Dillistone, F.W., *The Significance of the Cross* (Philadelphia: Westminster Press, 1946).

—*Jesus Christ and his Cross: Studies on the Saving Work of Christ* (Philadelphia: Westminster Press, 1953).

—'The Atonement', in *Christian History and Interpretation: Studies Presented to John Knox* (ed. W.R. Farmer, C.F.D. Moule and R.R. Niebuhr; Cambridge: Cambridge University Press, 1967), pp. 35-56.

Dodd, C.H., *The Meaning of Paul for Today* (London: George Allen & Unwin, 1920).

—*The Epistle of Paul to the Romans* (London: Hodder & Stoughton, 1932).

—*The Bible and the Greeks* (London: Hodder & Stoughton, 1935).

—*According to the Scriptures* (London: Lowe & Brydone, 1952).

—'The Mind of Paul', in *idem, New Testament Studies* (New York: Scribners, 1952), pp. 67-128.

Donfried, K.P., 'Justification and Last Judgment in Paul', *ZNW* 67 (1976), pp. 90-110.

—(ed.), *The Romans Debate* (Minneapolis: Augsburg, 1977).

—'Romans 3.21-28', *Int* 34 (1980), pp. 59-64.

Downing, J., 'Jesus and Martyrdom', *JTS* 14 (1963), pp. 279-93.

Drummond, J., 'On the Meaning of Righteousness of God in the Theology of St Paul', *HibJ* 1 (1902), pp. 83-95.

Dunn, J.D.G., 'Paul's Understanding of the Death of Jesus', in R. Banks (ed.), *Reconciliation and Hope*, pp. 125-41.

—*Unity and Diversity in the New Testament: An Inquiry into the Character of Earliest Christianity* (Philadelphia: Westminster Press, 1977).

—*Romans 1–8* (Dallas: Word Books, 1988).

—*Romans 9–16* (Dallas: Word Books, 1988).

Dupont-Sommer, A., *Le Quatrième Livre des Machabés* (Paris: Champion, 1939).

Eco, U., *A Theory of Semiotics* (Bloomington, IN: Indiana University Press, 1976).

—*The Role of the Reader* (Bloomington, IN: Indiana University Press, 1979).

—*Semiotics and the Philosophy of Language* (Bloomington, IN: Indiana University Press, 1983).

Eichrodt, W., *Theology of the Old Testament* (trans. J.A. Baker; 2 vols.; Philadelphia: Fortress Press, 6th edn, 1961, 1967).

Elliot, J.K., 'The Language and Style of the Concluding Doxology to the Epistle to the Romans', *ZNW* 72 (1981), pp. 124-30.

Elliott, N., *The Rhetoric of Romans: Argumentative Constraint and Strategy and Paul's Dialogue with Judaism* (JSNTSup, 45; Sheffield: JSOT Press, 1990).

Ellis, E.E., *Paul's Use of the Old Testament* (London: Oliver & Boyd, 1957).

—'Christ Crucified', in R. Banks (ed.), *Reconciliation and Hope*, pp. 69-75.

Endicott, T., 'The Style of St Paul the Apostle in the Letters to the Corinthians and Romans' (unpublished paper, Oxford, 1982).

Feuillet, A., 'La citation d'Habacuc 2.4 et les huit premiers chapitres de l'Epître aux Romains', *NTS* 6 (1959–60), pp. 52-80.

Fiore, B., ' "Covert Allusion" in 1 Corinthians 1–4', *CBQ* 47 (1985), pp. 85-102.

Fischel, H.A., 'Martyr and Prophet', *JQR* 37 (1947), pp. 265-80.

—*Rabbinic Literature and Graeco-Roman Philosophy: A Study of Epicurea and Rhetorica in Early Midrashic Writings* (Leiden: Brill, 1973).

Fitzer, G., 'Der Ort der Versöhnung nach Paulus', *TZ* 22 (1966), pp. 161-83.

Fitzmyer, J.A., 'The Letter to the Romans', in *JBC*, pp. 291-331.

—'Pauline Theology', in *JBC*, pp. 800-27.

—'The Targum of Leviticus from Qumran Cave 4', *Maarav* 1 (1978), pp. 15-17.

—*To Advance the Gospel: New Testament Essays* (New York: Crossroad, 1981).

—'The Pauline Letters and the Lucan Account of Paul's Missionary Journeys', *SBLSP* (1988), pp. 82-90.

Flusser, D., 'The Dead Sea Sect and Pre-Pauline Christianity', *Scripta Hierosolymitana* 4 (1958), pp. 215-66.

Forbes, C., 'Comparison, Self-Praise and Irony: Paul's Boasting and the Conventions of Hellenistic Rhetoric', *NTS* 32 (1986), pp. 1-30.

Forsyth, P.T., *The Work of Christ* (London: Independent Press, 1938).

—*The Cruciality of the Cross* (London: Independent Press, 1948).

Francis, I.S., 'An Exposition of a Statistical Approach to the Federalist Dispute', in *The Computer and Literary Style* (ed. J. Leed; Kent, OH: Kent State University Press, 1966), pp. 38-78.

Frazer, J.G., *The Golden Bough: A Study in Magic and Religion*. VI. *The Scapegoat* (London: Macmillan, 1913).

Frend, W.H.C., *Martyrdom and Persecution in the Early Church: A Study of Conflict from the Maccabees to Donatus* (Oxford: Basil Blackwell, 1965).

Fridrichsen, A., 'Aus Glauben zu Glauben, Röm 1.17', *ConNT* 12 (1948), p. 54.

Friedrich, J., W. Pöhlmann, and P. Stuhlmacher (eds.), *Rechtfertigung: Festschrift für Ernst Käsemann zum 70 Geburtstag* (Göttingen: Vandenhoeck & Ruprecht, 1976).

Fryer, N.S.L., 'The Meaning and Translation of *Hilasterion* in Romans 3.25', *EvQ* 59 (1987), pp. 99-116.

Fung, R.Y.K., 'The Forensic Character of Justification', *Themelios* 3 (1977), pp. 16-21.

Funk, R.W., 'The Apostolic Parousia: Form and Significance', in *Christian History and Interpretation* (ed. W.R. Farmer, C.F.D. Moule and R. Niebuhr; Cambridge: Cambridge University Press, 1967), pp. 249-68.

Furnish, V.P., *Theology and Ethics of Paul* (New York: Abingdon Press, 1968).

Gager, J., *The Origins of Anti-Semitism: Attitudes Toward Judaism in Pagan and Christian Antiquity* (Oxford: Oxford University Press, 1973).

Gamble, H., *The Textual History of the Letter to the Romans* (Grand Rapids: Eerdmans, 1977).

Garland, D.E., 'The Composition and Unity of Philippians: Some Neglected Literary Factors', *NovT* 27 (1985), pp. 141-73.

Garnet, P., 'Atonement Constructions in the Old Testament and the Qumran Scrolls', *EvQ* 46 (1974), pp. 131-63.

—*Salvation and Atonement in the Qumran Scrolls* (Tübingen: Mohr, 1977).

—'Qumran Light on Pauline Soteriology', in *Pauline Studies: Essays Presented to F.F. Bruce on his Seventieth Birthday* (ed. D.A. Hagner and M.J. Harris; Exeter: Paternoster Press, 1980), pp. 19-32.

Gaston, L., 'Paul and Jerusalem', in *From Jesus to Paul: Studies in Honour of Francis Wright Beare* (ed. G.P. Richardson and J.C. Hurd; Waterloo: Wilfrid Laurier University Press, 1984), pp. 61-72.

—*Paul and the Torah* (Vancouver: University of British Columbia Press, 1987).

Geller, S.A., *Parallelism in Early Biblical Poetry* (Missoula, MT: Scholars Press, 1979).

Gibson, A., *Biblical Semantic Logic: A Preliminary Analysis* (Oxford: Basil Blackwell, 1981).

Glombitza, O., 'Von der Scham des Gläubigen: Erwägungen zu Röm 1.14-17', *NovT* 4 (1960), pp. 74-80.

Goodspeed, E.J., 'Gaius Titius Justus', *JBL* 69 (1950), pp. 382-83.

—'Some Greek Notes: III Justification', *JBL* 73 (1954), pp. 86-91.

Gordis, R., 'The Structure of Biblical Poetry', in *Poets, Prophets, and Sages: Essays in Biblical Interpretation* (Bloomington, IN: Indiana University Press, 1971), pp. 61-94.

Grant, R.M., 'Like Children', *HTR* 39 (1946), pp. 71-73.

—'Hellenistic Elements in Galatians', *ATR* 34 (1952), pp. 223-26.

—'Hellenistic Elements in I Corinthians', in *Early Christian Origins: Studies in Honor of Harold R. Willoughby* (ed. A. Wikgren; Chicago: Quadrangle, 1961), pp. 60-66.

Grayston, K., ' "Not Ashamed of the Gospel": Romans 1,16a and the Structure of the Epistle', in *Studia Evangelica* (Berlin: Akademie–Verlag, 1961), II, pp. 569-73.

—''ΙΛΑΣΚΕΣΘΑΙ and Related Words in LXX', *NTS* 27 (1980–81), pp. 640-56.

Grenfell, B.P., A.S. Hunt and D.G. Hogarth (eds.), *Fayum Towns and their Papyri* (London, 1900).

Grube, G.M.A., *A Greek Critic: Demetrius on Style* (Toronto: University of Toronto Press, 1961).

Grundman, W., 'The Teacher of Righteousness of Qumran and the Question of Justification by Faith in the Theology of the Apostle Paul', in *Paul and Qumran* (ed. J. Murphy-O'Connor; London: Chapman, 1968), pp. 85-114.

Habel, N., Review of *Gerechtigkeit als Weltordnung*, by H.G. Reventlow, *JBL* 91 (1972), pp. 544-46.

Hadas, M. (ed.), *The Third and Fourth Books of Maccabees* (New York: Segal & Nickelsburg, 1953).

Hahn, F., 'Taufe und Rechtfertigung: Ein Beitrag zur paulinische Theologie in ihrer Vor- und Nachgeschichte', in J. Friedrich *et al.* (eds.), *Rechtfertigung*, pp. 95-124.

Hansen, G.W., *Abraham in Galatians: Epistolary and Rhetorical Contexts* (JSNTSup, 29; Sheffield: JSOT Press, 1989).

Harrison, E.F., 'Romans', in *The Expositor's Bible Commentary* (ed. F.E. Gabelein; Grand Rapids: Zondervan, 1976), X, pp. 3-171.

J. Haussleiter, 'Der Glaube Jesu und der Christliche Glaube', *NKZ* 2 (1891), pp. 109-45, 205-30.

Hays, R.B., 'Psalm 143 and the Logic of Romans 3', *JBL* 99 (1980), pp. 107-15.

—*The Faith of Jesus Christ: An Investigation of the Narrative Substructure of Galatians 3.1–4.11* (Chico, CA: Scholars Press, 1983).

—' "Have We Found Abraham to Be our Forefather according to the Flesh?": A Reconsideration of Rom. 4.1', *NovT* 27 (1985), pp. 76-98.

—*Echoes of Scripture in the Letters of Paul* (New Haven: Yale University Press, 1990).

Hayward, R., 'The Present State of Research in the Targumic Account of the Sacrifice of Isaac', *JJS* 32 (1981), pp. 127-50.

Hebert, G., 'Faithfulness and Faith', *Theology* 58 (1955), pp. 373-79.

Heil, J.P., *Romans—Paul's Letter of Hope* (Rome: Biblical Institute Press, 1987).

Hengel, M., *Judaism and Hellenism: Studies in Palestine during the Early Hellenistic Period* (trans. J. Bowden; 2 vols.; London: SCM Press, 2nd edn, 1974).

—*The Son of God* (trans. J. Bowden; London: SCM Press, 1976).

—'The Expiatory Sacrifice of Christ', *BJRL* 62 (1980), pp. 454-75.

—*The Atonement* (trans. J. Bowden; London: SCM Press, 1981).

Hester, J.D., 'The Rhetorical Structure of Galatians 1.11–2.14', *JBL* 103 (1984), pp. 223-33.

Hicks, F.C.N., *The Fullness of Sacrifice: An Essay in Reconciliation* (London: Macmillan, 2nd edn, 1938 [1930]).

Hill, D., 'DIKAIOI as a Quasi-Technical Term', *NTS* 11 (1964–65), pp. 296-302.

—*Greek Words and Hebrew Meanings: Studies in the Semantics of Soteriological Terms* (Cambridge: Cambridge University Press, 1967).

Hillyer, N., 'The Servant of God', *EvQ* 41 (1969), pp. 143-60.

Hirsch, E.G., 'Right and Righteous', in *Jewish Encyclopedia*, X, pp. 420-24.

Hooker, M.D., *Jesus and the Servant: The Influence of the Servant Concept of Deutero-Isaiah in the New Testament* (London: SPCK, 1959).

—'Adam in Romans 1', *NTS* 6 (1959–60), pp. 297-306.

—'Interchange in Christ', *JTS* 22 (1971), pp. 349-61.

—'Interchange and Atonement', *BJRL* 60 (1978), pp. 462-81.

—*Pauline Pieces* (London: Epworth Press, 1979).

—'Interchange and Suffering', in *Suffering and Martyrdom in the New Testament* (ed. W. Horbury and B. McNeill; Cambridge: Cambridge University Press, 1981), pp. 70-83.

Howard, G., 'Notes and Observations on the "Faith of Christ" ', *HTR* 60 (1967), pp. 459-65.

—'Rom. 3.21-31 and the Inclusion of the Gentiles', *HTR* 63 (1970), pp. 223-33.

—'The "Faith of Christ" ', *ExpTim* 85 (1974), pp. 212-25.

—*Paul: Crisis in Galatia—A Study in Early Christian Theology* (Cambridge: Cambridge University Press, 1979).

Hughes, F.W., *Early Christian Rhetoric and 2 Thessalonians* (JSNTSup, 30; Sheffield: JSOT Press, 1989).

Hultgren, A.J., 'The PISTIS CHRISTOU Formulation in Paul', *NovT* 22 (1980), pp. 248-63.

—*Paul's Gospel and Mission: The Outlook from his Letter to the Romans* (Philadelphia: Fortress Press, 1985).

Hurd, J.D., 'The Jesus whom Paul Preaches (Acts 19.13)', in *From Jesus to Paul* (ed.

G.P. Richardson and J.D. Hurd; Waterloo: Wilfrid Laurier University Press, 1984), pp. 73-89.

James, E.O., *The Origins of Sacrifice: A Study in Comparative Religion* (Port Washington, NY: Kennikat Press, 1971).

—*The Nature and Function of Priesthood: A Comparative and Anthropological Study* (New York: Vanguard Press, 1955).

—*Sacrifice and Sacrament* (London: Thames & Hudson, 1962).

Janzen, J.G., 'Habakkuk 2.2-4 in the Light of Recent Philological Advances', *HTR* 73 (1980), pp. 53-78.

Jeremias, J., 'Chiasmus in den Paulusbriefen', *ZNW* 49 (1958), pp. 145-56.

Jervis, A., *The Purpose of Romans: A Comparative Letter-Structure Investigation* (JSNTSup, 55; Sheffield: JSOT Press, 1991).

Jewett, R., 'The Form and Function of the Homiletic Benediction', *ATR* 51 (1969), pp. 18-34.

—'The Agitators and the Galatian Congregation', *NTS* 17 (1970–71), pp. 198-212.

—*Paul's Anthropological Terms: A Study of their Use in Conflict Settings* (Leiden: Brill, 1971).

—'Major Impulses in the Theological Interpretation of Romans since Barth', *Int* 34 (1980), pp. 17-31.

—'Romans as an Ambassadorial Letter', *Int* 36 (1982), pp. 5-20.

—'The Law and the Coexistence of Jews and Gentiles', *Int* 39 (1985), pp. 341-56.

—'The Redaction and Use of an Early Christian Confession in Romans 1.3-4', in *The Living Text: Essays in Honor of Ernest W. Saunders* (ed. R. Jewett and D.E. Groh; Washington, DC: University Press of America, 1985), pp. 99-122.

—*The Thessalonian Correspondence: Pauline Rhetoric and Millenarian Piety* (Philadelphia: Fortress Press, 1986).

Johnson, L.T., 'Rom. 3.21-26 and the Faith of Jesus', *CBQ* 44 (1982), pp. 77-90.

Johnson, P.F., 'The Use of Statistics in the Analysis of the Characteristics of Pauline Writing', *NTS* 20 (1974), pp. 92-100.

Johnson, S., 'Paul and 1QS', *HTR* 118 (1955), pp. 157-65.

Jones, A.H.M., *The Cities of the Eastern Roman Provinces* (Oxford: Clarendon Press, 2nd edn, 1971).

Jonge, M. de, *The Testaments of the Twelve Patriarchs* (Assen: Van Gorcum, 1953).

Judge, E.A., 'The Early Christians as a Scholastic Community', *JRH* 1 (1960–61), pp. 4-15, 125-37.

—*The Social Pattern of Christian Groups in the First Century* (London: Tyndale, 1960).

—'Paul's Boasting in Relation to Contemporary Professional Practice', *AusBR* 16 (1968), pp. 37-50.

—'St Paul and Classical Society', *JAC* 15 (1972), pp. 19-36.

Judge, E.A., and G.S.R. Thomas, 'The Origin of the Church at Rome: A New Solution', *RTR* 25 (1966), pp. 81-94.

Jüngel, E., *Paulus und Jesus: Eine Untersuchung zur Präzisierung der Frage nach dem Ursprung der Christologie* (Tübingen: Mohr [Paul Siebeck], 2nd edn, 1964).

Käsemann, E., 'Zum Verständnis von Römer 3,24-26', *ZNW* 43 (1950–51), pp. 150-54.

—'Liturgische Formeln im NT', in *Religion in Geschichte und Gegenwart* (Tübingen: Mohr [Paul Siebeck], 3rd edn, 1958), II, pp. 993-96.

—*New Testament Questions of Today* (trans. W.J. Montague; London: SCM Press, 1969 [1965]).

—*Perspectives on Paul* (trans. M. Kohl; London: SCM Press, 1971).

—*Commentary on Romans* (trans. G. Bromiley; Grand Rapids: Eerdmans, 1980 [1975]).

Kautzsch, E., *Über die Derivate des Stammes TSDQ im alttestamentlichen Sprachgebrauch* (Tübingen: Mohr [Paul Siebeck] 1881).

Kaye, B.N., ' "To the Romans and Others" Revisited', *NovT* 18 (1976), pp. 37-77.

Kearns, C., 'The Interpretation of Romans 6.7', in *Studiorum Paulinorum Congressus Internationalis Catholicus 1961* (Rome: Pontifical Biblical Institute, 1963), pp. 301-307.

Kelly, J.N.D., *Early Christian Doctrines* (San Francisco: Harper & Row, 1960).

Kennedy, G.A., *The Art of Persuasion in Greece* (Princeton: Princeton University Press, 1963).

—*Quintilian* (New York: Twayne, 1969).

—*The Art of Rhetoric in the Roman World: 300 BC–AD 300* (Princeton: Princeton University Press, 1972).

—*Classical Rhetoric and its Christian and Secular Tradition from Ancient to Modern Times* (Chapel Hill, NC: University of North Carolina Press, 1980).

—'An Introduction to the Rhetoric of the Gospels', *Rhetorica* 1 (1983), pp. 17-31.

—*New Testament Interpretation through Rhetorical Criticism* (Chapel Hill, NC: University of North Carolina Press, 1984).

Kertelge, K., *'Rechtfertigung' bei Paulus* (Münster: Aschendorff, 1966).

—*The Epistle to the Romans* (trans. F. McDonagh; New York: Herder & Herder, 1972).

Kessler, M., 'A Methodological Setting for Rhetorical Criticism', *Semitica* 4 (1974), pp. 22-36.

—'An Introduction to Rhetorical Criticism of the Bible: Prolegomena', *Semitica* 7 (1980), pp. 1-27.

Kirby, J.T., 'The Syntax of Romans 5.12: A Rhetorical Approach', *NTS* 33 (1987), pp. 283-86.

—'The Rhetorical Situation of Revelation 1–3', *NTS* 34 (1988), pp. 197-207.

Kittel, G., 'πίστις Ἰησοῦ χριστοῦ bei Pauline', *TSK* 79 (1906), pp. 419-36.

Klein, G., 'Righteousness in the New Testament', *IDBSup*, pp. 750-52.

—'Gottes Gerechtigkeit als Thema der neuesten Paulus-Forschung', in *idem*, *Rekonstruction und Interpretation* (Munich: Kaiser, 1969), pp. 225-36.

Knox, J., *Chapters in a Life of Paul* (New York: Abingdon Press, 1950).

—*The Death of Christ* (New York: Abingdon Press, 1978).

—'Romans', *IB*, IX, pp. 353-668.

Koch, D.A., 'Der Text von Hab 2:4b in der Septuaginta und im Neuen Testament', *ZNW* 76 (1985), pp. 68-85.

Koch, H., 'Römer 3.21-26 in der Paulusinterpretation der letzten 150 Jahre' (unpublished PhD dissertation, University of Göttingen, 1971).

Koch, K., 'Die israelitische Sühneanschauung und ihre historischen Wandlungen' (unpublished *Habilitationsschrift*, University of Erlangen, 1956).

Koch, K., 'tsdq', *Theologisches Handwörterbuch zum Alten Testament* (Munich: Kaiser Verlag, 1976), II, pp. 507-30.

König, E., *Stilistik, Rhetorik, Poetik* (Leipzig: Theodor Weicher, 1900).

Kraft, R., and G.E. Nickelsburg, *Early Judaism and its Modern Interpreters* (Atlanta: Scholars Press, 1986).

Kramer, W., *Christ, Lord, Son of God* (trans. B. Hardy; Chatham: SCM Press, 1966 [1963]).

Kümmel, W.G., *Römer 7 und die Bekehrung des Paulus* (Leipzig: Hinrichs, 1929).

—'Πάρεσις und Ἔνδειξις: Ein Beitrag zum Verständnis der paulinischen Rechtfertigungslehre', in *idem, Heilgeschehen und Geschichte: Gesammelte Aufsätze, 1933–64* (Marburg: N.G. Elwert, 1965 [1952]), I, pp. 260-70.

—*Man in the New Testament* (trans. J.J. Vincent; London: Epworth Press, 1963).

Küng, H., *Justification: The Doctrine of Karl Barth and a Catholic Reflection* (trans. T. Collins, E.E. Tolk and D. Granskou; New York: Nelson, 1964).

Kuss, O., *Der Römerbrief* (2 vols.; Regensburg: Friedrich Pustet, 2nd edn, 1957).

Ladd, G., 'Righteousness in Romans', *Southwestern Journal of Theology* 19 (1976).

Langdon, S.H., 'The Hebrew Word for "Atone"', *ExpTim* 22 (1910–11), pp. 320-25.

Lanham, R.A., *A Handlist of Rhetorical Terms: A Guide for Students of English Literature* (London: Cambridge University Press, 1968).

Lausberg, H., *Handbuch der literarischen Rhetorik* (2 vols.; Munich: Hueber, 1960).

—*Elemente der literarischen Rhetorik* (Munich: Hueber, 8th edn, 1984).

Leach, E., *Genesis as Myth and Other Essays* (London: Jonathan Cape, 1969).

Leaney, A.R.C., 'The Eschatological Significance of Human Suffering in the Old Testament and the Dead Sea Scrolls', *SJT* 16 (1963), pp. 286-96.

—'The Righteous Community in Paul', *Studia Evangelica* (Berlin: Akademie-Verlag, 1987), XI, pp. 441-46.

Leenhardt, F.J., *The Epistle to the Romans: A Commentary* (trans. H. Knight; London: Lutterworth, 1961 [1957]).

Leggett, D., *The Levirate and Goel Institutions in the Old Testament with Special Attention to the Book of Ruth* (Cherry Hill, NJ: Mack, 1974).

Lindars, B., *New Testament Apologetic: The Doctrinal Significance of the Old Testament Quotations* (London: SCM Press, 1961).

Lofthouse, W.F., 'The Righteousness of Yahweh', *ExpTim* 50 (1938–39), pp. 341-45.

—'The Righteousness of God', *ExpTim* 50 (1938–39), pp. 441-45.

Lohse, E., *Märtyrer und Gottesknecht: Untersuchungen zur urchristlichen Verkündigung vom Sühntod Jesu Christi* (Göttingen: Vandenhoeck & Ruprecht, 1955).

—*The Formation of the New Testament* (trans. M.E. Boring; Nashville: Abingdon Press, 1981 [1972]).

—*Die Einheit des Neuen Testaments: Exegetische Studien zur Theologie des Neuen Testaments* (Göttingen: Vandenhoeck & Ruprecht, 1973).

Longenecker, B., *The Ideological Background of the Philippian Hymn and its Significance for Interpretation* (unpublished MRel dissertation, Wycliffe College, University of St Michaels, Toronto, 1986).

Longenecker, R.N., *Paul, Apostle of Liberty* (New York: Harper & Row, 1964).

—*The Christology of Early Jewish Christianity* (London: SCM Press, 1970).

—'The Obedience of Christ in the Theology of the Early Church', in R. Banks (ed.), *Reconciliation and Hope*, pp. 142-52.

—'Ancient Amanuenses and the Pauline Epistles', in *New Dimensions in New Testament Study* (ed. R.N. Longenecker and M.C. Tenney; Grand Rapids: Zondervan, 1974), pp. 281-97.

—*Biblical Exegesis in the Apostolic Period* (Grand Rapids: Eerdmans, 1975).

—'The Faith of Abraham Theme in Paul, James, and Hebrews: A Study in the Circumstantial Nature of New Testament Teaching', *JETS* 20 (1977), pp. 203-12.

—'The Pedagogical Nature of the Law in Galatians 3.19–4.7', *JETS* 25 (1982), pp. 53-61.

—'On the Form, Function, and Authority of the New Testament Letters', in *Scripture and Truth* (ed. D.A. Carson and J.D. Woodbridge; Grand Rapids: Zondervan, 1983), pp. 101-14.

—*New Testament Social Ethics for Today* (Grand Rapids: Eerdmans, 1984).

—'Romans' (lecture series, Wycliffe College, University of St Michaels, Toronto, 1986).

—*Galatians* (Dallas, TX: Word, 1990).

Lorenzi, L. de (ed.), *Battesimo e Giustizia in Rom 6 e 8* (Rome: Abbazi S. Paolo fuori le mura, 1974).

Lührmann, D., 'Rechtfertigung und Versöhnung: Zur Geschichte der paulinischen Tradition', *ZTK* 67 (1970), pp. 437-52.

Lund, N.W., *Chiasmus in the New Testament: A Study in Formgeschichte* (Durham, NC: University of North Carolina Press, 1942).

Lundbom, J.R., *Jeremiah: A Study in Ancient Hebrew Rhetoric* (Missoula, MT: Scholars Press, 1975).

Luther, M., *Lectures on Romans* (trans. W. Pauck; Philadelphia: Westminster Press, 1961).

Lyonnet, S., 'De "Iustitia Dei" in Epistola ad Romanos 1,17 et 3,21-22', *VD* 25 (1947), pp. 23-34.

—'Pauline Soteriology', in *Introduction to the New Testament* (ed. A. Robert and A. Feuillet; New York: Tournai, 1965), pp. 820-65.

Lynonnet, S., and L. Sabourin, *Sin, Redemption, and Sacrifice: A Biblical and Patristic Study* (Rome: Biblical Institute Press, 1970).

Lyons, J., *Semantics* (2 vols.; Cambridge: Cambridge University Press, 1976).

McKnight, E.V., *The Bible and the Reader: An Introduction to Literary Criticism* (Philadelphia: Fortress Press, 1985).

McNamara, M., *Intertestamental Literature* (Wilmington, DE: Michael Glazier, 1983).

McSorley, H., *Luther, Right or Wrong?* (London: Augsburg, 1969).

Maier, W.A., 'Paul's Concept of Justification and Some Recent Interpretations of Rom. 3.21-26', *The Springfielder* 37 (1974), pp. 248-64.

Mailloux, S., 'Truth or Consequences: On Being against Theory', in *Against Theory* (ed. W.J.T. Mitchell; Chicago: University of Chicago Press, 1985), pp. 65-71.

Malherbe, A.J., 'The Beasts at Ephesus', *JBL* 87 (1968), pp. 71-80.

—'Athenagoras on Christian Ethics', *JEH* 20 (1969), pp. 1-5.

—'The Structure of Athenagoras: "Supplicatio pro Christianus"', *VC* 23 (1969), pp. 1-20.

—'The Apologetic of the *Preaching of Peter*', *ResQ* 13 (1970), pp. 203-17.

—' "Gentle as a Nurse": The Cynic Background of I Thess. ii', *NovT* 12 (1970), pp. 203-17.

—'Cynics', *IDBSup*, pp. 201-13.

—*Social Aspects of Early Christianity* (Philadelphia: Fortress Press, 2nd [enlarged] edn, 1983 [1977]).

—'The Inhospitality of Diotrephes', in *God's Christ and his People: Studies in Honour of Nils Alstrup Dahl* (ed. J. Jervall and W.A. Meeks; Oslo: Universitetsforlaget, 1977), pp. 222-32.

—'Ancient Epistolary Theorists', *Ohio Journal of Religious Studies* 5 (1977), pp. 3-77.

—(ed.), *The Cynic Epistles* (Missoula, MT: Scholars Press, 1977).

—'Pseudo-Heraclitus, Epistle 4: The Divinisation of the Wise Man', *JAC* 21 (1978), pp. 42-64.

—'Medical Imagery in the Pastoral Epistles', in *Texts and Testaments: Critical Essays on the Bible and Early Church Fathers* (ed. W.E. March; San Antonio: Trinity University Press, 1980), pp. 19-35.

—'Exhortation in First Thessalonians', *NovT* 25 (1983), pp. 238-56.

—'Self-Definition among Cynics and Epicureans', in *Jewish and Christian Self-Definition. III. Self-Definition in the Greco-Roman World* (ed. E.P. Sanders and B.F. Meyer; Philadelphia: Fortress Press, 1983), pp. 46-59.

—' "In Season and Out of Season": 2 Timothy 4.2', *JBL* 103 (1984), pp. 235-43.

—(ed.), *Moral Exhortation: A Greco-Roman Sourcebook* (Philadelphia: Westminster Press, 1986).

—*Paul and the Thessalonians: The Philosophic Tradition of Pastoral Care* (Philadelphia: Fortress Press, 1987).

—' "Pastoral Care" in the Thessalonian Church', *NTS* 36 (1990), pp. 375-91.

Man, P. de, *Blindness and Insight: Essays in the Rhetoric of Contemporary Criticism* (New York: Oxford University Press, 1971).

—'Semiology and Rhetoric', *Diacritics* 3 (1973), pp. 27-33.

—*The Rhetoric of Romanticism* (New York: Columbia University Press, 1984).

—*The Resistance to Theory* (Minneapolis: University of Minnesota Press, 1986).

Manson, T.W., 'ΙΛΑΣΤΗΡΙΟΝ', *JTS* 46 (1945), pp. 1-10.

—'The Argument from Prophecy', *JTS* 46 (1945), pp. 129-36.

—'St Paul's Letter to the Romans—And Others', in *The Romans Debate* (ed. K. Donfried; Minneapolis: Augsburg, 1977), pp. 1-16.

Marcus, J., 'The Circumcision and the Uncircumcision in Rome', *NTS* 35 (1989), pp. 67-81.

Marshall, B.A., *A Historical Commentary on Asconius* (Columbia: University of Missouri Press, 1985).

Marshall, I.H., 'The Development of the Concept of Redemption in the New Testament', in R. Banks (ed.), *Reconciliation and Hope*, pp. 153-69.

—*The Origins of New Testament Christology* (Leicester: Inter-Varsity Press, 1977).

Martin, J.P., 'The Kerygma of Romans', *Int* 25 (1971), pp. 303-28.

Martin, R.P., *Carmen Christi: Philippians 2.5-11 in Recent Interpretation and in the Setting of Early Christian Worship* (Cambridge: Cambridge University Press, 1967).

Mason, S., 'Paul, Classical Anti-Jewish Polemic, and the Letter to the Romans', in *Self-Definition and Self-Discovery in Early Christianty: A Study in Changing Horizons* (ed. D.J. Hawkins and T. Robinson; Lampeter, UK: Edwin Mellen Press, 1990), pp. 181-223.

Meecham, H.G., 'Romans 3.25f.; 4.25—The Meaning of διά c. Acc', *ExpTim* 50 (1938–39), p. 564.

Meeks, W.A., Review of *Galatians*, by H.D. Betz, *RelSRev* 7 (1981), pp. 304-307.

Metzger, B.M., *A Textual Commentary on the Greek New Testament* (n.p.: United Bible Societies, 1971).

Meyer, B.F., 'The Pre-Pauline Formula in Rom. 3.25-26a', *NTS* 29 (1983), pp. 198-208.

Michel, O., *Der Brief an die Römer* (Göttingen: Vandenhoeck & Ruprecht, 1957).

Micklem, N., *The Doctrine of our Redemption* (London: Eyre & Spottiswoode, 1943).

Milligan, W., *The Ascension and Heavenly Priesthood of our Lord* (London: Macmillan, 1892).

Minear, P.S., *The Obedience of Faith: The Purposes of Paul in the Epistle to the Romans* (London: SCM Press, 1971).

Moffatt, J., *A Critical and Exegetical Commentary on the Epistle to the Hebrews* (Edinburgh: T. & T. Clark, 1924).

—'Romans', in *idem*, *An Introduction to the Literature of the New Testament* (New York: Charles Scribner's Sons 1925), pp. 130-49.

Moody, R.M., 'The Habakkuk Quotation in Romans 1.17', *ExpTim* 92 (1980–81), pp. 205-208.

Moore, G.F., *Judaism in the First Centuries of the Christian Era: The Age of the Tannaim* (3 vols.; Cambridge, MA: Harvard University Press, 1966 [1927–30]).

—'Sacrifice', *Encyclopaedia Biblica*, II, cols. 4183-233.

Morris, L., 'The use of ἱλάσκεσθαι etc. in Biblical Greek', *ExpTim* 62 (1950–51), pp. 227-33.

—*The Apostolic Preaching of the Cross* (London: Tyndale, 1955).

—'The Meaning of ʼΙΛΑΣΤΗΡΙΟΝ in Romans III.25', *NTS* 2 (1955–56), pp. 33-43.

—*The Epistle to the Romans* (Leicester: Inter-Varsity Press, 1988).

Mosteller, F., and D.L. Wallace, 'Inference in an Authorship Problem', *Journal of the American Statistical Association* 58 (1963), pp. 275-309.

—*Inference and Disputed Authorship: The Federalist* (Reading, MA: Addison–Wesley, 1964).

Moule, C.F.D., 'The Biblical Conception of Faith', *ExpTim* 68 (1957), p. 157.

—*An Idiom Book of NT Greek* (Cambridge: Cambridge University Press, 2nd edn, 1959).

—'The Sacrifice of the People of God (1)', in *The Parish Communion Today* (ed. D.M. Paton; London: SPCK, 1962), pp. 78-93.

—'Obligation in the Ethic of Paul', in *Christian History and Interpretation* (ed. W.R. Farmer, C.F.D. Moule and R.R. Niebuhr; Cambridge: Cambridge University Press, 1967), pp. 389-406.

—'Fulfillment-Words in the New Testament: Use and Abuse', *NTS* 14 (1968), pp. 293-320.

—'Justification in its Relation to the Condition κατὰ πνεῦμα (Rom. 8.1-11)', in L. Lorenzi (ed.), *Battismo e giusitizia in Rom 6 e 8*, pp. 176-201.

—*The Origin of Christology* (Cambridge: Cambridge University Press, 1977).

Moule, H.C.G., *The Epistle of St Paul to the Romans* (London: Hodder & Stoughton, 1894).

Moulton, R.G., *The Literary Study of the Bible* (New York: Heath, 1895).

Muilenburg, J., *Specimens of Biblical Literature* (New York: Thomas Y. Crowell, 1923).

—'Literary Form in the Fourth Gospel', *JBL* 51 (1932), pp. 40-53.

—'The Literary Approach—The Old Testament as Hebrew Literature', *Journal of the National Association of Biblical Instructors* 1 (1933), pp. 14-22.

—'The Literary Character of Isaiah 34', *JBL* 59 (1940), pp. 339-65.

—'Psalm 47', *JBL* 63 (1944), pp. 235-56.

—'A Study in Hebrew Rhetoric: Repetition and Style', *VTSup* (Leiden: Brill, 1953), I, pp. 347-65.

—'Isaiah', *IB*, V, pp. 381-773.

—'The Form and Structure of the Covenantal Formulations', *VT* 9 (1959), pp. 347-65.

—'The Linguistic and Rhetorical Usages of the Particle *yk* in the Old Testament', *HUCA* 32 (1961), pp. 135-60.

—'A Liturgy on the Triumphs of Yahweh', in *Studia Biblica et Semitica* (Wageningen: H.V. Veenman en Zonen N. Vt., 1966), pp. 233-51.

—'Form Criticism and Beyond', *JBL* 88 (1969), pp. 1-18.

Müller, C., *Gottes Gerechtigkeit und Gottes Volk: Eine Untersuchung zu Römer 9–11* (Göttingen: Vandenhoeck & Ruprecht, 1964).

Munck, J., *Paul and the Salvation of Mankind* (trans. F. Clarke; London: SCM Press, 1959).

Murray, J., *The Epistle to the Romans: The English Text with Introduction, Exposition, and Notes* (2 vols.; Grand Rapids: Eerdmans, 1959).

Neumann, K., *The Authenticity of the Pauline Epistles in the Light of Stylostatistical Analysis* (Atlanta: Scholars Press, 1990).

Nickelsburg, G.W.E., *Resurrection, Immortality and Eternal Life in Intertestamental Judaism* (Cambridge, MA: Harvard University Press, 1972).

Nicole, R., 'C.H. Dodd and the Doctrine of Propitiation', *WTJ* 17 (1954–55), pp. 117-47.

Nida, E.A., J.P. Louw, A.H. Snyman, and J.v.W. Cronjé, *Style and Discourse, with Special Reference to the Text of the Greek New Testament* (Cape Town: Bible Society of South Africa, 1983).

Nineham, D., Review of *Structuralist Interpretations of Biblical Myth*, by E. Leach and D.A. Aycock, *JTS* 37 (1986), p. 442.

Norden, E., *Die antike Kunstprosa* (2 vols.; Leipzig: Teubner, 1909).

Nygren, A., *Commentary on Romans* (trans. C.C. Rasmussen; Philadelphia: Muhlenberg Press, 1944).

O'Connor, M.P., *Hebrew Verse Structure* (Winona Lake, IN: Eisenbrauns, 1980).

O'Neill, J.C., *Paul's Letter to the Romans* (London: Penguin Books, 1975).

O'Rourke, J.J., '*Pistis* in Romans', *CBQ* 35 (1973), pp. 188-94.

—'Some Considerations about Attempts at Statistical Analysis of the Pauline Corpus', *CBQ* 35 (1973), pp. 483-90.

Oepke, A., 'Δικαιοσύνη θεοῦ bei Paulus in neuer Beleuchtung', *TLZ* 78 (1953), pp. 257-64.

Olford, D.L., 'Paul's Use of Cultic Language in Romans: An Exegetical Study of Major Texts in Romans which Employ Cultic Language in a Non-Literal Way' (unpublished PhD thesis, University of Sheffield, 1985).

Osterley, W.O.E., *Sacrifices in Ancient Israel: Their Origin, Purposes, and Development* (New York: Macmillan, 1935).

Parker, T.H.L., *Commentaries on the Epistle to the Romans, 1532–1542* (Edinburgh: T. & T. Clark, 1986).

Paton, W.R., and E.L. Hücks, *The Inscription of Cos* (Oxford: Clarendon Press, 1981).

Patte, D., *What is Structural Exegesis?* (Philadelphia: Fortress Press, 1976).

—*Paul's Faith and the Power of the Gospel: A Structural Introduction to the Pauline Letters* (Philadelphia: Fortress Press, 1983).

Penna, R., 'Les Juifs à Rome au temps de l'Apôtre Paul', *NTS* 28 (1982), pp. 321-47.

Percy, E., *Die Probleme der Kolosser- und Epheserbriefe* (Lund: Gleerup, 1946).

Perelman, C., and L. Olbrechts-Tyteca, *The New Rhetoric: A Treatise on Argumentation* (trans. J. Wilkinson and P. Weaver; Notre Dame, IN: Notre Dame University Press, 1958).

Petersen, N.R., *Literary Criticism for New Testament Critics* (Philadelphia: Fortress Press, 1978).

Piper, J., 'The Demonstration of the Righteousness of God in Romans 3.24-26', *JSNT* 7 (1980), pp. 2-32.

—'The Righteousness of God in Romans 3.1-8', *TZ* 36 (1980), pp. 3-16.

—*The Justification of God: An Exegetical and Theological Study of Romans 9.1-23* (Grand Rapids: Baker, 1983).

Platt, F., 'Atonement', in *A Dictionary of the Apostolic Church* (ed. J. Hastings; Edinburgh: T. & T. Clark, 1915), I, pp. 110-23.

Plevnik, J., *What are they Saying about Paul?* (New York: Paulist Press, 1986).

Pluta, A., *Gottes Bundestreue: Ein Schlüsselbegriff in Röm 3,25a* (Stuttgart: Katholisches Bibelwerk, 1969).

Pluta-Messerschmidt, E., *Gerechtigkeit Gottes bei Paulus* (Tübingen: Mohr, 1973).

Pobee, J.S., *Persecution and Martyrdom in the Theology of Paul* (JSNTSup, 6; Sheffield: JSOT Press, 1985).

Price, J.L., 'God's Righteousness Shall Prevail', *Int* 28 (1974), pp. 259-80.

Pryor, J.W., 'Paul's Use of *Iesous*—A Clue for the Translation of Romans 3.26?', *Colloquium* 16 (1983), pp. 31-45.

Quick, O.C., *The Gospel of the New World: A Study in the Christian Doctrine of Atonement* (London: Macmillan, 1944).

Rad, G. von, *Old Testament Theology* (trans. D.M.G. Stalker; Edinburgh: Oliver & Boyd, 1962 [1957]).

—*The Problem of the Hexateuch and Other Essays* (trans. E.W.T. Dicken; London: SCM Press, 1984 [1958]).

Räisänen, H., *Paul and the Law* (Tübingen: Mohr, 1983).

Rashdall, H., *The Idea of the Atonement in Christian Theology* (London: Macmillan, 1920).

Rayment, C.S., 'A Current Survey of Ancient Rhetoric (1939–1957)', and 'Ancient Rhetoric (1957–63)', in *The Classical World Bibliography of Philosophy, Religion, and Rhetoric* (London: Garland, 1978), pp. 371-96.

Renehan, R., 'The Greek Philosophical Background of Fourth Maccabees', *Rheinisches Museum für Philologie* 115 (1972), pp. 223-38.

Reumann, J., 'The Gospel of the Righteousness of God', *Int* 20 (1966), pp. 432-52.

—*Righteousness in the New Testament* (Philadelphia: Fortress Press, 1982).

Reventlow, H.G., *Rechtfertigung im Horizont des Alten Testaments* (Munich: Kaiser, 1971).

Rhoads, D., and D. Michie, *Mark as Story* (Philadelphia: Fortress Press, 1982).

Rhyne, C.T., *Faith Establishes the Law* (Chico, CA: Scholars Press, 1981).

Richardson, A., *An Introduction to the Theology of the New Testament* (London: SCM Press, 1958).

Richardson, G.P., *Israel in the Apostolic Church* (Cambridge: Cambridge University Press, 1969).

Ridderbos, H., *Paul: An Outline of his Theology* (trans. J.R. de Witt; Grand Rapids: Eerdmans, 1975 [1966]).

—'The Earliest Confession of the Atonement in Paul', in R. Banks (ed.), *Reconciliation and Hope*, pp. 76-89.

Riffaterre, M., 'The Stylistic Approach to Literary History', *New Literary History* 2 (1970), pp. 39-55.

—'Interpretation and Descriptive Poetry: A Reading of Wordsworth's *Yew Trees*', *New Literary History* 4 (1973), pp. 229-56.

—'The Self-Sufficient Text', *Diacritics* 3 (1973), pp. 39-45.

—*Semiotics of Poetry* (Bloomington, IN: Indiana University Press, 1978).

—*Text Production* (trans. T. Lyons; New York: Columbia University Press, 1983).

Robert, L., *Etudes épigraphiques et philologiques* (Paris: Champion, 1938).

Roberts, D.R., 'Introduction', in *idem* (trans.), *Demetrius On Style* (London: Heinemann, 1953), pp. 257-93.

Robinson, D.W.B., 'Faith of Jesus Christ', *RTR* 29 (1970), pp. 71-81.

—'The Priesthood of Paul in the Gospel of Hope', in R. Banks (ed.), *Reconciliation and Hope*, pp. 321-45.

Robinson, J.A., *St Paul's Epistle to the Ephesians* (London: Macmillan, 1922).

Robinson, J.A.T., *The Body: A Study in Pauline Theology* (London: SCM Press, 1952).

—*Wrestling with Romans* (London: SCM Press, 1970).

Roehrs, W.R., 'Covenant and Justification in the Old Testament', *CTM* 35 (1964), pp. 583-602.

Ropes, J.H., ' "Righteousness" and "The Righteousness of God" in the Old Testament and in St Paul', *JBL* 22 (1903), pp. 211-27.

Rupp, G., *The Righteousness of God* (New York: Philosophical Library, 1953).

Russell, D.S., *The Method and Message of Jewish Apocalyptic* (Philadelphia: Westminster Press, 1964).

Sanday, W., and A.C. Headlam, *A Critical and Exegetical Commentary on the Epistle to the Romans* (Edinburgh: T. & T. Clark, 2nd edn, 1896).

Sanders, E.P., 'Patterns of Religion in Paul and Rabbinic Judaism', *HTR* 66 (1973), pp. 455-78.

—*Paul and Palestinian Judaism: A Comparison of Patterns of Religion* (Philadelphia: Fortress Press, 1977).

—*Paul, the Law, and the Jewish People* (Philadelphia: Fortress Press, 1983).

Sanders, J.A., 'Habakkuk in Qumran, Paul, and the Old Testament', *JR* 39 (1959), pp. 232-44.

Saussure, F. de, *Course in General Linguistics* (ed. C. Bally, A. Sechehaye and A. Riedlinger; trans. W. Baskin; New York: McGraw–Hill, 1959 [1915]).

Schatkin, M., 'The Maccabean Martyrs', *VC* 28 (1974), pp. 97-113.

Schechter, S., *Some Aspects of Rabbinic Judaism* (New York: Schocken, 1961 [1909]).

Schlatter, A., *Gottes Gerechtigkeit: Ein Kommentar zum Römerbrief* (Stuttgart: Calwer, 1935).

Schlier, H., *Der Römerbrief* (Freiburg: Herder, 1977).

Schmid, H.H., *Gerechtigkeit als Weltordnung* (Tübingen: Mohr [Paul Siebeck], 1968).

Schmidt, H.W., *Der Brief des Paulus an die Römer* (Berlin: Evangelische Verlagsanstalt, 2nd edn, 1966).

Schoeps, H.J., 'The Sacrifice of Isaac in Paul's Theology', *JBL* 65 (1946), pp. 385-92.

—*Paul: The Theology of the Apostle in the Light of Jewish Religious History* (trans. H. Knight; London: Lutterworth, 1961).

Schrage, W., 'Römer 3,21-26 und die Bedeutung des Todes Jesu Christi bei Paulus', in *Das Kreuz Jesu: Theologisches Überlegungen* (ed. P. Rieger; Göttingen: Vandenhoeck & Ruprecht, 1969), pp. 65-89.

Schrenk, G., and G. Quell, 'δικαιόω, κτλ', *TDNT*, II, pp. 210-25.

Schüssler-Fiorenza, E., 'Rhetorical Situation and Historical Reconstruction in 1 Corinthians', *NTS* 33 (1987), pp. 386-403.

Schütz, R., 'Die Bedeutung der Kolometrie für das Neue Testament', *ZNW* 21 (1922), pp. 161-84.

Schweitzer, A., *Paul and his Interpreters* (trans. W. Montgomery; New York: Schocken, 1964 [1912]).

—*The Mysticism of Paul the Apostle* (trans. W. Montgomery; New York: Seabury, 1968).

Schweizer, E., *Lordship and Discipleship* (London: SCM Press, 1960).

—'Dying and Rising with Christ', *NTS* 14 (1967), pp. 1-14.

—'υἱός', *TDNT*, VIII, pp. 334-92.

Scott, C.A.A., *Christianity according to St Paul* (Cambridge: Cambridge University Press, 1927).

Scroggs, R., 'Rom. 6.7 ὁ γὰρ ἀποθανὼν δεδικαίωται ἀπὸ τῆς ἁμαρτίας', *NTS* 10 (1963), pp. 104-108.

—*The Last Adam: A Study in Pauline Anthropology* (Oxford: Basil Blackwell, 1966).

—'Paul as Rhetorician: Two Homilies in Romans 1–11', in *Jews, Greeks and Christians: Essays in Honor of William David Davies* (ed. R. Hamerton-Kelly and R. Scroggs; Leiden: Brill, 1976), pp. 271-98.

Seeley, D., *The Noble Death: Graeco-Roman Martyrology and Paul's Concept of Salvation* (JSNTSup, 28; Sheffield: JSOT Press, 1990).

Segal, A.F., 'He who did not Spare his Own Son... Jesus, Paul and the Akedah', in *From Jesus to Paul: Studies in Honour of Francis Wright Beare* (ed. J.C. Hurd and G.P. Richardson; Waterloo: Wilfrid Laurier University Press, 1984), pp. 169-84.

Sharp, D.S., 'For our Justification', *ExpTim* 39 (1927–28), pp. 87-90.

Shedd, R.P., *Man in Community: A Study of St Paul's Application of Old Testament and Early Jewish Conceptions of Human Solidarity* (London: Epworth Press, 1958).

Silva, M., *Biblical Words and their Meaning: An Introduction to Lexical Semantics* (Grand Rapids: Zondervan, 1983).

Skinner, J., 'Righteousness', in *Dictionary of the Bible* (ed. J. Hastings; Edinburgh: T. & T. Clark, 1902), IV, pp. 272-81.

Sloan, T.O., 'Restoration of Rhetoric to Literary Study', *The Speech Teacher* 16 (1967), pp. 91-97.

Smit, J., 'The Letter of Paul to the Galatians: A Deliberative Speech', *NTS* 35 (1989), pp. 1-26.

Smith, C.R., *The Bible Doctrine of Salvation: A Study of the Atonement* (London: Epworth Press, 1941).

Smith, D.M., 'Ο ΔΕ ΔΙΚΑΙΟΣ ΕΚ ΠΙΣΤΕΩΣ ΖΗΣΕΤΑΙ', in *Studies in the History and Text of the New Testament in Honor of Kenneth Willis Clark* (ed. B.L. Daniels and M.J. Suggs; Salt Lake City: University of Utah Press, 1967), pp. 13-25.

Smith, M., 'A Comparison of Early Christian and Early Rabbinic Tradition', *JBL* 82 (1963), pp. 169-76.

Smith, W.R., *Lectures on the Religion of the Semites: The Fundamental Institutions* (London: A. & C. Black, 3rd edn, 1927 [1888–89]).

Snaith, N.H., *Distinctive Ideas of the Old Testament* (London: Epworth Press, 1944).

Snodgrass, K.R., 'Justification by Grace—to the Doers: An Analysis of the Place of Romans 2 in the Theology of Paul', *NTS* 32 (1986), pp. 72-93.

Snyman, A.H., 'Style and the Rhetorical Situation of Rom. 8.31-39', *NTS* 34 (1988), pp. 218-31.

Snyman, A.H., and J.v.W. Cronje, 'Toward a New Classification of the Figures (ΣΧΗΜΑΤΑ) in the Greek New Testament', *NTS* 32 (1986), pp. 113-21.

Sousan, A., 'Essay on the Interpretation of Genesis IV 1-16, The Story of Cain and Abel', (unpublished MA dissertation, University of St Michaels, Toronto, 1985).

Southwell, P.J.M., 'A Note on Habakkuk ii. 4', *JTS* 19 (1968), pp. 614-17.

Spencer, A.B., 'An Apologetic for Stylistics in Biblical Studies', *JETS* 29 (1986), pp. 419-27.

Spengel, L. von (ed.), *Rhetores Graeci* (3 vols.; Leipzig: Teubner, 1853–56).

Stacey, W.D., *The Pauline View of Man, in Relation to its Judaic and Hellenistic Background* (London: Macmillan, 1956).

Stambaugh, J.E., and D.L. Balch, *The New Testament in its Social Environment* (Philadelphia: Westminster Press, 1986).

Stanley, D.M., *Christ's Resurrection in Pauline Soteriology* (Rome: Pontifical Biblical Institute, 1961).

Staples, P., 'The Unused Lever?: A Study of the Possible Literary Influence of the Greek Maccabean Literature on the New Testament', *Modern Churchman* 9 (1965–66), pp. 218-24.

Stauffer, E., *New Testament Theology* (trans. J. Marsh; London: SCM Press, 5th edn, 1955).

Stendahl, K., *Paul among Jews and Gentiles* (Philadelphia: Fortress Press, 1976).

Stephens, G.B., 'Righteousness in the New Testament', in *Dictionary of the Bible* (ed. J. Hastings; Edinburgh: T. & T. Clark, 1902), IV, pp. 291-84.

Stevens, W.A., 'The Forensic Meaning of δικαιοσύνη', *AJT* 1 (1897), pp. 443-50.

Stewart, J., *A Man in Christ: The Vital Elements of St Paul's Religion* (London: Hodder & Stoughton, 1935).

Stibbs, A.M., *The Meaning of the Word 'Blood' in Scripture* (London: Tyndale, 1947).

Stowers, S.K., *The Diatribe and Paul's Letter to the Romans* (Chico, CA: Scholars Press, 1981).

—'Paul's Dialogue with a Fellow Jew in Rom. 3.1-9', *CBQ* 46 (1984), pp. 707-22.

—'Social Stature, Public Speaking and Private Teaching: The Circumstances of Paul's Preaching Activity', *NovT* 26 (1984), pp. 60-82.

—*Letter Writing in Greco-Roman Antiquity* (Philadelphia: Westminster Press, 1986).

—'ἐκ πίστεως and διὰ τῆς πίστεως in Romans 3.30', *JBL* 108 (1989), pp. 665-74.

Strack, H.L., *Introduction to the Talmud and Midrash* (New York: Atheneum, 1969 [1931]).

Strack, H.L., and P. Billerbeck, *Kommentar zum Neuen Testament aus Talmud und Midrasch* (6 vols. [vols. 5–6 ed. J. Jeremias and K. Adolph]; Munich: Beck, 1922–28 [vols. 1–4], 1956-61 [vols. 5–6]).

Stuhlmacher, P., *Gerechtigkeit Gottes bei Paulus* (Göttingen: Vandenhoeck & Ruprecht, 1966).

—'Recent Exegesis on Romans 3.24-26', in *Reconciliation, Law and Righteousness: Essays in Biblical Theology* (trans. E. Kalin; Philadelphia: Fortress Press, 1986 [1975]), pp. 94-109.

Surkau, H.W., *Martyrien in jüdischer und frühchristlicher Zeit* (Göttingen: Vandenhoeck & Ruprecht, 1938).

Swetnam, J., *Jesus and Isaac: A Study of the Epistle to the Hebrews in the Light of the Aqedah* (Rome: Biblical Institute Press, 1981).

Talbert, C.H., 'A Non-Pauline Fragment at Romans 3.24-26?', *JBL* 85 (1966), pp. 287-96.

Tannehill, R.C., *Dying and Rising with Christ: A Study in Pauline Theology* (Berlin: Töpelmann, 1967).

Tasker, R.V.G., 'The Doctrine of Justification by Faith in the Epistle to the Romans', *EvQ* 24 (1952), pp. 37-46.

Taylor, F.J., 'Blood', in *A Theological Wordbook of the Bible* (ed. A. Richardson; London: SCM Press, 1950).

Taylor, G.M., 'The Function of ΠΙΣΤΙΣ ΧΡΙΣΤΟΥ in Galatians', *JBL* 85 (1966), pp. 58-67.

Taylor, V., *Jesus and his Sacrifice: A Study of the Passion Sayings in the Gospels* (London: Macmillan, 1937).

—'Great Texts Reconsidered', *ExpTim* 50 (1938–39), pp. 295-300.

—*Forgiveness and Reconciliation: A Study in New Testament Theology* (London: Macmillan, 1941).

—*The Epistle to the Romans* (London: Epworth Press, 1955).

—*The Atonement in New Testament Teaching* (London: Epworth Press, 1958).

Thornton, T.C.G., 'Propitiation or Expiation?: Ἱλαστήριον and Ἱλασμός in Romans and 1 John', *ExpTim* 80 (1968–69), pp. 53-55.

Todorov, T., *Theories of the Symbol* (trans. C. Porter; New York: Cornell University Press, 1977).

Torrance, T.F., 'One Aspect of the Biblical Conception of Faith', *ExpTim* 68 (1957), pp. 111-14.

Townshend, R.B. (ed.), *The Apocrypha and Pseudepigrapha of the Old Testament in English* (Oxford: Oxford University Press, 1913).

Trebilco, P.R., 'Women as Co-Workers and Leaders in Paul's Letters', *Journal of the Christian Brethren Research Fellowship* 112 (1990), pp. 27-36.

Trumbull, H.C., *The Blood Covenant: A Primitive Rite and its Bearing on Scripture* (Philadelphia: Wattles, 1893).

Turner, N., *A Grammar of New Testament Greek. IV. Syntax* (Edinburgh: T. & T. Clark, 1963).

Uitti, K.D., *Linguistics and Literary Theory* (Englewood Cliffs, NJ: Prentice–Hall, 1969).

Vaux, R. de., *Ancient Israel: Its Life and Institutions* (trans. J. McHugh; Toronto: McGraw–Hill, 1961).

Vermes, G., *Scripture and Tradition in Judaism* (Leiden: Brill, 1961).

Via, D., 'Justification and Deliverance: Existential Dialectic', *SR* 1 (1971), pp. 204-12.

Walker, W.O., 'The Burden of Proof in Identifying Interpolations in the Pauline Letters', *NTS* 33 (1987), pp. 610-18.

Wallis, W.B., 'The Translation of Romans 1.17—A Basic Motif in Paulinism', *JETS* 16 (1973), pp. 17-23.

Warfield, B.B., '"Redeemer" and "Redemption"', *Princeton Theological Review* 14 (1916), pp. 177-201.

—'The New Testament Terminology of "Redemption"', *Princeton Theological Review* 15 (1917), pp. 201-49.

Warren, A., and R. Wellek, *Theory of Literature* (New York: Harcourt, Brace & World, 1949).

Watson, D.F., 'The New Testament and Greco-Roman Rhetoric: A Bibliography', *JETS* 31 (1988), pp. 465-72.

—*Invention, Arrangement, and Style: Rhetorical Criticism of Jude and 2 Peter* (Missoula, MT: Scholars Press, 1988).

—'A Rhetorical Analysis of Philippians and its Implications for the Unity Question', *NovT* 30 (1988), pp. 57-88.

—'A Rhetorical Analysis of 2 John according to Greco-Roman Convention', *NTS* 35 (1989), pp. 104-30.

Watson, N.M., 'Some Observations on the Use of ΔΙΚΑΙΟΩ in the Septuagint', *JBL* 79 (1960), pp. 255-66.

Wedderburn, A.J.M., 'Adam in Paul's Letter to the Romans', *StudBib* 3 (1978), pp. 413-30.

—*Baptism and Resurrection: Studies in Pauline Theology against its Graeco-Roman Background* (Tübingen: Mohr [Paul Siebeck], 1987).

—*The Reasons for Romans* (Edinburgh: T. & T. Clark, 1988).

Weiser, A., *The Psalms* (trans. H. Hartwell; London: SCM Press, 1962 [1959]).

Weiss, J., 'Beiträge zur paulinischen Rhetorik', in *Theologische Studien: Bernhard Weiss Festschrift* (ed. C.R. Gregory; Göttingen: Vandenhoeck & Ruprecht, 1897).

—*Der erste Korintherbrief* (Göttingen: Meyer, 1910).

—*Das Urchristentum* (Göttingen: Vandenhoeck & Ruprecht, 1917).

Wengst, K., *Christologische Formeln und Lieder des Urchristentums* (Gütersloh: Gütersloher Verlagshaus, 2nd edn, 1973).

Wennemer, K., 'ΑΠΟΛΥΤΡΩΣΙΣ Römer 3,24-25a', in *Studiorum Paulinorum Congressus Internationalis Catholicus, 1961* (Rome: Pontifical Biblical Institue, 1963), I, pp. 283-88.

Westcott, B.F., *The Epistle to the Hebrews: The Greek Text with Notes and Essays* (Cambridge: Macmillan, 1889).

—*The Epistles of John: The Greek Text with Notes and Essays* (London: Macmillan, 4th edn, 1902).

—*Saint Paul's Epistle to the Ephesians: The Greek Text with Notes and Addenda* (London: Macmillan, 1906).

Whiteley, D.E.H., *The Theology of St Paul* (Oxford: Oxford University Press, 1964).

Wilckens, U., *Der Brief an die Römer* (3 vols.; Zürich: Neukirchener Verlag, 1978).

Wilder, A.N., *Early Christian Rhetoric: The Language of the Gospel* (New York: Harper & Row, 1964).

—'The Rhetoric of Ancient and Modern Apocalyptic', *Int* 25 (1971), pp. 436-53.

Wiles, M.F., *The Divine Apostle* (Cambridge: Cambridge University Press, 1967).

Williams, J.W., 'The Interpretation of Romans 3.21-26' (unpublished PhD dissertation, University of Manchester, 1973).

Williams, S.K., *Jesus' Death as Saving Event: The Background and Origin of a Concept* (Missoula, MT: Scholars Press, 1975).

—'The "Righteousness of God" in Romans', *JBL* 99 (1980), pp. 241-90.

—'Again *Pistis Christou*', *CBQ* 49 (1987), pp. 431-47.

—'The Meaning of Faith: ΑΚΟΗ ΠΙΣΤΕΩΣ in Galatians 3', *NTS* 35 (1989), pp. 82-93.

Wrede, W., *Paul* (trans. E. Lummis; London: Philip Green, 1907).

Wright, N.T., 'The Messiah and the People of God: A Study in Pauline Theology with Particular Reference to the Argument of the Epistle to the Romans' (unpublished DPhil dissertation, University of Oxford, 1980).

Wuellner, W., 'Paul's Rhetoric of Argumentation in Romans: An Alternative to the Donfried–Karris Debate over Romans', *CBQ* 38 (1976), pp. 330-51.

—'Greek Rhetoric and Pauline Argumentation', in *Early Christian Literature and the Classical Intellectual Tradition* (ed. W.R. Schoedel and R.L. Wilken; Paris: Editions Beauchesne, 1979), pp. 177-88.

—'Where is Rhetorical Criticism Taking Us?', *CBQ* 49 (1987), pp. 448-63.

York, A.D., 'The Dating of Targumic Literature', *JJS* 5 (1974), pp. 49-62.

Young, F.M., ' "New Wine in Old Wineskins": XIV. Sacrifice', *ExpTim* 86 (1974–75), pp. 305-309.

Young, N.H., 'Did St Paul Compose Romans III.24f.?', *AusBR* 22 (1974), pp. 23-32.

—'C.H. Dodd, "*Hilaskesthai*" and his Critics', *EvQ* 48 (1976), pp. 67-78.

—' "*Hilaskesthai*" and Related Words in the New Testament', *EvQ* 55 (1983), pp. 169-76.

Zeitlin, S., 'The Legend of the Ten Martyrs and its Apocalyptic Origins', *JQR* 36 (1945), pp. 1-16, 209-10.

—*The Second Book of the Maccabees* (trans. Sidney Tedesche; New York: Harper, 1954).

Zeller, D., 'Sühne und Langmut: Zur Traditionsgeschichte von Röm 3,24-26', *TP* 43 (1968), pp. 51-75.

Ziesler, J.A.T., *The Meaning of Righteousness in Paul* (Cambridge: Cambridge University Press, 1972).

—'Romans 3.21-26', *ExpTim* 93 (1981–82), pp. 356-59.

—*Pauline Christianity* (Oxford: Oxford University Press, 1983).

—*Paul's Letter to the Romans* (London: SCM Press, 1989).

Zweck, D., 'The *Exordium* of the Areopagus Speech, Acts 17.22, 23', *NTS* 35 (1989), pp. 94-103.

INDEXES

INDEX OF REFERENCES

OLD TESTAMENT

CHRISTIAN WRITINGS

CLASSICAL RHETORICAL TEXTS

INSCRIPTIONS AND PAPYRI